Torture and Dignity

Torture and Dignity

An Essay on Moral Injury

J. M. BERNSTEIN

The University of Chicago Press
Chicago and London

J. M. Bernstein is University Distinguished Professor of philosophy at the New School for Social Research. He is the author of many books, including *Adorno: Disenchantment and Ethics, Against Voluptuous Bodies: Adorno's Late Modernism and the Meaning of Painting,* and *Recovering Ethical Life: Jürgen Habermas and the Future of Critical Theory.*

The University of Chicago Press, Chicago 60637
The University of Chicago Press, Ltd., London
© 2015 by The University of Chicago.
All rights reserved. Published 2015.
Printed in the United States of America

24 23 22 21 20 19 18 17 16 15   1 2 3 4 5

ISBN-13: 978-0-226-26632-9 (cloth)
ISBN-13: 978-0-226-26646-6 (e-book)

DOI: 10.7208/chicago/9780226266466.001.0001

Library of Congress Cataloging-in-Publication Data

Bernstein, J. M., author.
  Torture and dignity : an essay on moral injury / J.M. Bernstein.
    pages cm
  Includes bibliographical references and index.
    ISBN 978-0-226-26632-9 (cloth : alk. paper)—ISBN 978-0-226-26646-6
  (e-book)   1. Torture—Moral and ethical aspects.   2. Rape—Moral and
  ethical aspects.   3. Trust—Social aspects.   4. Beccaria, Cesare, marchese di,
  1738-1794.   5. Ethics—21st century.   I. Title.
    HV8593.B475 2015
    174'.936466—dc23

                                                          2014050162

♾ This paper meets the requirements of ANSI/NISO Z39.48–1992
(Permanence of Paper).

For Susie, who knows what matters most

CONTENTS

ACKNOWLEDGMENTS

This work has been long in the making, which means I have drawn on the goodwill, generosity, wisdom, philosophical acuity, and moral passions of friends, colleagues, students, and interlocutors in unusual abundance. My gratitude to them all is immense.

For criticism, conversation, and advice, I would like to thank the following philosophical friends and colleagues (and ask forgiveness of anyone whom I unintentionally omit): Ariella Azoulay, Sara Beardsworth, Seyla Benhabib, Alice Crary, Gregg Horowitz (who, as always, provided invaluable assistance at moments of crisis), Rahel Jaeggi, Paul Kottman, Hans-Peter Krüger, Beatrice Longuenesse, Eduardo Mendieta, Christoph Menke, Vida Pavesich, Adi Ophir, David Plotke, Sonja Rethy, Jill Stauffer, and Ann Stoler.

I owe a special debt to Judy Butler, whose own telling work on moral injury was the immediate provocation for the ideas that have emerged here. I know she disagrees with much that I say, but she has always understood where I was going and why, and encouraged me. In my visits to Berkeley, she and Wendy Brown were tireless in their hospitality, patience with arguments without end, and sense of occasion—memorably even once providing a small earthquake. It wasn't necessary, really.

I have presented parts of this work to audiences at a variety of universities and colleges, and always benefitted from their questions and responses: UC Berkeley, CUNY Graduate Center, Emory University, Haverford College (and the 2009 graduating seniors who asked me to be the Altherr Symposium speaker), Humboldt University, University of Leuven, University of Potsdam, Siena College, Southern Illinois University, University of Tel Aviv, Vassar College, Xavier University, and Yale University.

I have been gifted with a remarkable crew of graduate students at the

New School for Social Research whose enthusiasm for my work, their astute criticism of it, and the inspiring reach of their own research have proved invaluable: Roy Ben Shai, Matt Congdon, Adam Gies, Gabriel Gottlieb, Grace Hunt, Karen Ng, Katharina Nieswandt (while visiting from Pitt), Janna van Grunsven (who also heroically proofread the text in its final stages and compiled the index), and Rocio Zambrana.

I am grateful to two spirited anonymous reviewers for the University of Chicago Press and especially to my editor there, Elizabeth Branch Dyson, who has been an icon of encouragement.

I am deeply grateful to the American Academy in Berlin for awarding me a John P. Birkelund Fellowship that allowed me to spend the winter of 2013 in its Wannsee home doing the final researches for this work.

Some of these chapters have appeared in earlier or different incarnations, and I am grateful to the following journals for permission to reprint updated versions of these arguments: *The Berlin Journal* (chapter 1), *Political Concepts* (chapter 2), *Constellations* (chapter 4), and *Metaphilosophy* (chapter 5). An earlier version of chapter 6 appeared in Magdalena Zolkos (ed.), *On Jean Améry: Philosophy of Catastrophe* (Lanham: Lexington Books, 2011), 39–60.

This book would not have come to be without Susie Linfield, literally! It was she who introduced me to the writings of Jean Améry, whose thought is the continual resource on which this work leans. Susie has also been my continual conversational partner and spiritual anchor through all the highs, lows, and even worse lows that are the companion of writing a text such as this one. She has worried over the years that I would dedicate this book to her, thanking her for teaching me all I needed to know about torture. So little faith, my dear! It is, of course, for the opposite of all that that my gratitude knows no end.

INTRODUCTION

Torture and rape are paradigms of moral injury, which is the topic of part 1 of this work. In part 2, I argue that dignity is to be understood as the standing or status of persons considered as having intrinsic worth; dignity is what gets injured and even destroyed ("devastated" I will say) by the brutalizing and violative acts of torture and rape. Torture and rape are thus considered not only in themselves, but centrally as paradigms of moral injury; so understood they become a means for reconstructing the very idea of moral experience: what morality is and how it functions. Torture and rape are only rarely considered by moral philosophers, perhaps because they are so indisputably morally atrocious acts; or perhaps because they seem so remote from ordinary moral consciousness (to which one may object: for whom are they so remote?); or perhaps because they are such immediately repugnant sources of moral unease and disgust; or perhaps because their specific mode of suffering cannot be accounted for by reigning moral theories (a claim to which we shall return). Whatever the source of the resistance to looking attentively at these phenomena, by making them pivotal to the understanding of morality in general my intention is to throw into question the dominant schools of modern moral philosophy, and to attempt to restructure moral experience and understanding on the basis of the formations of suffering they make salient. Morals, I will argue, emerge from the experience of moral injury, from the sufferings of the victims of moral harm. For us moderns, morality at its most urgent and insistent is, finally, a victim morality. Justification for this claim and the procedures it assumes will become evident as my argument unfolds; what I can do here, before offering a brief outline of what is to follow, is explain some of the philosophical motivation for making torture and rape, moral injury, and moral suffering the central elements necessary for the reconstruction of morals.

Let me begin with two moral scenes. In the first, he stands above you, fist raised, quaking with fury, poised to batter and bruise, to pummel and pulverize you, and as your terror mounts in anticipation of the pain, the suffering, the brutalization you are about to undergo, your thought is not that the attacker is about to do a most terrible thing: breaking the absolute moral rule that thou shalt not thrash one's fellow human being. In the second, you watch while another—your child, a friend, a complete stranger—is about to be viciously assaulted, and your thought is wholly focused on the harm they are about to suffer, and what you can do to prevent that violent act and its painful consequences from occurring; your thought is not that you must prevent the attacker from breaking an overriding obligation not to act cruelly. The idea that in dire circumstances— call it the scene of morality—the stakes of what is about to occur depend on whether or not a moral rule, principle, or commandment is about to be broken is absurd, nearly unthinkable, or would be thought absurd and unthinkable were it not for the fact that moral philosophy for the past several centuries has kept the question of morals obsessively focused on the authority, force, and rationality of moral rules and principles. Because rules and principles are abstract things, mental things perceived and appraised through the mind's eye, such moral philosophizing has equally presumed that the question of what morality is like—why we should be moral and how we can be moral—is a question about reason and rationality, about how moral principles are deliverances from reason, and how reason can rule over the unruly, raucous, causally determined emotions, affects, and interests that lead us astray.

I do not want to say that no one ever struggles to overcome a self-aggrandizing inclination in order to hold true to a moral principle; but as a general picture of moral life, this is wildly implausible. It is not moral rules or principles or commandments that are broken when morally wrongful things happen; it is persons—their flesh, their bones, their sense of inner worth—that get bruised and broken. In the first instance, morals concerns the harm done to persons, their pains and sufferings and indignities; morals is, minimally and if nothing else, our awareness of these violations and their hurt as what should not happen, as above all what should not happen *to me*. And it is because of my intense awareness—however hidden from focal consciousness—of how utterly vulnerable I am, of how I would suffer if my bodily integrity were violated if I were beaten and thrashed, that I can be brought to the thought of how (most) others are like me, vulnerable and injurable, and how they too would wish never to undergo the torments of physical harm or savage humiliation. It is not the magic of obligations, the hallucinatory power of principles, the "mesmeric force" of the word "ought"[1] that move us to heed the ideal of doing unto others as we would have them do unto us; rather, it is our robust understanding of our own vulnerability, our own fear of pain and suffering, our deeply personal sense that these things *should* not happen, that their occurring at the hands of others would *wrong* me in my very being, that they would discount or injure the value I am (my sense of inner worth or dignity) and the knowledge that others are like me and share that understanding of our shared predicament of vulnerability. If moral principles matter to us at all, it is because they capture and reflect primitive experiences of individual worth in relation to experiences of moral injury, and thus of our shared awareness of a pervasive and unavoidable vulnerability. Nonetheless, in this scenario, the primitive experience of moral wrong is one of moral injury, to oneself and to others.

In a remarkably brave essay published in 1958, Elizabeth Anscombe argued that philosophers were wasting their time doing moral philosophy because the basic concepts they were using belonged to a theological framework that made no sense in a secular world. The idea of moral duty and moral obligation, the idea that there are things we *morally* "ought" not to do—for example, that one "ought" not to kill or steal—make no sense in the absence of the religious setting in which these "ought" statements appear as laws commanded by the creator of the universe. Inside the theological setting, to break the law given by God is a *sin* because it is an extreme act of disobedience against the author of the world who gives to each of His creatures their meaning and worth. If there were a further human intelligibility to the commandments to not murder or steal or commit adultery, it would be a cognitive bonus beyond the core normative command to obey. Law, virtuous obedience, and sinful disobedience form a constellation whose center points up and back, so to speak, to the origins of the law rather than down to the effects of breaking it.[2] Whatever the reasons offered for giving God the authority to make law, once that authority is offered or acknowledged, then the law story of morals becomes, at least, consistent and compelling: a familiar form of human relationship involving hierarchy, power, threat, command, and obedience is offered as an account of the authority of normative requirements and prohibitions generally. Moral principles are, finally, commands we obey or disobey; breaking them is at least disobedience and often defiance. Patently, obedience and disobedience can have nothing to do with morals for us. Removed from a theological setting and without the backdrop of a framework of law and command, the language of moral duty, obligation, ought, principle, and rule idles, becoming useless and empty— "It is as if the notion 'criminal' were to remain when criminal law and criminal courts had been abolished and forgotten"[3]—and hence, Anscombe urges, should be jettisoned. Although she is less than transparent in the inference she draws from this, I take Anscombe to be suggesting that when terrible moral events happen, it is not a moral rule or moral principle or moral commandment that is broken. Why on earth should we secular moderns care about a rule being broken? What fetishism is necessary to give a rule that frisson of overriding authority? When terrible moral events occur, it is living people who are injured, harmed, demeaned, and degraded. It is not broken rules that matter, but broken bodies and ruined lives.[4]

What might it mean to heed Anscombe's injunction to jettison the discourse of moral reason with its penumbra of moral rules, principles, and obligations? How might moral philosophy be pursued if not through the attempt to vindicate the deliverances of an autonomous moral reason? Anscombe's own preferred route is the provision of "an adequate philosophy of psychology,"[5] by which she means a critical appropriation of Aristotle's moral psychology (with the notion of "moral" sufficiently bracketed), a suggestion that has had its followers. But one might have a worry about this procedure that has the same form as Anscombe's critique of moral obligation and moral law—namely that without the ballast provided by Aristotle's metaphysical naturalism, the particulars of his virtue ethics lack the setting necessary for its intelligibility.[6] Without an appropriate understanding of moral injury and moral harm, recourse to an antique moral psychology will be of little avail. If what makes an action wrong is that it harms a person, then the primary phenomenon of modern moral life is *moral injury*. The claim, then, is not that there are no moral rules; it is that broken rules stand for broken bodies and ruined lives (and the bruising, wounding, humiliating, and general injuring that are parts or anticipations of such breakings and ruinations), and hence that whatever meaning and authority we might suppose moral rules to have will be parasitic upon our understanding of moral injury. Of course, in calling a scene of intentional injuring the production of a *moral* injury, a question is begged, but not, it will turn out, viciously. Equally, the forms of moral injury are many. There are all the direct forms in which one person violates another: battery, assault, murder, rape, torture, abuse; but also deceiving, betraying, humiliating, demeaning, insulting; and there are too the grand forms of institutional domination and exploitation—political, economic, and social—premised on differences of race, gender, class, religion. Having in mind the range of the types and forms of moral injury is important, but also idle until we have some core conception of what moral injury is against which the various forms, types, and cases can be tested.

A consideration of moral injury requires a larger reversal of philosophical procedure than is immediately obvious; after all, does not utilitarian ethics instruct us to minimize pains and sufferings? And in so instructing us, does it not implicitly acknowledge the primacy of moral injury? Put aside for the present utility's bizarrely naïve psychology of seeking pleasure (no matter how complexly figured) and avoiding pain (no matter how reductively considered); put aside as well its obliviousness to the intrinsic worth of persons, its bland willingness to quantify, to make no life worth *anything* if it stands on the wrong side of the maximizing happiness, minimizing pain tally, and thus, ironically, its inability to make suffering and, above all, loss meaningful. The more stringent reminder necessary here is that utilitarianism is either a crude decision procedure or a philosophy that operates in the same law-centered way that Anscombe is inveighing against, placing us under the absolute obligation to bring about the greatest happiness (or the least misery) for the greatest number. Although adopting recognizable pleasures and pains as its content provides utility with immanent materials befitting a secular ethics; and although its employment of an instrumental and calculating conception of reason matches one significant idea of secular reason; nonetheless, as a *morals*, utility either weds itself to the discourse of law, obligation, principle, and ought (as most committed utilitarians do), or collapses into a crude decision procedure for social engineers (as it does for the cynics who consider utilitarian modes of calculation a successor to traditional ethics).

The reason why even utilitarianism accedes to the law concept of morality is because traditional moral philosophy has been obsessed with moral agency, with explaining to the moral novice, the self-interested brute, the skeptic, the lurking sinner in us all why we should be moral, and how having a moral scheme in working order can lead to morally salubrious action of a kind sufficient for action coordination in a society of morally indifferent associates. And, since the point of a morality is to govern action, explaining how this is possible and why we should heed and remain faithful to what morality demands would appear to be both necessary and appropriate. This becomes even more urgent when one is attempting to construct a translation manual from the religious to the secular, from God commanding to reason (or community or habit or sentiments) commanding. How can pure practical reason obligate? Yet, again, outside a context of law-command-obedience, it is massively unclear that constructing and instructing moral agency is the appropriate frame for the understanding of moral experiences and moral phenomena. With only the empty husk of the religious idea of moral rules to work with, the effort of philosophical construction and moral instruction converge on turning ordinary statements—"Keep your promises!"—into fetish objects with unprecedented powers to oblige, to order, to direct, to suppress competing claimants, and to inspire the tawdry grasping and clamoring self. Rather than presume the position of the moral knower, the moral instructor, the moral authority, a more modest procedure that attaches closer to everyday moral experience would be to interrogate the phenomena of moral injury itself by taking up the position of the *victim*, the person harmed by a morally wrongful act—which from time to time is each of us. Doing so allows us to focus on the nature of harm rather than slipping into the moralizing question of why we should not commit harmful acts, to which, anyway, the best answer is: because they are harmful. Worse, if the validity of morals depends on the validity of the rules governing moral reason, then if it cannot be demonstrated that a set of moral rules is rationally overriding and obligating—and to date no such demonstration has succeeded—then we are forced to the conclusion that morality is an illusion.[7] But none of the skeptical machinery that so easily shreds the claims of moral reason touches the phenomena of moral injury: that this person is suffering here and now from an injury intentionally inflicted by another for no reason of self-defense or its like. The victim certainly knows and believes "This should not be," and since each of us is (actually or potentially) such a victim, then each of us knows "This should not be." If Anscombe—and Nietzsche—is right about the genealogy of modern moral reason, then its falling into the clutches of skeptical despair was fated. By turning toward the phenomena of moral suffering and moral injury we keep in view what makes morality matter to us moderns who care nothing about saving our souls or perfecting our wills or becoming virtuous—empty ideals from another age; and by making the victim the cynosure of reflection we avoid the presumption and self-righteousness of moral reason.

Torture and rape are paradigm moral injuries. Even as we allow a wide range of circumstances in which killing another human being, even a wholly innocent human being, might be justified ("collateral damage" is the contemporary moral euphemism for the claim to a justified killing of innocents), I cannot conceive of a set of circumstances of justifiable rape;

and even those who believe that torture is a legitimate weapon in the battle against terrorism agree that torturing remains morally atrocious—it is just that sometimes we must do morally atrocious things for the sake of the greater good. Even those who think torture is justifiable concede that the requirements for its use are more stringent than those for killing: if an intruder enters my home, I might well be justified in killing him; no matter the level of threat, however, I would not be justified in dragging him into my basement and torturing him. For us moderns, if rape is never justifiable, and torture is either never justifiable or justifiable only when the threat is of such magnitude and imminence that for the purpose of collective self-defense there is no conceivable alternative, then it becomes natural to consider torture and rape as exemplars of moral wrongness, of what is morally wrong if anything is utterly morally wrong. Yet, with respect to torture, this was not always the case. On the contrary, torture has *become* our idea of a paradigmatic moral wrong, but it was not always so considered. Throughout the better part of 700 years, well into the middle of the eighteenth century, torture was a routine and valued part of the Roman-canon legal system that dominated all European systems of criminal justice except the English. In England, as William Blackstone tartly states it in his *Commentaries*, the rack was "occasionally used as an engine of state, not of law."[8] Yet, even in England, whatever its differences from the Continent in the use of torture for criminal proceedings (and Blackstone slightly overstates English abstinence with respect to penal torture), the communal affect at public tortures was one of great festive celebration. In his diaries, Samuel Pepys records going to Charing Cross on October 13, 1660 in order to see "Major-General Harrison hanged, drawn, and quartered; which was done there, he looking as cheerful as any man could do in that condition. He was presently cut down, his head and heart shown to the people, at which there was great shouts of joy." After blandly stating that he had the chance to see the King beheaded and "the first blood shed in revenge for the King," Pepys records how he went home, where he became angry with his wife for leaving her things lying about the house, and in his passion "kicked the little fine basket which I bought her in Holland, and broke it, which troubled me after I had done it."[9] The cool equanimity and good cheer of Pepys's report of Harrison's being drawn and quartered compared to the perturbations of heart over the broken basket is chilling to contemporary ears.

In chapter 1, I track the seismic social transformation that led to the abolition of judicial (evidence-inducing) and penal torture throughout Europe in the course of the eighteenth century, the transformation from scenes of community-restoring jubilance and exhilaration of the kind reported by Pepys to scenes of communal horror and disgust at these public violations of bodily integrity, followed by torture's disappearance from both the private space of legal proceedings and, more slowly, from the public spaces of penal spectacle. By the early years of the nineteenth century, torture had virtually disappeared from Europe. This moment of the abolition of torture in Europe—arguably the culmination and fulfillment of the humanitarian revolution of the eighteenth century—marks the precise moment in which the fundaments of our ethical attitudes and our ethical sensibilities begin to take recognizable form. At this moment, it would have become intelligible for a great swathe of European humanity to agree that cruelty is the worst thing a person might do, to begin thinking that unnecessary human suffering should be prevented where possible, that not to respond with sympathy to another's suffering was a coldness of heart and thus an ethical failing of some grievous kind. As these sentiments coalesced and took on ethical form, some writers began thinking that all human beings should be considered as possessing equal moral standing and deserving of equal moral treatment.[10] A blunt way of capturing this moment is to say that torture had become the paradigm of moral wrong, a wrongness initially judged sentimentally rather than rationalistically; affective repugnance rather than principled opposition is what drove the abolitionist movement. Even the ever-dry Blackstone in his *Commentaries* adopts the sentimental stance of Cesare Beccaria's *On Crimes and Punishments* in his quietly devastating critique of continental torture practices: "because the laws cannot endure that any man should die upon the evidence of a false, or even a single, witness; and therefore contrived this method [the rack] that innocence should manifest itself by a stout denial, or guilt by a plain confession. Thus rating a man's virtue by the hardness of his constitution, and his guilt by the sensibility of his nerves."[11] Blackstone, who was never shy in offering arguments, takes these considerations as decisive: judicial torture's inhumanity is an echo of its transparent unreliability. Since the unreliability was well known from ancient times—Blackstone quotes from Cicero's *Pro Sulla* to hammer home the point—it was the rack's compelling "a man to put himself on trial; that being a species of trial in itself" that was the new humanist note; there is and could be nothing other than a man's sensible constitution that is put on trial by torture: if he is an insensible brute, he will be proved innocent; if he is a fragile daisy, he will be proved guilty. The whole meaning and significance of torture had devolved into its erratic effects on the individual body.

Beccaria's now almost unknown *On Crimes and Punishments* (1764) became the leading edge of the judicial and penal reform movements of the eighteenth century; a century later, it was still regarded, along with the writings of Voltaire, as uniquely responsible for the abolition of torture. Giving the leading role to Beccaria's book in the successful movement to abolish torture throughout Europe is the high point of the philosophical myth of the Enlightenment: the transformation of the moral and political landscape of Europe through ideas alone. Following the lead of Foucault's *Discipline and Punish*, I dismiss this myth by arguing that it was the emergence of a new conception of the bodily self—itself the product of a diversity of political, economic, social, and cultural forces—whose pains and sufferings are solely its own, a bodily self already patently present in Blackstone's words, that best *explains* the shifting ethical landscape of late eighteenth century Europe. But that still leaves two questions: why was Beccaria's text regarded as so important, and why has his achievement been forgotten? In answer to the first question, I argue that Beccaria's text did bring the humanitarian revolution to a culmination and fulfillment through proposing a *substantive* conception of the rule of law that is necessary for the abolition of torture to take on effective legal meaning. The core of Beccaria's considerations are not directly moral or even utilitarian, although arguably his text is the founding document of modern utilitarian thought (it was for Bentham). Rather, Beccaria is primarily concerned with what we now call due process considerations, especially the right against self-incrimination, the right to a fair and speedy trial, the right not to be punished until proven guilty, the right to demand that the state prove any charges beyond a reasonable doubt, and, centrally, the freedom from cruel and unusual punishments. Prior to Beccaria's writings, these due process procedures had no established place in the Roman-canon criminal legal system (their role in English law goes back to Magna Carta). Suddenly, Beccaria is insisting on them as the substantive framework necessary for a criminal legal system as such. What makes Beccaria's argument possible is the thesis that these procedural due process requirements are individually necessary and jointly sufficient to overcome the arbitrariness of the thin rule of law operative in absolutist legal regimes using torture. Procedural due process is, substantively, the determinate negation of the law of sovereign torture. Beccaria constructs the modern, substantive idea of the rule of law as a *negative ethics*; the rule of law draws its ethical substance from the history it remembers and negates; functioning as a remembrance of the suffering produced by the law of torture, the rule of law points aghast to the long history of state violation of the fragile human body and exclaims "Never again!" Beccaria's genius was to fill out his negative thought with detailed legal procedures; those procedures, one might say, constitute what it means for a state to recognize the human *dignity* of its citizens. Or, more accurately, through the adoption of procedural due process requirements that protect the bodily integrity and rights to appropriate legal treatment by the state, there begins to appear a new understanding of the status, standing, or worth of human beings: they are possessed of an unconditional dignity. This massive transformation in the structure of the criminal legal system tokens and implies an equally massive transformation in the general conception of the relation between individuals and the state; one might even say that the emergence of a substantive conception of the rule of law that consolidates and expresses the meaning of the abolition of torture adumbrates the new idea of the relation between state and citizen that climaxes in the American and French Revolutions.

Not only *should* modern morals be reconstructed from the vantage point of the victim, but in fact a founding moment in the constitution of modern political morality *did* transpire through a privileging of the perspective of the victim of violence. The abolition of slavery would be another such moment. But if morals can advance through experience, if structures of wrong can be righted, and if patterns of moral harm prevented through the elaboration of new moral ideals and codes, then the historical privileging of the victim is inevitable; it is just what learning through experience amounts to in this domain. The question remains whether the victim-structures determining historical transformation hold as well for concrete moral experience.

There are several reasons why Beccaria's achievement has been forgotten, all of them valid and telling. First, Beccaria was forgotten because he won the argument, because his critiques of judicial and penal torture, and his conception of, at least, procedural due process rapidly became jurisprudential and even ethical common sense; one could no longer imagine an acceptable criminal law system without the framework of these provisions. We are all Beccaria's legal offspring.[12] Second, if my negative ethics reading is correct, then the force of Beccaria's argument was contextual, not a free-standing deduction from first principles (although his text can read like a thin version of such an attempt), but an intervention into a political-legal context in which Beccaria could count on the majority of his readers sharing his initial ethical horror at torture practices and what they stood for, viz., the violative arbitrariness of the criminal law system. Without the context, without the vivid memory of arbitrary state violence against individual citizens, his words lost their practical premise and the normative aspiration of their end. Third, penal practices, no matter how refined, never did utterly remove traces of torture; in some jurisdictions, these traces of torture have grown rather than decreased over time. But the traces of torture in the penal system are not universally regarded as remnants of an unacceptable practice of torture, but rather as the quotient of punishment and pain proper to a penal system. Fourth, overt state violence against citizens was replaced by more insidious forms of penal violence, what Foucault denominates as *disciplinary regimes*. Fifth, even as states heeded the prohibition against torture at home, it was increasingly used in imperial and colonial adventures. Sixth, as Beccaria's construction was first emaciated in thin, liberal conceptions of the rule of law, and then forgotten, full-throated instrumentalist and positivist interpretations of the rule of law began to appear, interpretations that increasingly emptied the rule of law of any orienting ethical content. It is these thin, formal, instrumentalist conceptions of the rule of law that arguably are now dominant. Seventh, as the twentieth century wore on, with the rule of law ethically emptied, states could re-import torture practices from the colonies under the heading of "state security." In this last respect, Blackstone's original separation between torture being prohibited from use in the legal system but continuing as an "engine of state" has become standard operating procedure; as if unconstitutional and immoral legal procedures could be sanitized or legitimated simply by segregation: state action—"executive privilege" with the power to determine when a "state of emergency" amounts to a "state of [constitutional] exception" are the current terms of art—has become the paradigm for acts that subvert the ideal of the separation of powers, itself a key component of the rule of law, in its abuse of it. Eighth, above all, Beccaria could be forgotten because he employed a negative ethics; no affirmative ethical theory was ever constructed that provided a direct grounding for Beccaria's legal theory; no affirmative ethical theory was erected that began with the tortured body as its primary datum and attempted to interrogate the nature of that suffering, the precise character of the harm undergone that would make intelligible why that should not be done.

The effort to provide such an ethical theory is the project of the remainder of this work. What happens to the victim of a morally wrongful act that leads to the general acknowledgment that she should not have suffered what was done to her? What does she undergo and suffer? What makes the pains suffered morally wrongful ones? Before reading the remarkable chapter on torture in Jean Améry's *At the Mind's Limits*, I was unclear what an answer to these questions would look like. Améry offers an intense first-person account of his torture by the Nazis that shuttles delicately between the phenomenological, the confessional, and the reflective, while eschewing at each moment easy moralization of his experiences. Améry wants the terribleness of what occurred to him to be borne by the reflective account of his experience independently of moral concepts, categories, and forms. It is the absence of moral form and moralization that makes Améry's account so telling and persuasive. In chapter 2 I offer a partial reconstruction of Améry's account of his torture, seeking to illuminate its essential elements while following his lead in bracketing directly moral questions. Because Améry's little book details the character of his being *broken* by torture and life in concentration camps, and continues by reflecting on the meaning of living on as a broken and devastated being who has been overwhelmed and undone, I will throughout my argument return to Améry's reflections. Because the moral harm of torture is intimately connected with its power of *breaking* the victim, Améry's suffering will remain the lodestar for my reflections.

At a central moment in his account of his torture, Améry qualifies his analysis of his excruciating pain, a painfulness that severs the self's intentional relation to the world, driving it in on itself; how that pain was manipulated by the torturer; how his suffering lost its usual meaning of needing help and aid, becoming only a sign of vulnerability and exposure, a sign that more pain was possible; how the sense of exposure and vulnerability was coupled with a sense of isolation, a sense of being simultaneously utterly present as body and utterly absent as self for the torturer; how the torturer appeared simultaneously as god and anti-man, a being with supreme powers of life and death upon whom he was absolutely dependent, but for whom Améry's humanity meant nothing. In the midst of this scene of inescapable, disintegrating agony, Améry remarks that the experience was like a rape, where one person invades another's body without her consent. That rape has been used as a form of torture and that there is a sexual subtext to torture are well-known facts. Nonetheless, it has traditionally been assumed that the excruciating, inescapable, and so terrifying pains of torture are self-explanatory in their operation and function, remaining a different kind of suffering and harm from the violative undoing of the bounded self that constitutes a central aspect of rape. Améry's remark intends that something of the human meaning of rape, its particular form of harming beyond the harm of bodily pain and vulnerability, is equally at issue in torture. Torture and rape, I argue, are coordinate versions of the same form of moral injury.

Chapter 3 begins by noting how the categorial elements constituting Améry's account of his torture match, item for item, Susan Brison's categorial analysis of her rape. In considering torture and rape as a singular syndrome of moral injury, four categorial elements become prominent. First, what makes torture and rape possible is that, in the final instance, the self cannot separate itself from its body. The self *is* its body, and being a body is what makes the self vulnerable to assault and the violative depredations of the other. Second, the combination of the experiences of vulnerability, exposure, and inescapability reveal a dimension of selfhood otherwise absent or hidden from ordinary life: *existential helplessness*. What torture and rape demonstrate is that existential helplessness is not a matter of phases one passes through at the beginning and end of life, or a matter of singular failures of our normal relation to the world; existential helplessness is a dimension of selfhood. We are essentially dependent beings. Third, what enables us to rationally ignore, forget, overlook, and suppress our existential helplessness, what keeps this helplessness out of mind (when it is) is *trust in the world*. With a modicum of trust in the world we can take ourselves to be agents, having moderate control over our lives, capable of protecting ourselves from most physical and social harms through routine cautions and prudence; and, above all, in conditions of trust we take ourselves to have a standing for our social fellows that allows them to come dangerously close to us without fear that they will harm us. So trust in the world is, in part, a sense of one's self-worth with respect to socially relevant others. The sense that others respect me as one of them is one version of trust in the world. In torture and rape, trust in the world is destroyed. Losing one's trust in the world is losing a sense of one's standing in the world, a sense that one possesses intrinsic worth or value.

What I am here terming 'loss of trust in the world' appears in other literatures as *trauma*, and the continuance of traumatic suffering in post-traumatic stress disorder. As Brison's analysis of her 'devastation' (as I shall term it) and path of recovery make undeniable, standard accounts of trauma conflate the symptoms—depression, hypervigilance, sleep disorders, recurring memories—with what is undone, overwhelmed, and destroyed in a traumatic event. What is undone is the self in its constitutive world relations, relations that are normally sustained by trust in the world. Collapse of trust in the world marks the dissolution of the relations *constitutive* of the self in its relation to the world. Fourth, then, in order for this thesis to make sense, in order to understand how the otherwise perfectly accurate medical diagnosis of trauma mistakes symptoms for phenomenon, we need to say that what the medical and psychological accounts of trauma miss is that the self *is a normative construction that is so constituted through its relations to others*. Selves are relational beings who are inescapably *dependent* on others for their standing or status as a human self—as a person.

Chapter 3 interrogates how we can best understand the moral harm of rape and torture. I begin with rape because Améry claims that his torture was like a rape, hence shifting the emphasis away from the problem of pain; also, the philosophical literature on rape and its moral harm is better developed than are accounts of the moral harm of torture. A premise of my reflections is that although lack of consent is a reasonable *criterion* for rape being morally wrong, nonconsent does not capture the moral *harm* of rape. Consent matters in the way it does because it is a social practice that protects, fosters, and elaborates essential aspects of autonomy, especially bodily autonomy; consent provides the practical means through which selves become capable of declaring and effectively making their bodies their own. Consent as a normatively structured set of social exchanges gives practical and material shape to the very idea of my body being "mine." But a body being one's own is more than a legal fact; if the idea of the body being *violated* is to carry normative weight such that its occurrence might be devastating, then two thoughts need to be connected, one relating to a normative conception of the body, the other to the idea of moral injury itself. Part of what is at issue here, then, is the very idea of moral injury. In this work, I attempt to refashion the idea of moral injury first developed in Jean Hampton's Kantian analysis of rape. Hampton compellingly shows why the Kantian idea that persons are and should be treated as "ends-in-themselves" and never as a mere means distorts our understanding of the moral world if it is used as only a criterion for governing moral deliberation. If from the point of view of deliberative agency, treating others as ends-in-themselves involves taking them as a limit to my actions, from the other's point of view she is the *recipient* of actions that acknowledge or fail to acknowledge her intrinsic worth. The idea of a moral injury involves turning the idea of individuals as ends-in-themselves away from the perspective of the agent and toward the perspective of the victim. Moral injury, Hampton urges, is what is suffered by a self, both expressively and actually, when he or she is treated in a manner that fails to correspond to the idea of his or her being an end-in-itself—that is, when the self is treated as if it were a beast or a thing or a lesser human. Hampton is tempted by the idea that this mistreatment cannot touch the moral-metaphysical essence of a person, and hence is only an appearance of devaluing and degrading. The actuality of devastation makes nonsense of that claim. When violated, a person *is* degraded and suffers that degradation. In order for this thesis to make sense, then being a human in the full sense, being an end-in-itself, must be a social status or standing that calls forth appropriate treatment, and that status can be harmed and even lost when the appropriate behavior is not forthcoming. The status of being an end-in-itself is constitutive of the self.

So moral injuries are injuries to one's standing or status that become actual through modes of physical treatment. Moral injuries are dignitary harms whose most fundamental mode of becoming actual is through bodily harm. But this requires that our bodies be understood not as blank slates, not as morally neutral arenas of sensation and movement, but as morally saturated in themselves, as simultaneously physical and metaphysical things, to borrow Améry's phrasing. In this and the following chapter, I argue that we require a dual conception of embodiment in which we both *have* our bodies and *are* our bodies, where the relation between the living "body I am" (the body that sweats, blushes, stings, aches, laughs, and uncontrollably cries) and the agential/instrumental "body I have" (the intentional body that at its most eloquent disappears in the performance of successful actions) is a moment-by-moment *social achievement*, something I do or fail to do (which can be a source of shame) in accordance with more or less stringent social rules and norms. Understanding the precariousness of the achievement of bodily integration—that is, what is involved in appropriately sustaining the relation between the body I am and the body I have—is essential to understanding the harm of rape and torture. In both cases, the effort of the perpetrator is *to dispossess the self of its voluntary body*, to dispossess the individual of the body she has, and appropriate all bodily agency and will for itself, leaving the victim with only the body she is, her passive, suffering body, the body that rivets her to the natural world, the body that bears the experience of her mortality. The degradation occurs not just through loss of control, as humiliating as that can be, but through a radical and purposeful dispossession by the other who has always mediated the relation between the self I take myself to be and the self I am. This other here takes possession, appropriating for himself all agency, power, and will, leaving me with just this lacerated body, this quivering, penetrable body. Loss of trust in the world occurs through the recognition that I am absolutely dependent on the other for my *standing* as a self or person, even for myself, and hence that my existential helplessness is not a mere potentiality, but a present and now ever-present actuality. I am devastated.

Devastation is the extreme form of moral injury. In order to have a conception of the moral from the perspective of the victim is thus to ask "*What must a human be such that she can be devastated?*" Although in almost every arena of humanistic and social scientific thought, traumatic experience has become a pivotal notion for the understanding of the meaning of human suffering—trauma as the *persistence* of moral injury—the notion of devastation has hardly penetrated the precincts of modern moral philosophy. Is it possible to now have a conception of the meaning of morals without having near its center a conception of devastation? How can we understand what morally wrong action is if we do not know what moral suffering is?

Providing the rudiments of an answer to the question of "What must a human be such that she can be devastated?" is the task of part 2 (chapters 4–6). I understand devastation to be the extreme and endpoint of humiliation, and the experience of humiliation—of denigration and devaluation—to be both the primary, everyday form of moral injury and a constant reminder of the possibility of devastation. Humiliation and devastation reveal our radical dependence on others for our standing as a self in such a way that the recognition supporting that standing can be withdrawn at any time, leading to that standing being undone fully and utterly.[13] Such is the suffering we see in the experiences of Améry and Brison; rather than portraying themselves as heroes of resistance and overcoming—the moral story we prefer to tell ourselves—they portray themselves as being devastated, of being overwhelmed and undone; they describe the wrenching misery of that, and the ongoing terror of knowing that being human is being subject to such a fate. I take devastation to be the defining moral experience of human life; it may not have always been so, but it is certainly the most demanding moral actuality of the modern world. It is because torture and rape realize the devastation that is the promise in every act of humiliation that they have become for us paradigms of moral injury. It is *why* we think that torture and rape are, along the axis of justification, morally worse than killing; we cannot imagine worse than the devastations of torture and rape, because devastation is the endpoint of moral injury: incessantly suffering the dislocation of the living, sentient body I am from my intentional body, as the power of the other to deny my intrinsic worth as fully human. Devastation is always devastation of the human status; to lose that is to lose the necessary normative condition making life livable. It is my standing, status, or worth *as human* that is first riven and then dispersed.

Chapter 4 is the most philosophically technical of the entire book, and its arguments may be of interest only to philosophers. Throughout I have been connecting two claims about the nature of the self that depart from standard accounts: selves are values, normatively constituted such that to be a self is to sustain a normative ideal of what a self should be; and selves are relational, constituted through their relations with others to such a degree that they are causally and normatively dependent on those others for their standing as a self. I am aware of only one theory that attempts to hold the various normative and relational elements together in a way sufficient to account for the possibility of devastation—namely the theory of recognition first elaborated by Fichte and then Hegel. My interest in chapter 4 is not at all in Hegel commentary and scholarship; my effort is solely to provide the bare bones of a conception of subjectivity and self-consciousness of the "to be a person is to be recognized as a person" sort sufficient for the purposes of my overall argument. For these purposes, I adopt a theory of Robert Brandom's that elaborates the structure of human self-consciousness as a social reworking of the governing structures of animal desire and consciousness. Humans are animals who satisfy the entirety of their *animal life* through *social* means such that it comes to make sense to consider the desire for recognition as the replacement form of the drive for self-preservation. (What the arguments of chapters 5 and 6 must accomplish, among other things, is an explanation of how it is possible for the desire for recognition to be the driving force of social existence and yet it be the case that philosophers have been generally unaware of this fact.) In elaborating this claim, I simultaneously seek to demonstrate how the dual conception of the body—as both voluntary and involuntary such that one both has and is one's body—that we have seen as essential to the experience of rape and torture is equally the conception of embodiment necessary for a consistent conception of persons as constituted through practices of recognition that correspond to even our most minimal naturalist assumptions.

If devastation is loss of trust in the world, and trust in the world is what allows us to forget our existential helplessness, then trust must be both *deep*, connected to our most fundamental conception of who we are as persons, and *pervasive*, contouring and underwriting all our everyday social interactions (or explicitly not so doing when conditions of trust are palpably absent). Chapter 5 is the effort to make good on these two essential claims about the nature and role of trust in our lives. Following the lead of Annette Baier's groundbreaking work on trust, the first half of the chapter argues that trust is the *ethical substance of everyday life*. This is a peculiar claim since one might have thought that if it were true, it would not need to be established at all. But that misses what is most distinctive about trust: it is a set of attitudes, expectations, and normative relations that become visible or evident in direct proportion to their failure to function. Trust, we might say, is the invisibility of trust. And that invisibility matters since trust is the functionally operative set of ethical presuppositions associated with engaging in everyday activities with others; trust's invisibility is what permits everyday life to occur, allowing us to walk, travel, work, buy, sell, eat with our social fellows, allowing us to be together with others without anxiety or even a scent of moral deliberation or reflection. Trust is the fundamental ethical attitude holding in place our relations to others in everyday practices whose basic mechanism is to recede behind the cooperative actions it makes possible. Trust proposes the worth of self and other by allowing that worth to be taken for granted.

"Trust," Baier argues, "is accepted vulnerability to another's possible but not expected ill will (or lack of goodwill) toward one."[14] Trust commences from the victim position; trust commences from the acceptance of our vulnerability before social others, before whoever might come close enough to us (or those we care about most) to cause unspeakable harm. Unless we are bullies or thugs (who attempt to compensate for lack of trust in the world through threat and defense) or the socially deracinated who must expend all their energy on surveillance and protection, we are inserted into everyday life through trust relations. To trust another is to trust that she recognizes my human status (or usually something more parochial: being one of "us") as a limit to her actions. Relations of trust are relations of mutual recognition. Everyday life, on this accounting, is a massive ethical edifice binding us together in relations of mutual respect whose depth and force derive from the fact that they are or can be taken for granted; and when they cannot be taken for granted—the burden of distrust is massively unjustly distributed in accordance with gender, race, and class—this is felt as a wrenching tear in the social world. Failures in trust are experienced as failures of the social world to be as it ought to be. Conditions of trust and distrust are salient and experientially powerful mensurations of the degrees of functional order and justice in a society. However, that trust is not ethically self-sufficient—it will always require moral, legal, and political supplement and correction—does not prevent it from being the ethical substance of everyday life, of being the ethical premise and telos of everyday living. Hence the ethical substance of everyday life makes actual the necessity and pervasiveness of the victim perspective as the orienting moral structure of experience, which is one of the central theses I set out to prove.

Where does trust come from? How is trust possible? In the second half of chapter 5, I argue that because trust relations cannot be rationally chosen or rationally installed (although they are subject to rational evaluation and refinement), trust attitudes must be, in the first instance, the product of a developmental sequence. In the mode of trust, I assume the other will treat me in a way that confirms my self-worth: she will take me to be the morally valuable being I take myself to be. We think others will treat us well because we deserve to be so treated; and we deserve such morally respectful regard and treatment because we take ourselves to be intrinsically valuable

beings. Ethical life is unthinkable without each individual *expecting* normatively appropriate treatment that corresponds to an unreflective conception
of intrinsic self-worth. I argue that one can become a self-moving adult
only by becoming a being who has a value-conception of herself as intrinsically worthy. This self-conception, I argue, is the developmental product
of "first love": through detours and deferrals, the ethical pedagogy of good
enough first love is to produce a being who *expects* to be treated as having
intrinsic worth on the condition, which is often slightly more difficult to
instill, that such treatment is reciprocated. Because the other's regard of my
intrinsic worth is a necessary condition for becoming and being a social
agent as such, then my expectations here are both psychological and normative. Trust is thus the public form of the self-conception and normative
expectations formed by first love; trust, we might say, is the social actuality
of first love. Again, it is the joined vulnerability and value-assumptions of
the victim position that provide the surest inroad into moral life. In this
setting, I offer a stripped down mimetic account of how such a developmental sequence might go.

If the arguments of chapters 4 and 5 are valid, then I have provided the
core of an answer to the question of what must a human be such that she
can be devastated: she is a being whose normative conception of herself as
intrinsically valuable and worthy is a necessary condition for a practical,
empirically viable conception of herself that is held in place and made possible solely through practices of recognition. Love and trust are the forms
of recognition that first constitute and then sustain the intrinsic worth of
individuals whose human life is dependent on the will and regard of all
those around her. We are ideal beings, beings who in order to be must
sustain and value a conception of ourselves as intrinsically worthy (to a
greater or lesser extent); and we are social, relational beings, dependent on
the regard of others for holding in place our value conception of ourselves.
It is the joining of these two facts, understood appropriately, that make us
subject to devastation and explain why to be devastated *is* to suffer loss of
trust in the world.

If moral deliberation and reflection have as minor a role in ethical life
as I am proposing, and if further, the ethical substance of everyday life
comes down to the invisible workings of the trust system, then what is the
stuff of ethical life when it is not invisible and not solely combating conditions of endemic mistrust? Recall how Anscombe recommended that as
we desist from normative ethics, we replace it by work in moral psychology; if we substitute a modern moral psychology grounded in relations of
recognition for the Aristotelian psychology of the great-souled man, this

strikes me as the appropriate direction. I have already proposed that trust is a form of mutual recognition of intrinsic self-worth, and that the standard and exemplary form of moral injury is humiliation. Humiliation is a term of contrast involving a lowering in status; from the middle of the eighteenth century, rather than checking undue pride, humbling one who needs to be humbled, to humiliate came to mean a depressing of dignity or self-respect.[15] In honor societies, the loss of honor produced shame. For us, humiliation has overtaken shame as the bearer of intersubjective worth; humiliation is to structures of recognition what shame was to honor societies; and it is dignity and self-respect that have come to replace honor as the central affirmative concepts of practical self-worth.

In chapter 6 I attempt to provide an elaboration of what I term the 'dignity constellation': dignity, self-respect, respect, humiliation, love, and lovability. Rather than offer a directly analytic reconstruction of this conceptual family, I continue my procedure of tracking Améry's phenomenology of victim-existence in which dignity is the *explicit social* recognition of an individual's intrinsic worth; this makes dignity a status concept rather than a metaphysical possession. We can demonstrate the necessity of dignity, if we can demonstrate that the costs of its destruction are devastating. I use Améry's treatment of the Nuremberg Laws (depriving Jews of all civil and political rights, and disallowing sexual relations between Jews and their fellow German citizens) and the inaugural reception of the Holocaust as the materials appropriate to interrogate the fate of dignity: how Jews were deprived of their dignity by being deprived of the rights of citizenship, and the consequences of that as exemplified by their treatment in the extermination camps.

We can demonstrate the meaning and necessity of dignity by showing that it is the representation of an individual's intrinsic worth. How might such a demonstration go? The consequence of adequate first love is the expectation of appropriate treatment by relevant social others; the ethical term for such an expectation is self-respect; self-respect is thus the practical, first-person realization of an adequate appreciation of one's lovability. To believe oneself lovable is to have or come to have self-respect; self-respect is belief in one's intrinsic self-worth. Self-respect is the representation of an individual's intrinsic self-worth as it becomes manifest through resistance to what might threaten it. Because it is the revelation of intrinsic value in response to what is threatening that value, self-respect is also an essentially victim-based conceptualization of moral worth. What others respect, however, is not your self-respect, but your intrinsic self-worth, your dignity. Dignity is the ascriptive form of intrinsic self-worth; the ascription of dignity is thus an acknowledgment of the self-worth represented in actions expressing self-respect. In analyzing the nature of devastation as the undoing of a self's conception of her intrinsic worth before a dominating other, we have all along been analyzing the role of dignity in human life. Part of what distinguishes Améry's account of dignity from related status-based accounts is the degree to which he demonstrates that respect for dignity has an ineliminable corporeal dimension. I will argue that even human corpses can be deprived of their dignity. If this is so, then dignity must concern the mode or manner in which, again, the body I am and the body I have, my lived body (*Leib*) and my animate body (*Körper*), my voluntary (social) body and my involuntary (natural) body *are sustained* in relation to one another.[16] Achieving an appropriate relation between the body I am and the body I have is both something my consociates make possible for me, something I must achieve for myself, and, routinely, something my consociates help me to achieve when I cannot do so on my own. Burial rites are an extreme form of giving to the natural body—at the very moment it passes from the world of the living—the dignity of social agency. Finally, in a moving account, Améry demonstrates how physical struggle and revolt can be essential to the preservation of human dignity.

In my conclusion, which is intended only to flag some results and point to urgent areas for future research, I return to the question of the substantive rule of law in relation to the permissibility or impermissibility of torture, and connect it to the idea of human rights as set out in the Universal Declaration of Human Rights (1948). I then try to say something about why although torture and rape are nearly indistinguishable forms of moral injury, the moral opprobrium that attaches to torture has yet to fully attach to rape, at least if we take the persistence of rape as an accurate measure of the authority of its moral prohibition. The persistence of the law conception of morality in detaching us from an adequate appreciation of the devastating character of rape has not only aided the perpetuation of a rape culture, but alienated us all from our deepest moral impulses and judgments. The morality of law is worse than philosophically wrong; it produces a socially corrosive form of moral alienation.

For some readers, the first chapter's long historical preface to the reconstructive moral argument of the remainder of the book will feel more like a blockade than an invitation and scene-setting. For them, I have begun chapter 2 with a summary of the relevant philosophical results of the historical argument.

PART ONE

History, Phenomenology, and Moral Analysis

ONE

Abolishing Torture and the Uprising of the Rule of Law

I. Introduction

Our moral horror and unanimous moral disapproval of torture is a new—and perhaps still fragile—moral fact that arose only in the second half of the eighteenth century. Beginning with the installation of the Roman-canon legal system in the eleventh and twelfth centuries, torture had a central role in all European legal systems: first, as a pivotal element in the law of evidence; and second, as a dominating component of the penal system. In the Roman-canon legal system, crimes punishable by the death penalty, or by severe mutilation or maiming, required either the testimony of two eyewitnesses or a confession. This was a hard standard to satisfy—murderers tend not to commit their vile deeds before eyewitnesses, nor do they readily confess them; hence, torture was used as a supplement in order to produce new evidence or to "prompt" a confession. Without torture, the law of evidence would have been unusable for serious crimes. Yet, with breathtaking rapidity, torture was abolished throughout Europe in the second half of the eighteenth century. "So powerful was this revulsion against torture as a symbol of the enormities of the *ancien régime*," argues Edward Peters, "that not even the moral passion of the Revolution [with its murderous Terror] and the reaction that followed it inspired a return to torture . . . [The] real influence of writers like Voltaire and Beccaria: their work simply made torture unthinkable."[1] So complete was torture's abolition throughout Europe that in 1874 Victor Hugo could exclaim that "torture has ceased to exist."[2]

Running parallel to these events is the reception of Cesare Beccaria's *On Crimes and Punishments*. First published in 1764, it was almost immediately translated into twenty-two European languages; it went through twenty-eight Italian editions and nine French ones before 1800 (Voltaire produced a commentary that became a part of most editions); it was translated into English in 1767 (Jeremy Bentham becoming Beccaria's "apostle"), with multiple editions in both Britain and the United States (Jefferson copied long passages into his notebooks). It played a direct role in law reforms initiated by Catherine II, Frederick the Great, the Virginia Commonwealth, and those carried out in France before and during the Revolution.

Beccaria was among the most influential philosophers of the eighteenth century; everyone read him. Today he is virtually unknown. How can we explain the massive influence, and the almost complete forgetting of his work? More precisely: what was the historical import of the abolition of torture, and what was Beccaria's role in its abolition? In the nineteenth century, trumpeting an Enlightenment idea of historical progress, the argument went that it was the writings of Beccaria and Voltaire alone that had brought about the abolition of torture throughout Europe. This is a philosopher's "fairy tale,"[3] but not completely so: Beccaria's little treatise did bring to moral, legal, and political *fulfillment* the eighteenth-century humanitarian revolution by giving it principled legal form. In so doing, the Beccaria-informed abolition of torture grounds modern political morality. Without Beccaria, the legal formation of moral modernity would not have come to be; in forgetting Beccaria we have forgotten a founding moment of political modernity.

In the next section, I shall track the changed conception of body and pain presupposed by the abolition of torture. In section III, I reconstruct Beccaria's treatise as espousing the rule of law as the determinate negation of the conception of law implied by the practices of judicial and penal torture. I am tempted to say that the "dignified" modern bodily autonomous subject is a construction out of or emerges from the demands of substantive rule of law. Section IV tracks the development of what I call the "Beccaria thesis"—namely that the force of law is constituted by its unconditional eschewal of brute force as exemplified by torture, in the contemporary jurisprudential thought of Jeremy Waldron. In the final section, I argue that neither Beccaria's nor Waldron's defense of the rule of law as the determinate negation of the sovereign law of torture has generated a corresponding moral philosophy. Hence, the moral meaning of the abolition of torture remains unthought.

II. Abolishing Torture: The Dignity of Tormentable Bodies

In the opening pages of *Discipline and Punish*, Michael Foucault powerfully summarizes the scope of the humanitarian revolution with his memorable contrast between the 1757 execution by torture of the would-be regicide Damiens, and the terse list of rules that make up the daily timetable for a prison for young offenders in Paris in 1838. Damiens was to be placed on a scaffold, where "the flesh will be torn from his breasts, arms, thighs and calves with red-hot pincers, his right hand, holding the knife with which he committed the said parricide, burnt with sulfur . . . and then his body drawn and quartered by four horses and his limbs and body consumed by fire, reduced to ashes and his ashes thrown to the winds."[4] This gruesome image, that, with a hint of relish, Foucault continues quoting accounts of for another three pages, contrasts utterly with the numbing routine of the prison: "At the first drum-roll, the prisoners must rise and dress in silence, as the supervisor opens the cell doors. At the second drum-roll, they must be dressed and make their beds. At the third, they must line up and proceed to the chapel for morning prayer."[5] There then follows a precise structuring of the day: meals, work, schooling, more work until the boys are led back to their cells, undress in silence, and return to their beds for the night. To explain and understand the meaning of the abolition of torture cannot involve anything less than grasping the seismic shift in penal practices marked by the contrast between Damiens being torn to pieces by four horses and the boys in a workshop listening to a passage from an uplifting text read to them by their supervisor. Something of the moral meaning of modernity is lodged in this contrast.

The central motif here is Foucault's articulation of the transfigured role of the human body in the shift from torture to imprisonment, how the body disappears as a target of penal repression, and how thereby the theatrical representation of pain becomes excluded.[6]

> One no longer touched the body, or at least as little as possible, and then only to reach something other than the body itself . . . The body now serves as an instrument or intermediary: if one intervenes upon it to imprison it, or to make it work, it is in order to deprive the individual of a liberty that is regarded both as a right and as property. The body, according to this penality, is caught up in a system of constraints and privations, obligations and prohibitions. Physical pain, the pain of the body itself, is no longer the constituent element of the penalty. *From being an art of unbearable sensations punishment has become an economy of suspended rights.* If it is still necessary for the law to reach and manipulate the body of the convict, it will be at a distance, in the proper way, according to strict rules, and with a much "higher" aim . . . When the moment of execution approaches, the patients are injected with tranquillizers. A utopia of judicial reticence: take away life, but prevent

the patient from feeling it; deprive the prisoner of all rights, but do not inflict pain; impose penalties free of all pain. [7]

Although at the conclusion of this passage Foucault is leaping from the end of the eighteenth century into our own time, he is assuming that with respect to the new placement of the body in the penal system, our methods of execution are fully continuous with the introduction of the guillotine and the drop method of hanging: "an execution that affects life rather than the body." [8]

Consider the italicized sentence in the passage above as offering, in a nutshell, the meaning and essence of the humanitarian revolution. Two issues are prominent here: the body of individuals coming to have a new status, a new meaning, requiring a new regard; and, as cause or consequence of this new standing, the body's entering into a changed relation to the state. Let us consider the latter issue first. As opposed to the private and secretive character of judicial proceedings, penal torture and execution were great public spectacles. In a world in which there was as yet no police and no routine mechanisms of law enforcement, punitive public executions were certainly meant to terrify and deter. But these characteristics had a specific contour in monarchies in which the *authority of the law and the authority of the sovereign person were united*. In breaking the law, the criminal was attacking the very person of the sovereign, attacking his (or her) authority. Public executions thus had the juridical-political function of reconstituting the momentarily injured sovereignty; they "restore sovereignty by manifesting it as it most spectacular . . . Its aim is not so much to re-establish a balance as to bring into play, at its extreme point, the dissymmetry between the subject who has dared to violate the law and the all-powerful sovereign who displays his strength." [9] What the tortured body spectacularly demonstrates is the power of the sovereign, by which I mean the authority, validity, and legitimacy of the sovereign's laws, as well as the force of those laws. If it were only force that had been at stake, then there would have been no connection between the judicial proceedings and the penal finale, no truth in punishment, only vengeance; if tortured executions had just been occasions for terrifying the people, then they could not have been festive occasions. Sovereign power was an expression of the unity of the people with the sovereign and hence the unity of the people with themselves.

Giving expression to this unity was accomplished through the spectacle of torture: "Under the traditional understanding, the pains of the body did not belong entirely to the individual condemned person. Those pains

had the higher religious and political purposes of redemption and repara-
tion of the community . . . Public executions brought thousands of people
together to celebrate the community's recovery from the crime's injury."[10]
What was *seen* as the bodies of the convicted were ripped asunder was the
awesomeness of sovereign power. But to so experience the power of the
sovereign was what it was to experience the force of law; the lawfulness
of law was inseparable from sovereign power, where sovereign power was,
again, finally inseparable from its expression in the tortured body of the
condemned.

Sometime during the eighteenth century this ended; perhaps not the
terror, but its awesomeness, its ceremonial authority, its capacity to authorize the law, its power of uniting and renewing community. The carnival
was over. Suddenly, instead of seeing sovereign authority in the tortured
body, the people began to see vengeance and brutality; instead of gathering
community, public executions, came to feel like an attack on community,
a dismembering of it, as if the dismembered body of the individual now
stood for what was happening to the community through legal violence;
even criminals became objects of sympathy. Torture thus became an occasion for solidarity with the victim rather than with the sovereign, as if
the sovereign was now the primary threat to the community. Lynn Hunt—
whose argument is the basis for the one being offered here—states that
in the new state of affairs "cruel punishment exacted in a public setting
constituted an assault on society rather than a reaffirmation of it. Pain brutalized the individual—and by identification, the spectators—rather than
opening the door to salvation through repentance."[11]

Underlying the changed public reaction to the spectacle of torture was
a changed understanding of the locus and meaning of pain. Sometime
in the second half of the eighteenth century pain slowly stopped being
metaphysically meaningful; incrementally but emphatically pain stopped
having sacramental meanings that could be parlayed into political and
epistemological-juridical meaning and became, for all intents and purposes, meaningless, a blunt experience of what should not be, of what
should not be borne or suffered. Pain was no longer a sign to be translated
or a means of ennoblement.

Evidence for the disenchantment of the meaning of pain can be found
in the records of surgeons, those on the frontline in the treatment of pain.
In the sixteenth century, relieving even intolerable pains was considered a
side issue; because pain was the sign of a deeper cause, silencing pain could
be dangerous with respect to locating the cause. Pain inspired neither sympathy nor pity; it was still then a part of the Godly ordained natural course

of things that needed to be borne until the cause itself could be removed. By the end of the eighteenth century this had changed; pain itself was an issue, both for the sufferer, for companions and onlookers, and for the surgeon. Pierre Dionis, in his *A Course of Surgical Operations* (translated from the second French edition, 1733), writes: "There are surgeons who are offended at the cries of their patients, and who scold and chide them, as though they ought to be insensible to the tortures which they make them endure: these ways of acting are too cruel; a surgeon must have humanity, and exhort those under his hands to patience: *he must share their pain;* which, though he cannot help putting them to, he must, at least, leave them the liberty of crying and complaining."[12] Pain's sheer aversiveness has now become the primary fact about pain. Pain no longer circulates through the community as part of a divine political economy. Pain now belongs unequivocally to the sufferer. Because pain is an attack on the individual, the very thing that should not be, then to perceive another suffering in pain is to experience them as being attacked, destroyed, undone. To so see them is to see what should not be. We now cannot look on at another's pain without suffering with them. Dionis again: "We separate from [surgery] whatever is rough and barbarous, we retrench those burning irons and horrible instruments, which not only the patients, but the bystanders, could not see without trembling."[13] We tremble at the instruments that will cause the patient pain; in trembling we identify with the sufferer. Hume will use this very example of trembling at surgical instruments that will pain the patient in his account of sympathy.

Pain thus undergoes a double movement: on the one hand, pain becomes more emphatically and unconditionally what happens to the body of the sufferer; pain is possessed by the sufferer, belonging solely to him or her undergoing it. Pain individualizes and isolates; my body is mine in being the locus of my pains, pains that if not alleviated are my destruction. The self now draws in, becoming at one with the bounded body, the body that can be harmed and suffer pains. On the other hand, precisely because pain now portends the destruction of an individual without any broader significance, without any redeeming features, then pain becomes communicable in a new way: to see the other as another like oneself is to see that their sufferings should not be. The pain of others now calls for identification; the pained bodies of others call for sympathy and pity. Suddenly, to be unmoved by the pain of another would itself be a sign of immorality, of not knowing or understanding what being human was.[14]

In the course of the eighteenth century, bodily pains became no longer exchangeable, no longer part of a divine economy in which they might serve as payment or acknowledgment or communal resource. When each pain and each suffering is interpreted as impiety or punishment, as debt owed or sacred abandonment—"My God, my God, O why hast thou forsaken me?"—the body and pains of each cannot be fully her own, not irreducibly her flourishing or foundering, but are signs of innocence or guilt, purity or pollution, of being divinely loved or despised. All that eventually disappears with, let us say, the rise of modern individualism, with the modern thought that pains, whether accidentally incurred or intentionally produced, are properly suffered solely by the bodily being in which they take place, and they matter because they are a (sign of) harm to that bodily being. From hence forward, in my body being intentionally harmed by another, *I* am harmed in my very standing as a self or subject or person; with this is introduced the very idea of moral injury. The idea of moral injury so understood represents the utter secularization of the moral.

If moral injury is an acceptable way of recording the new contouring of body and pain, then we might say something like the notion of moral injury must have been experientially operative in the changed understanding of torture: from communal celebration to attack on the very underpinning of our being a community at all. This is not to claim that it was moral *arguments* that were essential to the abolition of torture; John H. Langbein and Foucault are right that those arguments occur at the conclusion of what was in reality an extended process (indeed far more extended than Foucault's ideal type presentation makes apparent). The claim is rather that the transfigured character of body and pain gave to suffering a new social meaning; if the words of the surgeons are an accurate capturing of what was occurring, then we must say that seeing others in pain became an *intrinsically moral experience*, perhaps for us moderns the paradigm of a moral experience. By "moral experience" is meant simply the thought that others being in pain was no longer viewed from a distance as what is fated or ordained or deserved; a sympathetic response to the pain and suffering of others, all others, even strangers, was coming to be identified as a primitive moral fact demanding direct response in the present and preventive response toward a foreseeable future: "For supposing I saw a person perfectly unknown to me, who, while asleep in the fields, was in danger of being trod under foot by a horse," Hume imagines, then "I shou'd immediately run to his assistance; and in this I shou'd be actuated by the same principle of sympathy, which makes me concern'd for the present sorrows of a stranger."[15] That sympathy should of a sudden become the fundament of a series of theories of morals—in Francis Hutcheson, Hume, Adam Smith, Rousseau, and later Schopenhauer—should in the first instance be considered as a component of a cultural transformation in which pain and suffering have been emphatically positioned in the body of the individual without further recourse. It is because the experience of others' suffering left the symbol-laden precincts of law, politics, and religion, and became a primarily "natural" (physical, causal) phenomenon and, thereby, experientially a moral phenomenon that the debate about torture could become available to moral argument. Moral argument tracks the moralization of the experience of the body. I shall return to the philosophical tracking of moral experience below.

What finally made the abolition of torture *necessary*, to the extent it retrospectively seemed so, is that the political-legal-theological regime in which its practice was embedded lost its authority, the torture spectacle becoming a force for political disintegration rather than integration. An essential feature of this collapse, I am arguing, is a transformed understanding of the social location of the human body and its pains, the latter adhering to the former in a radically new way. One way of expressing this occurrence is to say that Europeans were undergoing processes of emphatic social and cultural *individuation*: not only were individuals becoming more relatively independent as economic and social units, but bodily pains came to be primarily regarded as sources of individual destruction; these two movements together—the active and passive modes of individuation—lead to individual will and agency becoming sources of dignity or right. An immanent, experientially pervasive upshot of individuation was the moralization of intersubjective experience: each individual's pains, always implicitly and routinely explicitly, now making a claim on the onlooker's moral attention, a summons to at least sympathy or pity, and ideally a call to alleviating or reparative action; and the converse, indifference to another's pain, coming to be regarded as a perversion (Rousseau) or, at least, some form of moral failure.[16] Once intersubjective experience is moralized in this way, it places a constraint on the observable forms of state action and the presuppositions of lawfulness. As we shall see directly, the newly effective moral constraints on lawfulness is one of the central motives for the uprising of the modern rule of law.

The acts banning torture throughout Europe were the moral and legal reflection of this deeper ethical transformation—namely the gradual but emphatic emergence of the individual body as morally inviolable that was consequent upon the coming-to-be of the individualistic and wholly secular view that *pains* belong "only to the sufferer in the here-and-now."[17]

Only when pains are understood as belonging solely to the individual, solely as "my pains" does the body become inviolable and does the person come to be regarded as a being having intrinsic worth, or, as will be said later, an end-in-itself, a being with dignity, a being with natural rights—all these conceptual innovations reaching to express and articulate this transformation, this new understanding of the person.

The abolition of torture is the culmination and fulfillment of the processes of *societal individuation* and *cultural individualism* that generated what I wish to call "the moralization of intersubjective experience." Before the eighteenth century, morality in our sense—in which pain generally has the sense of sheer aversiveness, of what ought not to be, and hence as something that calls for sympathy and response—was morally marginal.[18] The secularization of pain is a central pillar of the humanitarian revolution. What made the abolition of torture capable of culminating and fulfilling the demands of the history producing the moralization of intersubjective experience is that it provided a principled legal articulation and moral expression of the transformed relation between the emergent bodily autonomous individual and the state. Even without democratic institutions, the abolition of torture as the exemplary moment of the rule of law provides for a radically new understanding of the relation between state and individual: once the bodies of citizens are legally beyond the direct physical "touch" of the state, which is what Foucault so powerfully documents, then the individual has acquired a new moral standing in relation to the state's legal claims against him.

III. Torture and the Rule of Law: Beccaria

Hunt and Foucault narrate the abolition of judicial and penal torture from opposing perspectives: Hunt perceives in the abolition an emphatic realization of the emergent experience of moral respect being accorded to the individual body that gathers up that experience and turns it into law, thereby forging and bringing to political self-consciousness the complex interconnection between societal individuation and cultural individualism. From the other side, Foucault, while acknowledging the law's new relation to the body of the accused and the convicted, underlines the coming into being of a new political economy of punishment that involves a combination of disciplinary surveillance with a redistribution of tolerated illegalities. The two narratives converge, however, not only on the law's retreat from its hold on the body, incrementally substituting the deprivation of liberty for the imposition of pain, but equally over the changed status of the authority of law. In the regime of the torture spectacle, the pain of the convicted served to reveal the authority of the sovereign, hence revealing the sovereign as the source of the authority of the law. In the new regime, the rule of law itself becomes immanently authoritative, its authority both drawing on the authority of the intrinsic worth of the individual body, recognizing that authority as its own, and in turn giving that authority back to the individual through its operations. For both Foucault and Hunt, Beccaria's *On Crimes and Punishments* provides the lynchpin to their analyses: a cold rationalization of legal and penal practice, and an agonized cry from the heart against the existing legal system's own barbarous cruelties.[19]

Foucault carefully documents how the collapsing sovereign system came to be viewed as arbitrary and irrational, where this change of perception is what lay behind the view that sovereign torture was a violent attack on the individual, as something personal and therefore not lawful, as arbitrary and therefore somehow extra-legal, beyond what legality could intelligibly be. The hollowness of sovereign authority was perceived as pervasive in the system as a whole by the reformers:

> There was too much power in the lower jurisdictions . . . [who] could carry out arbitrary sentences without adequate supervision; there was too much power on the side of the prosecution, which possessed almost unlimited means of pursuing its prosecution. . . . There was too much power in the hands of judges who were able to content themselves with futile evidence. . . . There was too much power in the hands of the . . . royal magistrates. . . . There was too much power exercised by the king, who could suspend courts of justice, alter their decisions, remove magistrates from office, or exile them. . . . This dysfunction of power was related to a central excess: what might be called the monarchical "super-power," which identified the right to punish with the *personal power of the sovereign*.[20]

Even as revised and modernized by the *Ordonnance Générale* of 1670, the authority of the Roman-canon legal system was unraveling as a consequence of the disintegration of (divine) sovereign authority; law increasingly came to appear as arbitrary and personal, the rule of men over other men, and, finally, the personal rule of the sovereign over everyone. In order to combat this, what was needed was a rationalization of the rule of law toward formality, procedure, the rights of the accused, and, dominantly, as deriving its status not from who commanded it, but in virtue of its satisfying the function of protecting the freedom and dignity of each from the arbitrary usurpations and violations perpetrated by the sovereign legal regime. Even as laws and statutes might remain the same, the modern idea of the rule of law begins, precisely and explicitly, as a repudiation of the sovereign authorization of law: sovereign law becomes the paradigm of unlawfulness, and torture the paradigmatic exposition of that unlawfulness. In refashioning the meaning of law, torture was fully transformed from standing for the authority of the sovereign to becoming the paradigm of arbitrary violation premised on inequality. For Beccaria, at least, the arbitrariness of the sovereign legal system tracked the societal structures of inequality in which it was embedded.

A routine misunderstanding of the influence of Beccaria's *On Crimes and Punishments* depends on the idea that Beccaria offered new or unheard of criticisms of judicial torture; this is implausible since the unreliability and potential unfairness of interrogational torture had been well known since ancient times. The immediate and singular impact of Beccaria's little book derived from four sources: first, timing—all the transformations in the economic, political, religious, and moral texture of everyday life, tending toward societal individuation and cultural individualism, were rushing toward culmination in the second half of the eighteenth century; thus, even prior to the efforts of Beccaria and Voltaire, Sweden (publically) and Prussia (at first secretly) could successfully abolish judicial torture. Second, Beccaria explicitly and emphatically placed his critique of judicial torture in the context of a compact and elegant defense of the rule of law, written, eloquently and powerfully, in the manner of the French *philosophes*, rather than in the technical jargon of systematic philosophy or eighteenth century jurisprudence.[21] Third, because he excludes natural law considerations from his analysis and proposals, Beccaria generates the first truly *critical* philosophy of law, offering an account, in broadly naturalistic terms, of what criminal law *should* be, drawing a clear line between is and ought, between, as Jeremy Bentham puts it, "expository jurisprudence" and "censorial jurisprudence."[22] Fourth, while lacking analytic detail, the argument consistently and almost unnervingly operates with a delicate and subtle reconciling of what became the most troubling philosophical dualisms of the time. Beccaria unites a utilitarian framework (which he is, for all intents and purposes, inventing here) with a Rousseau-inspired social contract theory; his penal theory makes deterrence legislatively primary while making retributive considerations essential to the application of law; the operation of the passions provides the motivational springboard for institutional design, while Enlightened reason, the standpoint of the reflective spectator, continually appears as precursor and consequence of those designs—reason thus having the power to control and determine the passions, and thus in practical terms capable of being an autonomous spring of action. Finally, if in standard social contract manner he makes individual freedom the premise of legitimacy, he continually makes inequality the fundamental threat to public welfare and the rule of law. Beccaria's philosophical *tact* makes a wholly secular, rationalized rule of law, with the abolition of torture and the death penalty at its center, appear as an emergent—Enlightened—jurisprudential common sense. It is the installation of this new jurisprudential common sense in which a morally substantive conception of the rule of law emerges as the necessary alternative to sovereign authority, as exemplified by the tortured body, that makes torture "unthinkable."

Part of what makes Beccaria's argument come together and have such wide impact is that he assumes that criminal law and the state's penal system can and should be seen as the exemplary locale for articulating state power: it is there, as nowhere else, that state and citizen come into contact with one another. For the ordinary citizen of the eighteenth century, for a world in which (constitutional) monarchy remained the dominant state form, the criminal legal system, the laws and their enforcement, *was* the actuality of the state. It is for this reason that judicial torture becomes the central image of a failing system, and its principled overcoming the core of a new ideal of political legitimacy; political legitimacy comes to be a function of the rule of law rather than vice versa. Arguably, it was the new egalitarian conception of the rule of law, with its social contract underpinnings and its protections of the bodies of citizens against arbitrary state violence, that fueled the flame of the rights revolutions that were to soon follow. Thus it was Beccaria's emphasis on the need for the rule of law in its modern, substantive sense and a generally rationalized penal system—a new "gentle way in punishment" as Foucault puts it—that gave his critique of judicial torture its force and authority.[23] Understood aright, and this is the crux of the matter: *substantive rule of law is the determinate negation of the law of sovereign torture.* Beccaria invented the modern rule of law as the principled pulse of criminal law and penal practice, which has at its core what I call the "Beccaria thesis": the very idea that the rule of law is constituted by the absolute incommensurability between the force of law and the kind of force represented by state violence to the human body. Beccaria does not argue from the possession of rights to the necessity for the abolition of torture, but, rather, from the devastation of torture to the necessity of the rule of law. I will reconstruct his argument in three steps: its social contract premises, its rule of law analysis of criminal justice and penal practice, and his arguments for the abolition of torture.

A. *The Social Contract.* Although the inherited Roman-canon legal system was secular and rationalized, it had come to appear as resting on nothing but tradition: "A few odd remnants of the laws of an ancient conquering race codified twelve hundred years ago by a prince ruling at Constantinople, and since jumbled together with the customs of the Lombards and bundled up in the rambling volumes of obscure academic interpreters—this is what makes up the tradition of opinions that passes for law across a large portion of Europe" (3). What the inherited body of laws palpably lacked was the governance of consistent *principles* through which their general authority and specific rationale could be evaluated. Beccaria thus begins, in effect, with a challenge to the tradition of legal positivism: rational principles were required in order to replace the rule of fading tradition and personal authority that positive law, in its bald positivity, implacably insinuated.

Nor was the jumble of inherited law merely arbitrary in its operation; the existing system concentrated power and the benefits flowing from its possession in the hands of a privileged few, "raising those few to the heights of power and happiness, and sinking everyone else in feebleness and poverty" (7). Inequality, structural and systematic, was the primary source of the personalization of power and arbitrariness. If the law stabilizes, legitimates, or perpetuates inequality, then, by that very fact, it perpetuates arbitrariness and moral violence.

The radical inequality of unprincipled monarchism ran from the organization of the state into the sinews of everyday life through the presumption that the state was composed of families, each with a little monarch at its head, rather than individual persons. Under the traditional family system, Beccaria argues, in a nation of one hundred thousand people, for example, with five persons in each family, "there will be twenty thousand persons and eighty thousand slaves" (60). Whatever Beccaria means by the public good, he never backs off from a moral and political individualism in which *each* has *equal* possession of his or her own freedom, each possessing the right to dispose of his or her freedom as desired within the bounds of law. Beccaria assumes that relations among persons must be conceived as, finally, voluntary, a matter of contract. He argues that the demand for "continual self-sacrifice to a false idol going by the name of the *good of the family*, which is frequently not the good of any of its members," is incom-

patible with the basic law of a republic, which is "made up of persons"
(61), not families. Beccaria's stringent moral individualism is, doubtless, in
significant part motivated by his repugnance at the sacrificial system of the
monarchial family. Beccaria broke with his own parents over his marriage
to a, in their view, socially inferior woman; he and Teresa named their first
child Giulia after the heroine of Rousseau's *La Nouvelle Héloïse*.[24] Under
conditions in which traditional communal forms were the bearers of social
position and status, only a moral individualism that replaced inherited position by voluntary association could satisfy the demand for freedom from
arbitrary authority.

Chapter 26, "Family Feeling," is a crucible for Beccaria's thoughts on the
appropriate relations between individual and society; not only did traditional monarchy repeat the arbitrariness of the miniature monarchy of the
family, but the logic of that inequality generated an illusory notion of the
whole—the good of the family, the good of society—to which the good of
the individual could be sacrificed. Part of the power of Beccaria's moral vision derives from his understanding of traditional social forms as not only
bastions of unequal privilege, but more severely, as squandering and pul-
verizing the claims of the individual beneath a sacrificial logic of the public
good that was most fully realized in penal torture. The utilitarian theory
that Beccaria invents in *On Crimes* is thus wholly unlike the utilitarianism
that Bentham developed on the basis of Beccaria's model. For Beccaria, a
central component of the arbitrariness and violence of the monarchial legal system was that it denied that the good of each be counted equally *and*
separately. Nonexchangeable individual worth, worth that cannot be sacrificed or traded-off against a collective good, operates as a moral premise
of his reflections—it is the moral substance determining his construction
of social contract theory. In inveighing against the practice of the wealthy
paying only fines for criminal assaults, Beccaria states what has become
the crux of the modern (Kantian) notion of human dignity—namely the
distinction between being a person and being a thing upon which a price
or value can be set: "There is no freedom when the laws permit a man in
some circumstances to cease to be a *person* and to become a *thing*" (50).[25]
Hence, from the outset a central principle of later utilitarian accounting
is denied; individual goods (pleasures or absences of pain) can never be
aggregated. Aggregated outcomes that ignore the good of each repeat the
sacrificial logic of family and state torture that Beccaria was overthrowing;
it is, Beccaria argues, "a false idea of utility . . . to separate the public good
from the good of each individual" (102).

Law, however, can only protect the personhood of each, preventing their becoming a thing to be sacrificed, if each is recognized as a legal person before the law. While the titles of chapters 20 and 21 are, respectively, "Violent Crimes" and "The Punishment of Nobility," their primary concern is equality before the law. Hence, after acknowledging all the different forms of social inequality, and leaving unanswered the question of their legitimacy and utility, Beccaria asserts that, nonetheless, "punishments ought to be the same for the highest as they are for the lowest of citizens. To be legitimate, every distinction whether of honour or wealth presupposes an antecedent equality based on the laws, which treat every subject as equally subordinate to them" (51). Beccaria's rule of law doctrine contends that whatever natural or social inequalities exist among persons must be irrelevant to their civic-legal standing: the law *makes the unequal equal*, giving to each equal legal and civic standing. Hence, the true meaning of law is its work of equalization, its *making* of each citizen a person through giving each equal legal personhood. As nearly every reader half understood, in the name of providing the terms for a nonabusive, nonviolative criminal legal system, under the cover of a procedurally governed conception of the rule of law, Beccaria was sotto voce projecting a new form of life, a new conception of the ethical life of the community, in which the legal institutions would provide the framework through which individuals *would become* free and equal citizens. Beccaria's social constructivism departed from the natural law tradition because he saw that only appropriate social practices could create the kind of freedom and equality that natural law promised.

It is this background social constructivist conception that underlies his defense of the idea of the social contract. Thus he argues that ideas of political justice are socially and historically variable; their variability demonstrates that their authority cannot be derived from either revelation or natural law since the authority of the latter are presumed to be constant and unchanging in light of local interpretations of them. Political justice rests on social conventions that, in order to be authoritative, must be agreed to by all; since agreement is the prerequisite for the authority of a convention, conventions should be regarded as "explicit or tacit compacts among men" (4); even more explicitly, laws, which have historically been tools of the powerful, "should be contracts among free men" (7). For Beccaria, laws are not commands of any kind but agreements, and hence forms of relations among persons, as Montesquieu construed them. Because revelation and natural law have already been shown to be inoperative then, with the withering of traditional authority, there is nothing else for laws to be but contracts of some kind. By elimination, the only possible ground for society is a social contract, however implicit; and since each individual is the possessor of his or her freedom, then a legitimate social contract is one made by free individuals compacting with one another. In Beccaria's hands, the social contract is a moral invention designed to elaborate the moral excess of each individual beyond the social whole of which she is a part. Like the burgeoning use of the notion of natural rights, the social contract is a philosophical invention and, eventually, a social construction of the very idea of moral individuality, of the individual's having an intrinsic worth that legal and political arrangements must be answerable to. (However naïvely earlier and later writers construed rights and social contract, there is no hint of that naïveté in Beccaria; his disillusioned constructivist habits of thought are precisely what Bentham most admired in his philosophy.) Beccaria's conception of social contract is thus the beginning of a normative reconstruction of lawfulness in opposition to the idea of sovereign lawfulness.

Beccaria employs a thin version of Hobbes's hypothetical state of nature as the motivation for forming the social contract: "Wearied by living in an unending state of war and by a freedom rendered useless by the uncertainty of retaining it, they sacrifice a part of that freedom in order to enjoy what remains in security and calm" (9). There is a precision in this claim: laws are a restriction on individuals' free movements; therefore, if the state of nature is a figure of the absence of law, then what individuals possess in it is their unconditioned freedom of action. Unconditioned freedom of action is thereby that which is intrinsic to a person. Consequently, the only thing that individuals can surrender is a portion of their freedom—that is, their freedom to do a range of actions. This tight little circle of thought intends to strip from the notion of law everything but its core function: to prohibit certain courses of action (and, occasionally, to require certain courses of action). The person with respect to the law is the autonomous subject.

Methodologically, Beccaria innovates a new form of logical naturalism in which normative terms compress "a train of reasoning" (12); normative concepts—rights, obligations, et al.—are logical fictions (Bentham's phrase) that do not name objects, the way nouns do, but rather are shorthand for the full sentences in which they belong. Normative concepts have uses, not objects, as their meaning.[26] Beccaria's primary example is the obligation of all to obey the law; this does not mean that there is some abstract "duty" commanding "Obey this law!"; rather, the obligation equals the thought that it is in the interests of all that contracts be observed, and hence we will sanction those who fail to do so. Analogously, sovereignty does not name the power of the sovereign. Rather, Beccaria contends, since persons intrinsically have nothing but their freedom as their natural endowment as persons, then in forming a social contract all they can conceivably surrender is some portion of their originally unconditioned freedom. The sum of those surrendered freedoms constitute "the sovereignty of the nation," and the sovereign is solely the "legitimate repository and administrator of these freedoms" (9).

Existing laws are a product of a messy and barbarous history. From this alone we can infer that for Beccaria the social contract refers to neither an empirical nor a hypothetical history; rather, the social contract is to be understood as a reflective mechanism for interpreting the meaning of laws; the device of the social contract announces the meaning of law beyond the sway of tradition, revelation and natural law. If the reason for leaving the state of nature is the uselessness of freedom without security, then the sole function or purpose of law is to make the exercise of freedom possible. We thus should judge the goodness of laws on the basis of their ability to satisfy the function governing their use. If we depart from the state of nature in order to avoid the *pains* of insecurity, fear, and the endless obstructions others place in the way of the pursuit of our satisfying our desires, then the principle governing the goodness of law is its capacity to enable each of us to maximally satisfy our desires. Laws, Beccaria says, should conduce to "the greatest happiness shared among the greater number [*La massima felicità divisa nel maggior numero*]" (7). In the first English edition of *On Crimes*, this was mistranslated as "the greatest happiness for the greatest number"[27]—issuing the usage Bentham adopted from it, and so generating two centuries of moral misdirection. Beccaria, cleaving to his conception of individual freedom and dignity, uses the notions "sharing" and the "greater number" in order to imply that the goal is not aggregation, but, on the contrary, the provision of conditions of action whereby *each* may attain the maximum happiness their individual free pursuit allows. The goal is not to maximize aggregate happiness, but to equalize the possibility of happiness by equalizing the conditions for its rational individual pursuit. On this reconstruction of Beccaria's thought, the principle of utility is not a self-standing moral principle, but an inference from the reasons for leaving the state of nature.[28] Binding maximizing calculations to social contract constraints is not a crude joining of disparate materials. Rather, it asks what principle autonomous subjects who have suffered the pains of the state of nature—and, by inference, present subjects who have suffered the arbitrariness and violence of the sovereign system of law—should employ in regulating their union; Beccaria's principle of utility tracks a path of practical reasoning rather than operating a deduction from first principles.

While surrendering the minimum portion of freedom necessary to guarantee the secure use of the remainder immediately leads to the principle—never stated by Beccaria but obviously implied—that each should have the maximum liberty compatible with every other having equal liberty, that principle is insufficient on its own: it detaches motive from principle, depriving the principle of the affective force necessary for its effectiveness. Further, and worse, it disconnects the rationale of law from the presumed motives for leaving the state of nature and those motives presumed to govern our continuing willingness to subject ourselves to the rule of law. Maximal distributive utility, as I shall call it, forms the social imaginary horizon of Beccaria's thought. His particular inflection of this idea sustains the emergent secular binding of pain to the individual, meaningless pain as, again, what a person most wishes to avoid. Assuming the primacy of avoiding pain over seeking pleasure, he understands the principle of distributive utility as the maximum elimination of unnecessary pains conducive to the pursuit of desire and the exercise of freedom. He summarizes his version of negative distributive utility this way: "Not everything which is useful to the commonwealth ought to be directly ordained, although everything which is harmful ought to be banned. Hence, all laws which restrict men's personal freedom must be limited and guided by necessity . . . The proximate and efficient cause of actions is the flight from pain, their final cause is the love of pleasure. Hence, the customs of a nation are determined more by the evils which beset it than by the pleasures which it enjoys and expects" (157). It is precisely the negative version of the principle of distributive utility that regulates the departure from the state of nature.

B. The Right to Punish and a New Logic of Penal Practices. Negative distributive utility makes possible a natural synthesis of social contract and utilitarian considerations in the construction of a just criminal system. Only those actions should be prohibited that materially cause pain or interfere with others' equal use of their freedom (with the underlying assumption that these considerations tend to converge). Beccaria's way of expressing his negative yet egalitarian ideal is to claim, once more, that the right to punish is nothing but the sum of those smallest portions of freedom men surrendered to the public repository consistent with the protection of the freedom of all. Beccaria elaborates the effective notion of "smallest portion" through the notion of necessity: "Every punishment which is not derived from absolute necessity is tyrannous . . . [hence, the foundation of the right to punish is equal to] the necessity of defending the repository of public well-being from the usurpation of individuals" (10).[29] Or, working the same thought from the direction of justice: "And by 'justice' I mean nothing other than the restraint necessary to hold particular interests together, without which they would collapse into the old state of unsociability. Any punishment that goes beyond the need to preserve this bond is unjust by its very nature" (11).

Justice is conceived in minimalist terms with respect to both laws and punishments; *thus I take Beccaria to be arguing that we require the minimal punishments necessary to sustain the authority and effectiveness of the minimal laws necessary to sustain a functional social order that (maximally) respects the equal freedom of each.* Legal and penal minimalism in accordance with the principle of distributive utility is meant to supply an image of legitimacy, which in its turn is intended to generate conditions of confidence, security, and trust—all of which were absent in the previous system. The series of minimal conditions, as given by negative distributive utility, is meant to generate an *image* in which what is socially authoritative are *laws*, not persons. One component of that image is that the body of laws, together with the corresponding state of affairs their successful implementation would yield, is to be considered "the repository of public well-being," where an irreducible component of that well-being corresponds to the affective mode of the law's reception—*trust, confidence, and a sense of security* as replacements for the awe and fear inspired by sovereign authority. Social order and the laws provisioning that order are irreducibly social goods; therefore, any trespass on the law is an attack on society as a whole. So the thought runs: while an individual's pain is the direct harm of an assault upon him, that harm is simultaneously a harm to all, since the law providing freedom from assault is constitutive of our (just) relations with one another; it is our bond. Harming a single individual harms the weft of our life together. Beccaria's immediate inference from this is that the "one true measure of criminality is the damage done to the nation" (22) or "harm to society" (24). Hence, the worse crimes are those directed at the immediate destruction of society, and the least harmful crimes are those that do a minor injustice to a private individual. Harmfulness is proportional to an action's effect on the rule of law itself—that is, its effect on our collective sense that the law operates in way conducive to our maximal *trust* in its effectiveness and fairness, recalling that effectiveness without fairness is tyranny once more. Thus, one version of the commitment to the rule of law is that such rule is a figure of our life together; *we* can be and routinely are pained by law-breaking, not just through empathic identification with the victim, but because the fragile normative bonds of legality constitutive of our life together are being undone. We are invested in social order not merely as a matter of security (the Hobbesian desideratum), but equally as the material embodiment of ideal justice: peaceful, egalitarian social relations in accordance with substantive rule of law are justice realized, and hence respect for the personhood of each citizen is realized.

Because Beccaria considers the rule of law as projecting a distinct egalitarian form of life, he views the law as something like a pervasive ethical substance, contouring, shaping, giving ethical significance to each and every aspect of everyday living. Hence, when Beccaria says that within "a country's borders there should be no place which is outside the law. Its power should follow every citizen like a shadow" (92), he is once more urging that no one be outside the law or above the law; to suppose that there could be such locales would be "to create many little sovereign states" (92), little islands of tyranny. Either law is the ethical substance of the polity, or it is an instrument of the most powerful; there is nothing in between. It is an austere and demanding vision.

The rest of the treatise works to fashion a system of criminal law procedures and the principles governing practices of punishment sufficient to sustain this image, this idea of the rule of law. It is in Beccaria's elaboration of the rule of law that we find both the commencement of modern high ideals for a just criminal law system, and the beginning of the rationalization of the penal system that, as Foucault expresses it, in turning away from torture and toward a new technology of subjection, seeks control and reform, working to inhabit and transform the soul of the prisoner rather than brutalizing his body—"the soul is the prison of the body."[30]

Beccaria's first set of inferences from his foundational principles are: laws alone should decree punishments for crimes; the authority for determining punishment must reside with the legislator who, bound by the idea of public good, represents the whole of society; because in a society of law formed by contract, no one escapes mutual obligations, although it is the responsibility of the sovereign to frame laws in accordance with principle, he may not judge particular cases (there must be a categorical separation of powers); judicial discretion in the interpretation of the law is to be eliminated, the task of judges being solely to adjudicate whether a case falls under a law; laws should be stated in unequivocally clear terms (the obscurity of laws is an evil) so that what falls under them is transparent to both citizens and judges; laws should be published and widely disseminated; to remove inequality from the system, trials should be by peers (a practice of English but not continental law at the time), and the accused permitted to dismiss a certain number of potential jurors without cause; as opposed to the secrecy of sovereign legal proceedings, verdicts and the proof of guilt should be public in order that opinion, "which is perhaps the only cement holding society together," can influence the passions by perceiving the justice system as one proper to free persons, protecting rather than enslaving them (36). Justice must be seen to be done.

All these and related proposals aim to make the law legislatively just, transparent in its meaning and in its operation, and judgment of individual cases fair, constrained, and, again, transparent. In the language of contemporary jurisprudence, Beccaria is engineering a double transformation of the rule of law: from a "thin" to a "thick" conception of the rule of law in accordance with "substantive" principle, so making the "thick" conception itself substantive. The thin conception of the rule of law is intended to provide a wedge separating law from personal command: coercive government powers can be legitimately exercised only if they are the product of recognized legislative practice. Legitimate legislative processes beget legitimate legal products. It was this rule-of-recognition conception of the rule of law that Beccaria was protesting against since patently the right to make law does not entail the making of right law; even if laws derive from a legitimating source, those laws may be not only unjust and unfair, but lacking in even those syntactical and formal features requisite for "lawfulness" in general. The idea of a "thick" or procedural rule of law stipulates the principles that Beccaria is elaborating in the requirements in the previous paragraph, roughly: generality, prospectivity, clarity, and neutrality.[31] For Beccaria, however, we adopt these formal and procedural thick rule of law and due process requirements not for formal reasons alone, but above all in order that the conditions for our equal protection from civil violence— the provision of a system of criminal justice—not become a form of legal, state violence as exemplified by arbitrary laws, arbitrarily applied, backed by judicial and penal torture. Hence, for Beccaria, procedural rule of law considerations have a substantive basis in equal respect for, and thus the equal standing of, each citizen.

The provision of that basis is always elliptical in *On Crimes* because Beccaria so emphatically eschews the use of natural law and natural rights considerations; their adoption, he argues, is always and necessarily historically provincial and thus, whatever the intention, conventional once more—just "our" provincial conception of what natural law requires or what natural rights we possess.[32] In place of natural law and natural rights, Beccaria discretely places before us, as the rhetorical and moral center of his argument, the broken bodies of the tortured and the long history of morally horrific legal state violence. If we cannot agree that *that* is wrong, then no further moral or legal agreements are possible. Even Beccaria's deployment of the ideals of moral freedom and equality as premises for his argument takes its force as a determinate negation of palpable forms of social domination, state violence, unfreedom—the various ways in which we are enslaved—and inequality. Beccaria's elaboration and imaging of substantive rule of law arrangements is the transfiguration of a massive, enduring, and finally all-too-visible history of legal state violence into an image of justice and public well-being. Beccaria's rule of law doctrine, we might say, erects an image of a dignified civil body out of the remnants of its repeated sovereign mutilation through a process of determinate negation: What must a system of laws, criminal procedures, and practices of punishment be that would prohibit all the excesses, vices, arbitrariness, and cruelty of the system of sovereign torture? What idea of *lawfulness* can be offered as an alternative to the idea of sovereign law? The sovereign law of torture had entered into a fatal self-contradiction: the very practice that was to demonstrate the authority of the law had increasingly come to demonstrate its arbitrariness and violative nature. A determinate negation of the sovereign law of torture could *constructively progress* beyond it by demonstrating that *each* of its new principles was the negation of an assumption governing the sovereign practice. We think of the joining of these new principles as nothing other than substantive rule of law. But, again, what makes these otherwise formal and procedural principles substantive is their coming to be as determinate negations of the sovereign law of torture; what is right constructively emerges *from* the overcoming of wrong.[33] Hence, substantive rule of law in its first announcement arises as nothing other than the determinate negation of sovereign torture or, what is the same, a remembrance of suffering. By its restraint, the rule of law remembers past suffering as that which should never be repeated. Beccaria's arguments concerning just punishment, and against torture and the death penalty, are thus pivotal moral moments in the construction of his doctrine.

What does punishment become under this new understanding? Beccaria's first thesis here is that severe punishments, even if they could be shown to serve the public good by their deterrent effect, are nonetheless contrary to enlightened reason because they turn citizens into "a herd of slaves among whom timorous cruelty is rife" (13). The broad principle underlying Beccaria's reflections on this topic, which will circulate throughout his treatment of torture and the death penality, is that we cannot trust and feel secure in a legal system that does not itself respect the bodily autonomy and intrinsic worth of its citizens; hence, if the operation of the legal system is *cruel* in any of its standard practices, where cruelty is the exemplary act of denying individuals their standing as intrinsically worthy persons, then the legal system denies the humanity of its citizens. Once public torture is seen to undermine sovereign authority, and social contract considerations become publically available, then the "return effect of punishment on the punishing authority and the power that it claims to exercise"[34] require consideration: cruel punishments speak unfailingly of the cruelty of the punishing apparatus. Hence, while the brutalizing of the citizenry is a sufficient moral criticism to require radical penal constraint all by itself, Beccaria also presumes that since the nation is the *We* corresponding to each *I*, then its treatment of criminals sets the standard or norm of who *We* are. The state as realization of the general will necessarily posits in each of its actions an image of our ideal self. Cruelty by the state thus invites and encourages citizens to act likewise. But this thought is simply the converse side of the revulsion at cruel punishment we have already heard. This articulated revulsion is a new voice in political self-consciousness: "The body, the imagination, the pain, the heart to be respected are not, in effect, those of the criminal that is to be punished [although they are that too], but those of the men who have subscribed to the [social] pact . . ."[35] Once laws are understood as conventions, and conventions as the product of contract, then state action takes on the visage of the signatories to the contract—in principle, all of us. Cruel treatment of the condemned becomes our cruelty— which is a *further* intolerableness beyond the intolerableness of the treatment itself.

While by repute, Beccaria's argument is said to be governed by utilitarian principles, in fact we find at almost every crucial juncture in his argument a turn toward an expressivist conception of law: laws express a broad moral consensus about the limits of acceptable action; crimes violate a society's collective conscience; and punishments are a conventional device to express indignation or reprobation.[36] Even if neither deterrent nor retributionist defenses of punishment were sufficient, arguably expressivist considerations would be enough: if crimes are the violation of norms essential to our self-understanding, of what matters most to us as a collective, then we require mechanisms for the sustaining and reassertion of those norms when they are broken. As Durkheim claims, violations *demoralize*, and hence we require mechanisms to reaffirm and demonstrate the worth of what has been violated; to leave violations unremarked upon is equivalent to saying that the norms do not matter, that *we* do not matter to ourselves. Punishments, ideally, demonstrate our conviction in the rightness of our legal norms. But if punishments express our condemnation of violative actions, then they equally must express our moral temperament generally;

cruel punishments would hence simultaneously express both an extreme disapprobation for the criminal deed and our affirmation of the appropriateness of acting cruelly—a contradiction Beccaria exploits to the full.

Beccaria understood, as no one previously quite had, that the state must bear the burden of preserving *our* sense of the worth of citizens found guilty of a crime if its treatment of them is not to undermine the principles of mutual regard constitutive of the very idea of the rule of law as a product of social contract. This is a terrible burden because the task of the legal system is also to *uphold* the law; hence its sanctions must be sufficient for that purpose—protecting us from criminal trespass. The design of a penal system must then satisfy two unconditional masters: the maintenance of legal order and respect for citizens once taken up by the criminal legal system. All by itself this eliminates retribution, "the undoing of a crime already committed," as a legitimate feature of legal justice: "Can the wailings of a wretch, perhaps, undo what has been done and turn back the clock?" (31) It is worth reminding ourselves that Beccaria's treatise came into being because the reigning legal system had failed absolutely and utterly in this regard: "[it] provided an entrenched and legitimised example of cold-blooded atrocity. And yet, the groans of the weak, sacrificed to cruel indifference and to wealthy idleness, the barbarous tortures that have been elaborated with prodigal and useless severity, to punish crimes unproven or illusory, the horrors of prison, compounded by the cruelest tormentor of the wretched, uncertainty, ought to have shaken into action the rank of magistrates who guide the opinions and minds of men" (8). These words are not mere rhetorical flourishes; they perform the image of legal destruction to which the Beccarian rule of law forms the counterimage.

Given his simple pleasure-pain construction of human motivation, Beccaria assumes that it is the force of self-interest that attracts us "like gravity, to our own good," requiring "equal and opposite obstacles" to be controlled (19). Punishments are thus to be conceived of as, in a beautiful phrasing, "political obstacles" whose task is to eliminate the evil effects of self-interest "without destroying the moving cause, which is the very sensibility inalienable from man's nature" (19). Again, the all-but-impossible equation is to make the obstacles to criminal wrongdoing in the form of punishments sufficient without their destroying the very sensibility the law is designed to protect; the aim is to reform the criminal without breaking him. Because obstacles to wrongdoing are what is needed, the purpose of punishments is deterrence: to provide reasons for the criminal not to repeat his actions, and to deter others from acting likewise. Beccaria's constructive principle to elaborate this demand begins engineering the civilizational seismic shift from the affliction of pain to the remaking of the soul: "Punishments and the means adopted for inflicting them should, consistent with proportionality, be so selected as to make the most efficacious and *lasting impression on the minds of men with the least torment to the body* of the condemned" (31; italics JMB). Later Beccaria summarizes the idea this way: "In general, the severity of a punishment and the consequence of crime ought to be as effective as possible on others and as lenient as possible on him who undergoes it because a society cannot be called legitimate where it is not an unfailing principle that men should be subject to the fewest possible ills" (48). The satisfaction of this proportionality would equal a penal system premised on the rule of law alone; in time, the processes ignited by this principle throughout Europe led to the disappearance (at least temporarily) of explicit penal acts of tormenting the body.

The primary strategic rule organizing Beccaria's proposals is: all citizens should have clearly and forcibly in mind the association between "the two ideas *crime* and *punishment*" (49). If punishments are to be obstacles, then they must appear to the mind of the potential lawbreaker as an invariable concomitant of the crime, and, cleaving to the minimal severity principle, be the least possible punishment necessary to deliberatively outweigh the advantages of the crime. Because it is an association of ideas that is driving the system, then the "pain" that matters most in penal practices "is not the actual sensation of pain, but the idea of pain, displeasure, inconvenience— the 'pain' of the idea of 'pain.'"[37]

Beccaria's signature innovation is to argue that satisfying the requirement for the association of ideas does not depend on the severity of the punishment or spectacular presentation; rather, it requires: (i) that crimes routinely and consistently be punished; it is "not the harshness of its punishment, but the unerringness of punishment" (63) that most effectively puts a brake on crime—thus generating, in time, the need for an active police force; (ii) that the punishment should follow the crime in the shortest possible time, thus generating the demand for speedy trials; and (iii) that the punishment should fit the crime in a manner that makes the association of ideas between the two—*this* crime associated with *this* perfectly matching punishment—imaginatively persuasive. While this idea of a poetics of punishment was widely popular at the time, and pursued with inventive abandon by Bentham, Beccaria's own suggestions are modest: social parasites should be banished; injuries to honor should lead to disgrace; wealthy thieves should be deprived of all their riches; poor thieves should be sentenced to hard labor to pay back to society what they have taken; and violent crimes of assault should be subject to some form of corporal punishment. What Beccaria meant by this last is unclear—probably even to him—since it cannot include any form of torture; this is also Beccaria's only capitulation to the model of corporal afflictive punishment. Its presence nonetheless requires the concession that the *spirit*, and thereby the content of the rule of law doctrine Beccaria constructs, surpasses the letter of his theory.

C. Abolishing Torture. My contention has been that the eager reception of Beccaria's critique of judicial torture derives from its placement in the context of a defense of the rule of law, which, by means of a synthesis of social contract, utilitarian, and expressivist principles, systematically reorganizes the relation between the state and the bodies of citizens. It is equally a fundamental rule of law consideration that orients and drives his critique of judicial torture (those forms of torture that are used for the sake of acquiring evidence necessary for conviction or acquittal): "No man may be called guilty before the judge has reached his verdict; nor may society withdraw its protection from him until it has been determined that he has broken the terms of the compact by which that protection was extended to him" (39). The idea that only the guilty should be punished belongs to the retributive tradition where punishment is a direct response to the evils committed by the convicted and punishment of him is for just those crimes. Retribution, in its backward-looking search for redress, for a balancing of the scales, necessarily restricts punishment to the individual wrongdoer solely for the crime committed; his guilt is a condition for and licenses his punishment. Conversely, if deterrence considerations alone governed penal practices, then the state would be entitled to punish not only the wrongdoer but anyone to whatever extent as long as it served the purpose of maximally deterring crime. Deterrence in this sense ill suits Beccaria's deepest commitments; as we have seen, for him the principle of distributive utility is for the sake of realizing the ends of the social contract itself; hence it is the maximum equal well-being of each that is sought, making the freedom and well-being of each individual the primary element in his political calculus. How, then, within a criminal justice system designed for the sake of deterrence, can the intrinsic value of each citizen register? One might express Beccaria's synthesis here by urging that: "whilst the [legislative] *purpose* and rationale of punishment was utilitarian, its [judicial] *application* had to be limited by retributivist considerations of guilt."[38] Retributivist considerations enter not as a purpose but as a *constraint* on deterrent ambitions in the precise manner that we have already seen operative generally in Beccaria: aggregative operations are unacceptable since they deny equal intrinsic worth, placing only a relative and corrigible value on individual lives. Because Beccaria nowhere allows aggregative utility, one might also say that the operation of the penal system is another example of his conception of distributive utility, his placing together of individualist assumptions with utilitarian ends.

The principle that a person is innocent until proven guilty is precisely what is denied by legal torture for purposes other than punishment. Beccaria lists the primary uses of torture at the beginning of chapter 16: "whether to compel him to confess to a crime, to exploit the contradictions he runs into, to uncover his accomplices, to carry out some mysterious and incomprehensible metaphysical purging of his infamy" (39). Judicial torture takes possession of the body of the accused anterior to the proceedings that are for the sake of determining innocence or guilt. This is contradictory, however, only if it is assumed that criminal justice is for the sake of protecting the freedom and well-being of citizens through the establishment of the rule of law. One might say that the presumptive innocence of the accused follows from individuals' *moral independence* from the criminal justice system, whose existence depends on their voluntary adherence: conceptually and morally the state must be conceived of as a voluntary association. Only by being found guilty of, effectively, breaking his contractual promise does the citizen lose more than the portion of freedom originally surrendered in consenting to the social compact; any earlier interference in his liberty and well-being usurps his freedom, his legal personality, and thus his standing as a person.

As Foucault underlines, the judicial system that used torture as both a *means* to establish the truth and as a punishment at the conclusion of the criminal process must have regarded innocence and guilt not as opposites—one is either innocent or guilty—but as poles along a continuum; hence, the suspicion of guilt, the mere fact of being charged with a crime is sufficient to establish that there is a degree of guilt; and once a degree of guilt is assumed, then torture as the punishment for the crime can be applied also as a means for establishing the truth of what is already assumed. Beccaria elaborates this collapsing sovereign logic thus: "The laws torture you because you are guilty, because you may be guilty, or because I want you to be guilty" (43). Although Beccaria will lodge a series of empirical criticisms against the use of torture—showing its fundamental uselessness with respect to the purposes for which it is employed—his fundamental critique of judicial torture is neither primarily aimed against its uselessness nor is it humanitarian (although its cruelty matters). Rather, it is that its judicial uses for purposes other than punishment run contrary to the very idea of the rule of law. To employ the means of punishment prior to the establishment of guilt involves government employing a power that no one has given to it; it denies that the individual charged has moral standing, and it transforms the rule of law into the rule of the greater force, reintroducing the very arbitrariness that the rule of law was meant to overturn. Nothing could be worse for an individual than to lose the very freedom for the sake of which he agreed to the social contract in the first instance. Hence, not only must an individual be presumed innocent until proven guilty, but also, Beccaria insists, nothing less than a moral "certainty" is adequate for the sake of establishing guilt (34)—guilty, we now say, beyond a reasonable doubt.[39]

Once the principle of the presumption of innocence is accepted, the further arguments Beccaria provides either directly support it or go to demonstrate the irrationality of the practice of judicial torture in its own terms. So, judicial torture willfully confuses proper legal procedure by requiring a man "to be at once accuser and accused" (39); it transgresses what should be a right against self-incrimination,[40] and in asking a man to accuse himself, it denies the ordinary psychology of self-love and attempts to create in him "a heroic self-hatred" that will lead him to denounce himself, "telling the truth even when your muscles are being torn and your bones dislocated" (43). Twice Beccaria reminds his readers that even the Romans restricted the use of judicial torture to slaves, "who were denied the status of persons" (42). And he reminds us further that judicial torture's "shameful crucible of truth" is a "standing monument to the law of ancient and savage times, when ordeal by fire, by boiling water and the lottery of armed combat were called the *judgments* of God" (41). While it might appear that the difference between ordeal and judicial torture is patent since the latter arose in order to displace the former, depending solely on the will of the criminal, the difference is illusory: "Telling the truth in the midst of spasms and beatings is as little subject to our will as is preventing without fraud the effects of fire and boiling water" (41). In truth, the will of the criminal is the very thing most directly canceled by torture; hence, judicial torture is not the secularizing of the ordeal, but the reversion of secular procedures to external influences outside the purview of human reason and will. It is no more intelligible that torture should happen on truth than that ordeals should, where it was the inadequacy—the arbitrariness, unreliability, unintelligibility, and brutality—of ordeals that motivated the development of the secular law of proof in the first instance.

This last consideration opens up the more familiar epistemological worries about the unreliability of torture as a mechanism for the production of truth, and how reliance on that mechanism further transgresses the principle of the presumption of innocence. First, sensitivity to pain and the capacity to withstand it is unevenly and randomly distributed. As a consequence, judicial torture will systematically reward the insensitive brute and brutalize the guiltless but sensitive man. Second, because judicial torture requires that confessions be repeated outside the torture and, where the free confession is not forthcoming, that the torture be repeated, it follows that "the innocent are in a worse position than the guilty . . . and that the innocent man cannot but lose and the guilty man may gain" (43). Third, given pain's ability to absorb "the whole sensory field, it leaves the torture victim no freedom to do anything but choose the quickest route to relieving himself of the immediate pain" (41); because relief from intense pain becomes the overwhelming motive of the torture victim, the natural and rational response to torture is to tell the persecutor whatever the victim believes the torturer wants to hear. Torture conduces not to truth but to what will make the pain stop. No matter how refined and sophisticated torture has become, no mechanisms have been discovered that can *reliably* bridge the abyss between pain and truth. But this entails that all forms of interrogational torture contain an essential surd: they naturally tend toward an end indifferent to the purpose for which they are employed.

Judicial torture is unjust, canceling the presumption of innocence, and necessarily unreliable; it rewards guilty ruffians and penalizes sensitive innocents. What of penal torture? Although Beccaria allows corporal punishment, he nonetheless emphatically disallows penal torture, first because it is materially insufficiently refined, pivoting from tolerable pain to unbearable suffering almost without interval, where that pivot point itself varies randomly from person to person. This lack of refinement and gradation fails to accord with the dual requirements of discrimination required for legitimate punishments: that they should be based on the degree of harm against the nation in the crime, and that they should be only as severe as necessary for their deterrent force. Second, penal torture presupposes an incoherent and, finally, merely vengeful logic of retribution. The presumed purpose of penal torture, other than deterrence, is the purging of infamy, which Beccaria immediately translates into the demand that a man "confirm his own testimony by the dislocation of his bones" (40). While the absurdity of this is patent, it opens onto the whole logic of body and debt to which Beccaria is objecting. A crime is a "civil stain," that is, a moral relation; how is the causing of pain, which is a bodily sensation, meant to purge, cleanse, or transform that relation, to remove the stain, so to speak?

Beccaria is aware of the religious origins of the idea of cleansing impurities; he simply denies that, once pain has been thoroughly secularized, these ideas can be secularized and thereby given a clear civic function. On the contrary, he contends that infamy for us moderns is not a mysterious state of the soul, but a matter of regard and public opinion; from this he infers that torture "itself causes real infamy to its victims. Therefore, by this means, infamy is purged by the infliction of infamy" (41).

Beccaria elaborates on the stakes of his calling penal torture an "infliction of infamy" in his third and final argument against the death penalty. There he explicitly argues that *the rule of law should function as a counterinstance to the rule of force and violence*: "If our passions or the necessity of war have taught how to spill human blood, laws, which exercise a moderating influence on human conduct, ought not to add to that cruel example, which is all the more grievous the more a legal killing is carried out with care and pomp" (70). If the purpose of law is to preserve and protect human freedom and dignity, then the operation of the law, its means, should be continuous with that ultimate purpose. To act contrary to that purpose is to legitimate the very thing the law as law opposes. Again, Beccaria takes the law to be an expression of who *We* are, what *We* take as fitting, and what actions *We* prohibit because they deny our standing as free and dignified persons. When the state acts, *We* act; if the state acts viciously and cruelly, then *We* are willing such viciousness and cruelty. So he continues his argument: "It seems absurd to me that the laws, which are the expression of the public will, and which hate and punish murder, should themselves commit one, and that to deter citizens from murder, they should decree a public murder" (70). What holds for murder, holds, ceteris paribus, for the relation between violent crimes and penal torture.

If cruelty emerges in the course of the eighteenth century as the worst thing one human might do to another, then what sense can be made of state cruelty, of cruelty in accordance with the law? If the law commands and commends cruel actions, then the law not only justifies these actions, but is their vehicle: the law itself becomes a form of cruelty. Beccaria plaintively argues that when the law "with slow ceremony" and "cold equanimity" (70) drags a wretched man to his death, then the only message conveyed is that the law is a form of vengeance, that "these laws are nothing but pretexts for power and for the calculated and cruel formalities of justice; they are nothing but a conventional language for killing us all the more surely, like the preselected victims of a sacrifice to the insatiable god of despotism" (70–71). State cruelty as performed by penal torture and the death penalty, even when not performed as public spectacles, cannot avoid the logic of the torture spectacle, the logic of turning punishment into a demonstration of singular sovereignty whose authority is to be identified with its brute force, its might, its power over life and death, and hence for whom the body of the accused functions as a sacrificial totem to be used as a demonstration of the might and power of the sovereign. It was just this that the argument for the rule of law meant to overturn. State cruelty as performed by penal torture and the death penalty contradict, in principle and in practice, the very idea of what we have come to understand by the rule of law. For us moderns, the force of law is incommensurable with and opposed to any violation of bodily integrity as the bearer of human intrinsic worth—that is the substance of the rule of law. The rule of law is thus the *institution* of bodily integrity as the fount of human dignity. That thought is the pulse driving Beccaria's argument.

IV. The Beccaria Thesis

"Where cruelty exists, law does not."

—Alberto Mora, *General Counsel of the United States Navy*

In a manner that is still breathtaking, a moral wonder, Beccaria, Voltaire and the other reformers won the day, in theory and in practice. By the early part of the nineteenth century, judicial torture had virtually disappeared from Europe, and, as the century wore on, penal torture followed suit, coming to be replaced nearly everywhere by incarceration. When in 1911 the *Encyclopedia Britannica* heralded that as far as Europe is concerned, the "whole subject [of torture] is now one of only historical interest," it was doing no more than reporting a fact together with what it reasonably took to be an overwhelming legal and moral consensus. It is worth remembering that the architects of the liberal state—Hobbes and Locke most pertinently—did not explicitly attack the use of violence or offer explicit accounts of the sanctity of life or the moral integrity of the human body. Their argumentative efforts were primarily prudential, offering the idea of the social contract as a way of *regulating violence*—escaping and suppressing lawless violence and giving the state a monopoly over the remainder— not surmounting it. What Beccaria's treatise added to the social contract tradition was the argument that state violence—as exemplified by judicial torture, and the death penalty—involved a regression to the same tyranny that liberal rights were meant to be protections from. State torture was not a mechanism for protecting the public good, but an act of war against the citizen. Beccaria was thus proposing that the *rule of law* was to be construed as the counterimage to the *sovereign law of torture*; these were opposed ideas of the very idea of law.

Arguably, it was the great reformist critiques of judicial and penal torture, and the death penality that finally generated a conception of the liberal state as governed by the rule of law in which there was to be an uncrossable divide between the force of law and brutality. *Beccaria's thesis,* the great lesson that emerges out of the arguments against torture and the death penalty in *On Crimes and Punishments,* claims that *the very idea of the rule of law is constituted by the moral incommensurability between the force of law and state violence to the human body.* This statement of the thesis is from Jeremy Waldron's "Torture and Positive Law," an essay whose effort strikes me as the most philosophically urgent defense of the Beccaria thesis to have emerged out of the recent debates over state torture.

The need for a restatement of the Beccaria thesis is evident: we now know that the moral triumphalism involved in the unabashed consensus that torture was a thing of the past, and that a substantive rule of law doctrine represented a core element of Western political morality was naïve and premature. In the United States, the prohibitions on torture and on cruel, unusual, and inhuman punishment were, for nearly a century, bracketed or qualified by the continuance of chattel slavery, a practice that, for all intents and purposes, possessed the same deep structure as torture, the same hold over the subject through a hold over his body that torture exercised over the accused and convicted.[41] Further, everywhere in the North Atlantic civilization, penal practices continued to contain torturous elements; the new penal systems, even apart from the traces of torture in them, contained new forms of subjection, domination, manipulation that were and remain brutalizing, to the soul if not directly to the body. And most damningly, European states embarked on imperial and colonial endeavors that would contain all the brutality, all the cruel and inhuman treatment, all the torture that they had vanquished from their home practices. Under the title of civilizing the black races, the practices of torture continued, developed, were perfected anew until they were ready to be shipped back to mainland Europe ever more effectively as the twentieth century progressed.

Perhaps because it occurred after the atrocities of World War II, after the founding of the United Nations, in a country that had suffered Nazi domination, in a country that traditionally has been a champion of rights and liberal ideals, the use of torture by France—first in Algeria itself, and then against Algerians in France—has become a chilling marker for the return of torture in just those states where its abolishment was celebrated. In the opening paragraph of his *Torture: Cancer of Democracy: France and Algeria 1954–62* (1963), Pierre Vidal-Naquet poses a question that could have been written about the use of torture by the United States in Abu Ghraib and Guantánamo during its war in Iraq. Vidal-Naquet queried: "Can a great nation, liberal by tradition, allow its institutions, its army, and its system of justice to degenerate over the span of a few years as a result of the use of torture, and by its concealment and deception of such a vital issue call the whole Western concept of human dignity and the rights of the individual into question?"[42] In asking his question in this form, running from the illegal use of torture to the destruction of the Western concept of human dignity and the rights of the individual, Vidal-Naquet is presupposing a version of the Beccaria thesis: the nature of the moral cancer caused by the introduction of torture into the legal body of the state is one that destroys the lawfulness of the law by abrogating the dignity and rights of individuals from which the law draws its claim to normative authority; once the law rescinds its protection and upholding of human dignity, then that idea of dignity loses its social and political place—it is publically extinguished.

This is precisely the view taken by Alberto Mora, who was serving in the Pentagon as General Counsel of the United States Navy in December 2002, when he first learned about the torture practices at Guantánamo: "If cruelty is no longer declared unlawful, but instead is applied as a matter of policy, it alters the fundamental relationship of man to government. It destroys the whole notion of human rights. The Constitution recognizes that man has an inherent right, not bestowed by the state or laws, to personal dignity, including the right to be free of cruelty. It applies to all human beings, not just in America—even those designated as 'unlawful enemy combatants.' If you make this exception, the whole Constitution crumbles. It's a transformative issue."[43] Vidal-Naquet and Mora are each contending that the Beccaria thesis is at the very core of modern political morality, that the practice of torture and the rule of law are contradictories such that inclusion of the former entails the destruction of the latter.

Assumed by the lawyers advising and working for the Bush administration was that the various legal documents prohibiting torture—both the international conventions and their implementation in the United States Code—were nothing other than stand-alone pieces of positive law whose legal force and scope are exhausted by their explicit content; if one could show that the cases one was seeking to justify fell outside the scope of those restrictions, then one could claim to be doing all that is required by the letter of the law. But this view is, recall, precisely where, historically, Beccaria sought to intervene: traditional law was nothing other than a jumble of "odd remnants" handed down over the centuries. In "Torture and Positive Law," Jeremy Waldron begins in philosophically the same place, contesting the claim of legal positivism that the law is "a heap or accumulation of rules each of which might be amended, repealed, or reinterpreted with little effect on any of the others" (225).[44] The law rather must be conceived as having structures and patterns whereby one piece of law follows from or supports other pieces, and where a constellation of laws is conceived as having an aggregate meaning not reducible to any of the particular laws belonging to the aggregate. In Ronald Dworkin's jurisprudence, for example, like Beccaria's, laws are shaped, ordered, and colored by principles and policies. Policies are purposes like road safety, consumer protection, or orderly rules of inheritance. Principles are broad normative ideals like those of justice or fairness or some other fundamental moral commitment. So, for example, Dworkin contrasts the *rules* regulating inheritance (e.g., the number of witnesses necessary for a will to be valid) as opposed to the *principle* that no one should profit from a criminal act she committed; you may indeed be the legally recognized legatee of a bequest, but you do not get to inherit if you murdered to get there.[45] The principle of not profiting from one's own criminal act does not specify which criminal acts it covers; it is the ongoing case-by-case task of the court to determine the scope and applicability of the principle, how it should be taken to constrain and regulate other law.

Waldron's great innovation in this area is to propose that certain laws should be regarded as *archetypes*. Archetypes are single laws within a particular cluster of laws that, while possessed of a specific content, also exemplify, embody, sum up, make vivid and perspicuous a principle, a purpose, or a policy that goes beyond that specific content; and, in light of their power of exemplification, such laws play a pivotal role in the adjoining legal terrain, ordering, supporting, and providing normative orientation to the related pieces of positive law surrounding them. Flagging this idea's origins in Montesquieu, Waldron states that a legal archetype "expresses or epitomizes the *spirit* of a whole structured area of doctrine" (228; italics JMB).

Consider habeas corpus statutes; specifically, habeas corpus petitions require prison officials or their representative to bring to the court persons in their custody in order to demonstrate that their detention is legally justified when they are so requested by a prisoner or his representative; if grounds for imprisonment cannot be demonstrated, the prisoner must be released. All by itself this is deeply important since it provides legal redress for improper imprisonment. But its reach is patently wider and deeper; for Waldron, habeas corpus is "archetypal of the whole orientation of our legal tradition towards liberty, in the physical sense of freedom from confinement. It is archetypal too of law's set against arbitrariness in regard to actions that impact upon the rights of the subject" (228). One might say that habeas corpus is a constitutive component of the idea of the rule of law in that, in requiring the state to bring a detained individual to court to show just cause for detention, it is (by that narrow requirement) simultaneously forced to recognize individuals as possessing a *legal personality* that provides them with a *standing in the law* before which the state itself must bow. It is by virtue of that standing that liberty rights can have effect at all. Since imprisonment is the most prominent and extreme form of state action against the individual—leaving aside the death penalty (which typically is preceded by imprisonment)—then if individuals had no legal recourse against arbitrary, groundless, or presumptive detention they would effectively have no rights apart from those operative for those already detained. Habeas corpus has reverberated in the way it has because it is simultaneously a concrete statute and a law about the nature and reach of the law, a law about what lawfulness involves. Without habeas corpus the principle of "innocent until proven guilty" would be eviscerated.

The Beccaria thesis claims an analogous scope and meaning for the prohibition on torture. What is the rule against torture archetypal *of*? Waldron contends that the rule against torture explicates the relation between law and force, the kind of force that the law legitimately possesses versus the kind of force the law must abjure if it is not to revoke its own claim to authority. Waldron's word for the kind of force the law renounces in its being lawful is *brutality*.

> Law is not brutal in its operation; law is not savage; law does not rule through abject fear and terror, or by breaking the will of those whom it confronts. If law is forceful or coercive, it gets its way by methods which respect rather than mutilate the dignity and agency of those who are its subjects . . . [Even when the law forces individuals] to do things and go places they would not otherwise do or go to . . . they will not be herded like cattle or broken like horses; they will not be beaten like dumb animals or treated just as bodies to be manipulated. Instead there will be an enduring connection between the spirit of law and respect for human dignity—respect for human dignity even *in extremis*, even in situations where law is at its most forceful and its subjects at their most vulnerable . . . [The rule against torture] is vividly emblematic of our determination to sever the link between law and brutality, between law and terror, and between law and the enterprise of trying to break a person's will. (232–3)

The final clause of the final sentence here reminds us of what interrogational torture normally intends: to break a person's will. It accomplishes that purpose through terror and brutality (causing severe pain or intolerable mental suffering). Hence the severances between law, on the one hand, and brutality, terror, and breaking of the will, on the other, do no more than state what is flatly ordained by having a rule against torture. Waldron is contending that this flat ordination—because of what *brutality, terror,* and *breaking the will* are as practices—must bear a suprapositive content or become incoherent in its own terms. The reasons for there being a rule against torture in the first instance necessarily brings with it a moral commitment that must adhere to the *law as such* if the prohibition of torture is going to be meaningful *as law.*

Law is forceful and coercive in its operations; it can deprive people of their freedom, separating them from all that they might consider as what makes life worth living. Nonetheless, this form of forcefulness is to be regarded as absolutely constrained by the prohibitions entailed by the prohibition against torture. Waldron's governing effort is to attempt to make this distinction between two kinds of force—the forcefulness of law and the force of brutality—*morally decisive,* and not just the difference between two different styles or regimes of penal practice, as Foucault at his darkest might urge. As Waldron concedes, we cannot finally separate the two forms of force without fully unpacking the *moral content* behind the law's repudiation of brutality—the task pursued in the following chapters. Waldron does, however, point emphatically to the unavoidable region of concerns.

Law in its modern, post-torture formation can be forceful while at the same time recognizing that those within its power have an unconditional moral standing and status, which standing is incorporated in the law as both content and form (the rule of law itself). Waldron's first wedge into displaying that standing is to distinguish between having the power to make individuals go places they do not wish to go and do things they do not wish to do *versus* directly manipulating their bodies. Now since imprisonment is a form of corporeal manipulation, then something more fine-grained needs saying. In order for the business about not being herded like cattle or broken like horses to carry weight, what is minimally required is some notion of *bodily integrity.* Bodily integrity involves recognizing the body as a limit, so that to physically interfere with a person's body—to touch, to mark, to directly manipulate, to invade, to violate the body—involves crossing an absolute moral boundary. As I shall later attempt to express this idea: the physically bounded body is also a kind of moral whole, a normatively saturated physical totality. It is just this idea, as we saw earlier, that is at stake in the new idea of bodily individuation, that moment when a person's pains come to be experienced and recognized by others as being irreducibly her own. The body, then, must take on a certain normative contouring—say by becoming what must not be touched without its owner's consent—whose transgression we take as morally violating to the person herself. Hence we are committed to some idea of there being an identity between a person's body and the person herself. The normative saturation of the bodily person, or the identity between a person and her body, requires that being a person is equivalent to having a certain status or standing. Following recent custom, but without philosophical warrant as yet, we call what normatively saturates the body, giving it its standing and status, *human dignity*, and the acknowledgment that an individual possesses that normatively saturated bodily being *respect for human dignity*. When we are horrified by physical brutality, it is because (at least) the violation of bodily integrity is a violation/denial/destruction of an individual's intrinsic worth and so her human dignity—however compelling and obscure the latter concept is at present.

The forcefulness of law at its most coercive is to be distinguished from the brutality of torture in that the former must nonetheless respect the human dignity of the individual; it must recognize that the individual has standing and status that prohibits the law from crossing the inviolable boundary demanded by respect for bodily integrity. There cannot be a non-trivial prohibition against the use of torture without its involving some notion of the law respecting inviolable bodily integrity, some notion of bodily autonomy, some irreducible sense in which a person's body (including its pains and sufferings) are her own, and thereby some notion of human dignity. But if bodily integrity and human dignity are what must be respected if the prohibition against torture is to hold, then *generally*—anticipating the prohibition on torture's archetypal status—the law is prohibited from acts that would trespass upon bodily integrity and human dignity. And that is the morally decisive distinction between the forcefulness of law and the force of brutality. I shall take up the obvious objection to this thesis below.

Besides making vivid some wider principle, being archetypal also involves a law's being fundamental to the intelligibility of a surrounding body of laws such that were the archetype to be withdrawn, those other laws would lose support, intelligibility, authority, and legal force. While the law is not a deductive system, it is not a series of atomistic rules either. A body of laws can share ideas, principles, assumptions, have overlapping scopes, all in ways that make a body of laws possess a conceptual integrity that rationally requires their clustering together. Remove from the cluster its archetype, that law that captures the moving spirit of the cluster, and argumentative practice will have to shift in ways that will weaken the integrity or rational architecture of the cluster, potentially threatening its unraveling or collapse altogether. In order for socially recognized argumentative patterns to hold, they must be attuned to socially compelling distinctions, distinctions that govern social practices in fact as well as in idea.

How then does the prohibition on torture function as an archetype in American law? From the wording of the Eighth Amendment, we know that prohibiting the infliction of "cruel and unusual punishments" was inspired by the English Bill of Rights (1689), and that those words in their original setting and in their adoption by the framers were meant to legally underwrite "repugnance towards the use of torture" (236). I noted earlier that the persistence of slavery in America inevitably weakened the full force that would naturally attach to prohibiting "cruel and unusual punishments," as well as the provisions of the Fourth Amendment that are meant to guarantee protection against physical assault by the state—"The right of people to be secure in their persons . . . against unreasonable searches and seizures." The fundamental constitutional ideas driving the Fourth and Eighth Amendments that had been shockingly and palpably compromised by the existence of slavery are, belatedly, upheld and returned to their full natural meaning and force with the abolition of slavery. Although there was variation among the states, typically the body of a slave was subject to his master's authority such that "physical assault could yield no legal redress."[46] The abolition of slavery injects or recharges the relevant amendments with the idea of bodily integrity and autonomy, with some manner of normatively saturating the bodies of citizens against government incursion: "A constitutional prohibition of slavery," Seth Kreimer argues, "brings with it a presumption that the bodies of citizens are subject to neither the 'uncontrolled authority' of the state nor that of any private party."[47] The prohibition on slavery recalls constitutional law to its own orienting moral commitments: respect for the bodily autonomy of citizens as a founding moment in the constitutional settlement. We might say that the vileness of torture that lends its prohibition its archetypal status is funded by the vileness of slavery that makes its prohibition archetypal. Although we are concentrating on the archetypal status of the prohibition on torture, in America the authority of that prohibition cannot be disentangled from the history of slavery and its abolishment.

The prohibition against the use of torture in the full sense then operates as a model for the interpretation of the Eighth Amendment, in "what has been said in our courts about prison rape, about the withholding of medical treatment from prisoners, and about the use of flogging, hitching posts, and other forms of corporal punishment in our prisons" (237). For example, in his dissenting opinion in *U.S. v Bailey* (1980), Justice Blackmun argued: "The reasons that support the Court's holding in Estelle v. Gamble lead me to conclude that failure to use reasonable measures to protect an inmate from violence inflicted by other inmates also constitutes cruel and unusual punishment. Homosexual rape or other violence serves no penological purpose. Such brutality is the equivalent of torture, and is offensive to any modern standard of human dignity. Prisoners must depend, and rightly so, upon the prison administrators for protection from abuse of this kind."[48] What happens to the bodies of citizens legally matters once an individual is directly under state supervision and care, even when what happens is not itself a direct state action. Hence, if an inmate is not protected from being raped by other inmates, the systematic failure of protection counts as a state action, and therefore counts as subjecting the inmate to "the equivalent of torture." Justice Blackmun's further presumption here is that the wrongness implied by the measure of torture is an offense to human dignity—bodily violation is, morally and legally, a violation of dignity.

A further area where torture acts as an archetype is in decisions concerning procedural due process (roughly the idea that individuals are entitled to fair processes of adjudication) and self-incrimination. The opinion of Justice Frankfurter in Rochin v California (1952) is exemplary. Like a sequence from a police procedural, Rochin swallowed illegal drugs just prior to arrest; the police had a doctor force a tube down Rochin's throat into his stomach through which an emetic was given, making Rochin vomit up the evidence. Justice Frankfurter's decision deploys the model of torture to illuminate what is going wrong and going too far in Rochin's treatment. Because so much of this decision bears on the archetypal status of the prohibition against torture, I want to quote a large stretch of it; I have italicized crucial phrases.

> Applying these general considerations to the circumstances of the present case, we are compelled to conclude that the proceedings by which this conviction was obtained do more than offend some fastidious squeamishness or private sentimentalism about combating crime too energetically. *This is conduct that shocks the conscience.* Illegally breaking into the privacy of the petitioner, the struggle to open his mouth and remove what was there, the forcible extraction of his stomach's contents—this course of proceeding by agents of government to obtain evidence is bound to offend even hardened

sensibilities. *They are methods too close to the rack and the screw to permit of constitutional differentiation.*

It has long since ceased to be true that due process of law is heedless of the means by which otherwise relevant and credible evidence is obtained. This was not true even before the series of recent cases enforced the constitutional principle that the States *may not base convictions upon confessions, however much verified, obtained by coercion.* These decisions are not arbitrary exceptions to the comprehensive right of States to fashion their own rules of evidence for criminal trials. They are not sports in our constitutional law but *applications of a general principle . . .* It would be a stultification of the responsibility which the course of constitutional history has cast upon this Court to hold that in order to convict a man the police cannot extract by force what is in his mind but can extract what is in his stomach.

Coerced confessions offend the community's sense of fair play and decency. *So here, to sanction the brutal conduct* which naturally enough was condemned by the court whose judgment is before us, *would be to afford brutality the cloak of law. Nothing would be more calculated to discredit law and thereby to brutalize the temper of a society.*

Before they coerced the evidence from him, the police knew Rochin was guilty, perhaps (I am hypothesizing) even with a very high degree of certainty. And imagine that the ultimate crime Rochin was guilty of was more dangerous than possession of an illegal substance; imagine that we in the community have a large investment in seeing Rochin put away (he sells drugs to our children). Our criminal legal system requires the subsuming of all such considerations beneath those of due process; having standing as a citizen means entitlement to treatment of a certain kind irrespective of the substance of the criminal action. That is the grand discomfort and awkwardness and formality that the rule of law brings with it. Being "too close to the rack and the screw," being too close to torture is the measure Justice Frankfurter employs to judge the legitimacy of the police's procedures. Equally, the model of judicial torture is used to rule out confessions gotten by coercion; and the model of coerced confessions is in its turn used to rule out coercing the evidence from out of the defendant's stomach. So what "shocks the conscience" of the court, what fails the *moral test* regulating due process, are acts that in their utter proximity to torture violate bodily integrity. Rochin has, in fact, become "a keystone in the constitutional protection of bodily integrity against arbitrary invasion."[49]

Justice Frankfurter draws a clear line exactly where Waldron is arguing it must be drawn, between brutality and the force of law. What approaches torture, what appears analogous to torture crosses a line where the claim that the individual is regarded as having legal standing and status is lodged; once that line is crossed, there appears no further place or limit in which some idea of an independent life possessed by an independent living being could be recognized. Having legal standing is, necessarily, a form of moral protection. Finally, Justice Frankfurter is arguing a version of the Beccaria thesis, both as a moral content and as an expressivist doctrine: sanctioning brutal conduct under the cloak of law discredits the law, deprives it of its authority *as law*; such actions contravene the lawfulness of the law. In further claiming that such acts "brutalize the temper of a society," Justice Frankfurter must be taken as contending, either that such actions, because receiving the cloak of law, are implicitly morally legitimated, implicitly morally sanctioned; or that they brutalize the temper of society because *we* have done them. Likely, both claims are implied.

The prohibition on torture is archetypal in orienting how Fourth and Eighth Amendment law is interpreted; it informs issues of self-incrimination (drawing on the Fifth Amendment), as well as issues about both procedural and substantive due process stemming from the Fifth and Fourteenth Amendment—"nor shall any State deprive any person of life, liberty, or property, without due process of law; nor deny to any person within its jurisdiction the equal protection of the laws."[50] While I could go on citing cases and precedents (as Waldron and Kreimer importantly do), what should be now sufficiently patent is that large swathes of law do draw their sustenance from the prohibition on torture to such a degree that were that prohibition to be withdrawn then a whole body of law, precedent, and legal argument would cease to function and to mean in the way it does now.

I am tempted to say, that were the prohibition of torture withdrawn, the law *would become* merely positive. What thus explains torture's prohibition being archetypal is the Beccaria thesis: that is, the prohibition does more than offer principled intelligibility to a large swathe of interconnected constitutional law; it does so because the very idea of the rule of law gathers its authority from the state's repudiation of the authority to torture. Alan Dershowitz argues that because torture is bound to happen in times of emergency, then its use should be authorized and regulated by a judicially centered system of issuing torture warrants.[51] This idea flatly contravenes the very idea of the rule of law in the modern world, returning the law to its premodern status of regulating violence through the state's legitimate monopoly on it. It is a fundamental rule of law assumption that there cannot be a rigid divide between the judicial system and the engines of state: no individual shall be above the law; the state in its actions should be bound by the law; and all citizens are entitled to equal consideration under the law. Beccaria gave this idea a particular declension—namely that if the ordinary principles of the rule of law are to hold, then the state must renounce its power over the bodies of its citizens as exemplified by judicial and penal torture.

Waldron concludes his argument for the archetypal status of the prohibition on torture by arguing similarly that the idea of the rule of law should be animated by the prohibition on torture. If the engines of state are free to operate outside the law, then they will sap the law of its authority (as the state, men, will have risen above it), which will in turn further deteriorate the authority of the state until nothing is left but tyranny, arbitrariness, and brutality. Law, Waldron argues, "has set its face against brutality, and has found ways of remaining forceful and final in human affairs without savaging or terrorizing its subjects. The promise of the Rule of Law, then, is the promise that this sort of ethos can increasingly inform the practices of the state and not just the practices of courts, police, jailers, prosecutors etc. In this way, *a state subject to law* becomes not just a state whose excesses are predictable or a state whose actions are subject to forms, procedures, and warrants [the narrow construal of the rule of law]; it becomes a state whose exercise of power is imbued with this broader spirit of the repudiation of brutality" (251). For Waldron too, a substantive understanding of the rule of law underpins and projects an ethos, a distinct formation of ethical life, a valuable form of life in itself.

For Beccaria, sovereign authority above the law was the ultimate source of the arbitrariness and state violence exemplified by judicial torture. In using Hobbes's scenario of the state of nature yielding to a social contract, Beccaria means to invert Hobbes's theory, making even the sovereign subject to the rule of law—which, after all, is the driving idea behind the idea of the rule of law. Hence, Beccaria takes the inclusion of the engines of state within the rule of law not to be a matter of extending the archetype of the prohibition of torture to the state, as Waldron does; Beccaria thinks that inclusion is the necessary condition for the rule of law to come into effect within the judicial system itself. This is how everyone read Beccaria; it is what made his treatise one of the founts of the humanitarian revolution.

V. Forgetting Beccaria

There is one plain objection to this whole line of thought concerning torture and the rule of law—namely that there is no clear line to be drawn between the force of brutality and the force of law. The pulse of this claim depends on the thought that modern penal reform, from the eighteenth century to the present, no matter how well meant and humanely intended, fails to rid itself of torturous brutality. I understand this charge to compound three different possible claims. First, even stripped down to its basics, the system of incarceration cannot operate as punishment without additional elements that directly concern the body of the convicted—"rationing of food, sexual deprivation, corporal punishment, solitary confinement"[52]—to which, in the American case, can now be added severe overcrowding, the slow withdrawal of rehabilitative practices, the threat and actuality of rape, the tolerance of rape by authorities, and the use of its threat in the judicial system. These practices bespeak more than a "trace" (Foucault's term) of torture in the mechanisms of modern criminal justice; whatever the case in Europe, the American prison system, through design and neglect, has developed into a system that has torture in its heart.

Evidence for this thesis is not hard to find. Solitary confinement, which Foucault lists among the traces of torture remaining in the system in the American penal system affects some 80,000 men each day;[53] in chapter 7 of his *American Notes* (1842), "Philadelphia and its Solitary Prison," Charles Dickens offers a chilling account of a visit to a modern, "model" prison designed around solitary confinement, a practice that he concedes is, in intention, humane and meant for reformation.

> I believe that very few men are capable of estimating the immense amount of torture and agony which this dreadful punishment, prolonged for years, inflicts upon the sufferers . . . that there is a depth of terrible endurance in it which none but the sufferers themselves can fathom, and which no man has a right to inflict upon his fellow-creature. I hold this slow and daily tampering with the mysteries of the brain, to be immeasurably worse than any torture of the body: and because its ghastly signs and tokens are not so palpable to the eye and sense of touch as scars upon the flesh; because its wounds are not upon the surface, and it extorts few cries that human ears can hear; therefore I the more denounce it, as a secret punishment which slumbering humanity is not roused up to stay.[54]

The remainder of Dickens's account of his visit—the black hood placed over the convict's head as he is first led into the prison; the eerie silence broken only by the muffled sound of a lone weaver's shuttle or shoemaker's last; inmates denied all human interaction, all vision of other human faces; the unbending routine; and all for often nonviolent crimes (larceny), or no crime at all—adumbrates the idea that the regimentation, ordering, surveying, disciplining, and administration of bodies in modern prisons, without touching them directly, without leaving any physical scars or markings on them, nonetheless constitutes a savage deforming of the souls of the inmates that is "cruel" (Dickens's term) and inhumane. That disciplinary practices that leave no scars behind are themselves a form of brutality is the second of Foucault's charges against modern penal systems.[55]

Although it does not operate through imposing brutal force upon a vulnerable body, solitary confinement is a form of torture—it seeks to bend or break the will; it is used as a form of torture or as part of a connected series of practices that jointly are for the sake of breaking the will of the detained individual.[56] Although widely used in penal practice, solitary confinement (continuous with other forms of extreme psychological manipulation that are explicitly recognized as forms of torture like sleep and sensory deprivation), falls squarely on the brutality side of force. Solitary confinement is a paradigm of clean torture, torture that brutalizes without brutalizing the body directly. What Dickens's critique demonstrates is that the suffering sufficient for the breaking of the will can be accomplished other than through the direct infliction of bodily pain. Hence the distinction between the force of brutality and the force of law, required for the installation of the prohibition on torture, requires more than a conception of human dignity based on bodily autonomy narrowly construed. Respect for bodily autonomy is a necessary but not sufficient condition for respect for dignity. But to agree to this claim is to uphold, not undermine, the distinction between brutality and the force of law; it expands our understanding of brutality rather than drawing the force of law back into the domain of brutality.[57]

Foucault, however, has a third charge concerning disciplinary regimes that does not claim they are torturously brutal in the way that Dickens charges solitary confinement to be; nor does Foucault claim that these practices cause forms of suffering continuous with the suffering caused by torture; nor does he even say that these disciplinary practices fall afoul of the archetypal deployment of the prohibition on torture in the way U.S. courts have found various police and prison practices to be too close to the rack and the screw. Here is the third form of critique that drives the argument of *Discipline and Punish*: "Exercises, not signs: time-tables, compulsory movements, regular activities, solitary meditation, work in common, silence, application, respect, good habits. And ultimately, what one is trying to restore in this technique of correction is *not so much the juridical subject*, who is caught up in the fundamental interests of the social pact, *but the obedient subject*, the individual subjected to habits, rules, orders, an authority that is exercised continually around and upon him, and which he must allow to function automatically in him."[58]

Foucault is sometimes read as if he were concerned with opposing formations of cruelty and pain production. He is not; he is concerned with different formations of power, most centrally the opposition between sovereign and disciplinary power, where the latter is rhetorically decried because of its ability to disappear as power only to reappear in humanist dress as reformation, rehabilitation, and care for the soul of the prisoner. For all its bravura, however, Foucault's critique here falls squarely within the Enlightenment tradition of distinguishing an education for the sake of autonomy versus training for the sake of obedience, which is what he implicitly says in the passage just quoted. He goes on to make the claim explicit in the following sentence, arguing that modern penal practices may function in two quite distinct ways: either by restoring the "juridical subject of the social pact" or in accordance with a disciplinary regime seeking total power in order to "shape an obedient subject."[59] In fine, Foucault's critique of disciplinary power (which is narrower and less fierce than his critique of the penal system generally) is post-Beccarian and post-Kantian, presuming the normative authority of the idea of the juridical subject of the rule of law whose standing as citizen underwrites its power of autonomy. Foucault's argument, in line with much eighteenth- and nineteenth-century penal thought, implies that a necessary condition for dignity-respecting penal practice is that it seek to restore the juridical subject of the rule of law.

Beccaria unequivocally intended the repudiation of judicial and penal torture to fashion a comprehensive idea of the rule of law; Foucault's researches demonstrate that, although premised on the idea of the juridical subject, Beccaria failed to fully disaggregate the juridical subject from the obedient subject (in this regard, his utilitarianism overwrites his commitment to social contract theory). In order for that distinction to have force, Beccaria's lesson must be absorbed, forgotten, and extended. It is absorbed by the acknowledgment that the vulnerable bodies of citizens are beyond the reach of the state, that brute force must not be used on them, that they must not be touched or violated; and that the purpose of all these prohibitions is for the sake of realizing a (new) formation of human subjectivity, what Foucault usefully denominates in implacably Beccarian terms as "the juridical subject of the social compact." Once we as a civilization agree to this idea, once we agree that the state must renounce its power to violate the bodies of its own citizens—even as it continues making war and killing in ever-increasing atrocious ways that possess new increments of violative cruelty—a moral threshold is passed and our idea of the state is no longer formed as solely a *counterimage* to the image of the spectacle of torture. Rather, the idea of the modern state under the rule of law is constructed, again and again, from Kant to Rawls, through the *resultant* of that counterimage—namely through the idea of the autonomous, self-possessed citizen who no longer even remembers the spectacle of torture, and hence through an idea of autonomous subjectivity that is so sufficiently safe and secure in its moral identity that it is not at every moment urgently, with horror and fear, gathering itself up in resistance to threat of bodily violation. Philosophically, at least, we have forgotten the threat and the surmounting of the threat of bodily violation by the state as the fount of our idea of law. We have forgotten Beccaria, we have forgotten the Beccaria thesis, we have forgotten that a negative ethics constructed in horrified response to the cruelties of torture forms the moral premise and fundament of modern political morality.

At a certain moment, the forgetting of the Beccaria thesis, the active effort of absorbing and suppressing its lesson, was the sign of its overwhelming civilizational triumph. We were no longer *beholden* to the image of Damiens—his flesh being torn from his breasts, his being drawn and quartered by four horses—as what must never be done to a citizen by the state; hence we were no longer beholden to our outrage and terror in order to form for ourselves the idea of a state acting wholly within the bounds of law. What would it have involved in order for us to remember *at each and every moment* the image of torture as the counterimage of what we wanted from the rule of law? To conceive of that imagination of imminent destruction as the moral source of the authority of the rule of law would be to imagine the rule of law as not fully present; it would be to imagine that what we were meaning to leave behind by turning to the rule of law remained, viscerally haunting us at every moment. Everyone in the eighteenth century read Beccaria; the forgetting of Beccaria is, I am claiming, part of a dialectical logic through which the impact of his claim was achieved; the Beccaria thesis was and logically could have been fully realized *only through its being forgotten,* its being turned into an affirmative morals of *rational autonomy* rather than a negative ethics directed at the living products of state violence; its forgetting was the sign of its establishment. Nonetheless, we have paid a terrible price for that forgetting: to have torture reemerge as an almost taken-for-granted instrument of state security.

Where this forgetting is most patent, however, is in the abyss separating the best constitutional reflections on the archetype of the prohibition on torture and the moral philosophy that would need to be present in order to found it. As Waldron modestly comments, the issue of legal archetypes is a "second-tier issue" in comparison to the "moral issue of the deliberate infliction of pain, the suffering that results, the insult to dignity, and the demoralization and depravity that is almost always associated with this enterprise [of state torture] whether legalized or not" (259). Justice Frankfurter's impassioned judgment almost certainly gathers its moral force not from an articulated set of moral ideas, but rather from the fact that we have vividly before our eyes the image of Rochin having a tube forced down his throat, being force-fed an emetic, and then uncontrollably vomiting what will be politely called "the evidence" of the crime—too much like state-sanctioned rape, too vivid a picture of helplessness to pass as reasonable police procedure.

Modern moral philosophy is, for the most part, significantly post-Beccarian; modern moral philosophy emerges *after* the individuation of the modern body has taken place, after its dependencies on others no longer arrive as a collective achievement; rational autonomy is now firmly embedded in social and legal practice, so firmly installed that it is capable of being taken for granted as a matter of social and legal fact. (All these presumptive facts are always, for reasons I shall come to, less true for women than men, and more evidently, less true for African-Americans than white persons.) Modern moral philosophy operates in near-perfect forgetfulness of Beccaria, both literally and philosophically. Beccaria's triumph, however partial and however temporary, by igniting a conception of the rule of law that made the body beyond touch, simultaneously made it possible for philosophy to forget its bodily investment, to have only an untouched and untouchable body before it, hence forgetting how the idea of human dignity and bodily autonomy must be entwined; the forgetting of Beccaria made possible an idea of *rational* autonomy that forgets and even repudiates its bodily dependencies to become the taken-for-granted starting point for serious moral reflection. Worse, by assuming for itself the idea and ideal of the autonomous subject, modern moral philosophy suppresses the deepest stratum feeding this idea of autonomous subjectivity—namely that in the horrified response to torture there was implied a trembling recognition that a human being can suffer *devastation*, that what makes us human is the possibility—beyond mortality and depravity—of an individual losing her *standing* as human for herself and her others. If a moral philosophy had arisen in the eighteenth century that had been equal to the meaning of torture and the moral necessity of its repudiation, it would have had to be a philosophy of devastation. *Beings possessed of dignity are beings subject to devastation.*

My effort in this chapter has not been to provide a reminder of what we have forgotten, although if my reading of Beccaria should lead others to seek out his little treatise, I shall not be disappointed. But Beccaria's book arose directly out of a moment of immense social, moral, and finally legal turbulence. That turbulence is the source of the intelligibility and force of Beccaria's argument. *On Crimes and Punishments* gathered up its time in thought, shaped its legal conversation, insinuated the rule of law with its modern meaning as the premise of modern political morality, and thus permitted that world to move on, to become our own. My effort has been to remind us of our forgetting, to see that forgetting as the triumph and disaster it has proved to be. No moral philosophy matching the impetus and demands of Beccaria's jurisprudence ever did arise. What is required now is not a work of memory—it is too late for that—but a reactivation of the origin, an effort to erect now a moral philosophy of devastation, to demonstrate from the instance of torture as the paradigm case of moral harm and devastation what our moral commitments must be, what conception of human dignity is demanded by the counterinstance of torture, and hence why the recognition of human dignity requires the principle that "Everyone has the right to recognition everywhere as a person before the law."

TWO

On Being Tortured

I. Introduction

Chapter 1 argued for a connected series of theses; central among them were:

In the second half of the eighteenth century, in the period leading up to the abolition of torture, there occurred a transformation in the social placement and understanding of bodily experience: increasing societal individuation was accompanied by an emergent cultural individualism. A central feature of this double transformation was the disenchantment of pain, whereby pain ceased being experienced as a component of a (divine) metaphysical scheme—as debt or payment or punishment or curse—and came instead to baldly signal harm and injury to the individual's body on which it was inflicted or in which it occurred.

The abolition of torture was a signature culmination of this process, morally and legally inscribing the new status of the individual: even when brought directly under state control, the individual's body is not to be touched or violated or have pains inflicted on it. Even when one is brought within the criminal justice system, one possesses legal personality. To be subject to torture, or to cruel or inhuman treatment, is to be deprived of moral or legal standing: if the state were permitted to violate the human body in those ways, then its powers would be effectively without limit, and the person without moral standing.

Bodily integrity thus became the marker for a new idea of intrinsic human worth: each individual possesses inviolable human dignity.

The role of Beccaria's *On Crimes and Punishments* in this process was to inscribe this new standing of the individual through the substantive idea of the rule of law. In Beccaria, the rule of law is constructed as the contextually inscribed determinate negation of, and thus the counterimage to, the rule of sovereign law exemplified by the tortured body. That construction remains legible in Constitutional law.

Because it arose as a determinate negation of its antecedent—rather than through the implementation of an already existing set of moral principles and postulates—the moral force and urgency of the rule of law remain tied to its being the counterimage to the sovereign law of torture such that every abrogation of the rule of law is experienced, implicitly or explicitly, as a threat to the very idea of human worth it inscribes. At present, we would not be able to make fully intelligible to ourselves either our understanding of the rule of law or our idea of human dignity if the connection between the rule of law and its formation as a counterimage to the sovereign law of torture were severed.

But this severance has occurred, and it is a part of ethical culture. In fact, the severance between the negative ethics recoiling before the tortured body and the rule of law was, in part, a *product* of the installation of the modern rule of law. Even as we have come to equivocally accept Beccaria's thesis separating the force of law from brutality, the construction of that thesis as the counterimage to the sovereign law of torture has been forgotten (even though, as I will argue in my conclusion, it is faithfully repeated in the Universal Declaration of Human Rights).[1]

Simultaneously with the rule of law becoming an orienting fundament of modern political morality, a singular and surprising result of the dialectical forgetting of the sovereign law of torture—the way in which the Beccaria thesis has triumphed by its origin being forgotten—has been the propounding of affirmative moral philosophies of rational autonomy that extirpate, to the point of oblivion, the negative ethics of the tortured body as moral source. Rather than portraying the human as that which is capable of devastation, modern moral philosophy has returned to the intellectualist tradition of portraying the human in terms of capacities for reason, reflective choice, linguistic communication, rule-following, self-consciousness, cooperative behavior. The forgetting of devastation, its actuality and its role as marker of the human, offers at least a partial explanation for modern moral philosophy's analyzing of moral wrongness in terms of acting wrongly, and analyzing acting wrongly in terms of breaking a moral norm, rule, ideal, or principle. This rationalist picture of morality presents moral rules as descending from an affirmative source (God or reason or benevolent nature), as opposed to the more obvious idea that moral rules articulate those actions a society does *not* want to happen to its members because, minimally, they cause bodily pains and harms, threatening the security of persons and goods; and, maximally, they cause death and devastation, and because permitting actions regularly experienced and perceived as harmful threatens antecedent affective bonds together with the reproduction of social order. The thesis that the rule of law is sourced by a negative ethics opposing torture would permit the shift mentioned in the introduction in which the notion of "morally wrong" is replaced by "wrongs someone": *people* not principles are what get harmed, broken, violated in morally wrongful behavior.[2]

The eighteenth century *experience* in which torture was transformed from communal festival to individual assault is now beyond recuperation for productive purposes. In order to reactivate the moral source of the modern rule of law, what is required is a modern rendition of torture in which the account of the experience of torture is already set within the framework in which the pains of the body have been disenchanted and the value of the individual is taken for granted. But if this account of torture is going to play a role analogous to the eighteenth-century experience of torture, then what is needed, in the first instance, is a provisioning of the *experience* of torture: some depiction in which the undergoing of torture is elaborated in terms experientially rich enough to guide further philosophical reflection. I have read numerous, often graphic accounts of torture, but only one has the reflective depth necessary for constructive purposes. Jean Améry's *At the Mind's Limits: Contemplations by a Survivor on Auschwitz and Its Realities* provides a searing portrait of Améry's imprisonment, his torture, and his experience of being a damaged survivor of that brutal history.[3] His account of his torture has become canonical in torture literature. Améry concedes from the outset that what happened to him was hardly the worst form of torture: "No red hot needles were shoved under fingernails, nor were any lit cigars extinguished on my bare chest." Nonetheless, on the basis of what he did suffer, he contends, "torture is the most horrible event a human being can retain within himself" (AML, 22). In a more philosophical register, this might be expressed as saying that torture is a paradigm of moral harm and moral wrong, a paradigm of a morally grievous occurrence. Améry was broken, undone, devastated; although he will revolt against his moral extinction, it is the power of torture and the camps to devastate him, to devastate the human, that Améry seeks to record. 'Devastation,' as I shall use this term, refers to the experience of being undone in one's standing as human, and to continue to experience the event of destruction as a present moral fact about oneself. Torture intends devastation, and it is his devastation through torture and in the camps that Améry is trying to understand.

The genre of Améry's interconnected set of essays is hybrid: more analytically acute, philosophically shaded, and reflective than standard survivor testimony, while nonetheless recusing itself from the requirements of explanation, explication, or understanding. So he says: "I had planned a contemplative, essayistic study. What resulted was a personal confession refracted through meditation . . . Confessing and meditating, I arrived at an examination or, if you will, an essence-description [a description of the essence] of the existence of the victim (*einer Wesensbeschreibung der Opfer-Existenz*)" (AML, xiii; trans. modified). Améry's confession and description of the essential elements of his existence as victim are what make his account invaluable; because it is the existence of the victim that absorbs him, questions of ethics and morality recede almost to the point of disappearance. By focusing on the experience of torture, Améry makes available to us a phenomenological profile, a philosophical ethnography of a paradigmatic grievous moral wrong without the coding or presuppositions of moral theory (about which, anyway, Améry would have been harshly skeptical). To make morality answerable to the experience of the existential profile Améry provides, to rewrite morality from the perspective of the victim, from the perspective of moral injury, would formally amount to a reactivation of the origin of the abolition of torture as the legal-moral pivot of the humanitarian revolution of the eighteenth century.

One preliminary clarification is necessary before beginning. For good reasons, we distinguish among the several purposes torture may serve: acquiring a confession (judicial torture); punishment (penal torture); acquiring information (interrogational torture); intimidation or getting a sufferer and relevant associates connected with the sufferer to act, or cease acting, in desired ways (terroristic or deterrent torture); to destroy the other without killing (dehumanizing torture); to please the torturer (recreational torture). A good deal of modern torture, including Améry's, is, at least officially, of the interrogational sort. In the era of national warfare states that began with the outbreak of World War I, torture returned as an essential instrument of state security. Tortured interrogations of those taken to be enemies of the state about their colleagues, places of habitation, storage of weapons, and their future plans of attack became widespread, routine, and clandestine. As state security has come to be seen as both more vital and fragile, torture becomes a more regular instrument for the purposes of knowledge acquisition. Interrogational torture is disenchanted torture,

torture as an engine of state and not as a component of the legal system, torture after the abolition of torture, late modern torture.

If presented with the category, Améry would have mocked the very idea of pure interrogational torture as an outsider's illusion incompatible with first-person experience. There are overwhelming reasons to think that the idea of pure interrogational torture is illusory. Consider the following, which we will investigate in more detail below: Assume that the goal of interrogational torture is truth; this entails that once the victim has offered the desired information, the purposes of the torture and interrogation have been satisfied, and the torture can end. In general, that simple progression is incapable of satisfaction. First, there is an incommensurability between method and outcome, torture and truth; the interrogator seeks truth, the victim seeks to avoid further pain. Beyond methodological incommensurability, there is, second, a reason why the sensitive innocent fares worse under torture than the callous terrorist (especially in time-sensitive situations): there are no internal criteria for truth; as a consequence, because there is no internal way for the torturer to know the truth has been given, there is no reason for him to stop. Formally, without external verification (or its equivalent: convergent testimony from several different sources) there is no determinate place or reason for the torture to stop. Interrogational torture is de facto limitless.

But these are just versions of the well-known arguments against torture's epistemic reliability and utility. They matter, however, because they place the torturer in a quandary: how can the gap between torture and truth be closed short of external verification? The infliction of pain is insufficient on its own for securing cooperation and hence truth. But to suppose sufficiency is to mislocate the role of pain in interrogational torture. Because the goal of torture is to make the victim answerable to the torturer, then *the purpose of the infliction of pain is to "break" the victim*; making the victim helpless and dependent is an essential and not merely ancillary or accidental feature of the process. For Améry, it is evident that interrogational torture must devolve into some form of dehumanizing torture in order to accomplish its own narrow (interrogational) purposes. For the torturer, breaking the victim is the mechanism for connecting pain to the extraction of truth.

Modern disenchanted torture works by breaking the victim; modern torture works through devastation; whatever its final purpose, torture is a process of devastation. It is the character of this devastation that is the object of Améry's reflections; he was undone, *overcome*—thus the original subtitle of the book: *Bewältigungsversuche eines Überwältigten*, literally, *Cop-*

ing Attempts by the Overcome. Améry was overcome, undone, devastated; the meanings through which his life had been meaningful were destroyed, and then he in his standing as a human was destroyed. What is it for a human being to be devastated? What is devastated in such torturous exchanges? Améry states that "for the torture-slave (*der Folterknecht*), the torturer is solely the other" (AML, 34); no longer are torture victims being tested by the gods. Torture in the modern age, what Améry calls "modern police torture," is torture stripped of its earlier religious trappings, which permitted a "theological complicity" between torturer and victim. Whatever the external goals or ends of torture are, torture now is a relation between two individuals (where the second individual stands for the state or some other collective body); that is, torture is now—or this is what Améry experienced and what he wants to relay to us—an exemplary exposition of the fate of the relation between a self and his other, nothing but self and other in a form whose characteristic articulation elaborates the very idea of being a self with an other. *To be human is to be subject to devastation through another.* That is the meaning of the human, the meaning of a victim-existence, that Améry experiences and means to elaborate.

Since, on any account, torture concerns the exploitation of the victim's pain, I will begin with some reflections on the nature of pain. Because torture is the systematic and ritual infliction of pain in isolation from other social forms and practices, it is prima facie plausible to treat torture as itself an exposition or living phenomenology of pain, a revelation of the meaning of human pain as a social phenomenon. Hence, torture takes the ordinary experience of pain and makes it the explicit and sole currency in the exchange between self and other. This marks the path I want to travel here: from the ordinary experience of pain to its installation as the bond between self and other in torture.

II. Pain: Certainty and Separateness

It matters to our hearing of Améry that his account of torture is in the first person, as much an expression of pain and a confession of the fragmenting of a human life as it is an interrogation of the process in which it occurs. Améry *presents* himself (AML, 2), his pain, and the severing of his relations to the world and others, which are the consequences of that pain.[4] The extremity of pain adheres to the first-person perspective as no other phenomenon does, and hence something significant in its reality eludes our ordinary conception of objectivity as what is shared or shareable from multiple perspectives: this table, this chair, this hand I see before me, the moon bone white in the night sky. In extreme pain the world around me collapses, dissolves, and reality seems to congeal at the very place in my body in which I am feeling the pain, and that feeling of pain becomes my body, fills it out until it becomes all of reality. I scream.

A familiar grammar of experience operates here: first, the disintegration of intentional relations to the world; second, as the world dissolves, receding from view, experience becomes lodged in a particular locale on or in the body, that locale becoming enormous, all else becoming background; third, as the adversity of the experience heightens, the sheer suffering of what I am undergoing begins to take on *living form*, forms itself, my body spontaneously and immediately expressing what is happening to it through posture (by crouching or bowing), behavior (by turning or fleeing), and sound (by yelping or crying). Loss of the world, the injured body filling out experiential space, bodily and vocal expression: these are pain's unchanging rhythm and beat. This simple grammar of pain is one we recognizably share with the higher animals.[5] Under conditions of torture, this grammar acquires an expanded form. In torture, pain takes on the full complexity of its intersubjective, social—and hence moral—meaning. In human life, pains *always* have, beyond their animal grammar, a social grammar of exposure and vulnerability to others, a grammar of expectation and need of aid from others, a grammar of expressiveness that automatically solicits acknowledgment, empathy, identification (or the denial of these moments). Pains are occasions in which human separateness and connectedness take on a unique physiognomy. Torture, in making explicit the social and moral meaning of pain, simultaneously reveals pain's human meaning, what it might mean generally and as such that we are the kinds of beings that suffer pain in the ways we do. It reveals that being vulnerable to physical pain and related psychological pains are constitutive of the human condition. And, at least in part, what is involved in understanding the moral and human meaning of pain is grasping how the two grammars of pain—the simple animal grammar of pain and its expanded social formation that torture articulates—interact and relate to one another. It is, finally, that relation that we are most interested in.

A first aside: acute pain, the kind of pain that is explicitly causally related to a bodily injury, is, in being bodily, located in space. When I stub my toe, knock my elbow, slice my finger, when I suffer from backache or bellyache, when my headache makes the top of my head feel like it is going to explode, when a blister on my foot forces me to hobble down the road, when my face stings with the slap it has just received, in each and every case the pain is felt in an exact place on or in my body.[6] In being felt in a particular place within the body's geometry—left or right, front or back, up top or down below, between the eyes or in the middle of the gut—pain acquires a precise spatial location. However "mental" pain is, however much pain is a function of the brain, it is not felt "in the mind" ("in the head") but where it is on or in the body, and for good reason: the location of the pain is determined by the location of damage, which in turn determines both modes of protection and defense, and the directions of repair and solace—the bandage or splint, the ice or hot compress or soothing touch applied "just there" where the hurt is. All this is obvious but for the fact that it is routinely philosophically forgotten or overlooked; pain invokes irrevocable worldliness, our bodily and spatial insertion into the world (even as the world as intentional object collapses with acute pains). Our feeling self with its pains and pleasures is a fully bodily self located in the same spatial world as pens, cauliflowers, ships, and stars.[7] How significant this is we shall come to.

We were tracking the simple grammar of pain, in particular its first-person character, how intense pain, in refocusing our attention, absorbing it, is qualitatively different from the experience of the world it interrupts. In interrupting the experience of the world, pain reverses the direction of attention: from world to self; but as we become painfully self-aware, self-absorbed, the quality of knowing shifts from a usually blind pragmatic confidence to an insistent self-certainty. Intense physical pain is thus like a skeptical mechanism: it brackets everyday knowledge of the world, turning attention inward, providing the sufferer with an experience incapable of being doubted. Pain, in tearing us out of involvement in the world and turning the gaze inward toward a coercive object of attention, parallels the movement of modern skepticism, with its doubt of the world and the overcoming of that doubt in self-certainty. That the grammar of pain and the logic of modern skepticism are parallel is probably no accident; modern philosophy instructs us that we come to self-consciousness, an awareness of the self in its separateness from the world, in retreat from violent attack: an evil demon disorganizing self-world relations, a war of all against all in a disordered state of nature, a life and death battle for recognition.[8] Pain individualizes, returning us from the self-forgetfulness of world involvements to an intense form of self-awareness; it is by virtue of the way in which pain individualizes the sufferer that pain's modes of separation and connection are set into motion.

Physical pain reorders our cognitive relation to the world to the point at which the extremes of the philosophical imagination become realities: to be in excruciating pain is for the suffering subject our model or paradigm of having certainty, while pain's very interiority, its lack of an intentional structure, and its resistance to language—that is, its sense of being anterior to language (its capacity to reduce the sufferer to cries, screams, and groans)—make an other's pain so emphatically inward in its primary significance that its becomes the exemplary instance of what can be doubted (BP, 4).[9] The abyss separating inward pain from outward manifestation is nowhere more sharply felt than when we discover we have been deceived by another's expression of pain; the acuteness of that discovery often causing a ruinous tear in the fabric of the relations that bind us. I understand the severity of such discoveries as a primary source of modern skepticism, a constant in its etiology: we do spontaneously treat the expressions of the body in pain as natural signs, immediate outward manifestations of inner suffering. When we discover that what appears to be almost a law of nature is not only breakable but manipulable and corruptible, we can become skeptics about the inner lives of others. Deceit in this domain of experience can leave in its wake severely frayed relations of trust.

I equally presume that we could not feel as betrayed as we do when so deceived unless we are generally justified in assuming that expressions of pain are as we unreflectively take them to be: the spontaneous concomitants of a living animal being in pain—groans and moans, flailing and grimacing as (culturally contoured) natural signs of pain. Our immersion in a shared pain-world is as thoroughgoing as its routine crises of isolation, these being two emphatic aspects of a single structure of experience; pain is both an intransigent source of human connection and a searing force of separation. Capturing the depth of pain's dual character—its power of connecting (consider empathic identification with another's pain) and separating—is part of what a successful analysis must achieve. Pain could not possess this complexity unless its prominent sensation aspect could be cognitively and affectively elaborated. Pain must be conceived as possessing sensational, affective, and cognitive aspects that structure its social appearances and exchange: to be in pain is always also to be in a self-relation to that pain—horrified, devastated, stoical—as a component of one's relation to others (isolated or bonded).

Pain, in opening up the abyss between my certainty and your doubt, makes the world cognitively divided and dissonant. This division possesses two distinct manifestations. On the one hand, it announces the separateness of persons; pain, I want to say, contours what we *mean* by the separateness of persons; it is a singular dimension of the experiential actuality of separateness.[10] In pain, others can feel terribly removed from me, distant as if nothing but the pain I am suffering can count as "near," because they cannot share or partake in what I suffer alone. Pain easily translates into isolation, desolation, existential loneliness; my pain is my world. Conversely, in the face of another's pain, we can feel impotent, irrelevant, outside the inner drama they are undergoing. All this I take as aspects of pain's interruption of world relatedness, its collapsing of intentional relations to the world, its reversing attention from world to injured self, and hence pain as an irreducible manner or modality of the self's being-in-the-world; being in pain is a way of existing. The refocusing of experience inward in pain draws the sufferer away from relations to others, making others distant, while you, the sufferer, in being remote, in being withdrawn from mutual interaction, become for those observing you an object of attention, a subject-object, a "thing" to be pitied or sympathized with, but still tinged with object-ness, socially abject. Hence we understand the awkward sense sufferers sometimes have of being a spectacle, just a "thing" to be passively stared at or done to: fed, washed, tended, or, worst of all, pitied. And, again, there is a half-truth here: if pain is a disconnection and withdrawal from the world, a severing and turning inward, then the sufferer and her proximate others are no longer sharing the world—jointly intending and attending to the world—in the way they were before the pain began. There are more benign ways in which this familiar scenario is played out—acts of care and sympathetic consideration that are felt to be such, unconditionally received as a vital necessity satisfied—but the isolation-and-spectator scenario reveals how pain provides a constitutive moment in structuring how the separateness of persons is experienced and understood. Attentive care of the right kind can mitigate or even relieve the isolation—the balm of a mother's touch—but it is a moment of stark separateness that is mitigated and relieved. Torture, as we shall see, radicalizes the isolation-and-spectator structure in a novel way.

On the other hand, pain also separates the suffering subject from his previous experience of the world. In the ordinary course of life, Améry claims, there is a steady congruence between our anticipation of events and the events themselves: my imagination of buying the morning newspaper and my buying the morning newspaper stand to one another as anticipation and fulfillment, and in my act I hardly differentiate myself from the millions of others who have performed the same act before me. Is my failure to differentiate myself sufficiently or fully a consequence of my failure to imagine the act in all its vivid detail? No imagination of an event is quite like the event, but the failure to differentiate myself from others in imagination or act is of a different order; it occurs "because even in direct experience everyday reality is nothing but a codified abstraction. Only in rare moments of life do we truly stand face to face with the event and, with it, reality" (AML, 26).

Améry does not suppose that everyday experience in any sense lacks reality or objectivity or validity. Perhaps we should say of the everyday that it cognitively unfolds independently of certainty or doubt, of being abstract or concrete, dull or vivid, that normally those categories are simply inapplicable. However, in claiming that everyday reality is "nothing but a codified abstraction," Améry does mean to say that normally we encounter events, objects, and others through categories, concepts, habits, and practices that are indifferent to their sensuous uniqueness and affective charge because, normally, sensuous particularity and affective significance are not at issue in the encounter. Codified abstraction corresponds to the pragmatically interested way in which we routinely negotiate the world: my shoes disappear in my walking, and my fork and knife disappear in their uniqueness as I cut the asparagus in half, and place the piece at the end of my fork in my mouth. More reality than is necessary for pragmatic coping and functional fitness would be neither practicable nor satisfying. Everyday acts of attending are task rather than object or event related. And what holds for objects and events, holds equally for oneself: intense self-awareness would cut one off from the world, not make one's experience of it richer. We do not need much "reality" for the purposes of everyday living.

Améry casually remarks that one does not require something as extreme as torture in order to be brought face-to-face with reality: "Arrest is enough and, if need be, the first blow one receives . . . Everything is self-evident, and nothing is self-evident as soon as we are thrust into a reality whose light blinds and burns us to the bone" (AML, 26). Améry's half-ironic tone is his rhetorical mechanism for creating sufficient distance between himself and what he suffered for its communication to leave space for understanding. So here what is self-evident is strictly unwelcome, almost intolerable, and that it is self-evident in this modality is what equally makes nothing self-evident, since the intensity of this experience lifts self and objects from their quotidian state of codified abstraction into, what? Not the fine-grained, emotionally heightened awareness that occurs in art or lovemaking, but just sheer presence of self and all but sheer absence of the world. In the extremity of pain that occurs with torture, the body is transformed from the nearly invisible instrument of our access to the world, our openness to the world as our way of inhabiting it, being in it, into worldless sentience itself, the outraged feeling of a pain from which there is no escape.

In tortured pain "each source of strength and delight, each means of moving out into the world or moving the world in to oneself, becomes a means of turning the body back in on itself, forcing the body to feed on the body: the eyes are only access points for scorching light, the ears for brutal noises . . ." (BP, 48). Our body can provide access to the world—both perceptually and in action—only because it is sensationally open to the world. Openness to the world has as its direct corollary vulnerability to the world. Openness and vulnerability are often of the same power under different aspects, vulnerability being the inward-looking dimension of a world-directed power of receptivity. In providing access to the world, the body recedes from view in favor of the world; in pain, the world recedes from view as the body comes to have itself as its primary object. The absolute certainty of the body's presence in severe pain, a state in which doubt is impossible, that very state that modern philosophy has imagined as its ground or fundament or realization, bursts into existence as the disappearance of the world. Here, in the torture cell, skeptical doubt, the systematic disappearance of an articulated world of things and events, and certainty simultaneously achieve their perfect existential realization. (The idea of the torturer as a malevolent deity, an evil demon, is not far from Améry's reflections.)

Améry contends, for reasons we shall come to, that "whoever is tortured, stays tortured. Torture is ineradicably burned into him, even when no clinically objective traces can be detected" (AML, 34). To say "whoever is tortured, stays tortured" means in part that the affective experience and cognitive disorder that is the immediate consequence of extreme physical pain occurring under conditions of torture is etched into the very being of the victim, and hence necessarily marks his engagements with the world even after the original pain and its marks have disappeared. In *At the Mind's Limits* this is a matter of both content and tone: the skepticism imposed by tortured pain becomes a skepticism about the durability and solidity of civilization's spiritual achievements; the separation of persons becomes a traumatized loneliness, and, later, an unrelieved resentment and insatiable desire for retribution.[11] Everywhere there is a tone of mock irony to hide the impossible hurt and rage; there is the cool language of analysis that becomes fractured by the insistence of the bodily memory of suffering, the resurgence of the "I" as the only reality, and the presumption of the incontrovertible authority that this suffering affords, the certainty of its pronouncements. It is as if beneath the quiet flowing of his communicative language we can hear still Améry's scream, that he, his body, cannot stop screaming.

Although, then, this work is a series of "contemplations," an analytic search for the meaning of the events told, the role of the confessional voice in it is indelible; but this indelibility is not the standard excess of a subject's saying something over what is said, the performative fact of each human statement, but the experiential remnant of the inversion of the cognitive order of the world that extreme pain produces. Pain's primary actuality is first-personal. One aspect of this is to say that, especially in cases of severe pain, the relation between a pain and its manifestation is one of expression rather than, say, report or avowal, thus making a stretch of human pain behavior continuous with animal pain behavior. Ludwig Wittgenstein contends that when a child learns to talk, "the verbal expression of pain replaces crying," by which he means that initially assertions like "I have a tummy ache" play the same role in expressing the ache as did the child's previous moaning while holding her stomach.[12] What grammatically looks and sounds like a report about an independently existing state of affairs is in fact another manifestation of it. This hypothesis makes sense if expression belongs to the simple grammar of pain shared by animals and humans.[13] I also hear in Wittgenstein's claim the thought that even in the most fact-stating, first-person statements about pain—"I would say that on a scale of 1 to 10 my pain now is a 5"—there remains a kernel of expression; it is difficult to conceive of a first-person, present-tense pain report that would contain no tinge of expressiveness.[14] To imagine first-person statements as wholly lacking in expressiveness is to imagine the assertion in question as not actually being about the speaker, thus calling for neither response nor acknowledgment—an imaginary exchange that is often a part of the strange actual exchanges that occur between doctors and patients. Expressiveness belongs to the grammar of first-person present-tense statements about being in pain; and, when the pains were sufficiently horrendous, we feel the same about past-tense statements from others, requiring us to demonstrate appropriate sympathy or concern—"Oh, how awful to have had to suffer that. It must have been terrible for you."

Something is lost from the understanding of pain if it is viewed only from the outside, from a third-person perspective. This is all the more the case when the pain being suffered is intentionally brought about by another. This is why we need to begin, in a phenomenological vein, with Améry's account of his torture. Torture, one might say, is the exposition of the body's capacity for pain, the articulation of the body's capacity for suffering and injury, and the mechanism through which those features of bodily existence are so absolutely inscribed upon the body that it can never recover, making the tortured body, whenever and wherever, the walking testimony to human injurability. Torture elaborates pain in revealing it as a social relation; pain's social relationality is stamped by torture into one of its categorial modalities. The exorbitance of tortured pain is not just its intensity, but its intersubjective constitution, pain becoming relational in its meaning and being undergone. Tortured pain doubtless is sometimes excruciating, unbearable; but what distinguishes it is that it is devastating. Devastation is the fullest realization of the social actuality of pain.[15] Torture tells us about our vulnerability before others, its structural features and unavoidability. All those things belong to the pain of torture and its character of being devastating.

This is also part of what Améry wants to say about torture, with the extra inflection that the Third Reich somehow took the torture form and turned it into a political form, a way of being in power and dominating those under its authority.

III. Améry's Torture

Before an analytic of torture can be given, we need a description of the event itself.[16] In July 1943, Améry—born in Vienna as Hans Meyer—was arrested by the Gestapo for handing out fliers for the small, German-speaking organization of the Belgian resistance movement to which he belonged. Améry considered himself a hardened expert on the Nazi system, and hence had, he thought, no illusions about what was in store for him once he was picked up by the men in leather coats and drawn pistols: "Prison, interrogation, blows, torture; in the end, most probably death. Thus it was written and thus it would happen" (AML, 25), a routine circuit well known to all members of the resistance and beyond. After his hands are chained together, Améry tells the police that he will not attempt an adventurous escape and that they can count on his cooperation. He is informed that unless he confesses he will be sent to Breendonk, the small SS-controlled concentration camp, called by the Nazis a "reception camp," that still stands midway between Brussels and Antwerp.

Because of the artful organization of the resistance, Améry is unable to provide the police with the information they want concerning accomplices and hiding places. His confession of ignorance is met with derision by the officers, and it is then he feels the first blow, the one that tells him, in a manner wholly unexpected, that he is *helpless*. Améry recalls Proust's dictum that "nothing really happens as we hope it will, nor as we fear it will," not because it goes beyond the imagination, as if it were a quantitative matter, "but because it is reality and not fantasy" (AML, 25). The blows keep raining down on him, but despite the visual and acoustic disorientation they bring about, because they act as their own anesthetic, they are strangely bearable, and this offers Améry the possibility and hope of stoic resistance.

Since beating him has gotten them nowhere, Améry's captors become tired of hitting him. Thus it is that he is sent, wrists shackled, twenty-five kilometers across the Flemish countryside to "Reception Camp Breendonk." He is first taken to the "business room" where he is efficiently and quietly processed: possessions taken away, his information carefully recorded. After the processing is finished, into the room steps a stocky figure with a sanguine face, a horsewhip hanging from his wrist, on whose field-gray uniform can be seen the black lapels of the SS: Herr Leutnant Praust, who played the role of a torture specialist. "Now it's coming," he quips to his prisoner in a "rattling and easygoing way" as he leads him through a series of corridors, dimly lit by reddish bulbs, "in which barred gates kept opening and slamming shut" (AML, 32). While the possibility of later being able to control a foreseeable pain reduces its experiential awfulness, the anticipation of pain without the possibility of control amplifies it significantly. Torture rituals amplify the pain they anticipate.

Améry arrives finally at a windowless vault, from which no scream can penetrate to the outside. "In the bunker there hung from the vaulted ceiling a chain that above ran into a roll. At its bottom end it bore a heavy, broadly curved iron hook. I was led to the instrument. The hook gripped into the shackle that held my hands together behind my back. Then I was raised with the chain until I hung about a meter over the floor. In such a position, or rather, when hanging this way, with your hands behind your back, for a short time you can hold at a half-oblique through muscular force. During these few minutes, when you are already expending your utmost strength, when sweat has already appeared on your forehead and lips, and you are breathing in gasps, you will not answer any questions. Accomplices? Addresses? Meeting places? You hardly hear it. All your life is gathered in a single, limited area of the body, the shoulder joints, and it does not react; for it exhausts itself completely in the expenditure of energy. But this cannot last long, even with people who have a strong physical constitution. As for me, I had to give up rather quickly. And now there was a crackling and splintering in my shoulders that my body has not forgotten until this hour. The balls sprang from their sockets. My own body weight caused luxation; I fell into a void and now hung by my dislocated arms, which had been torn high from behind and were now twisted over my head. Torture, from the Latin *torquere*, to twist. What visual instruction in etymology! At the same time, the blows from the horsewhip showered down on my body, and some of them sliced cleanly through the light summer trousers that I was wearing on this twenty-third of July 1943" (AML, 32–33).

IV. Pain's Aversiveness

Any form of intense pain—from accident or injury to disease or surgical aid—is sufficient to install the grammar of pain.[17] The primary feature of pain is its sheer aversiveness. Aversion refers to the action of turning away from oneself, and so against oneself. Pain is the occurrence of such a turning: pain is an attack on the body, the sensational experience of negation, a feeling of something being against one, which is always with pain one's body itself. With pain one's own body turns against one; in pain one is turned against oneself. At least part of the awfulness of pain derives from its being an experience that occurs within one's own body while nonetheless being felt as something utterly against and outside it. One's body turns against itself, attacks itself, so some part of me turns against me; I would cut it off (or tear it out) if I could. Who has not sought to silence an intense pain by paining another portion of his body, attacking himself again to suppress the agony of a first attack? The cracking and splintering of his shoulders, the balls springing from their sockets, each twists Améry's body to a point of perfect aversion. Strappado, the torture practice being employed on Améry, is like an allegory of pain in using the body against itself: the body's own weight, the simple fact of it, becomes first a threat, an enemy, and then, finally, the very thing, the weapon, that breaks it. Torture uses the victim's body against him, making his own body the site not just of vulnerability but of betrayal. Because pain is the body turning against itself, and vulnerability is access to the world turned into openness to pain, then in torture vulnerability becomes how the other can turn my own body against me. In torture, the body's capacity for pain becomes the vehicle or instrument of the torturer, and the being in pain under conditions of torture becomes the victim's primary self-relation: in pain I exist against myself.

Intimately related to pain's aversiveness is the way in which it monopolizes how the agency of pain, its activity of "being against," operates simultaneously as internal and external. So, on the one hand, even where there is an external object causing the pain, such as a whip, it is not the whip that one feels, but the sting, the sensation of one's own body hurting one, while on the other hand, the hurt in one's body is standardly described through the kind of instrument or event that might bring it about, "a sense apparent in our elementary, everyday vocabulary for pain: knifelike pains, stabbing, boring, searing pains. In physical pain . . . one feels acted upon, annihilated, by inside and outside alike" (BP, 53).

Torture ratchets up and objectifies pain's aversive character. In torture, pain is "made visible in the multiple and elaborate processes that evolve in producing it" (BP, 52). The very setting of torture turns the protecting shell of civilization into its opposite. So the vault or bunker into which Améry is taken, a place of ultimate safety, is now a place from which one's screams cannot be heard and in which there hangs from the ceiling the heavy, broadly curved iron hook; the physical world itself takes on the contours of a weapon that will be the cause of your intolerable pain.

For Améry, what makes torture the social or institutional elaboration of pain, pain's social actuality and institutional realization, is that in torture, pain's "againstness" is objectified by the torturer, a being who apparently wants nothing from you but your pain—not your death or disappearance, but just the self-attack of pain, of you attacking yourself in the most acute form possible and yet surviving. Here, the other is not just an enemy or even *the* enemy—another who is opposed to you—but rather an embodiment of aversiveness, a source or origin of self-attack. In torture, Améry underlines, all social arrangements lapse, from the benefits of the social contract to, even, the reprisals of an eye for an eye. There are no rules regulating your relation with the torturer; you cannot opt for any rules of interaction "when it is the other one who knocks out the tooth, sinks the eye into a swollen mass, and you yourself suffer on your body the counter-man (*den Gegenmenschen*) that your fellow man became" (AML, 28). This is at least part of why Améry considers torture the essence of Nazism; it was "the only political system of this century that up to this point had not only practiced the rule of the counter-man . . . but had expressly established it as a principle" (AML, 31). Even if we are not yet in a position to verify this thesis, the image of the torturer as "counter-man" eloquently captures how pain as aversiveness—its becoming the physical experience of negation and self-betrayal, self-attack—comes to be literally embodied by the torturer, how the fact of some part of me turning against myself is transformed by torture into the social bond connecting me to the world itself, which comes to stand for that aversiveness: my world-relation is self-attack.

Torture, I am suggesting, radically alters the simple grammar of pain. Normally, pain operates as a form of separation from both world and other subjects; in fortunate circumstances, others nurse, tend, care, so sustaining a connection even as the world recedes. Torture begins by making the victim helpless. Torture's effectiveness depends on removing from the victim every possible resource through which he might assert his independence. In making the victim helpless, returning him to the helplessness of the infant, making the victim absolutely dependent on his torturer, he comes to be exposed without limit to what, in normal circumstances, would count as outside him. Torture discloses helplessness as an existential dimension of the relation between self and other. In torture, helplessness is not isolation but constant vulnerability, a vulnerability whose constancy is made palpable by the combination of the pains produced together with the awareness that, in principle, there is nothing to prevent this production of pain from going on forever. Experientially pain feels to be without beginning or end, a terrible "infinite" (Emily Dickinson's term); knowing it will end makes acute pain more bearable (and chronic pain sometimes unbearable because it is without foreseeable end).[18] Torture as pain's social elaboration innovates the idea of an eternity of suffering, of suffering without end as the actuality of existential helplessness. To be helpless before the other is to be exposed to pain's unendingness; torture actualizes pain's infinity. Rather than producing a separation of inside from outside as does ordinary pain, tortured pain collapses the difference between inside and outside: as the body is turned against itself, both world and other become standing embodiments of that againstness, creating it, repeating it, making it absolute. In torture, the condition of being *in* pain becomes the incessance of one's *exposure to pain*. Améry's account of the meaning of torture in part turns on his elaboration of this collapse between inside and outside.

One might say that the collapse of the boundaries between inside and outside relates to the way in which extreme physical pain, as itself a non-intentional, non–object-involving state of consciousness, takes over consciousness, sentience utterly displacing sapience. The marks of this loss of relation to the world are revealed in tortured pain's relation to language. Physical pain has the ability to destroy language, where language is understood as both the means through which we articulate and give sense to the world, and that through which the world is perceived as already possessing sense and meaning. In ordinary pain, rather than outright destruction, there is semantic capitulation: one does want to talk about anything other than one's pain: its qualitative and quantitative attributes, its unfairness, one's need for assistance and relief. Or one retreats from language into silence. Torture shows the destruction of language as proceeding through a series of steps. Pain—or its threat—is first introduced as a focusing device: the prisoner speaks only when addressed; the primary form of discourse, apart from the threat, becomes the interrogation with its to and fro between question and answer. Even if seriously intended, interrogation through torture is a faulty weapon for truth seeking since the intensification of the pain at best makes the prisoner want to say something that will stop the pain, not speak the truth. But this every torturer knows, so in order to create a sluice capable of separating true from efficacious speech, he has only one weapon in his arsenal: the further intensification and/or refinement of the prisoner's pain. This, however, may lead only to the torturer's becoming the direct orchestrator of the prisoner's linguistic will, the prisoner capable of saying only what his torturer wants him to say, which might on occasion be the truth; or, as the pain is intensified, the torturer's effort to capture the will of the victim may overshoot its target, destroying rather than capturing the will, which in turn causes the collapse of language into the prelinguistic world of animal screeches and hollers. These two possibilities are joined if we recognize how the voice of the torturer has become only a weapon, while the body of the prisoner first becomes an expression of the torturer's will—the torturer's will becoming my will, every word I say, apart from "no!", a self-betrayal—and then, as the pain climbs, my will disappears, my body becoming nothing beyond the pain it suffers and the scream it emits (BP, 46).

Améry underlines how the destruction of language in pain is an aspect of pain's resistance to language. After offering a series of inadequate analogies for the pain inflicted on him, he complains that "one comparison would only stand for another, and in the end we would be hoaxed by turn on the hopeless merry-go-round of figurative speech. The pain was what it was. Beyond that there is nothing to say. Qualities of feeling are as incomparable as they are indescribable. They mark the limit of the capacity of language to communicate. If someone wanted to impart his physical pain, he would be forced to inflict it and thereby become a torturer himself" (AML, 33). As stated, this is a lazy and unconvincing argument. It is true of *any* sensory episode that it can never be fully communicated in speech ("this" shade of red must be seen to be believed); but that is just a truism marking the difference between language and experience. Further, there is an ordinary language of pain that operates analogically through specifying a hypothetical cause for the pain ("like a pin being stuck in my ear") or the form of the damage being suffered ("as if my eardrum were about to break open"), or through the special language of pain itself (throbs, aches, cramps, pounding). Pain is no more resistant to language at this level than any other feeling or sensation, even if, unlike perceptual experiences, pains have no intentional objects, and hence no correlates to which one could direct another's gaze. This last thought, however, is the point of Améry's final statement: in cases of pain, the analogue of directing the other's gaze to the same object could only be causing the other "this" pain. But it is this fact that does pull the argument into shape. To say that pain destroys language and is resistant to language means to connect the second thought with the first: pain literally destroys language by reducing the speaking being to a howling and moaning animal; and *this* experience is resistant to language—"The pain was what it was"—because its primary and overriding experiential quality is its aversiveness, its power of negation. This is to acknowledge that the primary fact here is pain's destruction of language, and that we comprehend pain's resistance to language through comprehending the significance of that destruction, how it tokens our utter undoing as speaking beings who can intend the world at all. Pain's power to destroy language underlines how the primary pain-language relation is necessarily expressive rather than descriptive.

Extreme pain resists language as the negation of language. What follows from or coordinates directly with this claim is that it (also/thereby) obliterates the contents of consciousness: Améry writes "I fell into a void . . ."; the void Améry fell into was the worldless void of pain itself, which is equally to say that his pain became total. In pain becoming total, however, a new experience of embodiment occurs: "Whoever is overcome by pain through torture experiences his body as never before. In self-negation, his flesh becomes total reality. . . . Only in torture does the transformation of the person into flesh become complete. Frail in the face of violence, yelling out in pain, awaiting no help, capable of no resistance the tortured person is only a body, and nothing else beside that" (AML, 33). Pain totalizes. As Elaine Scarry states the idea: "Pain begins by being 'not oneself' and ends by having eliminated all that is 'not itself.' . . . Terrifying for its narrowness, it nevertheless exhausts and displaces all else until it seems to become the single broad and omnipresent fact of existence" (BP, 54–55). Torture aspires to this totality of pain, to make pain the whole of the prisoner's reality and existence; under conditions of torture in which all possibility of help and resistance are removed, this aspiration can be achieved.

Torture completes pain; it is the social actuality of pain. This has two direct consequences. First, the tortured victim becomes his body; his bodily self and his self become one. Because of the relative character of our control over our bodies, we are all naturally tempted by the Cartesian locution that humans only *have* bodies, where the extreme version of this thought is that the subject is a separate existence from the body he has. In that mode, the stoic might want to say that *my* body is being pained, and *I* need to distance myself from it—it, this body, being beyond my control. Only what I can fully control is truly me. Extreme pain, like some other limit conditions—including laughing and crying—reveals how the body that cannot be controlled, that is out of control, *is* nonetheless *me*: I am my body. When I cry in grief, although overwhelmed, convulsed in sobbing, in a state of bodily disorder, that bodily disorder is *my* fullest response to the grief being felt; it is my cognitive and affective acknowledgment of what has occurred. The experience of grief—or sexual joy—demonstrates that bodily disorder concerns not only what happens to me but that it can be a means of self-expressiveness, the action of my suffering self—shivering in delight—and hence that the notion of the self cannot be reduced to the rational will or whatever mental or bodily states whose current orderliness is presumed to be a direct consequence of my agency, as if all suffering were antithetical to the very idea of being a self.[19] Pain's aversiveness brings the formations of bodily habitation into explicit conflict, the involuntary/vulnerable/suffering body undoing the voluntary/agential body, the body I *am* overwhelming the body I *have*. Under torture conditions, being overwhelmed is experienced as irrevocably mine, what my life has come to. Pain reveals how we not only *have* bodies but also *are* our bodies. The dual axes whereby we both have and are our bodies in a manner requiring coordination is constitutive of the specificity of human embodiment.[20]

The transformation of the person becomes complete in torture because the victim becomes the body he already is, while it is the torturer who, effectively, *has* (possesses) the victim's body. All activity and voluntariness are in the hands of the torturer, while only passivity and suffering are left to the victim. In torture, the dual axes of individual bodily life, the having and being of a body, the body as voluntary and involuntary, become divided between torturer and victim, the torturer aspiring to activity without exposure while the victim is reduced to flesh; the torturer aspiring to independence without the stigma of dependence while the victim is revealed, in his very being as a person, to be a wholly dependent being. Such is dispossession; such is devastation.

What initially appear as competing conceptions of our relation to our bodies must both hold: as well as having bodies, we are our bodies. Torture, in rendering the sufferer helpless, and thereby unconditionally vulnerable, a being for whom pain is his horizon of possibility, makes emphatic the second thesis: the victim is his body, for here there is nothing else he can be. Torture reveals how the sufferer is his body by extinguishing to the point of irrelevance the possibility of his having a body. In being made helpless, in the overturning and ruination of his will, the victim is made to be his body. It is as bodily creatures that we are always vulnerable to the effects of others; our bodily being is our primary exposure to others and to the harm they might cause. Torture perfects this exposure, makes it complete: "My body, debilitated and encrusted with filth, was my calamity" (AML, 91).

Again, if it can be said that the "having a body" axis abides at all, it abides in the will of the torturer, since it is he who truly has the victim's body; this is what the lapse of the power of resistance entails. This leads into the second aspect of torture being the social reality of pain: the fact of exorbitant pain is doubled, repeated or reiterated, in that the torturer is not only indifferent to the victim's pain, but is its absolute source, the counter-man. Pain's aversiveness is emptied of its usual human significance, indeed even its animal significance, by its not being recognized by the other *as* aversive, as the very thing whose utter againstness (to the self, to life, to meaning) spontaneously sounds as a call for relief: this should not be. Trivially, the sufferer's pain must be recognized by the torturer since it is what he is bringing about, making and repeating it as the means and conditional end of his action. And further, the torturer recognizes that the pain he is making is an attack on the sufferer; it is his way of attacking the sufferer. But the ways in which the torturer recognizes pain are ways or modes of, at the same time, not recognizing pain, not recognizing what pain effectively and fundamentally means: its essential aversiveness.

How might torture be the recognition and nonrecognition of pain? In what sense does the torturer fail to recognize the pain he is bringing about? To say he fails to recognize that the pain is "bad" or "wrong" begs the question at stake, since without recognizing pain's aversiveness the torturer would have little reason to engage in his cruel activity. Torture exploits bodily vulnerability for the sake of exploiting pain's aversiveness. Pain's aversiveness must then mean in a manner not yet canvassed.

V. Pain: Feeling or Reason?

I have been tracking pain's aversiveness, its emergence and experiential qualities. I now want to broach two of the ways in which that very aversiveness means. At the level of the simple grammar of animal pain, pain is not only experienced as an attack upon the self; pain experiences typically occur when, in fact, that body has been injured, and injured in a manner that is, minimally, harmful to its continued healthy functioning, and, maximally, threatening to the continuance of its life.[21] Pain experiences are not only sensations of particular kinds, but are experientially averse because they have a functional role in the economy of animal life. Their qualitative character must be integrated into and seen as a component of their functional role: normally, pain signals a state of affairs that, being against the self, threatens its continuance, and therefore should not be. Our spontaneous desire to hack off the injured part is the spontaneous desire to remove the pain. Pain is for the body what ought not to be, and hence the body's natural signal to act in ways that will stop it. The natural meaning of pain is of a state of affairs that "should not be" (or whose indefinite continuance should not be); it is thus a sign of what should be altered, stopped, prevented, and, when these are unavailable, then at least soothed, quieted, eased. Hunger and thirst are usually weak forms of pain that move those who suffer from them to the actions of eating and drinking that will stop those pains. Cold is that form of pain that leads the sufferer to seek warmth, just as being too hot leads the sufferer to seek the relief of coolness. When pain or its cause cannot be immediately removed, as is often the case with injury, we seek physical solace: cold compresses, hot baths, aspirin, sleep. Pains move us to those actions that will remove or ease them.

There are two standard accounts of the relation between pain sensations and action. On the first—empiricist—view, pain sensations are intrinsically normative entities: pain's painfulness, its characteristic feeling of awfulness is constitutive of what is bad; it is because raw sensations of pain feel the way they do that we are inclined—afterward or as a consequence—to do those actions that will remove it. What is implausible about this thesis is that while pain's feeling of being awful is made intrinsic, its leading to those actions necessary to remove the bodily state of affairs designated by it are taken as only a conceptually contingent consequence. This makes pain sensations things in themselves logically cut off from their biological function, as if the whole meaning of a painful feeling could be simply what it is like, the sheer painfulness of pain, its intrinsic horribleness, apart from what an animal does in response to that feeling, what painful feelings imply, what they mean in the life of the sufferer. It would be hard to think of there being such things as pains if they were not signals of something amiss, signs of injury, prompting us to do those things necessary for well-being and healthy continuance. Pains are not raw givens; like limbs and organs, and other bodily events, pains have a functional role in the life of the organisms in which they occur. Pains are not pure mental events, but events in the life context of animals; the antecedents and consequences of pain are constitutive of the meaning of pain. Said differently, without some sense of the causes and effects of pain, of what the normal and appropriate responses to pain are, and why those responses are appropriate, pain's being aversive becomes all but unintelligible, which is what it becomes for the torture victim; it is *made* practically meaningless.

This is rightly the starting place for the opposing—Kantian (rationalist)—view. For it, pain's sensation character fades into the background behind its functional role in giving the sufferer a reason to fight against it, to fight against what is attacking him. Christine Korsgaard thus argues that since pains could mean nothing in the repertoire of human lives unless they provoked actions to remove what causes them, then physical pain is primarily an impulse to change your condition; pains are the perception of a reason to perform some action or actions. One important argument in favor of this view is that pains are themselves experientially disparate; that is, pain comes in radically different kinds of sensations. What unites these disparate sensations, making them all *pains*, is that they all provide reasons to act to remove them (by removing their cause) or to ease the fact of their unavoidable presence: "What do nausea, migraine, menstrual cramps, pinpricks, and pinches have in common, that makes us call them all pains? (Don't say they're all horrible; that's just repeating yourself.)"[22] Korsgaard also seems at least partially right when she urges that if "the painfulness of pain rested in the character of the sensations rather than in our tendency to revolt against them, our belief that physical pain has something in common with grief, rage and disappointment would be inexplicable."[23] What Korsgaard is pointing out in these cases is that the meaning of pain is not given solely through its sensational aspect. But she wants to say more; she wants to urge that the painfulness of pain *is* the perception of a reason to change your state, making its relation to the range of feelings which we normally think of as painful purely contingent. She aims to fully invert the empiricism thesis.

Korsgaard doth protest too much. She does not deny the existence of the qualitative dimension of pain sensations, but she does want to absorb— philosophers would say "sublate"—that characteristic of pain inside its being "the perception of a reason"[24] to change one's condition. If this is true of humans, it will be true of animals as well. Here is how she makes that argument: "The animal has a reason to eat, which is that it will die if it does not. It does not know that it has that reason, but it does perceive it. The sensation in question is the sensation of hunger, not pain. But an animal is designed to perceive and revolt against threats to the preservation of its identity, such as hunger. When it does that, it is in pain."[25] There is something important here that is worth underlining. All animals, including human ones, are living beings designed to maintain and reproduce themselves; they possess what might be called a "self-maintaining form"; that is, they are organized so as to maximally maintain the coherence and integrity of their living form.[26] In broad terms, we might say that all animals naturally seek to preserve their own identity as realized in their living form, that preserving one's own identity is how the instinctual drive to self-preservation is practically manifest. An animal's forms of sentience are, in part, the perceptual means through which it becomes aware of what it needs for its continued existence as well as imminent threats to it. The feeling of hunger signals the need for food and triggers food-getting activity. Pain is the experience of an injury to the integrity of one's animal identity or a sign of its malfunctioning or neediness, which, if not reversed, could (would) be fatal. Pain, we might say, is the natural sign within sentient beings that the integrity of their living form has been damaged, their continued existence, their life, threatened, and hence that action is necessary.

Korsgaard rightly locates the meaning of pains in the context of their function in the lives of the animals having them. Nonetheless, because she wants to talk about reasons for action, she ends up rigidly separating the qualitative character of painful feelings from the functional role they play in animal life. By bracketing the qualitative character of pain sensations, she makes what should be transparent opaque—namely, why do just *those* types of sensations lead to just *those* types of palliative and preventive action?

The characteristic feelings of painful sensations matter to what they are and their role in animal and human life. If we were the sorts of beings for whom there were no intermediary feelings between a body part's becoming diseased or injured and doing those actions necessary to remove or resolve the problem, if the relay system between injury and action were sensationally silent, we would be like invertebrates or what we now think of as automatons or robots. I would be walking along, and then suddenly have the thought in my head that I must stop and take off my shoe and place a bandage around my big toe because it is blistered. No feelings, just the thought popping into my head that some remedial actions are necessary now, and then the actions. And what would torture be like? Unless I knew that the next turn of the screw would undo me completely—and how might I know that?—I would have no reason to divulge information until that point was reached. There would be no torture, just the flat threat of "speak or be killed."[27] And think how wonderful it would be to have tooth extractions but no toothaches, or to have open-heart surgery without the need for an anesthetic, or to give birth without labor pains. Chronic pain would cease to exist. And pity the poor masochist forever deprived of pain's exquisite jouissance. Again, Korsgaard does not deny there are sensations related to pain, but she does think that pain "really is less horrible if you can curb your inclination to fight it," and, even more deflating of the sensational side of pain, that "pain wouldn't hurt if you could just relax and enjoy it."[28] There is something morally obscene in telling the victims of torture that their suffering is their fault for fighting against the pain, but this is the upshot of fully subsuming the painfulness of pain under its role of giving sufferers reason to act in particular ways, as if humans could be like earthworms and other invertebrates, whose responsiveness to injury is not mediated by sensation.

Animal and human lives are not like those of earthworms or automatons—or Korsgaard's idea of Buddhists[29]—because pains are not just functional signals to fight against a particular state, but a range of feelings that despite their diversity share both some qualitative characteristics—their aversiveness, their capacity to become all-consuming, their capacity to interrupt world-relatedness, to refocus attention on the self—as well as the defining functional role of providing a reason to fight against it. The sensational aspect of painful sensations, their awfulness, is *how* they accomplish their functional role of alerting sufferers that they are in a parlous physical state, which is why, from a biological perspective, one important pathology of the pain system—chronic as opposed to acute pain—is the occurrence of the sensation even when there is no apparent injury or disease of which the pain is a symptom.[30] The misery of chronic pain is the detachment of the qualitative awfulness of pain from its functional role: there appears to be nothing to do but suffer. Another form of dissociation that directly makes the argument against Korsgaard is *pain asymbolia*, in which the patient has a "pain" sensation—a sensation in the place where the tissue damage is occurring—but it is not painful, not awful, not felt as aversive. While the sensation does accurately locate the region of the tissue damage, because the sensation is not one of awfulness the patients are not moved to ordinary pain behavior—withdrawal, protection—but instead laugh nervously. Without the awfulness of the pain sensation, it does not function to trip the appropriate behavior.[31] On any reasonable account of pain, its phenomenal aspect and its functional role are utterly intertwined without either aspect being fully reducible to the other: its aversive aspect, its qualitative horribleness, naturally leads to its role of prompting actions to change one's condition, including the protection of the injured region and enforced inactivity in order to give the body time to heal; its functional role explains why its characteristic feel had to be one that has the aversive features it does, features that can *bring about* the interruption of ordinary life and refocus all attention to the broken body in the appropriate way (avoiding, protecting, resting, etc.).

This much should now be evident: although in the normal course of things, the sensational and the reason-giving features of pain are thoroughly intertwined with one another, they are not just one thing, but (at least) two irreducible aspects of a unitary phenomenon. When we are unable to do anything about either the condition causing a pain or the pain itself, then the connection between sensation and the perception of it as a reason to perform a particular range of actions is severed. Chronic pain is the common form of the severance between feeling and reason; biologically, that severance is construed as the primary pathology of the pain system, its systematic malfunctioning. *Torture is the social creation of a severance between feeling and reason*; torture is the social pathology of the pain system, making the acute effectively chronic. Torture is the systematic exploitation of pain's Janus-faced aversiveness, its sensational horribleness as what is suffered while its being a reason for action is socially silenced, denied. Torture reveals the two-sidedness of pain by isolating sensational pain from its functional role. Torture extinguishes pain's being a perception of a reason to change the body's condition, leaving only its sensational horribleness— all danger and damage. The separation of the sensational and reason-giving aspects of pain is common, too common. What distinguishes torture as a form of action is that it depends on that two-sidedness for its possibility; torture works the distinction, relishing the sensational and extinguishing the reason-giving. Torture intends to categorically sever pain sensations from pain's reason-giving force. As the possibility of responding to reason's prompts for action recede, there are only the excruciations of the pain itself.

VI. Sovereignty: Pain and the Other

All cruelty exploits and revels in pain's two-sidedness. What distinguishes torture as a social form of pain making? What kind of social form of pain making and perception is it? Améry's analysis is, again, primarily phenomenological, not moral or strictly psychological; he means to render his experience of torture, his sense of what happened to him, how it felt from the inside. In the stretch of analysis I am about to examine, he is not interested in demonstrating, for example, that if a fellow human is in extraordinary pain and you are in a position to render aid, then you *ought* to give aid, you are morally obligated to do so. However, Améry does want to say something about how we *expect* to be aided when injured, and what it means to have that expectation utterly undone. The experience of loss and failure here happens below the level of morality as it is normally taken in part because it is being told from the perspective of the victim, not from the perspective of moral agency, and in part because it focuses on the rupturing of spontaneous, taken-for-granted expectations, rather than on being the recipient of another's transgression of a moral obligation. What is thus at stake is the social meaning of the systematic effort to sever pain sensations from pain reasons.

If my pain is a natural signal to me that I am injured and palliative actions are necessary, then a fortiori, as a being whose life has been entangled from its very first moments with and utterly dependent on others, will not my pain directly mean to proximate others that I require aid? Why should pain *mean* anything different for proximate others than it means to me? Why should the expressions of pain not be counted as manifestations of pain sensations bearing their usual rational sense?[32] I see you quaking and chattering from cold, *therefore* I wrap a blanket around you. It is what your cold calls for, elicits. Here is another scenario: We are alone; you are quaking and chattering from cold, and I am standing opposite you watching, just watching, not saying or doing anything. Even if there are reasons for nonaction here, my doing nothing and saying nothing about doing nothing is odd, strange, off. You are puzzled, disappointed, angry, and rationally so: something human is broken here. Independently of moral norms and principles, your being in pain and my proximity yield a "natural" expectation, an expectation that derives simply from the reason-for-action component of the grammar of pain in its direct social actuality.[33] The nonsatisfaction of that expectation arguably necessitates the need for some explanation, some accounting, some word; the nonsatisfaction of your expectation emerges as a small surd in the relations linking us.

The experience of torture leads Améry to conclude that in the human form of life, a necessary and fundamental experience is the *expectation* that if one is injured and in pain, aid will come ("the certainty of help" [AML, 28]). This he regards as a necessary stratum of the social contract, the place where human sociality meets with animal solidarity.[34] Generalizing from the grammatical connection between pain and aid, Améry takes it as impossible for there to be anything like a functioning and intelligible human society where an individual's being in pain is not in the first instance perceived as a reason for helping him, even when that reason is (for some socially general or contextually contingent compelling reason) rebuffed.[35] If pain is a signal of damage that gives a reason for its sufferer to try and remove it and the injury causing it, then the minimum condition of mutually dependent lives requires that one individual's pain is equally a reason for another who is perceiving that pain to render aid. At this level of analysis, this is not intended as a moral statement, not yet a question of what anyone deserves or merits or has a right to, although it is doubtless the stuff from which morals are made. Rather, the claim is that perceiving another in pain is directly a reason to provide aid, where because that is what perceiving someone in pain *is*, failures to render aid strike the sufferer as demanding explanation or justification—some bit of pain, its reason-giving force, has been negated, silenced, stopped meaning altogether. Nothing morally atrocious occurs here; there is just the sheer oddness of your quaking and my doing and saying nothing. I do not know how better to state the thought than to say that for social animals like us, the relation between pain and aid is grammatical, as close, I would say, as the relation between pain and expression.

But this reflective claim is also—and this is Améry's point—a fundamental experience, *a material a priori of ordinary life*. As children we expect each discomfort, sickness, injury, hurt, each pain to be tended to and removed by our parents. Because infants and small children are helpless (and remain functionally helpless for years), then for them the reason-for-action aspect of pain *immediately and necessarily* passes to the adult caregiver. Hence, the original intelligibility of pain for the child is relational, a turning toward the parent in the expectation of relief. *For humans, the logical grammar of pain is originally social, intersubjective* (and grammatical and not just causal because it is social and intersubjective). Originally, it evokes a simple expectation that, in response to their expression, pains will be cared for, that pains are the sorts of things that spontaneously and automatically bring down upon one the solicitous attention, if not the loving concern, of others—and when this fails to occur, then the experience is one of rebuff and rejection.[36] Only subsequent separation and individuation will generate the ordinary first-person structure of pain. Thus, even if a child must undergo the disillusionment that her parents' powers are limited, that sometimes only sympathy and not the removal of the pain is forthcoming, nonetheless, the expectation is that her pain matters to them, that the sure and continuous evidence that she matters to them—that she is loved—is that her pain is as awful to them as it is to her, awful to them because it is awful to her, awful not because she finds it awful but because it is awful. It is not the child's natural narcissism that generates the expectation of aid; rather, the social actuality of pain's aversiveness is its reason-giving force: the expectation of aid is the social actuality of pain as it perceptually presses on surrounding others. If my pain were not a reason for others to aid, then, logically, I could not matter to them; I would be as nothing to them. If pain's mattering constitutes an element of how any life matters, then pain's mattering is constitutive of the lives of others mattering. More broadly then, if anything like the child's view of mattering to others carries over to the adult world—and I shall argue below that it must—then any adult's *assumption* that he or she matters to others is utterly bound up with the existential or grammatical assumption that his or her pain matters to proximate others, ideally any proximate others, but at least those others with whom she shares her active life in whole or in part.

In adult life, it is often the doctor who is the stand-in for society; it is her task to acknowledge and cope with pain, to keep the grammar of pain in place and operative.[37] Even on the battlefield, Améry states, injured soldiers expect their comrades to help, for the Red Cross to come. These expectations are moderated for most adults, and qualified even further by those worst off in a society—they know that their pains do not matter because their lives do not fully matter to their fellow citizens, and hence when they suffer the tribulations of bodily vulnerability that no hand will be stretched out to them. To be socially dispossessed is this: to have one's suffering severed from the expectation that aid will come.[38] Stoicism, as a routine virtue, embodies the lesson that help is not always possible, that pain must be sometimes endured until it disappears on its own, or even endured permanently because it cannot be alleviated. But all these modifications and qualifications are of an underlying expectation: "In almost all situations in life where there is bodily injury there is also the expectation of help; the former is compensated by the latter" (AML, 29). We say "compensated" because in the expectation of aid we are lifted out of the isolation of pain; the expectation is the material a priori assumption that my suffering automatically matters to others, that I matter to others, that my pain is not just a bodily thing but also a social thing, something that enters into the social world, enters as a reason for others to care and aid.

For Améry, this structure of expectations is not a theoretical inference from pain's reason-giving force, but the realization of that force from the devastation of its denial. With the first blow from the policeman's fist, Améry reports, he knew that there would be no help forthcoming; he knew that his pain was not a sign to a fellow being that he should be aided, and hence he knew that the most basic fact of his life—namely that it was dangerously threatened—had no natural meaning for his persecutor. Discovering, through its cancellation, how deep and how structural is the assumption that help will come is pivotal for what Améry wants to understand and convey. One aspect of this experience emerges with the claim that "if no help can be expected, this physical overwhelming by the other then becomes an existential consummation of destruction altogether" (AML, 28). One can be destroyed in many ways, at many rates, and in many different circumstances. To claim that in torture there is an "existential consummation of destruction" is to claim that with torture all the salient negatives that belong to the destruction of a particular human life are there united, experienced and undergone: the helplessness, the pain, the futility, the suffering without end, and, above all, the permanent cancellation of one's life as a meaningful entity, as something that affirmatively matters to proximate others; torture consummates pain into devastation. It is the cancellation of one's mattering, and thus one's standing as human, to the all-powerful other that pulls the string that gives all the other elements of analysis their specific tortured salience, since they all can exist in non-torture circumstances. The unavoidable authority of the other as counter-man, the power quietly incubating in every other, turns endless pain into devastation.

That one's life does stop mattering in this sense is not a singular event, but rather a transformation of it into a different register, permanently: with the first blow, against which there was no defense, and with no helping hand either present or foreseeable, "a part of life ends and it can never be revived" (AML, 29). In pressing the thought that the pain-aid relation is grammatical, I have been urging that the expectation is deeper than an inductive inference or a well-formed habit: as the social actuality of pain's reason-for-action aspect, it belongs to the structure of the self in its social contours. Under conditions of torture, a single instance appears power-ful enough to cancel the grammatical connection and so the structure of self denoted by it. Something of the self breaks, never to be fully repaired. Devastation is the incessance of the injury. We might now be tempted to think that Améry is here beginning to analyze something like an experi-ence of trauma. He is, but Améry's achievement is to give an account of this phenomenon that, while overlapping and compatible with psychological materials, makes independent philosophical sense. We might think of his account as being a form of existential moral psychology—hence my turn to the concept of devastation.

Améry is trying to reveal and understand a situation of helplessness and pain where one's pain no longer carries its natural expectation of aid; on the contrary, it is as if the sound of pain, which everywhere is the sound that triggers the human-animal response to provide balm and solace, in-spires in the torturer only the response that more pain is possible. In tor-ture, the production of pain is in part for the purpose of canceling pain's reason-giving force. This possibility, or its near relations, can and does oc-cur elsewhere in experience: small boys in pulling the wings off flies or the legs off spiders, or in yanking the tail of the cat have their satisfaction solely in their power to produce the pained response, a wriggle or yowl; the bully wants nothing from his victim other than whimpering fear; the domestic abuser, inspired by misogynist hatred or resentment, needs his victim's pain, helplessness, and fear to bolster his unsure authority. The sadist relishes the pain of his victim. Torture is the perfection of this pos-sibility; it is the ritual and dramatic realization of pain's power of negation because in it the other appears only as a counter-man, as perfectly against, and therefore in *active* nonrecognition of the sufferer's humanity: in torture "instead of the person's pain being subjectively real but unobjectified and invisible to all others, it is now hugely objectified, everywhere visible, as incontestably present in the external as in the internal world, and yet it is simultaneously categorically denied" (BP, 56). Pain is *present* as feeling and the all-too-visible expressions of feeling (sounds and bodily postures), and blisteringly *absent* as a reason for action. Not only does the counter-man actively not recognize his human other, but conversely the pain, helplessness, and absolute dependence of the victim are the existential source of the torturer's sense of self. The master torturer depends on the tortured victim's pain for his sense of being absolute.

In making this claim, Améry means to be constructing what the standpoint of the torturer must existentially mean as the reverse side of a relationship in which the experience of the victim is understood in terms of the destitution of existential helplessness. What does the victim's helplessness mean for the torturer? Améry's wedge here is perfectly simple: if the apotheosis of existential destitution borne by the victim resides in his helplessness, where helplessness is revealed as an existential or categorial feature of human existence, then the act of torturing is the effort of categorically repudiating that existential conditionality. In making the other absolutely helpless, the torturer seeks to remove the stain of helplessness from his own existence. Améry designates the one who reduces his other to helplessness through torture "sovereign."[39] Modern police torture, exemplified in Nazi torture, is an existential ritual through which the torturer seeks to establish "his own total sovereignty" by rendering his other, who in this setting, "in an entirely specific sense, is 'hell' for him," nothing, but a nothing who can nonetheless testify to and be the sign of his authority (AML, 35). Being transformed into flesh, the victim is all but nothing, but a living nothing that screams in testimony to the absolute reality of his torturer. But this is a strange and fictitious exchange, since the torturer must make purely spiritual capital out of the purely physical pain of his victim, his ego or sense of self expanding, inflating, as the victim is increasingly reduced to sheer body.

Elaine Scarry's rendering of this moment is penetrating, but partial; she effectively obfuscates the existential structure of this moment by returning it to the logic of the sovereign law of torture: "In the very processes [torture] uses to produce pain within the body of the prisoner, it bestows visibility on the structure and enormity of what is usually private and incommunicable, contained within the boundaries of the sufferer's body. It then goes on to deny, to falsify, the reality of the very thing it has itself objectified by a perceptual shift which converts the vision of suffering into the wholly illusory but, to the torturers and the regime they represent, *wholly convincing spectacle of power*. The physical pain is so incontestably real that it seems to confer its quality of 'incontestable reality' on that power that has brought it into being" (BP, 27; italics JMB). The italicized phrase in the passage above indicates that Scarry is still operating with the sovereign spectacle of early modern torture in much the same terms in which Foucault analyzed it. It does not seem utterly false to say that when modern regimes cancel the rule of law and institute torture practices, some of the spectacle of early modern torture remains. But modern torture is secret and private, not a communal activity in the way early modern torture was; and, again, this is because for us the scene of torture, even when imagined as a justified act, still involves the violation and destruction of bodily integrity and human dignity, and hence appears as something morally repugnant (sometimes, we say to ourselves, we must do these morally repulsive things). Affective indifference, for ordinary persons, requires a difficult learning. Thus, even if something about the exchange of pain into power rings true, it is operating here in the wrong social space. Again, Améry insists that in modern police torture, for the tortured "the torturer is solely the other" (AML, 34).

Améry is contending that there is a fundamentally existential structure at the core of all modern torture. This transformation is not pain into state power, but agonized helpless into sovereignty. There is to torture an existential dimension and existential satisfaction that trumps its other aspects. As Améry notes, he saw on the serious, tense faces of his torturers nothing like sexual-sadistic delight, although doubtless such delight has accompanied much torture throughout the ages and must have been a subtext even here; rather, he perceived a concentration bent on murderous self-realization: "With heart and soul they went about their business, and the name of it was power, mastery over spirit and flesh, excess of unchecked self-expansion" (AML, 36; trans. modified).[40] What power means here is something existential rather than the power of the sovereign law of torture.

It would be nice to think that the fabulous transfer of pain into sovereign power was wholly fictitious, a fiction of the torturer. But that would be to suppose that power and sovereignty were solely ideal phenomena entirely separate from the reality of strength and force, which is implausible, and implausible not just theoretically but practically. Améry confesses that there were moments when he felt a kind of "wretched admiration for the agonizing sovereignty" they exercised over him: "For is not the one who can reduce a person so entirely to a body and whimpering prey of death a god, or at least, a demigod?" (AML, 36) This dreadful confession is, logically, the converse of existential helplessness; it shows the victim completely surrendering his perspective upon the world to that of his master—and, again, not without reason since the torturer does, delicately or crudely, easily or awkwardly, with infinite finesse or impatient indifference, hold the life of the victim in his hands, the pain of the victim's body to be played like a musical instrument, each note a hymn to the torturer's mastery and the victim's existential destitution. And that mastery is a mastery over life and death themselves. As Améry notes, no path traveled by logic can cancel the opposition between life and death; but through pain, perhaps, a path of feeling can be paved, leading to the equation: Body = Pain = Death. This is the godlike knowledge the torturer possesses, and it is the equation he writes on the body of his victim. Tortured pain aims to blot out "the contradiction of death and allow us to experience it personally" (AML, 34).

"Whoever was tortured stays tortured. Torture is ineradicably burned into him . . ." (AML, 34). This, to Améry, indubitable truth is the germ of all his speculations; it is what he is trying to understand. And near the center of that understanding lies the notion of sovereignty, of the other as one in possession of a sovereign power whose only meaning is his pain: "If from the experience of torture any knowledge at all remains that goes beyond the plain nightmarish, it is that of a great amazement and a foreignness in the world that cannot be compensated by any sort of subsequent human communication. *Amazed, the tortured person experienced that in this world there can be the other as absolute sovereign*, and sovereignty revealed itself as the power to inflict suffering and to destroy" (AML, 39; italics JMB). The sovereign is he who believes that he is absolutely autonomous and self-sufficient, that nothing about his being depends upon others; the more different others are, and the closer to him they appear, then the more they threaten the fantasy of independence.[41] Torture is the ideal practice for asserting sovereignty, even if the notion of absolute sovereignty remains contradictory. The contradiction is patent: like Hegel's idea of the relation between master and slave, the relation of sovereign torturer and victim is one that cannot achieve satisfaction because the torturer is dependent for his sense of sovereignty, his feeling of independence, and above all, his sense of possessing unconditional authority on the squealing, writhing testimony of another, but another whose worth he does not recognize. The torturer *depends* upon the "nothing" to which he reduces his victim for his independence; the torturer lives off the victim's helplessness and the certainty of the victim's pain as the source and confirmation of his absolute being, his authority over living being.

This contradictory core to the relation between torturer and victim is one of the reasons why dehumanizing torture has no natural end, no fully satisfying conclusion: the torturer's independence is never complete, his authority never utterly absolute, the word of the victim never certain and reliable. Bored, tired, impatient, in need of another fresh fix, dissatisfied, the torturer ends the torture with either the victim's death or his now useless life returned. Nonetheless, the victim is—must become—absolutely dependent on the torturer, which is why even the slimmest shred of stoical resistance, the slimmest withholding of information or withholding of acknowledgment of his suffering is felt by the victim as an overwhelming victory; it is the remnant of his life as *his*. A victim is broken when nothing further can be withheld. And for this to occur, the torturer knows that the victim must become absolutely dependent upon him for his being and being thus. Nonetheless, what the sovereign cannot do is fully and completely transform the factual dependence of the other into his absolute independence—he needs the agonized scream of his victim. The victim can never suffer enough, surrender enough, be helpless enough for his (physical) dependence to be unconditionally transfigured into the torturer's (spiritual) independence.

This is why Améry adopts Sartre's locution that hell is other people; this is untrue as metaphysics, but becomes true in the Third Reich: the German cannot bear his dependence upon the Jew. Whether or not this is any kind of explanation of the Nazi movement—something in which Améry is uninterested—it does fit perfectly camp and torture practice. There the Jew must be destroyed as his torturer's other in order that the German might attain to an untrammeled and pure ethnic identity, and hence the torturing community attain to a position of pure sovereignty. This need for sovereignty is thus built on a paradoxical recognition and nonrecognition of the Jew: he is recognized as the other—the chosen people—who must be eliminated as other (unchosen). The paradoxical or aporetic character of the recognition is carried over into the practices of camp and torture: the Jewish other must become nothing and in his nothingness offer complete testimony to German sovereignty. The state of becoming nothing but a body in pain is the state of nothingness and complete testimony. Sovereignty, then, derives from the other's pain; the sovereign "boundlessly asserts" his existence through reducing the victim to nothing but flesh and death; and hence the victim's certainty of his bodily pain is continuously transfigured into the other's sovereign power. This is not the obliteration of the relation between self and other; such obliteration is common in human affairs, and in these circumstances would be welcome. This is far worse, for here one's perpetual dying at the hands of the other, at his behest or through his rules, itself becomes the bond that keeps you and he connected, self and other: a couple.

If Améry is right, anti-Semitism, racism, sexism—all those forms in which a group is assigned the place of being "the other" in relation to some "the one" (Aryan, white, male)—are shields or covers or occasions for a deeper existential logic—namely the desire for sovereignty, the desire for radical independence, the desire to eliminate the existential depth of dependence which is, finally, each and every one of us being existentially helpless. There are other reasons for exclusion and domination, but the intolerableness of dependency—rooted almost certainly in the necessity of surmounting the dependencies of infancy and childhood[42]—is persistent. Racism and sexism are best understood as social means, sovereignty the end. My hunch is that the sovereignty structure is the essence of sexual and racial domination; it is why these forms of domination become rape, torture, slavery, and genocide. In each case an otherwise threatened or fragile system of self-worth is translated into the illusory ideal of individual or collective self-sufficiency. The sovereign structure represents the attempt to resolve the dilemma of self-worth by negation. But this is to acknowledge that racism and sexism, and related forms, answer to deep existential anxieties; they will not be surrendered easily.

The state of helplessness is the most radical form of the state of dependence, but it is also an element of all dependence, since if one cannot escape dependence on others (and even the perfect torturer cannot so escape), then there is no escape: we are helpless. Our inaugural and potential physical helplessness connects with and is underwritten by the myriad ways—physical, psychological, and moral—in which we remain permanently dependent on our social others. Finally, because we are all inelim-inably physically dependent on others, we are potentially helpless before them. Because we are forever potentially physically helpless, we suffer metaphysical or existential helplessness, helplessness as one abiding aspect of human finitude. Existential helplessness is a categorial structural property of the relation between self and other; it thus belongs to the existential structures composing human self-consciousness. Whatever other function they perform, racism and sexism (misogyny and patriarchy) are also social mechanisms for the repudiation of existential helplessness. Conversely, it seems plausible to suggest that religion has been the most persistent social practice for moderating the anxiety consequent on the recognition of existential helplessness; acknowledging absolute dependence on God is the means for ritually and reflectively working through the unconditionality of existential helplessness. This is perhaps religion's most resounding civilizational achievement; arguably, it is this achievement that secular society has yet to fully fathom or make its own.[43]

Torture is the attempt to escape from the existential helplessness that is at the core of all human relationships; given the stakes, its fundamental operation is wonderfully simple: to render the victim helpless. In rendering the other absolutely helpless—the other's will now belongs to the torturer; the other's body now belongs to the torturer—the torturer thinks to rid himself of his own helplessness. The effort is doomed to failure. But, unlike the original model of master and slave, the failure of this relationship is without an inner dynamism, there is no inner mechanism of development in the relationship between sovereign and victim. It is a kind of hell.

VII. Without Borders: Loss of Trust in the World

We are not yet at the end of these reflections on the meaning of torture, although Améry's astonishment that there can be an other in the world who wants nothing from him but his perpetual pain and dying, and his astonishment that his dying is a condition for the realization of sovereign power and authority, points toward that end. What we have not yet discovered is how this claim about sovereignty, the idea of the other as counter-man, reverberates with what it means to say that one who has been tortured *stays tortured*. I have been suggesting that the relation between torturer and victim is the most collapsed, eviscerated, static, destructive version of a logic binding self and other imaginable that nonetheless sustains a relation, keeps it in place, rather than becoming a sheer fury of destruction that would end the relation. This is a terrible scene of recognition and nonrecognition jammed together; in this setting, a final fury of destruction would be a relief. Here there is no relief.

Part of what is at issue here is a shift in register from, let us say, a material to an existential-normative understanding of intersubjectivity. Because bodily pain is pivotal to the kind of torture Améry suffered, it made sense to consider the existential structures of mutually dependent lives as if they were narrowly material, as if bodily vulnerability before the other were the sole source of dependency, and hence as if the other's physical authority over the helpless victim were identical with his spiritual authority. Patently, Améry considers the bond between self and other as more complex. For example, if torture severs the material a priori expectation of aid by severing the grammatical connection between pain-as-sensation and pain-as-reason-for-action, then what is severed is the grammatically normative structure belonging to the constitution of the self in its relation to the other. But if bodily pain is already configured in socially normative ways, if bodily experience is already contoured as posing a normative relation to the other, then the self's relation to its own body is mediated by its relation to the other. If *At the Mind's Limits* has as its purpose the revelation of the life of the *victim*, then, in stating that for the torture victim the torturer is always the other, Améry is interpreting torture and the experience of the camps as revealing the depths of human dependency on social others, depths that are, to use his terms, physical and metaphysical at once, simultaneously bodily and normative. Implicitly, each accounting of an existential structure of dependency until this point should be regarded as having a spiritual dimension, a dimension in which social, practical, and normative elements are interconnected. I now want to begin making these implicit structures explicit in the specific way Améry provides.

The final paragraph of Améry's account of his torture begins thus: "Whoever has succumbed to torture can no longer feel at home in the world. The shame of destruction cannot be erased. Trust in the world . . . in the end, under torture, fully, will not be regained. That one's fellow man was experienced as the counter-man remains in the tortured person as accumulated horror. It blocks the view into a world in which the principle of hope rules" (AML, 40). It is a constant in the literature on torture and the camps that it is the victim, not the torturer, who carries the burden of shame, since it is the victim who experiences his body as no longer his, as beyond control, as if the wrenching shamefulness of being unable to publically control one's natural bodily functions—being unable to publically control bladder or bowel—now attaches to one's body *as a whole*, one's body as a whole becoming an involuntary thing, a thing of spasms, howls, leaks, bursting and shriveling, all as automatic responses to the prod, poke, punch, slap of the torturer. It is humiliation without relief.[44]

Coordinated with this abiding sense of shame is something worse, a loss of trust in the world. This loss I take to be the core of the claim that the one who is tortured stays tortured; loss of trust in the world is the experiential actuality of devastation. Améry poses loss of trust in the world as the existential corollary of the discovery that there can be in this world an absolute sovereign. Absolute sovereignty, I have suggested, turns on taking the existential core of human dependence, our final helplessness and impotence in the face of the other, and in wild rebellion against it seeks to transfigure the helplessness of the victim into spiritual independence. The sovereign counts the other as *worth* nothing; his action means to reveal that worthlessness, to realize it by turning the other "into a shrilly squealing piglet at slaughter" (AML, 35). And this *devaluing* can be accomplished; Améry suffered it. His physical dissolution mattered because it precipitated his spiritual devastation; not only did Améry talk, accusing himself of "invented absurd political crimes," but the surrender never stopped occurring: "It was over for a while. It still is not over. Twenty-two years later I am still dangling over the ground by dislocated arms, panting and accusing myself" (AML, 36). The physical injuries can be recovered from; wounds heal. To be dangling there off the ground still, twenty-two years later, is the incessance of the injury, being overcome still, being undone still. This is devastation; devastation is a dimension of human suffering that shows not only a fatal entwining of the physical and the moral, but through its incessance a stratum of the human that is in itself both normative, value constituted or value laden, and destructible. The dangling man is the one who remains accompanied by the sovereign other; because he cannot but remain accompanied by the sovereign other, the dangling man is the one who has lost trust in the world. Torture exposes the deepest—because it is ineliminable—dimension of human helplessness.

It is because helplessness cannot be overcome that we can have a world at all only if we can trust proximate others not to exploit our helplessness, not to exploit our vulnerability. More precisely, having trust in the world is not having to face the full impact of existential helplessness. Trust in the world, *Weltvertrauen*, is the foundational normative concept in Améry's thought; for him, it specifies the fundamental normative structure of the bond connecting self and other that relates to that stratum of the self that is value constituted and destructible. Part of my conviction that Améry's account of torture is right turns on my conviction that his contention about the loss of trust in the world is compelling. What trust in the world amounts to in detail and why it must have the status and role Améry claims for it is the sole topic of chapter 5. But it is a curious normative concept, behaving in ways not usual for fundamental normative concepts. As a first approximation: trust relates to our willingness to thoughtlessly allow to come close to us those who are capable of doing us terrible harm. In trusting the other, we no longer guard ourselves against him. More generally then, we have trust in the world when we can "forget," so to speak, our helplessness and vulnerability, when we can take for granted that our mere being in the world matters to relevant others, that we are recognized in ways that involve their respecting us, respecting our humanity, say, where the inferential link connecting pain with aid is so utterly taken for granted that it can remain *outside* conscious awareness. Our taken-for-granted, thoughtless confidence that our life matters means that we are never forced to bear the burden of our existential helplessness. The "accumulated" horror of torture—and related infamies like rape and domestic abuse—is that having faced an absolute sovereign, I cannot forget my helplessness, cannot forget that there are those for whom my humanity means nothing, that I am absolutely exposed and vulnerable, devastated in my standing as human.

In the midst of considering how the first blow generates the experience of helplessness, Améry explicitly and emphatically sets aside the presumptive moral account of what happens: at the first blow the victim loses his human dignity. To which Améry replies: "I must confess that I don't know exactly what that is: human dignity" (AML, 27). After running through a variety of things dignity might be, Améry remains dissatisfied, uncertain. "Yet," he continues, "I am certain that with the very first blow that descends on him he loses something we will perhaps temporarily call 'trust in the world'" (AML, 28). Although Améry will eventually restore dignity to a place of honor, he is here contending that trust in the world forms a deeper stratum of our habitation in the world than our possession of dignity: to be able to comport oneself in a dignified manner or to be treated by others as having dignity already presupposes a world which one can call one's own, inhabit, trust. Morals, in the way we usually think of them, as rules or principles or obligations, both presuppose trust in the world as a background condition, and, when understood aright, function to hold that trust in place by erecting borders and boundaries and limits, paths of action and responsiveness that jointly carve out a space through which an individual can take for granted and presuppose some version of the thought that "this body is mine" since only if my body is mine can my (practical) life be mine.

This situation of exposure, vulnerability, and helplessness, the actuality of not being recognized by the sovereign, has then everything to do with pain and embodiment. Améry acknowledges that trust in the world is a multifaceted and complex phenomenon; some part of it will include a blind confidence that, for example, the standard causal laws will continue into the future as they have in the past, and further that events have causes, that things can be explained. Call this "predictive trust." Although not as ironclad, my trust in the social world is akin to the kind of trust I require and have concerning the natural world. By reason of an unwritten social contract, I must, Améry argues, have certainty that the other person "will respect my physical, and with it also my metaphysical, being. The boundaries of my body are also the boundaries of my self. My skin surface shields me against the external world. If I am to have trust, I must feel on it only what I *want* to feel" (AML, 28). Call this "moralized trust." Moralized trust is predictive trust in normatively contoured social relations; it is trust in others' normative regard for me.[45] Améry consistently describes the harm of torture, its particular transgression, as a border violation, or rather, as the experience in which the idea of a self having boundaries and borders disappears. But the idea of one's having borders and boundaries is what it is for one to have standing in the world, to matter at all to others. And to matter at all to others is the condition of trust in the world, to feel one has a place and that one will not be arbitrarily or indifferently harmed, injured, damaged, pained by one's fellow beings. So the very being of the self in the world is the sense that one counts, that one's self counts, that one's skin counts, and that one's self counts is shown by one's skin counting. The skin is central here because it is a natural boundary; in order for the world to affect me it must somehow touch my skin. Again, my senses and skin (which in its touching mode is also a sense) are modes of access to the world; they can give access to the world only through their capacity to be affected by the world. Each mode of access is a mode of vulnerability that is capable of emphatic harm and injury: scorching light, blasting sounds, disgusting or noxious smells and tastes, and all the blows and stabbing and burning and freezing and twisting that skin and limbs can suffer. Because I am so hopelessly and radically vulnerable as a sensible being, I can have a sense of self only if I can, *thoughtlessly,* trust those around me to acknowledge my skin and senses as mine so that I will only feel on them what I want to or should feel.[46] This, we might say, is what the humanitarian revolution of the eighteenth century meant to accomplish, its promise, what it means for my pains to be mine because my body is mine. It is what Beccaria meant when he urged that the power of the law should follow every citizen like a shadow.

"At the first blow . . . this trust in the world breaks down. The other person, *opposite* whom I exist physically in the world and *with* whom I can exist only as long as he does not touch my skin surface as border, forces his own corporeality on me with the first blow. He is on me and thereby destroys me. It is like a rape, a sexual act without the consent of one of the two partners" (AML, 28). That Améry draws on the analogy of a rape is consequential for his argument, since there it is the lack of consent and not necessarily the physical harm itself that makes the crossing of the boundary of the victim's skin a violation. Rape is traumatic not because of the physical injury done, but because the victim's skin is no longer *counted* as a boundary of any sort, and hence her body no longer *counts* as hers, her bodily vulnerability is used against her. She no longer has standing before the other. Améry supposes that the victim of rape experiences her rapist as sovereign, and in so experiencing the other she loses, briefly or permanently, a sense of herself as having a world. Rape is a form of losing trust in the world in which it can be the case that one who is raped stays raped, just as one who is tortured stays tortured.

What it means to stay tortured or raped is that one senses that there are others who take themselves to be sovereign. If there are beings who take themselves as sovereign, then there are beings who take me to be as nothing. In torture and rape, the other is experienced as an absolute sovereign. When the world is viewed through these eyes, it is a permanently threatening place: "One who was martyred is a defenseless prisoner of fear. It is *fear* that henceforth reigns over him" (AML, 40). Trust in the world is gone. Forever. So to live in the world without perpetual and insistent fear is to have trust in the world.

The analogy with rape introduces a further refinement in Améry's analysis, since in cases of rape the *violation* and *transgression* need not involve the infliction of significant bodily pain (although they often can and do). Hence, while what is at stake is still a bodily violation, the self is most radically undone through the destruction of the normative social bond that secures self-worth through trust in the world. This thought yields two consequences: first, although loss of trust in the world invokes a destruction of the value of self for both self and other, Améry does not spell out in the torture chapter an intersubjectively constituted conception of self-worth that explains how loss of trust in the world bears with it a destruction of self-worth. How must we understand the self in order that destruction of trust in the world corresponds to a destruction of the self? In fine, despite the long path traveled, we still do not fully comprehend *what* is destroyed through torture. Second, as Améry's mention of "consent" in the context of the analogy with rape underlines, the nature of the dependency of the self on the other that yields the self's vulnerability and helplessness before the other that is betrayed in torture and rape is not reductively physical. There is a social and normative dependency of the self on the other to the extent that the *standing* or *status* of the self as an autonomous being worthy of respect depends on the other. This, again, is part of the sense of self at stake in trust in the world.

Plainly, it is the form of spiritual dependence that is employed in so-called clean torture practices, forms of torture that leave no scars behind. Clean tortures still involve the infliction of pain, of using the body against itself, of separating the voluntary from the involuntary body, of severing the grammatical link between pain as sensation and pain as reason for action, depositing the victim with the body he is, leaving agency in the power of the sovereign torturer. The infliction of pain need not break the skin: stress positions, sleep deprivation, exposure to extremes of heat and cold, waterboarding, exhaustion exercises, noise, the use of drugs and irritants all operate for the sake of wringing from the victim an acknowledgment of existential helplessness and dependency. The CIA KUBARK manual that elaborates its methods of torture is clear that the purpose of torture is the regression to a previous stage of spiritual dependency: "It is a fundamental hypothesis of this handbook that these techniques, which can succeed even with highly resistant sources, are in essence methods of inducing regression of the personality to whatever earlier and weaker level is required for the dissolution of resistance and the inculcation of dependence."[47] We know all too well now that the "dissolution of resistance," the loss of the border between self and other, and the inculcation of thoroughgoing dependence is devastating, the final consequence of which is a loss of trust in the world.

THREE

The Harm of Rape, the Harm of Torture

I. Introduction: Rape and/as Torture

The first chapter's interrogation of the abolition of torture was structured by Foucault's stark contrast between two images of punishment: the tortured body of the would-be regicide Damiens versus the austere disciplinary regime of the prison for young offenders. In light of this contrast, Foucault argues that punishment was transformed from "an art of unbearable sensations" to "an economy of suspended rights" in which the body is no longer touched. Beccaria's *On Crimes and Punishment* installs this contrast as one between two ideas of the authority of law: the sovereign law of torture as opposed to the substantive rule of law. The Beccaria thesis thus provisions the rule of law through the elaboration of an incommensurability between brute force and the force of law, in which the latter is determined by the moral axiom that the body of a citizen must not be touched, thus making bodily autonomy as that which the law must preserve as a condition for its own normative authority and legitimacy. The force of the moral axiom itself, I argue, draws all its authority in the first instance from being the determinate negation of the tortured body: what ought to be lives off of what must never be. In forgetting Beccaria, in simply accepting as a matter of fact the moral axiom of the body-beyond-touch, modern moral philosophy suppressed its own historical and material conditions of intelligibility, leaving the authority of the rule of law and the ban on torture (and much else besides) rationally exposed. Law must track social morality; fundamental legal wrongs are compelling only if they express the structuring and orienting moral postures of historically entrenched ethical life. Just this is occurring when Justice Frankfurter complains in *Rochin* that the police's methods of interrogation were "too close to the rack and the screw."

We thus turned to Améry's account of his torture for an image of what must not be, as what our moral philosophy must resource if it is going to entrench again the ban on torture as the moral foundation for the rule of law. Améry's depiction of his torture, his phenomenology of the victim, was offered as a contemporary experiential analogue for the eighteenth century experience of revulsion against sovereign torture. Améry's willingness to present his broken self without moralization, without moral commentary or the trappings of moral theory, provides the opportunity, if not a demand, for consequent moral reflection. This chapter is the first step in the construction of a moral understanding adequate to that experience, generating, through what amounts to a process of determinate negation, an accounting of what the moral harm of torture truly is.

A direct path to this conclusion is, however, not available. The conclusion of chapter 2 introduced what might appear to be almost a change in topic, from torture to rape. In quick succession Améry asserts that at the first blow his "trust in the world breaks down"; he can exist in the world only as long as the other person "does not touch my skin surface as border," only as long as he does not force "his own corporeality on me." With the first blow these conditions of existence are negated: the other person "thereby destroys me"; all this is "like a rape, a sexual act without the consent of one of the two partners" (AML, 28). We are meant to comprehend that rape somehow realizes the conditions of human existence and their destruction—rape as a further elaboration or articulation of the experience of torture. Even before Abu Ghraib, the intimate connection between extreme forms of sadomasochistic sex and torture was evident, etching the thought not only that certain forms of sexual practice bleed into torture,[1] but more importantly, that torture routinely possesses a sexual subtext: the particulars of rendering torture victims helpless, humiliating them, are seen and experienced as a feminizing of the victim, as if to be rendered so passive, vulnerable, and physically violated, to be an object capable of only involuntary responses were to lose not just one's human dignity, but to lose it through losing one's standing as a "man" and becoming a social woman.

The connection between torture and rape becomes an identity when rape is used as a form of torture, as it was in Algeria, in Bosnia, and as it continues (in 2013) to be used in the Congo. In such cases, the logic of comprehension works in the opposing direction; we understand the moral harm of rape through its likeness to torture: "A violent invasion into the interior space of one's body represents the most severe attack imaginable upon the intimate self and the dignity of a human being: by any measure it is a mark of severe torture. When a woman's interior space is violently invaded, it affects her in the same way as torture does. It results in physical pain, loss of dignity, an attack on her identity, and a loss of self-determination over her own body."[2]

In *Aftermath: Violence and the Remaking of a Self*, Susan J. Brison provides a moving and analytically acute account of the traumatic consequences of—and her slow recovery from—her violent rape and near death off a quiet road in rural France on July 4, 1990. Even at the time of its occurrence, Brison claims, she experienced the "assault as 'torture-resulting-in-murder' and, unconsciously recalling Holocaust testimonies, I heard my assailant speaking in what I later described as a 'gruff, Gestapo-voice'" (A, 88).[3] The phenomenological shape of Brison's first-person account, especially in the existential categories she employs, is uncannily similar to Améry's narration of his torture. Let me simply note some of the most obvious of these overlaps:

Silencing: In torture and rape, there occur forms of silencing that, in both cases, result in a breaking of the victim's "linguistic will," as it may be called—that is, the power to word the world for themselves, to speak the world as it appears to them and for them. In torture, the torturer attempts to take direct control of the victim's linguistic will, to orchestrate its responses, while nonetheless desiring that the victim's speech be veridical. Paining, as the means of achieving this end, routinely overshoots, leading to the destruction of the power of speech generally, forcing a regression into the expressive noises of groans, howls, yelps, and whimpers. In rape, the victim's protestations are taken as nil, or what is nearly the same, taken to mean the opposite of what such words (and gestures) normally mean, hence leading the victim to discover that her words have stopped meaning at all. Linguistic silencing is the way in which the victim's loss of an intentional relation to the world—which, again, is part of the grammar of acute pain—becomes manifest.[4]

Shame: Although utterly blameless, Brison felt ashamed at having been raped, a shame she did not feel about the violence of the assault itself, and suffered periods of intense self-blame (A, 3, 13). She understands the self-blame, if not the shame, as strategic: it is less painful to feel that there is some action one might have done to prevent what happened than to acknowledge loss of trust in the world. Oppositely, shame over a traumatic event "is a response to helplessness, the violation of bodily integrity, and the indignity suffered in the eyes of another person."[5] The existential contradiction of blameless shame and intense self-reproach provide an exemplary instance of an experience that can neither be owned nor disowned, that cannot be lived through but only suffered.

Body and Self-Betrayal: Prior to her rape, Brison had begun thinking that the traditional Christian and philosophical antipathy to the body, the flip side of philosophy's celebration of reason, was mistaken. The predominantly involuntary experiences of pregnancy, labor, and childbirth, against the background of a line feminist thought celebrating these as an acknowledgment of a particular formation of human embodiment, had come to appear to Brison as something she wanted to experience. Her rape abruptly severed that desire, transforming Brison's relation to her body: "My body was now perceived as an enemy, having betrayed my new-found trust and interest in it, and as a site of increased vulnerability" (A, 44). Traumatic events generally "violate the autonomy of the person at the level of basic bodily integrity. The body is invaded, injured, defiled."[6]

Life/Death: The full impact of being overcome by another, of being brought to the brink of death, of losing one's sense of having any control over the world, and of thus being forced in upon oneself, abandoned to oneself, is to suffer a kind of social murder, where to so suffer is to experience the line between life and death, which once seemed "clear and sustaining" as "carelessly drawn and easily erased" (A, 9, 91–92). The violation of the body's borders, their pollution, in exposing the bodily self beyond any possibility of protection blurs the line separating life and death; when that line is so blurred a kind of "soul murder"[7] or "soul death" or "social death" emerges.[8]

Existential Helplessness: What each of the above categories speak to is a reversal whereby a presumed relation to self or world is undone at the behest of an other, but undone so thoroughly and unconditionally that the victim loses any sense of being able to determine herself, her immediate environment, and, thus, her relations to the world in general: you experience yourself as in a state of existential helplessness (A, 45, 59, 73–74, 89). Brison notes that one definition of a traumatic event is "one in which a person feels utterly helpless in the face of a force that is perceived as life-threatening" (A, 39). In post-traumatic stress disorder (PTSD), the helplessness felt in the traumatic event carries on in its aftermath as a component of the victim's sense of self—it is that which reveals such helplessness as existential and categorial.

Loss of Trust in the World: The bulk of traumatic symptoms from rape—sleep disorders, heightened startle response, hypervigilance, nightmares—are physiological. According to Judith Herman, traumatic reactions involve the system of self-defense placing itself in high gear after it proved helpless in forestalling a horrific event; when "neither resistance nor escape is possible, the human system of self-defense becomes overwhelmed and disorganized," continuing to prepare the body for the very event it could not prevent.[9] However, neither these symptoms, nor the related involuntary psychological symptoms that accompany severe trauma—"depression, inability to concentrate, lack of interest in activities that used to give life meaning" (A, 40)—are what PTSD is *about*; they are, precisely, *symptoms* of the disorder. In showing a victim that she is unconditionally vulnerable and categorially helpless, traumatic events may lead to a dissolution of the conditions that make ordinary existence possible, the most basic of which is trust in the world—by which I mean, again, the rational and habitual suppression, overlooking, forgetting, or fortunate ignorance of each individual's utter dependence on surrounding others, and hence each individual's categorial helplessness. PTSD *is* a loss of trust in the world (A, xi, 9–10, 13–14, 44, 46, 56, 112);[10] it reveals how constitutive of selfhood and pervasive in our experience is the sense of trust whereby we presume our relative "safety," our sense that we have a standing in the world that matters to those around us (that we are not immediately and imminently in danger from them or immediately vulnerable before them), and that our capacity for severe harm can be sheltered by ordinary rational prudence. That the meaning of PTSD is to be found in loss of trust in the world— rather than in, say, the idea of "missed experiences," experiences that could not be affectively or cognitively digested at the time of their occurrence (A, 32)—coheres with our intuitive understanding of its routine causes: war, torture, rape, violent assault, child abuse, domestic abuse. In each of these cases, the experience is one of being overpowered and overwhelmed, as Améry has it, and thereby revealing dimensions of vulnerability, dependence, and potential helplessness that are normally hidden from consciousness, which hiddenness, in turn, enables a trusting and confident relation to an individual's personal, social, and material environment. The most touching and wrenching image of this loss of trust occurs when Brison has finally begun daring the world again by going for walks; lacking eyes in the back of her head, Brison compensated, in part, by getting a haircut so that she would look like a man from behind, in part by looking over her shoulder a lot and, for extra security, by punctuating her purposeful, straight-ahead stride "with an occasional pirouette, which must have made me look more whimsical than terrified" (A, 14). I find the image of the terrified woman pirouetting down the road nearly unbearable.

The Relational Self: What each of the previous categories addresses is a reversal in a constitutive relation to world and self that occurs through the savage depredations of the violator. There are only two explanatory possibilities here: either the psyche is so disordered by the experience of violence that it begins to systematically malfunction, or the self is constitutively dependent on others for both her relation to herself and her relation to the world, and once those dependencies appear impossible to sustain, her trust in them no longer possible or justifiable, then the self's relations to self and world necessarily collapse. In the second case, the self as self is undone *because* of her severed relations to others; it is not as if the self continues to exist as it always has, but now without relations to other persons and worldly possibilities of action; rather, because of the lack of appropriate relations to others, the self disintegrates, no longer able to do those ordinary activities that define normal functionality (A, 40–41, 61–62). If the first thesis were the whole truth, then we would be able to identify PTSD with its physiologically induced and psychological involuntary symptoms, which is to say, the response to trauma would be equivalent to just those features that are subject to pharmacological adjustment: with the right drug regime, the victim would recover. Brison does not deny the benefits of drugs, but sharply delimits their potential: "The chemically enhanced communication among my neurotransmitters may have facilitated my getting out of bed in the morning, but it didn't tell me what to do next. It made things seem more do-able, but it didn't provide me with any reason for doing them" (78).

Support for the thesis that the relational conception of the self is the source for the other features of subjection to torture and rape—shame, bodily self-betrayal, the permeability of the boundary between life and death, existential helplessness, loss of trust in the world—is provided by Brison's account of her recovery. Much of the effort of *Aftermath* is devoted to its defense of the role of "telling to live": of elaborating the role of therapy, and of how learning to narrate her experience for herself and to others began to make significant recovery possible for Brison. Working through, narrating, immersion in therapeutic relations are effective because in them the self is literally *recomposing itself through reconnecting with others*, connecting through narrating, finding terms of shareable and bearable existence by making them, and so creating ways of being with others that allow the self to be. If silencing is the dissolution of self-world relations, then those relations can only be recomposed through regaining the capacity to word the world for oneself. Narrating is wording the world in relation to the victim's experiential temporal path through it. One narrates oneself in relation to the world for others, letting the self appear in the world for oneself and others.

If I can be undone by others, then, a fortiori, others are also the source of my very being: others can both make me and unmake me, my life only being possible through them. In urging this, Brison borrows a beautiful formula from Annette Baier: *persons are second persons*, "essentially successors, heirs to the other persons who made them."[11] In brief, the trauma survivor can find a world at all only by establishing reassuring relations with others that enable her to have reflective confidence that, for the most part, others are vulnerable beings like her, not would-be sovereigns who would count her as nothing. Although to be raped is to stay raped (A, 20), because trust in the world once emphatically lost cannot be fully restored, it is through reconstituting conditions of connection and sharable habitation that a paled version of trust is possible, which in turn makes ordinary living more or less possible.

If Améry's and Brison's accounts of their respective experiences are anything like accurate, then the similarity in risk rates between torture and rape in leading to PTSD is best explained by their having more or less the same categorial structure:[12] rape and torture are flagrant forms of moral injury—even, or so I will argue, paradigms of moral harm.[13] Torture and rape are crimes of violence that are also "personal," their harmfulness essentially related to one person's intentional injury of another in a manner that makes the physical injury—which can be considerable—a component of a larger injury to, somehow, *the person* of the victim. It is that conjuncture of physical and moral injury, injury to the other in her very standing as a person, that is implied by Améry's and Brison's categorial accounts, and that is dimly echoed by the propensity of these types of crimes to cause PTSD—or so I will argue.

A further feature that Améry's and Brison's meditations share is their assessment that, whatever the dangers, an appropriate accounting of what they have undergone, the logic and meaning of their suffering, requires a first-person address. In part, their decisions to write in a partly first-person narrative mode reflects the kinds of crimes torture and rape are: "personal" ones. But it is just that characteristic of torture and rape that entails that there are larger issues for moral inquiry at stake in them. What is being marked by the shift from a third-person, objective approach to a first-person, confessional approach is something like a shift from seeing morality as fundamentally about what agents ought to do to seeing morality as initially an account of *how humans suffer*, and thereby what humans ought not to suffer and why we think that they ought not to suffer like "that." Ernst Bloch once wrote that the West has two great visions of the moral hero: Aristotle's depiction of the great-souled man and the suffering Christ on the cross. I think of this difference as projecting two contrasting approaches to moral thought. In the first, reason-based account, moral reflection draws from the fact that humans are distinct from the beasts by their possession of the capacity for rational thought the consequence that morality must track that distinctive trait of our nature. Traditional moral philosophy inquires into the governing reasons for action: how reason secures human flourishing (Aristotle), or allows for the calculation of the greatest happiness for the greatest number, or promotes the highest good, or how pure practical reason alone can secure moral behavior through demonstrating what reasons for action there are that would be good reasons for all rational beings, reasons all could share (Kant).

In the second, victim-based approach, our interest is in the nature of moral injury, in what should not occur and why, in what moral boundaries must not be crossed, in what human suffering is, in what its causes are, and in how suffering means to sufferer and spectator. In considering particular and precise forms of suffering, we connect moral reflection to historically and socially conditioned moral experience, giving moral experience a voice in the construction of morality. In so doing, we connect moral theory to everyday life in a systematic manner. Interrogating torture and rape as paradigm cases of moral injury is hence not an exercise in applied ethics, so-called, but rather a way of constructing an account of moral life grounded in the actualities of exemplary moral experiences. Morality is structured and transformed by moral experiences that are themselves part of wider social transformations—that is what occurred in the eighteenth century with the abolition of torture and the uprising of the rule of law.

Arguably, the emergence, theorization, and acceptance of the very idea of post-traumatic stress disorder, the idea that there are *traumatizing* events that are suffered long after the inaugurating event is over marks a transformation in our collective understanding of human suffering. Didier Fassin and Richard Rechtman have argued that the significance of trauma in our culture should be understood as giving a name to "a new relationship to time and memory, to mourning and obligations, to misfortune and the misfortunate."[14] This suggests that in the first instance trauma should be grasped as a moral rather than psychiatric category, a category that requires onlookers to acknowledge the duration of suffering, to acknowledge that an injury does not end when the event causing it ends: "In its compulsive repetition of the moment of utterly vulnerable victimization, trauma is the incessance of injury. It is not the incessant return of the past, but rather the persistence of the thing itself . . . in its persistence [it is] a broken-off piece of suffering."[15] Améry resisted the label of "trauma" because he did not want his condition medicalized and scientifically objectified, torn out of the history in which his suffering was an integral part and through which it arose. That Améry suffered from trauma—still dangling with dislocated arms twenty-two years later—is nonetheless without doubt. Brison accepts the diagnosis of trauma but narrates the limits of its medical explanation, persuasively resituating *the incessance of her suffering as the incessance of the moral injury of her rape.*

In conceptualizing trauma as a loss of trust in the world, Améry and Brison inaugurate the restitution of trauma to moral discourse—making moral discourse answerable to traumatic suffering. Adequately accomplishing this restitution requires giving conceptual and practical primacy to moral harm and moral injury; but moral injury can only live up to the demands of the idea of trauma if moral harms can make compelling how a duration of suffering that is a continuation of the moral injury undergone could become a *determining moral fact* about the sufferer. To ask these questions is equivalent to asking the question: What must a human be such that she can be *devastated*? To ask the question of the moral meaning of trauma is to ask after the possibility and meaning of devastation. Without the idea of devastation, of how a human being can be undone, we have no way of registering the moral harm of rape or torture. This is not to argue that only in light of devastation is the category of moral injury significant: devastation is, arguably, the ultimate wrong; on my construction, however, it is best understood as a radical version of the kind of devaluation or degradation at issue in experiences of *humiliation.* Humiliation is a form of degradation that adumbrates something worse; devastation is the realization of the destruction foreshadowed by acts of humiliation, which is why humiliations are so wrenching: we intuitively know that they token an existential helplessness that exposes us to worse possibilities. The requirement to acknowledge that we are the kinds of beings who can suffer devastation entails that the humiliation will become *a* or even *the* general type of moral injury. The acknowledgment of devastation is meant to yield humiliation—all the forms of devaluing, degrading, mortifying, embarrassing, shaming, debasing, dishonoring, etc.—as the negative core of everyday moral experience. (Recognition of devastation, I am assuming, was the new moral fact that began arising in the second half of the eighteenth century that made the pains of the torture victim morally exorbitant, the marker for what was becoming morally intolerable and politically egregious. What Améry presents to us is, finally, his devastation. What Brison asks us to acknowledge is that rape can be morally devastating—the meaning of that thought. Trauma is the *formal* recognition of devastation; the acceptance of the idea of trauma marks an inflection in the discourse of moral suffering for the sake of an acknowledgment of devastation.) Constructing the primacy of moral injury and the intelligibility of the incessance of injury are the necessary conditions for achieving the transformation of moral thought demanded by the social institution of trauma and the recognition of devastation. This would be the first step in philosophy catching up with and claiming moral suffering as constitutive for the meaning of moral life. Conversely, any moral philosophy that denies the conjunct of the primacy and incessance of moral injury, that denies devastation, would either delegitimize the idea of trauma without remainder or deposit it as a morally empty psychiatric syndrome, effectively denying that such suffering has any moral import at all.

In light of the categorial overlap in Améry's and Brison's accounts, I want in this chapter to examine the moral harm of torture and rape.[16] The overlap of the existential categories necessary for an adequate depiction of torture and rape tells us immediately that there is something wrong in standard reductive pictures of moral harm. The moral harm of torture is not only about the physical pain caused—torture that leaves no marks behind, stealth torture, torture "lite," has become its dominant form in the West;[17] and the wrongness of rape is not solely about the lack of consent; it is devastating. The reductive account of each phenomenon replays the duality between body (torture) and mind or will (rape) that distorts moral reflection generally: it must be all about pleasure and pain (utilitarianism) or all about individual autonomy (Kantianism). I take it that the existential categories necessary for the description of torture and rape converge, recalling again that rape is a form of torture, while the fact that the most natural ways of thinking about the harmfulness and thus wrongfulness of each point in opposing directions—toward exorbitant pain in torture or the destruction of the will in rape—provides a good reason to think that contemporary moral theory is a poor match for concrete moral experience.

There is now a fair convergence among legislators and philosophers that for the purposes of criminal law, rape can be defined as sexual penetration without affirmative, informed consent between competent adults.[18] Some of the difficulties in achieving successful prosecutions for rape would be overcome if criminal law shifted the onus probandi to defendants in cases where "logic tells us that the reasonable woman would not consent."[19] That apart, the literature on rape law is now sophisticated and refined, and it is no part of what follows to intervene in those discussions. Nonetheless, what permits the continuation of a vicious rape culture that fails to cause collective moral alarm, and prevents rape from being prosecuted in anything even approximating its actual occurrence is the cultural failure to fully acknowledge the moral devastation of rape; rape and domestic abuse are not perceived or treated with the moral seriousness, urgency, and sense of abhorrence with which we treat torture, yet forms of torture they patently are; I will come back to this issue in my conclusion. What, then, is sufficient for effective criminal laws prohibiting rape is far from sufficient for understanding the moral harmfulness of rape. Rape involves a "violation of bodily integrity," a violation of "the autonomy of the person at the level of basic bodily integrity. The body is invaded, injured, defiled."[20] These are the minimal first terms through which the moral devastation of rape must be understood. There is a gap between the legal and philosophical account of rape, and its everyday moral description. The ambition of my account is to close that gap so that notions like "violation," "bodily integrity," and "defilement" appear morally informative and explanatorily sufficient. We will discover that we cannot account for the moral harm of rape or torture without yielding to the categories necessary for their existential description, above all how the relational conception of the self and the bounded/bordered body contribute to a minimal conception of the moral subject, the concrete individual as a moral person, where such persons may be undone in their *standing* as persons, devastated.

Section II will begin with an interrogation of the moral ideal of bodily autonomy. In an important essay, Jean Hampton makes the radical, yet, once accomplished, obvious move of arguing that the Kantian categorical rule that we must treat others not as mere means but always at the same time as ends-in-themselves can be turned away from an account of rational agency and toward an account of moral injury and moral harm. Moral injury, she argues, should be interpreted as the perception and experience of acts that devalue and/or deny the other her *standing or status* as being an end-in-itself. In section III, I argue that the idea of possessing intrinsic value must belong to the *constitutive* self-interpretation of modern agents such that what occurs in morally injurious acts is for that self-interpretation of oneself as a being of intrinsic worth to become effectively unavailable.[21] Understanding moral injury is in part understanding how others can have such power over us. Roughly, we shall need to argue that social others must have a necessary (constitutive) role in assigning and sustaining for any individual her practical self-evaluation as being intrinsically worthy. Further, in order for the type of events that rape and torture are to be comprehensible, this notion of intrinsic self-worth must devolve from abstract self-consciousness to bodily self-awareness. We must be capable of conceiving how the idea of intrinsic self-worth, each taking herself to be an end-in-herself, can normatively saturate each individual's bodily self-understanding, a conception typically realized through the ideals of bodily autonomy and bodily integrity. Because my body is morally me and morally mine, then, within the bounds of ordinary custom (what occurs on crowded streets or subways or dance floors or in the course of contact sports, etc.), I immediately take my body to be untouchable without my consent, to be morally inviolable; that is, all things being considered, I can be touched only if I consent to being touched. Once these notions are sufficiently elaborated, section IV can proffer an analysis of the experience of rape, and section V can then explicate the moral injury suffered from it: rape transgresses the victim's bodily autonomy, denying that her body is morally hers, and thereby denies her standing as a person—rape is essentially devastating. The standing denial occurs through physical dispossession and violation—violation is the experience of dispossession. Section V continues by ramifying the notion of the body necessary to make this analysis intelligible, allowing section VI to provide a parallel account of the moral harm of torture and its devastation through a conversation with David Sussman's commanding essay "What's Wrong with Torture?"

Despite its length, all this chapter can accomplish is to make the relevant notions of moral injury and loss of trust in the world prima facie plausible. It will be the task of part 2 to make them rationally compelling.

II. Moral Injury as Appearance

Jane Larson builds into an understanding of autonomy in a sexual setting the requirement that autonomy be bodily actualized. Autonomy in a sexual context has three constituent aspects: "bodily integrity, sexual self-possession, and sexual self-governance." She continues: "Bodily integrity denotes the interest in maintaining secure physical boundaries, and includes a person's interest in controlling access to her body and sexuality. Sexual self-possession includes a person's interest in sexual self-expression through acts and with partners that satisfy her present desires and purposes." Conversely, nonconsensual sex is an act of "bodily and sexual *dispossession*: the aggressor appropriates the victim's body and sexuality for his own purposes."[22] *Dispossession* is a fundamental element of the experience of rape, yet at first hearing it sounds metaphorical: how can one be dispossessed of the body one is? I will understand 'dispossession' as tokening some sense in which the *mineness* of my body is undone, and further, that this has something to do with a *border* violation (a suggestion we first saw in Améry's account of his torture). Nonconsensual sex is a breaching or violating of bodily integrity; because the notion of bodily integrity is emphatically normative, its breach or violation is transgressing or breaking down a normative boundary. And this breach amounts to dispossession. The difficulty in thinking this is thinking how the normative and the physical/material are wed, how the notion of bodily integrity can avoid being reduced to two distinguishable items: something occurring materially—an act of penetration—and something altogether separate—a mental state of not having acquiesced to this occurring and feeling disrespected, even devastated thereby. Lack of consent seems a poor fit for causing devastation. Something is untoward in our basic phenomenology of embodied experience.

Consider again the puzzle from the perspective of the difference between torture and rape. In torture, the wrong of inflicting harm affecting bodily and/or psychological well-being is palpable, but what the acknowledgment of the intentional infliction of pain obscures is the relational harm whereby the sufferer experiences shame and a loss of dignity brought about by an experience of existential helplessness before (a sovereign) one who counts him as nothing. In rape, conversely, the relational harm of being devalued and having one's autonomy ignored is palpable while what is obscured is the pain of violation itself (where by "pain of violation" I do not mean the physical pain of violation, although that matters, but whatever pain corresponds to having one's bodily integrity nonconsensually broken, one's body invaded, one's possession of one's body transgressed upon and thereby being dispossessed). If these ways of setting up the problem are right, then two fundamental adjustments to moral theory are going to be required. First, against consequentialist habits of thought that take pleasures and pains as givens and generate norms through the aggregation and counting of them, trading off benefits against losses, we require a more intimate connecting of pain and normativity such that the transgressing of a norm itself can be understood as a cause of pain, a pain somehow continuous with physical and psychological pains, a kind of pain or suffering equal to the experience of devastation.[23]

Second, against standard Kantian moral theory where actions are evaluated against norms and principles, those norms must be relocated so that they are in the requisite sense embodied, a manner or mode of living one's body. Once norms are in the requisite sense embodied, then the transgressing of those norms is an action against a bodily being, harming it. Violation, again, is the crossing of a normative yet material boundary or threshold. To consider nonconsequentialist norms, norms presumed to determine in themselves what is right and what is wrong, as features or aspects of bodily experience entails that wrong and harm mutually determine one another, albeit not in the manner of standard consequentialism. I think of these two gestures as giving consequentialist (utilitarian) morality a nonconsequentialist twist, and Kantian deontology a naturalist twist: suffering matters; suffering results from the (physical) violation of embodied norms. What will join these two corrections is making the fundamental locale of moral experience and moral form the space of embodied intersubjectivity, so that morality itself becomes relational, entailing that the primary meaning of the notion of an action being morally wrong is that it *wrongs someone*.

Classical Kantian moral theory provisions moral meaning solely from the perspective of the moral agent, the doer of an action, forgetting the victim through the very gesture in which she is included. Roughly, the objects of actions are included in the stretch of practical reasoning leading to an action as rational considerations, as constraints on what is deliberatively understood as obligatory, permissible, or forbidden. In morally right action, I take the standing of another into consideration by limiting my actions to ones she and any other *could* share. In "Defining Wrong, Defining Rape," Jean Hampton's procedure is to take seriously Kant's idea that one must always treat others as ends-in-themselves by looking at it as an account of how we must understand what befalls the *victim* of morally wrongful behavior. Hampton calls her way of joining a wrongful action to its characteristic way of harming the object of that action "moral injury."[24] Her broad thesis is that a moral injury is done when an individual is the object of behavior that *represents* her value or worth as less than the value or worth she merits as a member of her community.[25] Moral injury is an injury to an individual in her standing, worth, or value; it is discounting or ignoring her value, and harming her thereby. Hampton supposes that moral injury does not require actual physical or psychological pain: some individuals do not experience the wrong done to them because the action never comes to their notice (I never see the debasing internet pictures of me), or, because of an already decimated self-esteem, they do not experience the action as wrong ("I deserve to be treated this way"); oppositely, an individual may feel their standing is injured—because a female or a black applicant is given a job that only white males should have—where nothing morally untoward has occurred.

Hampton presses the detaching of moral injury from particular actual experiences of physical or psychological harm because she wants moral injuries to be fully objective phenomena, and not dependent on whether an individual feels or believes she has been injured. Although, as I shall argue below, Hampton is wrong to systematically detach injury from experience, she does so in order to better isolate *what* is injured in a morally injurious act. And what is injured, she claims, is a person's value. In the way of speaking that Hampton is urging on us, persons do not simply have a value vis-à-vis other persons; one person is not worth more or less than others, since that way of considering persons relativizes their worth to some value or end external to their standing as persons. *Persons are values; their being a person is synonymous with their being intrinsically valuable.* This way of talking was originally religious: persons are of intrinsic value because they are made by God in his image; being made by God, their value is permanent and unchanging. Degradation is impossible here because "nothing that any human being could do to another can remove this value." [26] Kantian moral theory inherits this idea of the permanence of intrinsic value with two qualifications: now persons will be considered of intrinsic value because of their possession of rationality and autonomy rather than an immortal soul; and because persons are finite, then the value they are can be destroyed—it dies when they die. Those qualifications granted, Hampton contends that although the characteristics that give us intrinsic value can be damaged or extinguished, as long we remain alive, immoral actions cannot actually lower or degrade our value: "A Kantian theory of value insists that human beings *never* lose value as ends-in-themselves, no matter what kind of treatment they receive"; rather, what occurs as a consequence of a wrong action is the *"appearance of degradation"* (DW, 127, 128). There is a connection between Hampton's view that moral injury can be specified independently of experience and her thesis that the value a person is can be "flouted" and appear wrongly, appear degraded, but that her intrinsic worth nonetheless remains.

How does a flouting of the intrinsic value of an individual occur? As with autonomy itself, we need to distinguish between the ascription of a value and its actualization. Things can be said to be of a certain value, relative or intrinsic, only if their being of that value accords them particular kinds of treatment: rare diamonds are hoarded, great paintings kept free from defacement, good sweaters saved for special occasions, fine china handled with care, great wine savored, a family heirloom treated with respect. In each case, the ascription of a value is realized through a particular set of appropriate acts, with "wrongful," inappropriate acts treating an object in a manner only appropriate to some different kind of object— treating diamonds like paste, great paintings like doodles, fine china like everyday dinnerware. And in cases like these, it seems right to say that the "wrong" actions both empirically misuse the objects concerned and express an attitude that they are not really of the value the rest of us assume them to be. And while the sweaters and china may all be said to be of instrumental worth, the painting and the heirloom, while not of unconditional value, do appear as valuable in themselves and not as mere means to some value or end external to them; that is, although such items are bought and sold, there is another sense in which they are "priceless," nonfungible, and irreplaceable, having a worth that cannot be measured in relative terms. If *Starry Night* is shredded, then the world has less value in it. Diamonds belong in that strange territory in between instrumental and intrinsic.[27]

Humans are similar; the significance of humans being values, being ends-in-themselves, is that such a value generates entitlements to do certain things and not to have certain things done to them. Hence, a person's intrinsic value is flouted when they are treated in ways contrary to how their rights and entitlements dictate they should be valued. Hampton instances a case told by the dancer Bill T. Jones that he heard from his mother. In it, a white farmer deals with a complaint by a black farmhand by placing the farmhand and his four sons in large burlap bags, hanging the bags from a tree, and burning them (DW, 129; I've omitted repulsive details). The moral injuries here occur in two different ways according to Hampton. The farmer's deed is both directly "violative" of the victims' entitlements given their value, and it represents the victims as of no intrinsic value, while representing the farmer himself as possessing a value superior to and perhaps even incommensurable with the value of the farmhand and his sons. Part of the intrigue of Hampton's theory is how she connects the directly violative (what was done to them) with the expressive aspect of that doing (its announcement of the value of the object violated). Along the first axis, the moral injury damages the *realization* of the victim's value, while along the second axis the moral injury occurs as damage to the *acknowledgment* of the victims' value (DW, 132). The two forms of damage are connected in that both involve a value disparity between perpetrator and victim; in *doing* the action, the farmer physically treats the farmhand and his sons as lacking the value that would prohibit him from treating them in that way, and his action so understood *expresses* the attitude and judgment of his superiority lying behind the action. Actions not only accomplish things in the world, but in so doing they express the attitudes and beliefs of the doer about the object of his action: the farmer's act treats his victims as things to be bagged and burned, and expresses the view that such treatment is an appropriate valuing of them, and hence, further, that he is their moral superior who counts and is entitled to count them as nothing. He does actually *terrible* things to them that are a *degrading* of them, and that says so. Although it will take the remainder of this book to get there, establishing an essential connection between an action doing something *terrible* to its object (for its object) and that terribleness being a work of *degradation* is my quarry.

Wrong actions not only do what should not be done, but in their doing they act to diminish the value of the object wronged, and thus act in a manner that aims to either rearrange or make perspicuous a local map of appearing values—that is, an actual mapping of what objects possess what values, and hence, in light of their placement, what treatment each relevant object deserves. The concept of moral injury offers a mode of *representing the value structure of the appearing world* through the actual ways in which individuals are treated by one another in their actions. Morally injurious acts are representations of the world that reveal how perpetrators regard their victims, and how they evaluatively regard themselves relative to them and relevant others (which could be everyone). Not all wrongful acts involve moral injury, but paradigm cases of criminally and morally wrong acts do involve moral injury.[28]

What, it might be asked, does the conception of moral injury add to the standard Kantian view of moral wrongness? Part of the answer belongs directly to the logic of action. All actions are necessarily publically and socially legislative; to do or forgo a course of action, in the actual doing or forgoing itself, necessarily expresses the claim that this course of action is of a kind that is both worth doing (desirable) and right to pursue. The thesis that actions express a formal desire I take as transparent; formally, to do something is to do what one wants to do irrespective of how the want is formed (through inclination, reason, habit, social pressure, or moral suasion). But if actions are freely chosen, then they also claim for themselves a normative rightness; they state, minimally, that this is the kind of action that it is permissible to do, and, depending on circumstances, that this is the kind of action one should do in cases like this—it is what is to be done here. Call this *expressive universalism*; actions may or may not be truly shareable by all, and one may not actually believe that in doing some action it is the kind of action that any similarly placed agent should or should not be permitted to do (you may think you are special because you are a man, white skinned, or president of an investment bank). However, in the actual doing of any action, one is legislating it as universally permissible (or permissible for all those suitably the same as you) and thus expressing that the objects of the action are properly valued by it. *Because materially visible doings having recognizable social meanings, actions necessarily legislate the value of their objects.* It is because actions are socially legislative in this sense that we hold agents accountable for actions in the way we do; *we take* any individual's commitment to a course of action to involve a commitment to the rightness of that course of action, which is why anxious withdrawals of legislative authority—"Do as I say and not as I do"—and excuses—"These really are extenuating circumstances, and I would not be doing this otherwise"—belong to the logical grammar of action rationalizations: they acknowledge the legislative authority of individual actions in their retreat from that authority. This is also why we naturally take the unqualified claim "I am doing this action, but I sincerely believe it is wrong" to be simply contradictory; either there is an extenuation, in which case the claim is not unqualified, or we must take it that the agent is committed to the action's rightness. There is no middle ground.

It is because actions are necessarily socially legislative, logically committed to their own rightness, that they are necessarily expressive. Their logical claim to rightness entails the agent's attitude toward their rightness irrespective of what the agent actually feels or thinks he feels or says he feels; according to expressive universalism, actions necessarily speak louder than words. Both theses—that actions are legislative and that because they are legislative, they are expressive—concern the *appearing* of actions in the world. Although actions' legislative character matters to how agents must understand their actions—to do this act is to *commit* yourself to its rightness and all that follows from being so committed—my interest here is in how their legislative and expressive features immediately reveal one of the ways in which values emphatically appear in the world, how actions necessarily provide hierarchically structured appearances of the worth of agents in relation to the worth of the objects of their actions. Roughly, if some agent Smith does some action A to another agent Jones, then the action appears as "claiming" its own rightness, and in being right stipulates the worth of agent Smith relative to agent Jones. When the context demands it, we understand the evaluation of Jones as occurring not because of who she is or where she is, but because she belongs to a particular class of persons; when this occurs, the action stipulating the worth or value of Jones simultaneously legislates the worth and value of all the members of that class of persons.

Hampton is right in contending that the correspondence or failure of correspondence between an action (or its maxim) and the moral principle regulating it—the Categorical Imperative—locates an action's moral worth in the wrong kind of space, solely in the logical space of reasons and nowhere else, something to be seen by the mind's eye alone. Part of the attraction of Kant's doctrine of treating others as ends-in-themselves has always been that it not only brings the principle that maxims of action should be universalizable closer to experience, but that it also relocates the significance of morality from rational deliberation to how individuals morally appear with respect to one another as a consequence of the actions they do, and hence what and how modes of suffering morally mean. As a first crude approximation, this appearing world operates with a simple ethical geometry—individuals appear as higher, lower, or the same as one another; the representation of an individual's placement is accomplished by coordinating different types of treatment with different types of objects, where those different types of objects are themselves located on a crude hierarchy of being: human, less human, beast, tool, mere thing. There are appropriate ways of treating other humans, sub-humans, beasts, tools, and mere things: one lifts or lowers the standing of an object by treating it in ways like or unlike the typical members of its class. "Although," Hampton states, "all wrongful actions are 'disrespectful of value,' exactly *how* they deny value differs: What they all have in common is the fact that they convey—and work to effect—the wrongdoer's elevation relative to the victim (understood as an individual or as a class of individuals)" (DW, 134). Actions *are* evaluations of their objects. Hampton is urging that wrongdoing be understood in the first instance as being about degrading or diminishing the value of others, how their worth or standing is shown to be less than that of the perpetrator through his actions. Moral injury locates wrongdoing in the evaluation given to an individual relative to the perpetrator; in this respect, all wrongful actions express the idea of there being a moral inequality between doer and victim: victims are treated as worth less than the perpetrator, and the doing of the action is the effectuating of that (de)valuation.

Wrongfulness is located in "the expressive content of the action—in both its commission and its results" (DW, 135). Expressive content is not a mere attitude in the mind of the agent; rather it is the content of the action itself—its doing and the consequences of its doing—in its evaluation of the object of that action. Moral injury, as here understood, certainly begins to get at some of the moral awfulness of rape, how it involves the rapist necessarily representing himself as entitled to be raping his victim, and in being so entitled, representing the victim as being of lower worth and hence himself "as master and the victim as inferior object" (DW, 135). It also begins to get at how in many contexts, that representing and expressing of the worth of the victim as inferior is taken as representing and expressing the worth of all women.

Yet, in stipulating that all moral injury occurs in the sphere of appearance only, Hampton's theory withdraws from its own best insight. As she is aware, there is a puzzle about why we should care about the mere appearance of loss of value; her detractors ask why should we not, in the spirit of Nietzsche, simply shrug off crimes "as nuisances with respect to our value, ineffective in what they seek to establish given the permanence and equality of our worth as persons?" (DW, 133). This is a good question, but not the most urgent one. If to morally injure an individual is to injure the representation of their worth, how can that not matter to the worth itself? How can the worth of an individual be insulated from the damages incurred to its representation when those damages occur through acts directed at the object itself? Why does the work of devaluing stick to the action of devaluing but not to the object of the action? How can my value-image be devalued but not me? Do not the notions of *injury* and *harm* lose their primary significance in Hampton's usage? Hasn't she effectively reduced the material actuality of violation to its expressive aspect?

Again, Hampton says that moral injury occurs in the domain of appearances and not reality because she wants to insist that a person's being of intrinsic value is something she cannot lose no matter what happens to her. This is false. Things can lose their value, even the apparent intrinsic value of a painting or heirloom can simply be lost as reevaluations take place: It's not great art, just kitsch; An heirloom? It's just a knick-knack. Or things can lose their intrinsic value because they have become damaged: in ruining the painting, the flood destroyed the painting's beauty, making it valueless. Of course, for persons we want to say that their being treated as if worthless cannot by itself directly entail that they are worthless, but this is true of everyday objects too, where some treatment is objectively mistreatment: putting a moustache on the *Mona Lisa*—the one in the Louvre—would be a defacing of it; if we could not remove the moustache, we would be forced to say that the painting's value had been permanently damaged. On the other hand, we are amused by moustaches placed on her copied image. There is a difference between harming an object and harming its image.

What underpins Hampton's thesis that moral injury occurs in the domain of appearance only? It is, I think, no accident that Hampton articulates the idea of persons as ends-in-themselves as the effort to provide a secular equivalent to the religious idea that the intrinsic value of persons is grounded in the fact that their value is permanent, something that cannot be destroyed, although its bodily, earthly vessel can be destroyed. The only difference between the theological story and the Kantian story is that in the theological tale, permanence is "strong" because it persists even after death, while in the Kantian account the permanence of intrinsic value is "weak" because it does lapse with the death of the person. But this is a very slight concession indeed—and mysterious. An immaterial soul made by God has permanent value because literally nothing can harm it. Weak permanence makes the bare possession—potential or past—of rationality and autonomy unconditional guarantors of intrinsic value, and hence a value that cannot be actually damaged, broken, or lost, even though, patently, the capacities for autonomous action and rational behavior can themselves be damaged, broken, or lost. That magical inviolability, a value beyond damage and loss, is the theological remnant in Hampton's theory. The permanent value thesis systematically detaches essence from appearance, norm from its material realization, intrinsic value from appearing value, such that there is no connection between the two; nothing that happens in the domain of material appearance matters to what happens in the domain of rational essence; hence the harm persons suffer as a result of wrong actions is logically discontinuous with that wrongness.

Despite herself, Hampton has discounted the suffering of the victim once more. In the name of protecting the intrinsic value of the person, Hampton's devolved Platonism unhinges value from its materialization in the world, emptying moral suffering of any consistent sense. To say to those who have lost everything—whose dignity has been shattered, whose sense of self-worth has been decimated, who are suffering from agonies of shame, humiliation and self-loathing, whose sense of loss has spilled over into soul-death—to say to these individuals that their intrinsic worth is perfectly intact, that nothing in their essential standing as a human being has been harmed or injured, that everything in their moral personhood is exactly as it should be, sounds like a form of vicious cruelty. It denies the possibility that degradation, humiliation, and devastation might be *actual* in the lives of sufferers.

However we finally account for the authority of the norms underwriting the worth of individuals, and however we want to uphold a standing that has been injured—and nothing here is meant to contest our entitlement to authoritatively assert that no being having a human form *should* be degraded, or that in harming another the value of the human itself suffers degradation—it must not falsify the cold truth of the real injuries individuals suffer to the very fabric of their moral being through rape, torture, abuse, slavery. If moral injuries were appearances only, then Hampton's detractors would have a point: with Nietzschean insouciance, we could shrug them off (just as Korsgaard advised we should shrug off phenomenal pains). While claiming that all individuals having a human form deserve to be treated as persons regardless of how they have fared in the world is intelligible from the perspective of moral agency, it would make a bitter

mockery of the suffering of victims to infer from this that all those possessing the human form thereby are morally intact persons. If values are materially actualized, then they cannot be protected from suffering the kinds of
ruination and degradations that material objects having the characteristics
of living beings can suffer. This is the shift in moral meaning required by
the acknowledgment of humiliation and trauma: humans can be degraded,
devalued, and finally devastated.

If we drop the theological prop from Hampton's argument, four consequences immediately follow. First, the idea that *persons are values* must
shift from a direct metaphysical reality derived from the possession of a
trait (rational autonomy) into a socially instituted one: being *counted as
(fully) a person, an end-in-itself, is a standing or status bestowed by society.* Second, rather than individuals possessing intrinsic value unconditionally,
independently of how they are treated, value must be conditional and possessed in degrees; the possession of value is dependent on the general social recognition of that value by others in word and deed in ways that allow
that value to be actual, or not, in practice. In our standing as persons, as
ends-in-themselves, we are dependent beings. It is because we are constitutively dependent creatures that we are systematically morally vulnerable
to others. The depth of our concern for the moral is in direct proportion
to our implicit awareness of our constitutive dependence and the vulnerabilities consequent on that dependence. The far end of the recognition
of dependence is the experience of existential helplessness, or rather, existential helplessness of the kind suffered by Améry and Brison is only finally intelligible as the revelation of constitutive moral dependence—we
are always constitutively, which is to say morally and normatively, second
persons. Without the linking of moral dependence with existential helplessness, the shattering character of the exposition of the latter would be
left unexplained.

Third, then, embodied values must be conditional items also in that
they can be damaged and even lost. Hence the value of a person cannot
be insulated from experience. Améry's dignity evaporated almost instantly,
but we routinely lose standing in the eyes of others in ways that feel unde-
served, we routinely lose standing in our own eyes in ways others around
us do not share, and sometimes we are both seen as worthless and feel
worthless, being without self-respect or self-esteem or a sense of basic entitlements in a world where we are held to have none. Even if it is the case
that a moral injury can occur without its being experienced by the victim,
we count something as a moral injury because, internal to the social space
shaped by the concept of intrinsic individual worth, some actions *typically*

give rise to a certain harm, where that typicality can be located in and co-ordinated with the deep structures of human personhood; what is true for our bodies where certain types of action typically produce certain types of injury (stabbings producing painful bleedings) is equally the case for the moral person (curses launched at one are experienced as insults; rapes are experienced as violations). Moral injuries speak to the general ways we suffer from the doings of others; more precisely, the systematic harm that wrong actions bring about through devaluing the worth and standing of an individual is damage to her personhood: her possession of worth as revealed through posture and action, her sense of her own worth, her presentation of her worth to others, others' routine appreciations and diminishments of her worth, and hence the characteristic ways in which, as a consequence of a wrong action, the value-saturated life of the individual continues—scratched, tarnished, hobbled, damaged, broken beyond repair. It is to these features of the moral life of persons that the core concepts of our moral psychology—insult and injury, respect and disrespect, dignity and humiliation, shame and shamelessness—refer.

Fourth, rather than seeing the possession of rights and entitlements as flowing from individuals having intrinsic value, it must make more sense to see our standing and worth as accomplished through the ascription to us of rights and entitlements, where the idea of intrinsic value represents one specific regime for the distribution and assignment of rights and entitlements. Being bestowed a right is how the community both expresses and gives substance to its valuation of its members. We *institute* something like a true, secular equivalent of intrinsic value, a translation of it into the machinery of law and the practice of morality by, for example, banning slavery, requiring the consent of the governed, outlawing torture and cruel and unusual punishments, upholding the rule of law, providing for bodily autonomy, requiring consent for sexual relations, legally prohibiting child abuse and removing children from abusive homes, providing welfare rights and rights to health care, making education universally available, and by considering these practices as applying to, ideally, all beings with a human form. These practices, in their moral depth, *give* persons the equivalent of intrinsic value by providing a *standing* or *status* for themselves and others that gives maximal weight to their life as valuable. The very idea of intrinsic value is thus translated into the social practices through which individual autonomy and bodily integrity are made authoritative, and the individual person is thereby constituted as an object whose human dignity is deserving of general respect. But this, broadly speaking, is what social practices have always done: ideas of human worth, however sustained as components of a belief system, have been *realized and made actual* only through the social practices of the peoples concerned. Persons are normative constructions, but constructions tailored everywhere and always to the requirements of their material constitution, its needs, necessities, and limits.

Because it is so deeply a part of our modern moral self-understanding, I shall continue to use the idea of persons being of intrinsic value. However, I shall now mean by 'intrinsic value' or 'intrinsic worth' the conception of the person we attempt to fashion and uphold through modern moral and political norms and principles, and the practices coordinated with them. The rule of law, distinguishing the force of law from brute force, is an index and expression of the conception of the person as possessed of intrinsic value in the manner being here canvassed.

III. Moral Injury as Actual: Bodily Persons

The position that is slowly beginning to emerge is one in which what has sometimes been called "dignitary" or expressive harms, on the one side, and physical and psychological harms on the other, are not only systematically connected with one another, but folded into one another, fused. Recall, again, how Brison separated out the symptoms of her traumatic response to her rape that could be treated with drugs from the deeper injuries to her very person that concerned her sense of worth, her trust in the world, her sense of helplessness, bodily vulnerability and exposedness. These latter were injuries to her person, injuries to her as an end-in-herself; they were real and not merely appearing diminishments of her *as a person*. Personhood is not primarily an abstract moral idea whose role is to govern practical reasoning, rather it is the individual herself as realized in her constitutive relations to self, others, and world, relations actual in posture and comportment, in each spoken word and physical action, in the attitudes expressed as she raises or lowers her eyes in the presence of others; *personhood is the socially constructed practical self-evaluation of self-worth* that constitutes the way in which the self appears to itself in relation to others—as worth the same or more or less than they—and how the self appears to those others—as worth the same or more or less than they—and how those others routinely and standardly respond to those self-presentations. It is consequentially the raft of existential features, features that are neither reductively psychological nor merely physiological, and their related moral articulations (loss of autonomy, dignity, and self-respect) that are affected in injuries to the person in her personhood, in her standing as a person, that I want to identify as paradigmatic moral injuries.

Moral injuries are complex because the very items that are vulnerable and injurable are also, from the opposed perspective, the items whose authority, worth, and power form rights, entitlements, and limits, providing the agent with a secure border or boundary. However—and here is the fragility of the human—those limits receive their authority and ability to protect the agent from the same persons who can deprive her of them. *Our second-person sources of standing and safety are also the sources of our vulnerability.* Whoever offers me respect and dignity by recognizing my bodily autonomy can, just as easily, cross the boundary erected by that recognition and impose his body on mine, impose his fist on my eye. Nothing can stop him if he will not be stopped. Sometimes my sense of self-worth can survive such a pummeling intact, sometimes it cannot, sometimes it is damaged but will heal, sometimes the self is devastated; and whatever occurs will usually have deep individual and social causes.

The very idea of moral injury requires a reconfiguration of the structure and nature of moral space and simultaneously a reconfiguration of the meaning of embodiment. Again, the first aspect of that rearrangement of moral space is the demand to acknowledge the conditioning of persons as ends-in-themselves so that their being as ends depends in part on others; with this transformation, moral injury shifts from being only an appearance of diminishment to an actuality, injuries to the value-substance of persons as persons. It is because moral injuries do this—because acts of humiliation can effectively lower us, deprive us of standing—that they horrify us. By itself this points to, but fails to articulate, the kind of fusion of body and meaning, flesh and value required in order to understand the precise moral harm of rape.

In order to claim that moral injuries are *primary* harms to the value-substance of persons as persons, I need to refute the claim that moral injuries are secondary and derivative, a view that accords with much moral and jurisprudential thought. Peter Westin, for example, distinguishes between *dignitary harms* and *material harms*. Dignitary harms are the indignities that are inflicted upon an individual by another who is willing to abridge her "legitimate interests in order to aggrandize himself." [29] The badness of a dignitary harm derives from the victim's belief that a perpetrator is willing to override or ignore her standing as a person with rights, with dignity, as evidenced by the wrongful criminal deed; hence, a dignitary harm is an insult to the victim's legitimate sense of worth. In order to sustain the difference between a dignitary harm and a material harm, Westin contends that the dignitary harm of an act is the same whether the deed is completed or not; so the dignitary harm of an attempted rape and a completed rape would be the same, while in the case of the primary, material harm, it is claimed as obvious that an attempted rape and a successful one are criminally and morally different. In order to hammer home this somewhat speculative claim concerning rape, Westin argues that at least in the case of murder, the primary harm "is not the indignity A inflicts upon S by manifesting a willingness to kill her but the more serious material harm he inflicts by actually depriving her of life."[30] This is puzzling, since in the case of murder it is hard to see what the dignitary harm could be for Westin if the act is successful. If being alive is a condition for being harmed, and hence a condition for having legitimate interests, murder deprives an individual of his sense of self-worth by depriving him of the necessary conditions for his having a sense of intrinsic worth at all.[31]

What might be the material harm of rape that is wholly distinguishable from the dignitary harm borne by the act? Westin defines the primary harm of rape that the law seeks to prevent as "the material harm an actor A inflicts upon a subject S by subjecting S to a genital *invasion* for A's own sexual gratification *without S's having subjectively chosen* it for herself under the *conditions of choice* to which she is lawfully entitled."[32] This definition unnecessarily restricts the orifices that can be invaded and the instruments of penetration; let us assume the needed expansions. What the words italicized above point to are those *experiential* features of rape that are central to rape's being harmful, something that should not occur because it is systematically harmful—that is, something that is experienced as harmful as an inductive matter of fact, where those inductive facts can be shown to correlate with deep structures of personhood. Consent matters because of the values it fosters, above all that of bodily autonomy. Hence, the issue of "invasion" and that invasion's not being consented to, not "subjectively chosen," can only get its experiential force because it coordinates with the value-saturated, bodily self-conceptions of rape victims. As I shall argue directly, only the value-saturated body—my body as integrally and rightfully *mine*, my body as the corporeal realization of my being an end-in-itself, my body as me—can suffer the harm of rape. *The actual material harm of rape is fundamentally a dignitary harm, a harm to the very person of the victim, but a harm that is suffered bodily.*[33] The act of invasion, again, effectuates a *dispossession*, and thereby a *violation*. Without that type of experience of harm, there would be no wrong of rape (in our modern sense of it). And, again, what this assumes is that I constitutively have the standing or status of a person (or its equivalent), and I am a body; hence my body is me, and it is the body of a person. This will require some unpacking.

The harm of rape includes "invasion," a bodily experience. Hence a straightforwardly bodily experience, which can include only a small fraction of physical pain, or even none, is central to the experience of having one's person damaged, violated, injured. But this should be easier to document than it has been. Let me begin with the obvious—namely the norms regulating why we should not be physically harmed. Ignore for the moment the fact that it is we humans whose physical well-being is at stake here. The more general point would be that we have norms regulating what can occur to our bodies because our bodies are vulnerable and injurable, things that can be damaged beyond repair and subject to intolerable pains. If we did not possess those susceptibilities to pain, injury, and death, we would not need or have norms protecting us from attack. Vulnerability to damage, pain, and death provide *grounds* for the adoption of norms to prevent attack and violent trespass. If to simply be an ordinary functioning self in the world is to have a sense of one's standing as a person and thus of one's intrinsic worth, then the standard laws and moral norms protecting us from physical attack must be understood as internal components of individuals' value-saturated senses of self. There is all the difference in the world between slicing my finger while slicing the Sunday roast and your slicing my finger, or between being accidentally hit by a flying baseball bat and being intentionally beaten with one. Even in each first instance, I do not just feel a particular pain, but feel as well that a barrier has broken down, a protective layer pierced; and the pain afterward reminds me that these injuries to my body are injuries to my person, to me: while pain is felt in a particular region of the body, the pain is *to* the person whose bodily region is affected. When I accidentally cut my finger, I scream in pain, and I run my fingers under cold water.

These cases—the accidental slicing or being hit—are not moral injuries because I have not been morally diminished by them, at least not by any other, but they do or can inflect my occurrent sense of self: I might shrug them off, or I might approach the world more hesitantly, feel more fragile, stand less straight. And what of illness, where I become profoundly dependent on others? Here it seems right to say that you might temporally lose, or feel you have lost, some portion of your standing in the world because you literally cannot stand; in becoming an explicit dependent, or, more precisely, dependent in nonhabitual or nonroutine ways, some of your normal capacities for claiming dignified standing are modified or placed in abeyance. In illness, because of the loss of self-control, because the body stops being controllable in its characteristic ways, because you cannot regulate your relations with the world as previously, you might come to feel ashamed, humiliated, diminished, less worthy, less fully human. Tending to the ill is in part tending to their compromised state, physically and morally, showing them that the loss of some of the habitual conditions for personhood need not involve its actual diminishment, or that this state of affairs is morally idle, a routine bracketing of ordinary life with its moral demands while the body mends. The ambiguity here—our sense that when injured or ill or otherwise incapacitated we can feel ourselves to be somehow less fully a person, certainly less than the person we were—occurs because relative physical wholeness as routinely experienced, the socially routine experience of well-being, and moral standing cannot in the first instance be fully separated: sheer physical incapacity can turn one into a moral dependent, just as severe moral injury without physical injury may make it difficult to physically function.[34]

These thoughts converge with those about the nature of pain in chapter 2. To say that the experience of pain, its awfulness, has as an immediate consequence that I undertake ameliorating actions if I can, or scream for help if I can do nothing else, is to say that pain immediately provides reasons for action. But if pain immediately provides reasons for action, then susceptibility to pain and responses to it must belong to the *normative structure* of our sense of self. Pain and our responses to it are not autonomous systems independent of our self-consciousness; they belong to the deepest stratum of my understanding of what should or should not happen to me. Even disenchanted pain must "punish" the "organism for doing something dangerous, or for doing something that may worsen an existing injury."[35] Pain is for the sake of experiencing threat, danger, or damage to the integrity of the body. For persons, bodily vulnerability and susceptibility to psychological distress belong to their *sense* of self as having value and worth. To be a self is to care about pains and potential pains. We cannot pull apart the awfulness of pain from the way in which we have a care for the self at all, but our care for our self is one component of our sense of worth. Susceptibility to injury and illness in relation to the forms of pain they cause imposes on us—individually and collectively—primary modes of care and concern, and hence fundamental modes of orienting ourselves in the world in general. Having a vulnerable body organizes and generates a value-saturated sense of my body and its relation to the world.

But all this follows from just accidentally slicing my finger, or accidentally being hit with a baseball bat or having the flu. Now what makes a body the body of a person is that being a person is to have a sense of one's intrinsic worth for oneself and in relation to others; hence my value-saturated sense of my body is in fact mediated by or given with my intersubjectively generated and maintained valuation of myself as, ideally, a person, an end-in-itself. So the thought is not that finger-slicing pains me and, all things considered, I do not wish to be so pained, but that my finger *should* not be pained by slicing because slicings generally pain me and *I as living person* should not be pained. This *should* is not merely biological and prudential in even its bald form because the underlying claim is something like: given that I am a person whose standing in the world is borne by my fully functioning body, my body as the body of a person should be free of debilitation. For persons, *bodily integrity is a stronger-than-means value because, simply, my body is not a mere instrument for my habitation of the world, but is me, or at least one full realization of me, and if I am as a person an intrinsic value, then my body is intrinsically valuable, or at least the immediate bearer of my intrinsic value.*[36]

Now ask the question: What might it mean for my body to be intrinsically valuable once it is acknowledged that my standing as intrinsically valuable is constitutively dependent on others, and hence necessarily mediated by the regard in which others hold me? One feature of this must be the now authoritatively charged sense of my body as *mine*, mine and therefore not yours, and hence mine to control or use or have used in ways fully consonant with my standing as an end-in-itself. For us, the natural expression of this conception of the moral mineness of a body is the idea of having bodily autonomy, where this involves, following Jane Larson once more, some notion of "bodily integrity," and hence some right to maintain "secure physical boundaries," which itself involves an individual's "controlling access to her body and sexuality."

The first point to underline here is that bodily autonomy and bodily integrity are the active and passive versions of the same bodily conception: to possess bodily autonomy is to have authority over bodily boundaries, where having those boundaries protects or secures one's bodily integrity. If the notion of autonomy here as elsewhere points to actively determining oneself, what is here so determined are the movements of and access to one's body. Bodily integrity is the body as so determined, as secure, bounded, intact, uncoerced, its movements fully its own, its skin a habitually or ordinarily secure shield against the world. Bodily integrity is the bodily realization of bodily autonomy; a sense of bodily integrity is the bodily self-conception had by one who possesses normatively satisfactory bodily autonomy.

Bodily integrity is the normative appearance of a human body's normally possessed physical integrity, where it is understood that physical integrity for living beings is already biologically normative—they possess a self-maintaining, living form—if not always fully morally normative.

Bodily integrity in some minimal normative articulation belongs to even the appearance form of the human body, even where individuals claim entitlement to injure or mutilate the bodies of others—to, say, bag them and burn them. In so doing those others are being *injured or harmed or killed*, and hence some realizations of the human form are being caused to suffer intolerable pains or are being destroyed as the normatively saturated *forms* they are. Bodies are living forms and moral forms. Viciousness acknowledges the normative core of bodily integrity, its standing for what should not be passed beyond, in, and through the violation of it; otherwise the harming, paining, killing would mean nothing, would not be the viciousness, cruelty and savage degradations they are meant to be (and from another angle, meant to demonstrate). When we strike, we mean the other to bodily suffer, to suffer her pains *as diminishments and degradations*, for her to so suffer in the being she is through our trespassing bodily on her. We cross the boundary defiantly, with vicious intent.

Second, while bodily integrity has been considered through a variety of ideas and images, including, for example, purity and defilement, in light of the eighteenth-century institution of the body that should not be touched, modern notions of autonomy and embodiment depict the body's moral mineness and integrity in terms of boundaries and borders. As Judith Jarvis Thomson argues with respect to our right not to be bodily harmed: "A traditional metaphor for a person's claims is a boundary: all around a person is a boundary (a fence or film or membrane) such that to cross it is to infringe one of his or her claims. In light of that metaphor the name 'trespass' would have been a good metaphorical name for all claim infringement, for if I cross your (literal) boundary, I (literally) commit trespass . . . Trespass is claim-infringing bodily intrusion or invasion."[37] Notice first how the metaphorical boundary shifts from materially hard artifact (fence) into something more translucent, as if permeable (film), until with the concept of a membrane we have an analogue whose features are not unlike those of the skin itself. And this shifting and crossing is repeated in the idea that the literal crossing of a boundary, imposing my flesh on yours, literally commits a legal/normative trespass. By definition, *trespass* involves an unlawful act on the *person, property*, or *rights* of another committed with force actual or implied; hence it is an even-handed equality among bodily person, property, and rights, where, again, one would presume that the trespass against the first two items bears with it a trespass against the third (the material stuff trespassed on tokening the immaterial stuff having been trespassed on). Our linguistic repertoire in this area shuttles back and forth between the breaking of some law and the breaking of the body in ways that make that shuttling not a linguistic confusion of categories but the semantic force of these expressions. *Violation, transgression, intrusion, infringement, breach* all have one sense targeting something intrinsically normative—moral or legal—being broken, and another sense pointing to a (wrongful) breaking, rupturing, tearing, piercing, violently prizing open of the living body.

To repeat an earlier suggestion that should now have greater purchase: Broken laws stand for broken bodies; law is the inscription of the body in or as its integrity. It is difficult to resist the thought that *bodily integrity is for us moderns the first law, the lawfulness of law*, through which the very idea of what should not be first becomes manifest.[38] The body must be value saturated because its physical integrity is the very idea of value once the body becomes the body beyond touch, once, that is, the pains of my body become unconditionally and recognizably mine. Of course, this is a moral invention; in the strong form being proposed here, this is the idea of bodily integrity that emerged with the repudiation of the sovereign law of torture—where the body, again, was not in the final instance *mine*—and the uprising of the substantive conception of the rule of law. It is the moral elaboration of this claim that we are here on the track of as a condition for understanding the harm of rape and torture. (For example, it is only once an individual's body becomes and so *is* her own that rape can stop being primarily a matter of dishonor—to the victim, her husband, and her family—and become a matter of moral injury *to her*.)

Consider the normative boundary thesis from the angle of our notion of persons as intrinsically valuable. How does this insert itself in our midst? To regard someone as intrinsically valuable must, before anything else, involve seeing her as someone who is not to be caused unwanted pains, not to be assaulted, abused, violated. The primary sense of intrinsic value is derived from my bodily injurability, from the fact that bodily pain is aversive and hence should not be. Once pain is disenchanted, then the brute "should not be" of physical pain increasingly comes to anchor or orient what morally should not be, stamps it, so that the notion of intrinsic value can only begin to have real meaning through the coordination of the pains that naturally should not be and what should not, therefore, be done *to* one. Once pain is disenchanted and naturalistically relocated as being primarily or essentially an injury and harm to the body of the being in which it occurs, then the idea of bodily integrity as borne by the idea that each (animal) body seeks its characteristic freedom from pain can provide the first, emphatic content to the idea of persons as ends-in-themselves, as possessing intrinsic value—namely, ceteris paribus, that no human body should be caused to have the pains that such bodies characteristically seek to avoid.[39]

Thomson's way of pressing an analogous thesis is to say that whatever other rights or privileges we might imagine an individual to have, if he lacks a claim against bodily intrusion, all those other privileges are worth nothing: "Even his privileges of action (if he has privileges of action) would be of little value to him, for given he lacks claims against bodily intrusion, no claim of his stands in the way of anyone's preventing him from acting, by whatever ghastly laying on of hands we might choose to imagine."[40] Rights against intrusion are the metaphysical film wrapped tightly around the self-maintaining form of the human body because not to be trespassed upon, not to have one's body violated, is a necessary condition for the possibility of enjoying any other rights and privileges of action, including the most basic.

Because we conceive of bodily integrity through bodily autonomy, we construe the intactness or physical integrity of the body through the notions of boundary and border, where secure boundaries and borders are equated with having the right to determine access. Border and boundary talk should not, however, mislead us into thinking of the limit as something external to the body; rather, that thoroughly normative fence, film, or membrane begins where the body begins; it just is my skin or flesh in its normative bearing. And this is required because, as I argued in chapter 2, pain, unlike pleasure, is normally located on or in some specific bodily locale. No portion of my body can be exempted from normative contouring or forming because every portion of my body, as well as the whole thing, is experientially mine as what can be pained or moved (without my moving it). Once the principle of bodily integrity as normatively saturated is in place, once it is the case that my primitive bodily self-relation is saturated with the idea of being mine—where being mine is the condition for anything being mine, and hence being seen as of worth or value or standing— any breach or violation or trespass is a source of moral injury, depriving me of what must be mine and valued if anything is.

Thomson hilariously begins her account of trespass with a vignette: in a moment of boredom in the library, she suddenly finds herself infatuated with a lovely young man sitting opposite her; of a sudden, she walks around the table and kisses him on the back of the neck—a minor trespass, with no physical pain involved, but nonetheless a trespass. And if we now imagine that the boy is a philosophy student, fully aware of who Professor Judith Jarvis Thomson is, then he might well have the thought that his body is in systematic jeopardy, that he cannot fend off these kisses without threatening his degree, his whole future; hence the boy suddenly senses that he has been dispossessed of his first property. Innocent kisses and sexual harassment are fields apart, but how quickly the one slips into the other; how apparent innocence can tip into defilement concerns the thickness of meaning of the moral membrane that the kiss crossed. But we have all had minor versions of this experience with kisses from presumptuous aunts and uncles, where somehow being less than adult has placed one's body in a range where unwanted kisses cannot be rightfully resisted; if you feel defiled by the kiss, then you shall defiantly try to wipe it off your cheek. As almost-adults, we were all in fact subject to endless minor demeanings, humiliations, trespasses, all of which made us or kept us as less than full persons. If loved well enough, we shrugged off these minor moral hurts (learning the power of authority, the constitutive meaning of status, the structure of depredation); if we were unsure of our standing, they might have fired anxiety, doubt, and rage. Or consider the moment in adolescence when parents become alert to the claim that they are no longer entitled to kiss a child or to enter the bathroom when one is showering, that to presume they can involves a trespass or diminishment, a childing of their child. Well before rape is in the cards, bodily integrity is a fraught terrain, where the confusions and indeterminacy between licit and illicit infringements can provoke the whole panoply of diminishments that can accompany moral injury; if one is a woman in Western societies, these minor forms of trespass (availability to kissings and touchings and holdings) continue longer, continuing almost always with a hint of threat or warning in them. Up until quite recently, a whole range of verbal and physical behavior toward women was taken as permissible and not, as we now take them to be, as forms of sexual harassment. I offer these minor episodes in the career of bodily integrity, where small infringements can be felt as trespasses, warnings, threats, even as painfully wounding, in order to underline what the potential for severe damage from acute instances of moral injury might be. Why this is so will be the story of chapter 4.

I have been pressing the claim for an account of moral injuries being actual by urging that the locale, so to speak, of our standing as being ends-in-themselves is our bodily integrity, where the claim to bodily integrity is not merely the claim to have rightful control over a value-neutral body, but rather to have a sense of one's body as integrally one's own, so that any trespass from kiss to stabbing can be *felt* as injurious because it is a crossing of an invisible border that is at the same time perfectly physical and thereby perfectly visible: to perceive a human body appropriately is to *see a person*, where persons are understood to be ends-in-themselves, where to *touch a person* is to touch an end-in-itself. We can ramp up this claim one further notch by considering the relation between bodily autonomy and sexual autonomy. Sexual autonomy is a direct extension of bodily autonomy. The reasons why sexual autonomy is best understood as an extension rather than identical with bodily autonomy are, first, that we possess a modicum of bodily autonomy before sexual awakening; second, that due to the degree of bodily exposure and involuntariness involved in sexual activity, it is massively riskier and thus requires greater degrees of trust than standard social interactions, even moderately intimate ones; and third, because if characteristic forms of sexual activity occur in sex-differentiated ways, then the characteristic risks just noted are distributed differently between men and women.

IV. On Being Raped

Although he attempts to salvage sex through marriage, Kant's analysis of sexual relations makes them intrinsically immoral and degrading of human nature: each uses the genitals of the other for private satisfaction and enjoyment. Jean Hampton is intrigued by Kant's conception of sex as degrading, since it states about sex in general what she wants to argue about rape. In what at first glance is a surprising move, she turns to the writings of Andrea Dworkin, who agrees with Kant that heterosexual sex is degrading and debasing. Because Dworkin cannot, finally, make sense of sexual equality, her view is palpably false and illicit. Nonetheless, Hampton argues, Dworkin "deepens the Kantian objection to sex" through an analysis of "what the act of penetration means" (DW, 141). Hampton's engagement with Dworkin is extended (DW, 139–49); mine will be less so. Following Hampton's lead, I want to draw on some of Dworkin's phenomenology of sexual life as a means for giving phenomenological expression to the internal relation between dispossession and violation. Dworkin's paranoid metaphysics of gender has the virtues of a hyperalertness to the liabilities of sex in the setting of a patriarchal society.

Step one in her account is to use the idea of skin in its literal and metaphorical senses as a means for giving bodily meaning to the notion of border and boundary that seems essential in thinking about the relation between bodily autonomy and bodily integrity. In this, her analysis elaborates Améry's and Thompson's.

> The skin is a line of demarcation, a periphery, the fence, the form, the shape, the first clue to identity in a society . . . and, in purely physical terms, the formal precondition of being human. It is a thin veil of matter separating the outside from the inside . . . The skin is separation, individuality, the basis

for corporeal privacy and also the point of contact for everything outside the self. It is a conductor of all feeling. Every time the skin is touched, one feels . . . The skin is our human mask; it is what one can touch of another person, what one sees, how one is seen. It is the formal limits of a body, a person, and the only bridge to human contact that is physical and direct.[41]

Skin is where the body beyond touch and the body as eminently touchable meet. It would be difficult to underestimate the degree to which we are emphatically skin: in our separateness from one another, our sense of individuality, the persistence of the body as limit for the other; skin is what is seen but not to be touched, in being seen it bears our visible individuality. Our sense of our boundedness is inseparable from the skin as limit. But in this role as "line of demarcation, a periphery, the fence" the skin is simultaneously fully exposed: "The skin is electric . . . sensitive to every whisper of wind, chill, heat."[42] Skin can be scratched, torn, pierced, ripped, burned, scalded, wet, creamed, soaped, rubbed, stroked, tickled, slapped, tattooed; the touch of every item in the world on it feels distinctive in some way; it carries the memory of those feels in fear and anticipation. Skin is limit and vulnerability, fence and porous membrane.

Dworkin approaches the riskiness of sex in relation to skin, in relation to how the boundary that makes everyday life possible can, for all intents and purposes, collapse, and when sex is good, joyfully so. If bodily boundedness is a necessary condition for everyday existing, then part of the fascination of intense sexual experience is that in it, what ordinarily is a condition of existence is overridden.

Sometimes, the skin comes off in sex. The people merge, skinless. The body loses its boundaries. We are each in these separate bodies; and then, with someone and not with someone else, the skin dissolves altogether . . . There is no physical distance, no self-consciousness, nothing withdrawn or private or alienated, no existence outside physical touch. The skin as boundary collapses . . . There is only touch, no boundaries; there is only the nameless experience of physical contact, which is life . . .[43]

Sex is not always this skinless experience; indeed, it perhaps rarely is. But nearly every sexual act contains the collapse of skinned boundaries as a moment, potential or actual—a moment in which we are no longer safe, no longer separate, no longer secure behind the fence, film, or membrane. It is the moment in which bodily passivity and involuntariness is celebrated and enjoyed. If intact skin is one element of our bounded moral standing, then in sex we no longer have standing: we pass beyond it, we move from the vertical to the horizontal, we are stripped bare, exposed, without moral defense (without the resources of morality being employed defensively). Sex may be wondrous, but part of its wondrousness lies in its departure from the uprightness of moral standing, its dissolution of boundaries, its being "unspeakably, grotesquely visceral . . . unmediated by form or formal limits."[44] Again, sex is rarely so, but the moment of involuntariness—of touch, arousal, yearning, scintillation, penetration and orgasm—the moment of exposure tokens an *existential stratum* of the self in its relation to others. (Giving this stratum place in ordinary self-consciousness will be a task of chapters 4 and 6.) In recognition of this stratum of self in relation to others, critical moralists like Kant and celebrants of sex agree: sexual activity in itself passes beyond the ordinary terms of moral existence; it does away with boundaries and standing and choice; sexual activity involves (the actual or possible) shedding of one's civilized body for a skinless one. Sexual activity is not dignified; the sexual body is intrinsically violable, riven with involuntariness, and so without the separateness of dignity. Something of this is a part of all sex, which is why sex is inherently dangerous, risky, intense in its being beyond our capacity to fully shape or order or control. This is the bodily mattering of sex, how sex is bodily experienced, and hence why the sexed body, the body in its sexual being, cannot avoid (touching or being touched by) sex's amorality, its being beyond good and evil, as it were.

Sex intensifies the value-saturation of the body by letting the body become skinless, letting the body's exposedness and vulnerability become sources of connectedness and pleasure (even as they are denied, repudiated, disowned). Since the pleasures of sex are largely involuntary, a form of loss of control, of the body's feeling pleasure and being (blissfully) undone by it, then sexual activity must at some point surrender to the involuntary body; it must surrender bodily autonomy and moral protection and allow a moment of defenselessness. To be sure, we can protect ourselves against sex's improprieties by having sex become habitual or dutiful or ritual, by keeping the lights out, the body mostly covered, the act quick, and the mind fixed on quadratic equations. (And because human need is what it is, with sexual customs often *designed* to protect individuals from the amoral implications of sex, then in all likelihood [but how might we know this?] routinized sexual practices that maintain a secure distance from the full amoral implications of sexual life are perhaps the norm.) But those are precisely civilizational mechanisms of protecting the self from sex's incursions against the boundaries of moral order. The

Kantian judgment has a point: sex bears in itself the (threat or possibility of) bodily expulsion of the autonomous agent from her ordinary moral standing. Perhaps, then, we need to say this: sex is the bodily becoming of the value-saturated body into a body whose intrinsic value is no longer realized through its boundedness, but through its removal of borders, the body turned to shared life, the body in its intrinsic liveliness in relation to another living body, a shared bodily liveliness that is life itself, which I would suggest is another vision of intrinsic value, a vital purposiveness without purpose. Sexual pleasure, when it happens, is felt as good in itself, a happiness or meaning beyond moral meaning and beyond instrumental meaning, which is why religions police women's pleasures, attempting to subdue sexuality into the instrumental order of procreation. In sex, a moral fate of the person is played out in rigorously bodily terms.

If bodies are value saturated, they have been saturated in different ways in men and women. It is true that there are modes in which the body is value saturated as an end-in-itself (or its devaluation) other than a sex-differentiated one, say, racial ones; it is equally the case that the character of each value-saturated body possesses an aspect of irreducible idiosyncrasy, and increasingly there are settings in our culture in which the gendering of the body is socially idle, an empty marker. All that granted, for most of history in most societies, the possibility of being a person, or its premodern equivalents, have come in a sex-differentiated form: one is a male person or female person because one is recognized as a person only by or as possessing a sexual identity.[45] For the purposes of this argument, by sexual identity I will just mean one's social identification as male or female as given at birth—"It's a girl!"—which is socially sustained throughout a life through social practices that thematically magnify and exploit primary and secondary sexual characteristics as determinants of social identity. One is born a boy or girl, and one comes to adulthood, which is to say, to being a socially recognized and placed active member of society, by becoming a social male person or social female person with all the value-saturated bodily being that is appropriate to sex-differentiated personhood in that society. Exceptions, marginal cases, and hard cases prove the rule. One's personhood is sexually differentiated only if one's standing as a person is practically inseparable from one's being male or female for oneself and for all others; and this will necessarily be the case if, for social recognition of oneself and for all others, one *is* necessarily male or female. *When* personhood is sexually differentiated, then one's standing in a society at all is bound up with one's sustaining or at least accommodating one's sexual identity. Because personhood is sex differentiated, we can be morally injured in our standing as a person by having our sexual identity attacked, demeaned, humiliated, or by failing the demands appropriate to one's sex role—a man being treated as a social woman, a woman found inappropriately masculine.[46]

In attempting to reduce rape to battery, to keep sex and sexuality from being legally co-opted, Foucault urged "that there is no difference, in principle, between [pressing] one's fist into someone's face or one's penis into their sex."[47] Whether or not Foucault would consider the body as intrinsically value neutral, its meanings wholly derivative from the protocols of a particular practice, this passage is meant to de-differentiate bodies, to morally and legally make bodily kinds uniform (or indefinitely multiform, which means the same here) and anonymous, to take the sexual aspect of rape out of it by making the bodies of perpetrators and victims semantically and ethically homogeneous (or indefinitely heterogeneous). This is implausible. It is evident that the moral injury particular to rape now is borne by sexual difference, borne by the female body being violated in its anatomical specificity. Although she notoriously—and falsely—interprets ordinary heterosexual intercourse as metaphysically bearing the meaning of rape, Andrea Dworkin's accounts of intercourse aim to locate the value-charged significance of rape as a bodily experience for a woman's personhood generally: "this" is how that body is experienced as now raped and therefore rapeable, and "this" is how that bodily experience as such is intrinsic to a woman's understanding of her self-worth, how, that is, the rapist's act transfigures her sense of self-worth, injuring it, by invading her body and imposing on her a transformed body image, her transformed body image necessarily bearing with it a transformed conception of self-worth. *Dworkin rewrites the female body from the vantage point of its raped formation,* from the vantage point of the rapist, his act contouring the moral meaning of the woman's body. Her account is deeply morally offensive, repugnant, but the offense is the extreme moral destitution in the experience of rape itself.

> He has to push in past boundaries. There is the outline of a body, distinct, separate, its integrity an illusion . . . because unseen there is a slit between the legs, and he has to push into it. There is never a real privacy of the body that can coexist with intercourse . . . The vagina itself is muscled and the muscles have to be pushed apart. The thrusting is persistent invasion. She is opened up, split down the center. She is occupied—physically, internally, in her privacy . . . There is a deep recognition in culture and in experience that intercourse is both the normal use of a woman, her human potentiality af-

firmed by it, and a violative abuse, her privacy irredeemably compromised, her selfhood changed in a way that is irrevocable, unrecoverable . . . that slit that means entry into her—intercourse—appears to be the key to women's lower human status . . . she is intended to have a lesser privacy, a lesser integrity of the body, a lesser sense of self, since her body can be physically occupied and in the occupation taken over . . . this lesser privacy, this lesser integrity, this lesser self, establishes her lesser significance.[48]

Dworkin's passage powerfully fuses the moral and the sensible as they coalesce on features of the female body. Sexual activity in its dissolution of bodily boundaries is subject to moral difficulty because sexual activity imposes on the value-saturated body a departure from a person's standing as a moral being. Rape exploits the precise character of the body's skinned being and the skinless moment of sex to decimate the body's boundaries, which is to say now, to decimate the accumulated pulse of moral worth that is borne by the bounded body. "Occupation" is Dworkin's word for the place where dispossession—of boundedness—becomes violation of bodily integrity. The susceptibility to invasion thus takes on the continued moral meaning where "this lesser privacy, this lesser integrity, this lesser self, establishes her lesser significance." *Violation is degradation.* Rape is an attack on women in their sexual being, but for all that, is not itself a sexual act—that it might be so is the fantasy of the rapist.

V. Exploiting the Moral Ontology of the Body: Rape

Our quarry at the beginning of this discussion was to explain the moral harm of rape with an eye toward its features while simultaneously unlocking the moral harm of torture. I argued that a successful account must be able to explain the widespread intuition that rape is a paradigmatic moral injury, an intuition underlined by the risk of trauma from rape being nearly as high as it is for torture. The use of rape as a form of torture and the hypothesis that the existential structures of torture and rape are the same leverage the thought that torture and rape might represent deeply similar forms of moral injury and harm. In order for this to be the case, the harm of rape must relate to fundamental structures of personhood; the harm of rape must relate to how the body actualizes the fundamental structures of personhood; the harm of rape shows the bodily person to be intersubjectively constituted.

Three philosophical gestures have formed the pivot of my account. First, if transformations in personhood or self-worth are the felt terms of the experience of rape, as the loss of dignity and loss of trust in the world were the felt terms of Améry's torture, if something in the area of abysmal humiliation and degradation are what occur in cases like these, then we need an account in which moral worth can play a role not just in moral reflection and deliberation, not solely as a moment in practical reasoning, but also in the very character of moral suffering. Again, our moral psychology contains a minimum of the appropriate kind of language—insult, humiliation, denigration, shame, hurt, wound, disrespect, degradation, ignominy, dishonor, disgrace, abasement, mortification. Paradigmatically, immoral actions involve either a direct or indirect discounting or devaluation of the human worth of their object and/or the surrounding moral population. Immoral actions commit moral injuries.

My second gesture was to claim that once one builds the idea of individuals as ends-in-themselves into their actual standing for themselves in relation to all others, then that inviolable status becomes something that is attained and therefore can be lost; inviolability is not a metaphysical fact but an embodied normative achievement. My third gesture claimed that persons do not merely take themselves to be ends-in-themselves or the socially parochial equivalent thereof (being a full member of some relatively self-sufficient social group); being a person is not restrictedly psychological, an idea in the head; it is borne by value-saturated forms of embodiment and comportment, by posture and forms of movement, by bodily habits and sensitivities, and, centrally, by the way in which all these are elaborated and confirmed in everyday social practices. Persons are values (which is the true meaning of the primacy of practical reason). It is a necessary condition for everyday social activity to have the sense of one's body as being authoritatively "mine." The mineness of my body is constituted by the coordination between the social practices providing for bodily autonomy and bodily integrity. Like health, the normative authority of bodily integrity is *felt*, and so recognized, in and through its breach or collapse, its actuality known and experienced in its being lost or undone; hence, the normative force of bodily integrity typically withdraws in the light of its taken-for-granted achievement. Possessing the sense that one's body is securely normatively bound is the necessary condition for having trust in the world; in other words, *the sense that one securely possesses bodily autonomy and integrity is to have trust in the world.* This provides a first vindication of Améry's hypothesis that trust in the world is a necessary condition for living in the world as a person in general.

The normatively bounded body-person is doubly vulnerable. First, I am vulnerable because the normative authority that provides for my standing in the world, and hence is the source of my value as a person, is bestowed on me, given to me, through social practices of recognition that provide for my being in the world. However, what is bestowed can be retracted; recognition can be withdrawn, ignored, overridden, discovered to be without substance or weight, nothing to be counted upon. This means that my others are already there within me, since it is they who give me to myself as a person. If persons are second persons, if their sedimented and ongoing recognitions are the invisible threads holding uprightness in place, then one's standing as a person is systematically vulnerable to destruction. If I am for myself what I have been held to be by my others, then in ways terrible to discover, *they own me*—a fact which, if one is fortunate, one will never have to explicitly face or bear the full negative implications of. If the mineness of self and body is the glory of the autonomous subject, the fact that I am first owned by others, that my self is borrowed or on loan from my social world, is my misery.

Second, I am a bounded self through my skin's being a limit; unlike the limits we erect around ourselves—brick walls, fences, suits of armor, leather jackets, power suits—this limit is inherently permeable and fragile, and there are joys in throwing it off. Skin as border and boundary—where skin is a synecdoche for all the elements of bodily integrity—is like our being second persons in making the source of standing what makes us ripe for falling. Again, it is the dual or reversible structure of skin that is significant: the source of safety is the source of vulnerability. And this dual structure is heightened and intensified once we consider skin as the intrinsically saturated bearer of personhood, as the person realized, fully incarnated.

What makes rape and torture paradigms of moral injury is now easy to state. Both rape and torture exploit the dual character of the body boundary by turning the victim's body against her, and they both do so for the sake of morally degrading her, for the sake of decimating the boundary protecting the self and thus collapsing her standing as a person. Rape and torture exploit the intrinsic vulnerability of personhood by exploiting its intrinsic bodily realization; they exploit the duality of the body as source of standing and source of vulnerability in order to reveal and stamp one's dependence as a person on the other, and they reveal that constitutive dependence for only one purpose: in order to destroy the person, *to remove any claim to mineness that a subject may have over its body and life.*[49]

Rape takes the most precarious of human physical encounters and empties it of its usual meaning; it turns the victim's body against her by turning her power of enjoyment, her power of welcoming and joining the other into simple vulnerability, into what allows her to be invaded and violated, not merely in her body but in her self. Because one's intrinsic worth is wherever one's body is, and because our bodies are sexually differentiated, and our personhood carried by our sexually differentiated bodies, then we are ripe for sex-differentiated forms of violation, violations that seek to destroy the whole person, to reveal to her that there are those in the world who count her as nothing because she is a woman and can be invaded in this way. And this is devastating in the way it is because it brings to the fore the first vulnerability, the radical dependence of her standing as a person on (male) others, her internal relation to them, her final existential helplessness before them.

Rape devastates the self because it acts directly on the conditions of personhood, and its acts on them for the sake of depriving a woman of her personhood: "Because you are woman and can be invaded in this way, you deserve destitution." This argument does not presume that all rapists have this explicit intent. It only presumes that where personhood is given with sexual identity, then in a society that remains socially stratified along sex-differentiated lines (as most but not all societies have been[50]), a sexual assault is necessarily experienced as *marking* that form of personhood: a raped woman's body is not bound; it lacks worth except as it is used for the enjoyment of the perpetrator, and hence women's bodily formation is experienced as not a form of personhood recognized by the attacker or his class.[51] To be raped is—for the traumatized victim—to have suffered the communication *from the rapist* that she is intrinsically rapeable; hence, being a woman is to be rapeable, and in being rapeable she is therefore not fully a person. One is not possessed of full personhood because the necessary condition for it—namely to have one's body as one's own—has been brutally destroyed, and that brutal and terrible destruction can occur even if the rape is not physically violent and even if no physical force is used (its implied threat is enough). What is most intimately "mine," if anything is to be mine, is no longer mine: that is the communication of nearly every rape, and why rape is a fundamental form of moral injury.

It is equally why to be raped is to stay raped, why rape is traumatic and devastating: because moral injury is imprinted on the body-psyche of the rape victim, it is imprinted on her person. And this imprinting or stamping could not happen if the body were value neutral; the depth of undoing suffered by rape victims occurs because what might have been reflectively known and anticipated, as rape usually is in our society,[52] is now realized in bodily reality; but bodily reality is not equivalent to, say, an empirical confirmation of a well-known rule, like learning that fire burns. Rather, the bodily experience of invasion decimates the *moral body*, the body as bearer of personhood, the body as morally bound, and, as a consequence, imposes on the victim the apparent necessity to absorb and make part of her self-consciousness the revelation of that devastation. What Judith Herman says about the result of repeated trauma under circumstances of captivity corresponds to acute responses to rape: "Whatever new identity she develops in freedom must include the memory of her enslaved [raped] self. Her image of her body must include a body that can be controlled and violated. Her image of herself in relation to others must include a person who can lose and be lost to others."[53] Consider again the image of Brison walking down the road, anxiously pirouetting every few strides.[54]

Rape is a consistent exploitation of the moral ontology of the body. It is this that makes it a paradigm moral injury. Body and social recognition that were previously sources of bodily autonomy and integrity, a sense of oneself as self-moving and secure, are inverted, turned into nothing but a persistent sense of exposure and dependence. Think of the fence analogy: rape means to remove central slats in the fence permanently; the fence no longer can protect in the way it did; the body bears this as its persistent sense of being exposed; one can never feel safe in the way one felt before, one can never be the same in one's person; one's standing for oneself is forever fragmented, partial, morally injured. Devastated.

But this analysis is insufficient on its own since by tying rape to female embodiment so firmly, it severs it from the general existential structures of human embodiment. Such a severance would not make men and women different versions or aspects of the human, but nearly different species, as if only the species woman could be raped, reserving for the species man the privilege of torture, and hence deny that rape is a form of torture and that all torture now has a sexual subtext. Further, Dworkin's insistence upon the female form as designed for invasion is insufficient on its own since male-on-male rape is also invasive; but when this invasion happens to an unwilling man, a significant component of humiliating diminishment comes from its making the victim like a woman, feminizing his body.[55] And this matters to our understanding of torture because something in its manner of bodily violation has about it a sexual subtext, a humiliation through feminizing. In Abu Ghraib, the subtext became the text of the torture: posing naked or near-naked prisoners in sexual postures that on their own, without physical pain or bodily invasion, were sufficient to cause severe humiliation. Thus, the force of being capable of being invaded like a woman must have a further resonance, a resonance not reducible to the capacity to be penetrated itself, and thus a resonance connecting male embodiment to female embodiment in ways that have already undergone repudiation.

Two features of female bodily experience are connected here. First, as Brison notes, a signature feature of female bodily experience relates to bodily processes that are involuntary or at least not fully agential, like menstruation, pregnancy, childbirth, and lactation. Of course, these processes have been socially highlighted because they bear on the creation of life; nonetheless, these processes, if placed in a wider setting, should be taken as telling us something about human bodies generally—namely that there are constitutive features of the bodies of humans as living beings that are not directly connected to agency and will, processes that happen of their own accord and which because they happen of their own accord require particular civilizational practices and codes of concealment or keeping private. Privacy, it could be argued, is nothing but the cultural system whereby we attempt to place a civilizational border around those features of bodily life that are essentially disorderly because they are involuntary, privacy and concealment as modes of providing a border for those processes that do not recognize borders; hence, our systems of privacy and concealment are social mechanisms for regulating the difference between the voluntary and involuntary by giving what is involuntary, and therefore socially undignified, an out-of-sight place to occur, or a place suitably coded as private no matter how public it is in fact.[56]

Put those practices and codes aside (I shall return to them later). The first thought here is that those female involuntary bodily processes exemplify the *ontological* fact that the human body is not something that even potentially can be fully within our control, fully within the ambit of will and reason. It is not the distinction between active and passive, doing and suffering, that is primary; it is the distinction between the voluntary and the involuntary that is essential. Sexual practices and their reproductive consequences have been traditionally regarded as peculiarly animal or low because they are simultaneously necessary elements of human social practice that in their indelible involuntariness remain outside the fierce policing efforts of reason and will, law and civility; they can be curtailed but not controlled. This aspect of bodily experience refers to ways in which I simply *am* a body that undergoes bodily life as opposed to my *having* a body that is an instrument for realizing my purposes in the world.

It is thus not the anatomical specificity of being designed for penetration/invasion that marks the specificity of female embodiment, but rather it is the way in which the capacity to be invaded *stands for the involuntary body*, the body that spells out the human in its essential potencies and liabilities as a living being indebted to vital processes beyond reason and will. These features of embodiment reverberate with existential and moral significance: the involuntary body as the body one is, and hence the body as one's emphatic being naturally conditioned, as thereby drawn into and placed in the world, there for everyone, essentially visible and touchable, as a living, sensate object and not a rationally self-moving subject. The involuntary features of female bodily experience are thus culturally taken—when they are so taken—as standing for the human body as not a vehicle for human reason, will, and expression, but rather as a living thing, as quivering sensuous sentience, hence as insupportable fact, the body whose hurt is my hurt, the body whose death will be my death.

Because the involuntary body stands outside the full control and purview of reason and will, outside civilization's rules and regulations, outside the jurisdiction of law, in some societies it becomes equally something that requires repudiation, the body as calamity, as abject in itself. On almost any account of the history of male domination, men have, however equivocally and self-deceivingly, thought of themselves *as having bodies but not being their bodies*, while *projecting* onto women the full complexity of both having and being their bodies. But in projecting onto women the duality of bodily experience, men have essentially repudiated their own embodiment and, in a long-achieved division of spiritual labor, made women the social bearers of living embodiment generally.[57] Since involuntariness is a component of all embodiment—I am my body—and can be celebrated and embraced as well as repudiated, let me call the body in its involuntary or passive mode *as repudiated* the 'abject body.' I take it that one fundamental and often defining gesture of patriarchy is the disposing of bodily involuntariness onto woman, which becomes the marker for a differentiation in status. The status differentiation could not operate unless involuntariness was understood as itself degradation and liability. It is not involuntariness itself, which may be celebrated or reviled, but involuntariness as a stigmatized sign (of insufficient severance from nature, say) that forms the abject body.

The idea of woman as the bearer of the abject body points directly to a patent third element of rape that carries over into the structure of torture: rape pins a woman to her bodily being in its abject mode, in the very mode that men have repudiated and devalued. Rape but not sex isolates the involuntary body, the body I am rather than have, and reduces the victim to it precisely by the act being nonconsensual; consensuality, either as a social rite like marriage or a free-standing social practice, is the mechanism for placing a civilizational border around the involuntary joys and indignities of sexual life, allowing the involuntary to shift from danger to duty, from threat to invitation, from dissolution to delectation. Rape, by placing the act out of the range of choice, volition, and social legitimacy means to place a woman's sexuality out of the range of choice, volition or social legitimacy, where doing this nails her to a feature of her sexual identity—namely bearing the burden of repudiated embodiment. Rape as an act of will and force gives male sexuality an aura of pure agency—despite its all-too-evident involuntary aspects—while depositing sexuality's polluting involuntariness onto (into) the woman.[58] When this occurs, as Brison confessed, the woman's body becomes an enemy—polluted and vulnerable. This is how being a woman can become a site of shame.

The abject body is the body in its humiliating, shameful, disgusting, degraded role. In Western societies, this body has routinely borne the name "woman." In male-on-male rape and in torture, to be rendered helpless is to be left with only an abject body, a woman's body; it is to have lost all the conditions necessary for personhood, for self-worth. The tortured body in pain, the body invaded, the naked body coerced into sexual postures as if pleasuring or being pleasured all deposit the subject in the space of the abject body; in each occurrence, the victim is rendered into a form of embodiment which, in itself, is a site of humiliation and degradation—that is, already a site where the victim no longer has standing or worth for himself or for the torturer; he is "other" the way a raped woman is "other."

The abject body is one consummation of existential helplessness. This, arguably, is the tacit but governing effort of the rapist and torturer: to accomplish the severance of the victim's voluntary body from her involuntary body, with rapist and torturer appropriating all agency, power, and voluntariness for themselves while leaving their victim with only her involuntary body. In so doing they are abjecting the other, forcing the other to become only an abject body, a body without boundary or defense, a body reduced to involuntariness, to having no movements of its own but moving only as it is moved by them. *The rapist's severing of the voluntary from the involuntary body is the precise analogue of the torturer's severing of pain-as-feeling from pain-as-reason-for-action*; indeed, it is the same work of severing and abjecting, since the latter takes effect through the former.

Modern torture and rape attempt to force the victim to embody the whole of repudiated embodiment, the whole of everything about the body that, from the illusory heights of reason, makes it deserving of repudiation. At least part of the reason that rape and torture victims frame their degradation in terms of defilement and pollution, of being stained and dirtied, lies in the region of their literally becoming the scene of bodily abjection, the scene of the involuntary body that has lost any relation to the civilizational codes of privacy and concealment that might dignify it; their body has become polluted because they have been turned into oozing, writhing, involuntary life, life without civilizational refinement. The sovereign effort by rapist and torturer to appropriate all civilization for themselves—as *agents* of ruination—and leave the other deposited in abjection will fail: they are attempting to repudiate what cannot be repudiated. But that failure is of no consolation to the victim. He or she remains abject, devastated.

VI. Exploiting the Moral Ontology of the Body: Torture

In "What's Wrong with Torture?" David Sussman provides a compelling analysis of the moral harm of torture. In the course of his analysis, Sussman acutely situates torture with respect to other forms of harm and registers most of the salient materials necessary to explain torture's specific moral harmfulness. What prevents his account from being fully successful is that although he accurately portrays the specific interpersonal structure of the moral harm of torture, he lacks an interpersonal conception of subjectivity itself and therefore cannot adequately account for the continuance, the incessance of the injury (although he underlines the importance of the fact of continuance); and while making the undermining of dignity central, he emphasizes the idea of self-betrayal, of forcing the victim to use his dignity against himself without seeing how this incurs a destruction of the agent's status or standing. Hence, although Sussman's analysis gets right or nearly so some of the central dynamics of torture, it fails to capture the very moral extremity it intends, viz., the explanation as to why torture is "the most profound violation possible of the dignity of a human being," why torture is a paradigm of moral harm, something that "sets it apart even from killing, maiming, or imprisoning someone, such that the circumstances might justify inflicting such harms [but] would not even begin to justify torture" (WWT, 2, 3).[59] I shall conclude my account with a defense of this thesis.

Using Améry and Scarry as guides, Sussman's account of torture overlaps considerably with the one presented in chapter 2. Torture involves (i) the intentional infliction of great pain on an individual who (ii) is helpless both physically and legally or morally because (iii) the terms and structure of what occurs in torture are wholly within the control of the torturer; (iv) as a consequence, the "asymmetry of power, knowledge and prerogative is absolute: the victim is in a position of complete vulnerability and exposure, the torturer in one of perfect control and inscrutability" (WWT, 7; note how the asymmetry of control and vulnerability tips into the asymmetry of the exposed and the concealed); (v) because the torturer's will is absolute, it is equally experienced as arbitrary, as without limit or constraint; promises made or bargains struck are empty because they can be arbitrarily withdrawn; (vi) torture is thus without limit since even surrendering the truth—the presumptive point of the exercise—can require indefinite confirmation because it is distrusted and therefore subject to disbelief. Why would a torturer ever trust someone saying something for the sake of halting intolerable pain? Extreme pain can induce speech, but that speech, because it is a product of extremity, is indefinitely unreliable. Torturers are both all-powerful and powerless with respect to their victims; their powerlessness is what exacerbates the insistence of their practice, the necessity of its continuing indefinitely.

It is because interrogational torture has no internal possibility of completion that it necessarily collapses into pure torture, torture for the sake of humiliation, degradation, dehumanization, torture *for the sake of breaking the victim*, and hence a torture whose point is the asymmetry and nonreversibility of position between torturer and victim, the establishment of the absolute *authority* of the torturer. The torturer's absolute authority is meant to translate into the absolute submission of the victim to his will, which in its turn is meant to translate into the victim's saying what the torturer wants him to say: the truth. Hence, the apparently limited purpose of interrogational torture—namely the gathering of some particular bit of valuable information—is made possible through a practice that is structurally neither finite nor pragmatic, but rather turns on the destruction of the autonomous agency of the victim. The practice of torture itself, its means of acquiring truth, and not the purposes for carrying it out, are what make it morally awful.

In order to demonstrate the moral awfulness of torture, Sussman proceeds by first showing that neither Kantian nor utilitarian moral theory can capture the situation, each blind where the other is sighted: "The utilitarian focuses on the badness of the victim's agony but cannot readily grasp the significance of the characteristic interpersonal structure of torture. The Kantian can begin to make sense of that structure, but in turn has difficulty explaining why torture seems morally special because it specifically involves pain" (WWT, 14). This seems exactly right: the horrendous pain of the victim and the further destructive and corruptive features of a torture culture speak against it, but they capture nothing of the moral perversity of the relationship between torturer and victim—its patent ambition of degrading and humiliating. Conversely, the Kantian sees the abuse of the victim's rational agency but can make nothing of the victim's pain. The duality between Kantian and utilitarian approaches here perfectly matches the initial conundrum of rape: the bodily fact of physical violation and the

mental fact of lack of consent seem to inhabit different and incommensurable registers of moral meaning.

Sussman intends to extend Kantian morality to incorporate the dimension of pain, but before so doing he needs to explicate how he thinks the
standard Kantian model is inadequate here. As already noted, the Kantian
can do little with the role of pain in torture. What the Kantian can do is
argue that pain's characteristic power of driving out all other features of
mental life has the consequence that it either temporarily or permanently
undermines the conditions of rational agency. If it is the possession of rational agency that makes us persons, then the intentional infliction of pain
must be impermissible. But this includes and excludes pain at the same
time: pain is counted only because of what it brings about—the destruction of agency—but is discounted in that this account is unable to do justice to the necessary truth that pain hurts. If only the destruction of agency
is the issue, then tickling—which has its own increment of cruelty in it—is
as good as pain. The Kantian analysis sees in pain only what eventuates
from it for rational agency, and sees nothing about the characteristic phenomenal features of its occurrence, it awfulness (nor, I would add, what
the *infliction* means to achieve, communicate, express: its work of devaluing
the subject through transgressing a boundary, say).

Second, Sussman argues that "any approach that condemns torture
as a disruption of agency will have difficulty distinguishing torture from
killing" (WWT, 15). Compare the use of torture to killing in self-defense
and its collective extension, killing in a just war. All three cases involve
the disruption of agency—you cannot disrupt agency much more thoroughly than by ending it—yet the three cases are not morally equal; as
Sussman rightly comments, we do not think that it is appropriate to torture
in self-defense, and even those who defend the use of torture in extreme
and urgent—ticking bomb—cases, begin with the thought that there is a
presumption against torturing, thus requiring that the stakes be sufficiently
high in order to justify its use. We are much more demanding about torture
than about even killing the innocent, where the innocent can be "legitimately" regarded as unavoidable collateral damage. Something in torture
is worse than or significantly morally different from killing in self-defense,
in ordinary experience or combat, such that the requirements to even con-
template its use are more stringent. You enter my home, gun in hand, to
rob me; shooting you in self-defense might be justifiable, but torturing you
for days on end is not. Yet you might recover from the latter experience, but
cannot recover from the former. Of course, questions of excessive force can
always be a consideration when self-defense is at issue, but here the issue is

not one of *excessive force* but of *the wrong kind of force*, a force whose primary action appears, at least in the first instance, as indifferent to any possible instrumental ends. This is why justifications of torture are always empirically exorbitant—for example, a ticking bomb and thousands of lives at stake; justifications attempt to give a constructive purpose to a practice that is intrinsically value destroying. The exorbitance of the stakes is what is meant to allow the connection: in these circumstances, *any* acts that can save the lives of the innocent are presumed to be permissible. *Any* acts? Might we torture just anyone? Might we commit a preventive terroristic bombing against the presumed terrorist's village? Commit a minor genocide that would still save more innocent lives? That thought is morally absurd, but inevitable since the exorbitance necessary to establish a possible instrumental relation always establishes too much. There is no principled way to limit what might be done once the constraint on the moral character of the means has been finally silenced.[60] Put all that aside; the thought here is that ticking-bomb scenarios concede the moral point: torture is somehow more heinous than ordinary killing in self-defense and therefore in need of greater and more stringent justification.

No account of torture will be adequate that does not elaborate the infliction of pain in its relation to—and not mere cancellation of—the power of agency, and only if it does so in a manner that makes sense of torture's being interpersonal, a relationship between victim and torturer. As we have already seen, it is in the nature of pain that it connects a phenomenal awfulness with a "pure imperative . . . a bodily demand to change something about one's condition, to do something to silence this very demand" (WWT, 20). In order to satisfy these requirements, Sussman's suggestive thesis is that torture involves a particularly destructive form of *self-betrayal*: "torture forces its victim into the position of colluding against himself through his own affects and emotions, so that he experiences himself as simultaneously powerless and yet actively complicit in his own violation" (WWT, 4). In torture some part of the victim is "an eager agent of his tormentor": "The victim finds in his pain, and his own immediate responses to that pain, a surrogate for the torturer. The victim's own voice, the voice of his body, has come in part to speak the torturer's mind. This is why torture requires there to be a protracted process in which pain is both inflicted and withheld . . . in a capricious and unpredictable way" (WWT, 24).

Something like a logic of self-betrayal is clearly a fundamental mechanism of torture. My criticism of Sussman's thesis is that self-betrayal is an overly compressed statement of the underlying structures of bodily autonomy that are at stake; and further, lacking an appropriate setting, the notion of self-betrayal does not by itself amount to a profound violation of human dignity, a "turning dignity against itself in a way" that fundamentally dishonors it (WWT, 19); the notion of self-betrayal abstracts too quickly from the moral forms in which the structures of agency are embodied.

Being an accomplice to one's own undoing is humiliating, but by itself not obviously morally devastating. Consider again being tickled; children tickle one another, especially very ticklish children, as a way of exerting power, a way of wringing from the victim that his voice and values are no more than what the tickler wishes them to be: "Say I am the god of stamp collecting on Hillsborough Avenue or I will keep tickling you!" and in great hilarity the tickled one concedes all. Nonetheless, being unable to stop hysterical laughter can be deeply disconcerting; being made to so laugh by another often has a violent subtext; it can be an assertion of power by the tickler over the tickled that possesses a strong tinge of anger or resentment against the tickled. The tickled one knows this, which is why the humiliation of powerlessness can instantaneously turn an episode from hilarity into anger. Scenes of power tickling, as it may be called, seem an exact analogue of Sussman's vision of torture; indeed, it is a version of torture, the everyday way in which children torture one another (especially older siblings against younger ones), and how parents torture their children under the guise of having fun with them (and why children are always desperate to discover if their parents have ticklish spots—under the arms, on the soles of their feet—the way they do). The reason why tickling should have a structure and consequences parallel to those of standard torture is because even the production of pleasure, if that is the right word for the release of laughter on being tickled, sets the victim's body against his agency in a way that can become disorienting, even frightening, because, in uncovering a dimension of embodiment whose operations are intrinsically involuntary, the laughing victim discovers dimensions in which his body is not his own, ways in which he is his body but does not fully possess it because there are dimensions of it that remain outside his control. (One token of the incommensurability between the voluntary and involuntary body is that we seem to be unable to tickle ourselves.) Having this ticklish vulnerability exposes his body to someone else's owning it—becoming a god over him. I take the unpleasantness in coerced hilarity to derive not simply from the coercion itself, but from its revelation of the stratum of bodily involuntariness; it is the ongoing of the laughter, the not having access to mechanisms of defense or control, that tip the laughter into something very unfunny. Once we recall that children invite being tickled by their parents in order to become "helpless with pleasure,"[61] as the experience, premonition, and foretaste of the later helplessness with pleasure that all adults seek, then the sexual subtext of torture becomes patent: categorial helplessness in relation to others through our involuntary body comprises an ineliminable aspect of both one of our greatest joys and one of the most corrosive of moral injuries.

A first, simple worry then about the notion of self-betrayal is that it overstates or misstates the role of agency so that suffering is not merely something undergone in torture but "something *I do* to myself, as a kind of self-betrayal worked through my body and its feelings" (WWT, 21; emphasis mine, echoing the phrase "actively complicit" above). Pain's aversiveness does have a moment in it of "my body hurts me," but this is not me *doing* something to myself—say, hurting myself—but rather a vulnerability, an exposure to what harms or undoes me that is internal to and a structural feature of who I am. The parallel between tickled, out-of-control laughter and pain makes thinking of either of them as a component of one's agency curious. Pain is a sign of damage to the vital body, a destruction of the body's self-maintaining form; tickled laughter is not. That is why the former is necessarily more vicious than the latter. But tortured pain is an exacerbation and underlining of existential helplessness, an assertion of the absolute asymmetry of position, and thereby an effort of humiliating. In those central features of tortured pain, the parallel with tickled laughter remains.

Normally we consider self-betrayal as someone acting against some deep value under conditions in which they could have and should have resisted. Out of fear of embarrassment, Jones betrayed his commitment to the cause by publicly voting with the opposition; or Jones betrayed his love of his wife by giving in to temptation. The weaker sense of self-betrayal is inadvertently revealing (betraying) something about yourself that you meant to keep concealed. Neither sense tallies with what Sussman wants, because although torture sunders the self, turning the self against itself in terrible ways, in ways that can cause it to betray its highest values, that betrayal is neither normatively inappropriate—we don't blame you for speaking under torture, although you might forever blame yourself—nor inadvertent.

Two misfirings are jammed together here. First, Sussman places both our active and passive powers, our powers to do and to suffer, under the title of "agency"; only thus can my undergoing something be thought of as me *doing* something to myself. The justification for this, if there is one, is that on the Kantian construal of pain, it is an imperative to do something to change one's state; as an issuer of imperatives, it belongs to the rational structure of the will; pain immediately engages the will—"This should not be"—prior to deliberation or reflection. But it is just the immediacy of pain's moving the will that makes thinking of pain as a component of agency untoward; pain moves me as I naturally need to be moved, but my immediate and spontaneous actions from pain are not exemplars of self-determination; if anything counts as my being moved to act independently of reflective reasons for acting, it is acting on the basis of extreme pain. So immediate is pain's effect on the will, that what we must learn is to control our expressive outbursts and flailing behavior, to not let pain rule utterly. Pain typically displaces rational agency.

Second, Sussman attempts to build the structure of self-betrayal on pain's aversiveness, its being a sense of my body attacking me in ways that simultaneously constrict or undo my powers of agency. This short-circuits the role of the body. My suggestion in considering tickling was that the negative moment kicks in when the revelation of a stratum of embodiment is revealed as involuntary, and thus as "me but not mine." It is a surprising discovery that the slightest touch, with a feather, can set the body loose from rational control. But the notion of control is only a factual feature of the mineness of my body: it is something I can control to "this" extent, but it contains dimensions of not just resistance to control ("I'll never manage the fingering for that tune"), but involuntariness. Strata of involuntariness are at the same time dimensions of vulnerability: what I cannot control opens me to the control of another. Consider, for example, the depth of dispossession suffered by having to rely on the permission of another in order to go to the bathroom. Here the issue is not the fact of control over the body, but the relation between my vulnerability and the lack of my having normative authority over my body. My physical vulnerability reveals the limits of my moral authority: I can control my body only if it is recognized as mine. The mineness of my body intertwines bodily autonomy with bodily integrity; the moral harm of the intentional infliction of pain transgresses bodily autonomy by transgressing bodily integrity. Every intentional infliction of pain—every punch, kick, slap, or shove—is a small moral injury, an insult, because something in one's standing as indexed by one's bodily integrity has been crossed. How stinging and humiliating even a slap on the face can be, or being spat upon—even a drink thrown in the face. Even minor acts of breaching bodily integrity, even when done in humor, can carry degrading significance. Torture victims are often stripped naked both to make explicit their vulnerable helplessness, a humiliation in itself, and to make evident that every portion of their body is available for violation by the torturer. Being stripped naked is already dispossession, and everyone knows it.

If, for a Kantian, dignity equals the power of rational self-governance, then it just seems wrong to say that torture involves "turning our dignity against itself" (WWT, 19). Torture is destructive of human dignity, but it does not obviously turn the power of rational self-governance against itself through manipulation of the body. It transgresses bodily integrity under conditions in which bodily autonomy—the right of bodily self-control and self-movement—has already been removed. The stakes are not coercing the victim into self-betrayal—although self-betrayal occurs—but *dispossession*. Again, as children know, pain can be used to get someone to quickly say something against her will. The quickness of routine playground cases of fast torture—"Say uncle!"—suppresses the structural issue—namely that the rational will is dependent on the other for its independence in the first instance. What the duration of torture accomplishes is not only the psychological breaking of the victim, revealing to him time and again that he possesses no powers of resistance, but, further, the revelation that his will has *always* belonged to the social other whose place is now occupied by the torturer—the anti-man, the counter-man. It is the *relationality of the autonomous will*, the relationality of my personhood itself, that is exploited in torture: because we are second persons as a condition of our being first persons, then torture is the mechanism whereby we are forced back into the position of being a second person without the prerogatives of being a first person. That is, through the systematic infliction of pain under conditions of helplessness, the victim's voluntary body is severed from his involuntary body, dispossessing him of bodily autonomy, and thereby of moral standing. In torture, I do not so much betray myself as discover myself as always already betrayed, always already in the grip of another, unable to be myself for myself.

Torture could not be injurious in the way it is, a profound attack on the dignity of another, unless it did, indeed, exploit the structure of dignity. What is exploited, however, is the almost always suppressed dependence of the rational will on what appears as external to it: my standing as an end-in-itself is *a status I am given by the other*, just as the status of my body as mine, as a first property, is a state achieved in tandem with its being socially bestowed. Sussman locates human dignity too directly in the power of rational agency itself, which leads him to think of the problem of torture as a perversion of a mechanism, the agent-body being used against itself, rather than the traducing of a status that is both bodily and intersubjective. The process of pain infliction under conditions of helplessness is how, as a physical act, it is a spiritual act of traducing. The physical capitulation is entwined with a spiritual capitulation because the act of pain infliction in that setting both is and expresses the judgment of the victim's lack of standing as a person.

The moral harm of torture and rape is that they are devastating, a destruction of personhood through severing the voluntary body from the involuntary body and leaving the victim with only her involuntary body. This severance—accomplished through bodily invasion and the infliction of pain under conditions of helplessness—is the radical dispossession of the self from itself, and hence its utter discounting, devaluation and degradation.

What now of the claim that torture is a paradigm case of moral harm? Let me begin here with a word about justified killing. From the growing numbers of soldiers suffering from post-traumatic stress disorder and from the standard treatment of police personnel involved in shootings, there is strong evidence that even when acts of killing are morally justified, they are nonetheless routinely experienced as somehow inhuman, polluting.[62] We also know that the more intimate the kill, the more the victim has a recognizable face, the higher the rate of retrospective distress. Place these two claims together: the awfulness of killing is not that one has broken a moral rule—even a very internalized moral rule with religious origins and the whole weight of the super-ego backing it—because, first, the rule is against murder, not killing in self-defense, and second, even if the rule were against killing, the role of intimacy demonstrates that it is not the mere fact of having killed that is at issue. My hypothesis is that even justified killing is routinely experienced as somehow degrading to the perpetrator because the experience is one of ignoring or crashing through the moral boundary that is the simultaneously visible sense of the intrinsic worth of each human body and face; killing literally rips into the fabric of human worth through ripping into the body bearing it. Part of what is thus so obliterated is the value, worth, meaning of the human itself—of course only as embodied in this particular dangerous individual, an enemy, but still a being recognizably human, and as such exemplifying the human status. For good reason military leaders attempt to instill in their troops beliefs about the nonhumanity—the bestiality or animality or verminlike character—of the enemy. The human status is realized in each instance of the human, at least for us modern universalists. Justifications for killing are rules that override the claim of intrinsic value for some particular realization of that status; justifications for killing are products of the reflective comprehension of a context of danger: the more dangerous and threatening the context, the more justified the kill, so that even innocents can be justifiably killed. The rationales and justifications for killing are real enough; the fact that they are reflective does not entail that they do not impinge on some practical necessity. Nonetheless, the gap between the reflective rationale and the concrete act is abysmal: reasoning cannot close the gap between reason and event. Even a justified killing violates the human status of the individual killed, discounts it, counts it as here to be discounted.

Killing takes a life; torture and rape injure a life but leave it living. Yet the prohibitions against torture and rape are more stringent than those against killing. By hypothesizing that even justified killing is, as we might say, tragic, a destruction of something intrinsically valuable for contextually justified overriding reasons, I was trying to both make the account of killing converge with the general shape of my account of the moral injury of rape and torture and set up terms of moral comparison. Justified killing involves overriding the claim of the human status of the victim; if overriding must occur, if the status must be put aside, then the cleanest, fastest, most pain-free method must be preferable for both victim and killer. Killing cleanly and quickly honors the victim in the act of destroying him, while "purifying" the act itself as far as possible; killing without degrading respects the victim's standing while preserving insofar as possible for the killer his sense that the human status itself remains unaffected by his killing. For many if not most ordinary moral agents, no insulation is sufficient to protect them from the sense that the human status itself has been harmed in their killing act.

This is sufficient to demonstrate the extra quanta of moral heinousness in rape and torture. The short way with the argument is that, all things being equal, killing in self-defense overrides the human status of the victim but does not require devaluing, degrading, dehumanizing, undoing that status. A justified killing can at least claim to respect the enemy; historically, war enemies have even honored one another in death. Torture and rape are otherwise: they depend upon undoing the human standing of the victim, of removing her from the domain of beings deserving of human treatment. Killing, at its best, severs an insupportable relation; rape and torture are relations whose very dynamic requires the transformation of the relationship as a fully human one into something else: a relation between human and subhuman, say; they are relations whose terms require that the victim be shown that her standing as human is insupportable and unsustainable. Torture and rape are paradigm cases of moral harm because they are enduring and repeatable forms of human encounter in which one of its members dismantles the fabric of the human status of the victim by not merely overriding it, but by separating the living being from her bodily autonomy and integrity—her dignity.

My effort in this chapter has been to begin revealing how the physical and moral body are fused, how they are internally connected aspects of a complex unity. Rapist and torturer understand this fusion perfectly, since their perpetual effort is its separation into its constituent parts, to have the physical human remain, but without its standing or value as fully human, while their own standing as human becomes thereby inviolable—sovereign. (This should make us worry that the very idea of the human status as inviolable, although intended as an effort of raising and protecting, is, finally, a product of a form of mastery and domination over the living embodied being housing the inviolable core.) Rape and torture are, I have suggested, efforts of self-repudiation and abjection—a wild projecting of the whole of bodily involuntariness, the whole of the suffering body onto the victim.

What makes the effort of degradation possible in cases of rape and torture is that the human standing is compromised, conditioned from the inside. Our shorthand for this thesis is that first persons are second persons. Our standing as human is bestowed on us and remains dependent on relevant social others for its maintenance. Killing's awfulness for the killer acknowledges this fact, but killing itself does not exploit it. Rape and torture render the victim existentially helpless; their helplessness is the emphatic statement of their dependence, of their being utterly dependent for their human standing on this very one who is now not recognizing them, whose actions shred the fabric of bodily integrity through invasion or the intentional infliction of pain. We are not just, as a matter of fact, vulnerable before the depredations of others; in rape and torture we discover that we are categorically vulnerable, vulnerable in the very core of our standing as human. It is unsurprising that the raped and the tortured stay raped and tortured, or that they lose forever their trust in the world.

PART TWO

Constructing Moral Dignity

FOUR

To Be Is to Live,
to Be Is to Be Recognized

I. Introduction

Modernity begins in devastation, not the devastations of war or genocide or natural disaster, but in the recognition of sovereign torture as devastating to its victims, and hence as devastating in a new manner—namely as an undoing of their status as human, as persons. The recognition that to be human is to be capable of suffering devastation is the suppressed moral premise undergirding the emergence of the rule of law as the determinate negation of the sovereign law of torture, a premise that may or may not have been explicitly operative in the abolition of torture, but that has become explicit in our collective understanding of the meaning of torture and rape. Torture and rape are paradigm moral injuries because they are extreme versions of moral harm that reveal that the fundamental stakes of moral life concern the acknowledgment, or failure of acknowledgment, of individuals *as* persons, as having a certain standing or status that is intrinsic to what such a person is for herself in relation to others.

Standard moral theories—with their guiding ideas of autonomy, pleasure and pain, flourishing, and virtue, which are intended to tell agents what they *ought* to do—come nowhere near addressing the types of harm suffered in the two paradigm cases of wrongful violence, cases that are pivotal for our individual and collective self-understanding. Rape and torture require a thicker, more complex conception of what makes human lives injurable by human others, one which brings into view our standing for ourselves in relation to others as human. As should anyway have been evident from the long histories of slavery, racism, and misogyny, significant moral wrongdoing routinely involves the denial of the other's standing as either "like me" or "like us," and thereby as not deserving of (approximately) equal treatment. Such wrongdoings have always been cruel, degrading, humiliating, devastating, soul murder. While wrongdoing, as moralists keep harping on about, would not occur without heavy doses of selfishness, egoism, self-interest, greed, lust, and all those other self-absorbed vices, what those affects and inclinations do is blind the agent in question, temporarily or permanently, to the worth or standing of (some) others. But the long history of moral injury and suffering also tells us that narrow motives are rarely the full issue in extreme cases of forms of social suffering. To understand wrongdoing is first to understand what it does, what moral injury and moral suffering are, and hence why we have moral cares and concerns at all, rather than fixating on how best to chastise and control (potential) wrongdoers, which is done the way it always has been: by teaching, training, habituating, educating, and civilizing, and where they fail, by constraining and excluding.

To comprehend moral injury out of its exemplary instances sets the question that the remainder of this study must answer: What is the nature of the human such that it can suffer the harms of humiliation and devastation? Answering this question will immanently intrigue the requisite conception of morals.

The analysis of the moral harm of rape and torture implies a schematic outline of what elements must be included within a plausible account of the possibility of devastation:

- Because rape and torture deploy the body of the victim against her, then the human must be an essentially living and embodied being who stands in a relation to her body in a manner that makes dispossession possible; not a mere injuring of the body, but a transformation in the victim's relation to her body as a transformation in her relation to herself as a person is at stake.
- In order for dispossession to be possible, the human must be an essentially living being—subject to pain, death, and thus the requirements of the ongoing maintenance of its living form—and "more than" a living being, a being who stands in some particular relation to its life. The "more than" of a living being denotes the manner in which human life departs from being ordered by the laws of nature to become (relatively) self-ordering, to become the life-form of, to name some obvious candidates, cultural or social beings, norm-mongering or cooperative beings, linguistic or rational beings, self-conscious or free beings. From the perspective adopted here, these alternative formulations will be treated as mutually re-enforcing elements.
- In order for dispossession to be devastating the (social, rational, self-conscious) capacities through which a more-than-living being takes up a

relation to her living body must involve more than the mere exercise of those capacities; the possession of those capacities must be an ingredient in her self-understanding, such that they provide her with some standing, status, or worth that is taken to be intrinsic to who she is for herself and for (relevant) others.

· Minimally then, a being capable of devastation must be a self-interpreting being whose self-conception—*how* she understands herself—is in part essential to what she *is* as a living and more-than-living being. Human beings are the kinds of beings who by *taking* themselves to be essentially of a certain kind—as essentially members of a certain family, tribe, clan, nationality; as God-made souls; as philosophers, plumbers, policemen; as essentially male or female—*are*, in part, essentially that kind. One can only be dispossessed of an essential standing by a violent form of practice if that standing is one that one takes oneself to have and is subject not just to outright destruction, but also ruination.

· But dispossession and ruination at the hands of the other could not occur unless the standing or status one takes oneself to possess is in some manner essentially dependent on the treatment of others, on their endowing or acknowledging or sustaining that standing. Who one is for oneself must be essentially dependent on others.

· Loss of standing or status amounting to devastation is marked by loss of trust in the world. This presupposes that trust in the world is internally related to status and standing in a manner in which having trust is in part constitutive of an individual's relation to others.

It is because we are naturally and normatively in our standing and status as persons dependent beings that we are subject to devastation. Devastation, as the continuance of an original moral injury, is the reverse side of the fact that we are constitutively normative beings who are dependent on others for the maintenance and sustaining of our normative standing for ourselves. In more pedestrian terms, trauma is not only a type of breakage of ordinary psychological functioning, although it is certainly that; it is the undoing of the constitutive normative relations binding self and other, and hence the undoing of the normative presuppositions through which ordinary psychological functioning transpires.[1] Psychic life is the life of an essentially normatively constituted, dependent being; when the normative presuppositions of ordinary life collapse, so too will the psychological functions processing them.

My term for the constitutive, physical, and normative dependency of the human is existential helplessness; it was the experience of having their existential helplessness revealed and exploited that occasioned both Améry's and Brison's devastations. The only account of dependency and existential helplessness of which I am aware that does justice to its scope and depth occurs in theories of recognition that take up Hegel's claim in *Phenomenology of Spirit* that "self-consciousness exists in and for itself by way of its existing in and for itself for an other, i.e., *it exists only as a recognized being.*"[2] Or to put it another way, "A self-consciousness exists for a self-consciousness. Only thereby does self-consciousness in fact exist, for it is only therein that the unity of itself in its otherness comes to be for it."[3] My interest in what follows is not Hegel scholarship, but solely the elaboration of the bare rudiments of a conception of self-consciousness as mediated through, and so dependent on, the recognition of others sufficient for the explanation of the possibility of devastation as thus far conceptualized.

A theory of recognition adequate to the explanation of the possibility of devastation must elaborate our constitutive normative dependency on others in a manner that simultaneously captures our being living beings who are more than living beings. Judith Butler suggests a perspicuous way of weaving these two thoughts together: "It was Spinoza who claimed that every human being seeks to persist in his own being, and he made this principle of self-persistence, the *conatus*, into the basis of his ethics and, indeed, his politics. When Hegel made the claim that desire is always a desire for recognition, he was, in a way, extrapolating upon this Spinozistic point, telling us, effectively, that to persist in one's own being is only possible on the condition that we are engaged in receiving and offering recognition. If we are not recognizable, if there are no norms of recognition by which we are recognizable, then it is not possible to persist in one's own being, and we are not possible beings . . . Norms of recognition function to produce and to deproduce the notion of the human."[4] Human beings can only satisfy their desire to be—which elsewhere in nature occurs as the desire for self-preservation or the desire for life—through the satisfaction of the desire to be recognized, since only through being recognized can they have a standing or status of being a person and thereby a place in a social world, where having a recognized place in a social world is a necessary condition for *living* a human life. Because recognition is a normatively contoured social practice, one can only be recognized if one is recognizable in accordance with operative social norms, in whole or in part. The standing desire for recognition is equivalent to the desire to have one's standing as a self-consciousness, as a person, as one of us with a particular social identity, recognized; hence the desire to *persist* becomes the desire to persist in one's social identity. Being able to persist in a recognized social identity is to be able to live (a human life). Because recognition is a social achievement, it comes in degrees, is never pure, and lacks any final terminus. The desire for recognition is the ground desire to live a human life.

This is a surprising claim since it states that humans are overwhelmingly motivated by a desire that most persons would probably deny they have ever experienced, and that almost all philosophy and human psychology to date has blithely ignored. How can the desire for recognition be the ground desire to live a human life and yet have passed virtually unnoticed in the history of thought? A plausible account of recognition must simultaneously account for its virtual invisibility to most social agents and their observers.

In the previous chapter, the demand for recognition was presented as a certain inflection of Kant's idea of the demand to treat others as ends-in-themselves, and hence as a further elaboration of modern moral rationalism. In opposition to this rationalist way of proceeding, I am here pursuing the thought that the appropriate space for a theory of self-consciousness in terms of recognition is as a socialized naturalism, a consideration of human life as a form of animal life, a manner or mode of living an animal life. In the next sections, I will present a narrow and somewhat formal argument for this conclusion that concerns simply the question of the nature of self-consciousness, where self-consciousness is taken as one of the names for the human self or subject. In the following sections, I argue that not only is a relation to its being alive an essential component of such a self-consciousness (section II), but that a self-consciousness is a particular formation of animal embodiment, making some version of bodily autonomy a necessary condition for a human life (section IV). In the final section of the chapter, I offer a first pass at demonstrating how and why we should consider moral practices as a particular inflection of living, thus offering a way of making the transition from life-form to form of life, from *zoe* to *bios*, from nature to second nature in a manner that fully sustains the significance of our being embodied living creatures who must structure their lives together through normative practices of recognition. Although some of the materials necessary to demonstrate the possibility of devastation will be here put in place, it will take the realization of relations of recognition in practices of trust examined in the next chapter to complete the task. Chapter 6 will then be able to demonstrate that, in fact, the core terms of our moral psychology—dignity, respect, self-respect, et al.—are best understood in terms of relations of recognition, completing the task of answering the charge concerning invisibility begun in the analysis of trust.

II. To Be Is to Be Recognized

For our purposes, an adequate conception of self-consciousness—that is, what is involved in being a relatively self-determining human adult—must place together four weighty claims:

(a) Human beings are natural beings whose mode of living makes essential reference to their being living organisms whose lives are fundamentally akin to other animal lives.

(b) Human beings are not social beings simply as a matter of fact—hanging out together because we are gregarious or enjoy company or discover cooperative behavior is a necessary means for individual survival; rather, our being social beings belongs to our intrinsic nature.

(c) In light of (b), human beings are not just contingently, but constitutively dependent beings, whose very being *as* human—as more than living—depends in some structural way on how others regard and treat them.

(d) The way in which items (a)–(c) are articulated must itself coordinate in some essential way with those capacities for linguistic communication, rational thought, and cooperative social practices that have traditionally been regarded as what distinguish the human as human.

My narrow argument for considering relations of recognition as the manner in which essentially social beings *live* follows the path set out in Robert B. Brandom's "The Structure of Desire and Recognition: Self-Consciousness and Self-Constitution."[5] Brandom's account is useful for my purposes because he attempts to leverage a conception of recognition from materials descriptive of non-self-conscious animal living; self-consciousness takes over, so to speak, the structure of animal living, transforming it into the human form of social living through recognition. Self-consciousness is not added on to the protointentional structure of animal life, but rather constitutively transforms it such that the primary elements of protointentional animal life disappear into—are canceled and preserved in, sublated by (to use a Hegelian term of art)—the intentional life of self-conscious agency.[6] The thought here is not that human self-consciousness overcomes its animal origins—the preserving is even more important than the canceling; rather, the specificity of what makes us uniquely human, human subjectivity itself, is structured, contoured, given salient shape and meaning by the structure of animal living from which it originates. I am tempted to say that what is more than animal living in the human is nonetheless a mode of animal living.

Animal lives have their distinct shape through animal activities, and animal activities have their distinct shape through animal desires. Desires are
the springs of animal action; different animal desires—for nutrition, safety,
reproduction, warmth, etc.—structure the different action routines composing an animal life. Desire institutes an original mapping of the world of
the living animal, giving it practical meaning and salience with respect to
the overriding needs and prerequisites of animal life; the animal perceives
and negotiates its world as the internal correlate of the desires that move
it to action. Desires must then be understood as practically classifying and
ordering the animal world such that each item in it shows up in relation to
its character as potentially satisfying, not satisfying, or inhibiting the desire
in question. All this is to say that we can think of an animal's perceptual
takings of the world as structured by its desires, the world thus appearing
to the animal as articulated and contoured by its desires. Perceiving the
world from the perspective of its capacity to satisfy or block the satisfaction
of desires is the first installment of what we call a *subjective* perspective: the
animal's world is *its* world because the world surges up as meaningful, *as* a
world or habitat, solely with respect to what the animal needs from it. This
world is meaningful *for* the animal.

But this world should not be considered as narrowly subjective, a mere
appearing to the animal in the light of its longings, as every gamboling
lamb appears as a lamb chop in the balloon above the head of cartoon
wolves. Animals are necessarily invested in the reality of their subjective
takings since those objects must satisfy real needs and desires. Because actions mediate between the animal's desire and the object satisfying it in the
world, animal life opens up a distinction between appearance and reality:
how something *subjectively* appears in the light of a desire, as food to be
eaten, for example, is *objectively* confirmed if the eating of the object satisfies the desire, and is disconfirmed if it does not (not a lamb at all but a
disgusting fluffy poodle). The distinction between appearance and reality
is fundamental to animal life because the animal's world is structured from
the perspective of subjective desire, but the satisfying of those desires is a
matter of necessity for the animal's survival. One primary way of speaking
about animal action is thus to say that its effort of testing the reality of
a subjective taking is the first delineation of a concern for squaring how
things appear with how they are in the world, where the desire for squaring
or reconciling how things appear with how they are is the precise structural
meaning of how desire and action are internally related. Analogously, action must be conceived not merely as the "effect" of a desiring motive, but
as an ongoing means for mediating between appearance and reality, as a

junction in a feedback loop connecting the animal's inner life to the recalcitrant structures of the world. Thus, however instinctually programmed animals are to follow their multiple action routines, the diversity of those routines, the persistence shown by animals in executing them, the variability in their execution, and animals' capacity to distinguish between subjective significance and objective reality (and learn from it) makes considering action routines as brute causal sequences inapt.[7]

In light of animal desire classifying the world in practically significant ways, it makes sense to think of animal activities as purposive and thus protointentional. In reading animal actions in light of their precipitating desires, we attribute to them a meaningfulness: if an object is of significance in light of the desire that classifies it, then an action springing from that desire is one that *takes the object as something*, to be eaten or avoided, say. Eating is a way of taking something *as* food, just as fleeing is a way of taking another animal *as* a predator. Animal actions are primitive interpretations of the world that can be falsified through what they beget. Because desire is the starting point for animal activities—practically classifying the world in relation to necessary action routines—Brandom, with sly amusement, terms the relation among *attitude* (desire), responsive *activity*, and *significance* (what an object appears *as*: food, shelter, threat) the "tripartite structure of erotic awareness."

Brandom's forwarding of the tripartite structure of erotic awareness as the clue to the nature of self-consciousness derives from an attempt to make sense of Hegel's puzzling statement that "self-consciousness is *desire* itself."[8] In context, it is evident that Hegel is wanting to place self-consciousness—each subject's awareness of itself in its actions and judgments, actions and judgments taken as necessarily and inevitably *mine*, each subject's ability to say "I," the "I think" that Kant thinks must accompany all my representations since otherwise they would mean nothing *to me*—this sense of self-consciousness must be considered as a certain development of animal desire and action. There can be no significant mineness to how the world appears other than through the practical mineness or subjectivity that is a result of perceiving the world from the perspective of desire; desiring introduces a subjective orientation on to the world, yielding a being who the world is for and the world as an orderly structure of significances as what is seen from the perspective of that being. The thought of self-conscious subjectivity requires a space between how the world is for that subject and how the world is in itself that requires their continuing coordination such that the practical meaning of the world is the consequence of the continuous squaring of desire and reality through action.

The language of human knowing and the language of self-consciousness only make sense in the first instance from the point of view of practical striving, of being in the world as a creature needing to act in and on the world in order to survive at all.

In saying that "self-consciousness is desire itself," Hegel is, at least, meaning to institute this practical turn in the understanding of the nature of self-consciousness.[9] He is further, at least, commenting on the inevitable disparity between how things subjectively appear and how things objectively are for desiring beings, and further how the movement of action, in testing the reality of each subjective taking of how things as desired appear, is also thereby a movement striving for an integration and unification between appearance and reality, with satisfaction functioning as a criterion of objectivity and dissatisfaction functioning as a criterion for what is false or illusory. Striving for and seeking to achieve such a unification between appearance and reality, which might seem as if it were the highest and most lofty of theoretical pursuits, only becomes intelligible as the movement of a being possessed of an erotic structure, a movement that applies simply to animal lives and more complexly to self-conscious ones.

Hegel is thus urging that human mindedness should be understood from the direction of erotic striving rather than godly contemplation, as biologically practical rather than brain-in-a-vat theoretical, and hence that something in the manner of the tripartite structure of erotic awareness orienting animal life must itself be structural for human self-consciousness. There is a long history in which getting the analysis of the structure of animal awareness correct has been unconvincingly contested, swiveling haplessly between the reductively causal (animals as machines or automata) and the anthropomorphically inflated—as if there were no structural space between mechanism (body) and consciousness (mind). The debate about animal awareness has been useless because the premise of the debate is that there is no in-itself of animal awareness, only either human awareness or the nothing of what is mechanically determined. The implausible character of the debate about the nature of animal consciousness is thus a consequence of an implausible metaphysics in which mechanism and consciousness, *res extensa* and *res cogitans*, sweeps all before it, as if there were no life, no living things, no creatures with their own nature. Hegel insists on the great Aristotelian (Schellingian) reminder: if the possession of self-consciousness is not to be a piece of creation out of nothing, then life itself, and in particular animal life, requires separate acknowledgment, a separate accounting that permits ontological magic to be avoided. But if this thought is to do any philosophical work in making some aspects of human self-consciousness and subjectivity intelligible, then something in the character of animal awareness must be essential for being a human self or subject. Brandom is arguing that to be a subject is to be "something things can be something *for* . . . [that is,] a *desiring* animal, a subject of erotic awareness, an institutor of erotic significances, an assessor of the consilience or disparity of what things are *for* it or subjectively and what they are *in* themselves or objectively, the subject of the experience of *error* and the cyclical feedback process of revision-and-experiment it initiates and guides" (SDR, 34). All these features open the kind of space necessary for human self-consciousness.

Now—and this is Brandom's elegant insight—when Hegel states that "self-consciousness is *desire* itself," he must be using the structure of erotic awareness not only to open up the structure of self-consciousness; he is meaning to say that self-consciousness is a version and development of the tripartite structure of erotic awareness—namely one in which this erotic structure enters the analysis twice: first as subject of awareness, then as object of awareness—a being possessed of an erotic awareness becoming aware of another like being. Roughly, then, what is wanted is a story in which the erotic significance of a particular object for a desiring subject is that of being an object possessing an erotic structure of awareness; so the account of self-consciousness is to be arrived at through an account of the erotic awareness of a being coming to awareness of the erotic structure of awareness. In this account, the tripartite structure of erotic awareness is to occur as both subject and object; thus the object possessing the significance of being possessed of the tripartite structure of erotic significance could be either a different object or the apprehending subject itself. Comprehending the tripartite structure of erotic awareness in both the subject and object position should thus be a way of turning desire itself (i.e., the tripartite structure of erotic awareness) quite literally into self-consciousness. In order, then, for self-consciousness to be desire itself, it must be a being that not only *exhibits* the tripartite structure of erotic awareness, but equally one that has that significance for itself—that is, it must *take* itself to be a being governed by the structure of erotic awareness in which its subjective takings of how things are make a *claim* to authoritativeness generally, recalling that for a desiring being, its taking of the world to be thus-and-so is a subjectively ordered claim as to how things really are (SDR, 38).

Two questions arise here: First, what *actions* must a subject take in order that those actions involve treating an object of its awareness as possessing the tripartite structure of erotic awareness in the same way that *eating* is the action that treats objects as *food*? Second, what *desire* motivates the "*activ-*

ity and *assesses* the *success* of taking something *as* having the erotic significance of being," something possessed of the structure of erotic awareness? (SDR, 39) Because the presumption is that self-consciousness is structured through desire and action, then the relevant questions about the institution and apprehension of that structure can only be: what *actions* in the world interpret their objects as possessing that structure, and what must a subject *desire* when it desires to act toward an object in a way that takes that object to be one possessing an erotic manner of world apprehension?

Hegel answers these questions in an unexpected way: one can only *take* another being as essentially a being who itself institutes erotic significances by striving to have her take you to be a being who institutes erotic significances; that is, the erotic structure of awareness must itself become thematic as orienting your taking of another, and it can do so only if you solicit or summon the other to take you as a taker, take you as an authoritative institutor of erotic significances. This is what Hegel means by the desire for recognition; it is the desire that the other, who is herself taken as an institutor of erotic significances, recognize (and so desire) your desires as authoritatively instituting erotic significances. Almost everything that is central to this argument—the shift from natural to explicitly normative and the simultaneous shift from essentially solitary beings pursuing their own ends to essentially interdependent beings—funnels through the idea that self-consciousness emerges in and through the institutor of erotic significances becoming *authoritative*, its desiring-significances taking on a certain normative authority because they stem from a being possessing that authority. So, of a sudden, the standing or status of the institutor becomes the focal issue.

Because erotic significances are practical commitments about the meaning of objects and how they are to be treated, then another counts as treating you as an institutor of erotic significances only if she treats the actions that express your assessment and evaluation of what things are in light of how they appear to you as (prima facie) *authoritative* for her. The claim to *authority*—the claim that in erotically perceiving S as P, you are perceiving S as it *ought* to be perceived, and hence your inclination to issue judgments of the form "S *is* P"—is what becomes of the idea of being an institutor of erotic significances when they are not just acted on, the desire moving the subject to action, but made thematic, the erotic commitment to taking the world as "this way" and "not that way" becoming a claim as to how things are in the world. You do not just take the apple to be edible, but claim it is edible (to the other); the claim is the making self-conscious and explicit the original taking as one to which you are committed—commitments being an essential mechanism through which takings are made into claims. Your commitment to your claim, your holding it as something to which you are committed, expresses not subjective certainty, but a claim to correctness. Because objective correctness is at stake, your standing as an institutor of erotic significances is realized if you can get the other to recognize your authority, if you can get her to eat the apple because you have just taken a bite from it, where taking a bite and handing her the apple intends the thought "This apple is edible such that if you desire something edible, then you should take a bite from this apple." Behind this purely objective talk lies an erotic structure in which I am proposing my desire as *authoritative* for your desiring: you should desire the apple because I desire it, and so, finally you should desire my desire.[10] As we shall see, if in particular cases the test of satisfaction keeps the recognition of authority empirically constrained, no such constraint underpins the ongoing constitution of authority through recognition; that is why the wild and abysmal business of you desiring that I desire your desire in its stark purity—call it the demand for love—cannot be circumvented.

Again, what makes an individual an institutor of erotic significances is that she has desires that take objects to have a significance with respect to what would *satisfy* those desires; the test of satisfaction is what prevents the demand to desire my desire from being vacuous. In this regard, animals are already unselfconscious authorities as to the meaning of things. Further, since an erotic significance is effectively a *commitment* about the meaning of an object that is tested through action, then validity and truth, as the unification of appearance and reality through action, are implicitly already at stake in animal strivings. The implicit structure of commitment becomes explicit as a claim when I strive to have another institutor of erotic significances take my striving activity as authoritative for her striving. This is the momentous shift whereby the natural becomes explicitly normative, which it can do since it was already implicitly normative: my simple animal desiring is already a *commitment* about the objective meaning of an object, what it is not just for me, but in itself; commitments are the existential source of what become intersubjective claims. As we shall see more fully below, mimetic activity is exemplary here: in mimetically taking a bite of the apple after you have already done so and then handed it to me, I am taking your action of eating as authoritative for the meaning of the apple—which is why I eat it. Adam recognizes Eve as an authority about apples, and Eve recognizes Adam as capable of recognizing her authority. Adam and Eve mutually recognize one another. Their act is one of eating from the tree of *knowledge* because in it they each recognize the other as an authoritative institutor of erotic significances; in so recognizing one another they are, through their successful eating, establishing an objective truth about the edibility and so goodness of apples (for them). This knowledge, however, arises erotically: each desires that the other desires what they desire, and hence, finally, desires their desire. Knowing and desiring another's desire emerge together.

One might also state the mimetic claim this way: Eve's eating and handing the apple to Adam is meant to give him *a reason* to take a bite from it. Treating actions as interpretations where the agent is a presumptive authoritative issuer of significances just means that the agent's actions give others grounds or reasons for treating the object of that action the same. Reasons, it might be said, are what happens to erotic significances when they are authorized and so made explicitly normative, and reasoning is the way in which we support and challenge these authorized significances under the auspices of the requirement for unifying, and so squaring, appearance and reality. This way of thinking about actions explains the thesis of expressive universalism that states that we should treat each human action as legislative, as a norm-instituting claim as to what the appropriate action in "this" context is, how "this" object *should* be treated, and hence as a claim as to the correct evaluation of the object of the action. It is now evident that doing so involves treating human actions as (contestable) claims to authority. Expressive universalism is in this respect a partial delineation of the logic of ethical action from the perspective of beings who take themselves to be authoritative institutors of erotic significances.

When Eve hands Adam the apple and he accepts, and Eve accepts his acceptance as a token of her authority and of his power to authorize her authority, then their *joint action* makes them a "we"—a couple or community. Generally, on this account acknowledging that another has some general authority over how things are and, further, that we have the authority to authorize her authority is the mechanism through which the other is recognized as one of "us"; membership in a community *is* being recognized as possessing routine authority to institute (and challenge) erotic significances (SDR, 44), and membership in a community has until recently been the fundamental mechanism through which recognitions have been achieved, secured, and distributed. The very acts of mutual recognition that make us a "we" do so only because and insofar as they make each participant an "I," an authorized institutor of significances. One sense of a normative community is as a collective of authorized authorities, where each member has been authorized by relevant others as having the power to authorize the standing of every relevant other (either equally or unequally).

The focus on claim-making can be thought to hide rather than reveal the structure of recognition governing it, since the authority of claims ultimately depends on the commitments those claims express, not on the person who articulates them; that is, one could imagine these apple exchanges occurring in a manner never raising, nor needing to raise, the issue about one's desire being authoritative for another's desire—the underlying normative structure of such exchanges can remain hidden or suppressed.[11] In order for the appropriate underlying structure to become visible, all that is required is a small extension of the Adam and Eve story. Imagine that Adam keeps munching away on the apple, ignoring Eve altogether; in response, Eve becomes furious, demanding another bite of the apple. In response to this Adam does nothing; he just keeps munching away. In his indifference to Eve's anger, Adam has effectively voided the anger, emptied it of meaning to such an extent that it no longer appears as an unproblematic episode of *anger* (at him); by acting as if nothing were occurring, Adam has voided Eve's human presence to him. In this case, Eve's desire that Adam desire her desire no longer turns on the edibility of apples as an external constraint; there is just her desire itself—that is, the demand that Adam recognize her anger as lodging a demand for a response in kind, be it contrition or justification or angry retort. Nothing is at stake here other than Eve's standing as one whose claims—angers, hurts, words, needs, desires—*count because she counts*. Unless Eve can matter in this way to Adam, her claims about apples cannot *humanly* matter either. Eve's original eating and handing over the apple might have been, after all, like a lackey tasting food for her king—providing bald empirical evidence for the food's not being poisoned. For that episode to bear the weight of a recognition of authority, *she* must be recognized as the kind of being who can lodge authoritative claims. Recognizing her in this way is what raises the exchange from sharing information about the environment, as animals do, to a human exchange of normative claims. Claiming, however much leveraged by reliable exchanges of information becoming trustworthy sources of advice and counsel, all geared to surviving mutually dependent lives (that is what squaring appearance and reality accomplishes, after all), thus rests, finally, on the *pure* recognition of the other as a self-consciousness.

This shows that the original apple story is incomplete; although Adam and Eve do indeed treat one another as erotically aware, there is as yet no evidence that either is aware of this awareness, self-aware; while they act appropriately toward one another as self-conscious beings, nothing in their behavior demonstrates that they are aware that their *taking* claims *as authoritative* rather than practically useful is essential to them. Hence, neither is yet fully self-conscious. Equally, there is no reason to suppose that they are aware of themselves as instantiating a unique "we" structure that exceeds their individual sayings and doings over the apple business; joint actions— eating the apple because the other did so—can appear as a series of in- dividual actions to the participants.[12] We can begin getting the required further thought into focus by first noting that the difference between being an animal *taker* of significances and a human one is that a human must take her own takings *as* authoritative claims; hence she must take herself as a being who possesses the authority to lodge objective claims to which she is thus committed, and in light of that commitment required to do those actions that would *support* that commitment to relevant others. But demonstrating the fact and depth of commitments is insufficient unless that demonstrating somehow turns back toward the individual in a man- ner that reveals her instituting authority itself, and hence the way *she is staked on her authority to make claims*, thereby making the normativity of her previous doings explicit (without which, finally, there is no normativity). The idea that one's authority to make claims stakes one to that authority such that it becomes the essential component of one's self-understanding is worked out in Hegel's thesis that in order to demonstrate that one *is* a self-consciousness requires the risk of life, the risk of everything for the sake of that authority, the risk of life for the sake of being recognized as having that status and standing. I shall return to the necessity of the risk of life in the next section. My point here is to underline the inference from making claims to the entitlement to make claims such that the agent can- not claim this entitlement, this *status* for herself, other than by desiring and demanding that the other recognize this status, thus making her status objective. This is the question of authority once more. To be self-conscious of oneself *as* an authorized institutor of erotic significances is to be aware of oneself as possessing a certain status or standing. The human arises from the natural through turning the fact of instituting erotic significances into a claim that requires the claimer to have standing or status to issue claims, to issue reasons for others to act and be recognized as having the authority— the standing, status, rights, or entitlements—to do so.

Transparently, she can only take her recognition of the other seriously, the other's recognition can only *count* as a validation of her standing as in- stitutor of erotic significances, if she recognizes the other as an authoritative taker in turn. On the one hand, this implies that desire for recognition can be satisfied only if it is mutual. On the other hand, because it equally implies that her *status* as an institutor of erotic significances *depends* on the other's recognition of her authority, then her status is always in jeopardy, ready for questioning, challenging, denial, ready for exclusion and devastation. The difference between the animal and the human is that animals can be physically destroyed, but humans can also be normatively devastated—that is, humans can have their authoritative claims not only questioned, doubted, and held up to scrutiny by others (where doing so is a sign of respect for their authority), but others as recognized authorities have the power to question and deny one another's *standing generally* as authoritative institutors of significances. The upsurge of the human in the midst of the logical space of animal life occurs through the double movement whereby desires become claims, and the desiring being becomes a being with the *right* to make claims (the right to keep promises, Nietzsche would say). Although humans do, apparently, have some abilities other animals do not (or do not have in the same degree or way), the human is not to be distinguished from other animals solely through the noting of abilities; rather, it is our reflexive relation to our exercise of those abilities, our being self-conscious beings, that transforms the protonormative exercising of abilities into an explicitly normative affair: *there is no human without the claim to be human.* Typically, I will argue, in a manner that follows directly from the story of Adam and Eve, the question of standing gets played out through the rules and practices governing membership in a community: which individuals and how they are recognized as members (or not members) of a community establishes the manner through which effective authorization of individuals as self-conscious agents having the standing to authorize claims occurs.

Assume all this is broadly correct; it does not yet adequately locate the source of each person's constitutive vulnerability before the other. The issue of the necessary exposure of self to other begins, again, with the division between how the self is for itself, which is how the self desires to be, and what it is in reality, where this division itself arrives from simply taking humans to be primarily practical agents, the structure of whose agency derives from the structure of erotic awareness. Commenting on this moment of division between self-as-desired and self-in-itself, Robert Pippin states "The first hint of a practical turn [in the understanding of self-consciousness] emerges here when Hegel implies that we need to understand self-consciousness as *a unity* to be *achieved*, that there is some 'opposition' between self-consciousness and itself, a kind of self-estrangement, which . . . we are moved to overcome."[13] Pippin is pointing toward one result of self-conscious beings as having their very selves riven between how they desiringly take themselves to be and how they are in themselves; the erotic structure of consciousness both installs that divide between self-as-desired and self-in-itself, and requires its overcoming. When the object of self-consciousness is itself, then there is necessarily posited some self-conception, some self-interpretation, some particular way self-consciousness takes itself to be, the reality of which can only be established through the modes of action appropriate to having and satisfying the self-interpretation in question. A moment of self-estrangement thus becomes constitutive of self-consciousness in a manner demanding that it be overcome. To not care about that division would be to have no care or concern about who you are in virtue of what or who you take yourself to be. Perhaps this is the life of the wanton, or the Muselmann, or the self at the far end of Alzheimer's; they have lost a constitutive relation to themselves, and thus have only the force of their desires moving them. Such a being would have an animal life, but not a recognizably human one. What this reveals is the bald sense in which self-consciousness is not a piece of representational knowledge—consciousness observing itself the way it observes things in the world—but rather an ongoing movement toward whatever being unified with itself signifies for that self-consciousness: the movement to overcome self-estrangement and achieve unity is the movement to become the very meaning that self-consciousness takes or posits as what it takes itself to be—to become who you are.

All this original division at the core of self-consciousness, its original self-estrangement, and the life of striving after unity as the vindication of its original desire to be itself is fraught enough; but it is only the tip of the iceberg, since it transpires that the separation between what a self-consciousness takes itself to be and what it is in itself is at the same time a separation between that self-consciousness and its human others; the division *in* self-consciousness is also the division *between* one self-consciousness and another, entailing that the relation of a self-consciousness to itself—its striving to achieve unity between its taking and its being (where being is in part constituted by taking)—is mediated by its relation to others. It is into this very divide between self and self that the other enters: in order for a being possessed of an erotic structure of awareness to be fully self-aware, it must acknowledge that the erotically installed division between appearance and reality applies to its conception of itself; that is, it must acknowledge that there is a gap or division between its *taking* itself to be an authoritative institutor of erotic significances and its reality as such a being: the reality of being an authoritative institutor of erotic significances is made actual through being recognized and authorized. There can be no normative authority without authorization, and hence recognition. It is this that makes self-consciousness dependent on the recognition of some other institutor of erotic significances in order to close the gap between appearance and reality. Because both the desire for recognition and the dependence on the other are permanent, striving to close the gap is permanent. To be a self-conscious being is thereby a continuous effort toward closing a gap between how one takes oneself and how one is taken by the other that is in principle impossible to complete; there is operative here a conatus or a ground desire that "ceaseth only in death."

We are seeking to make compelling some idea of the way others mediate between myself and myself, making those others almost a part of me—my standing for myself arriving through their recognition—and impossibly distant, where there is nothing, finally, that I can do to wring recognition from them if it is not given. Without the recognition from another self, all an erotically self-aware being would have is what Hegel calls "self-certainty." Being self-certain leaves the claim to authority unauthorized, no more than a feeling. There is no action a self-certain being can do all by itself that can reassure it that its claim to being an authorized institutor of erotic significances is valid once another such being comes on the scene. It cannot be the mere possession of certain capacities—to reason or speak or perform complex actions—that directly make an individual a self-conscious agent, because being a self-consciousness is a practical achievement rather than a factual classification. Hence the exercise of those capacities must involve some idea of issuing authoritative claims, entailing that what is at stake is the standing of the agent as a being who has the authority to make authoritative claims; Eve's anger matters, truly is anger and not a mere animal howl of frustration, only if it can generate an appropriate response in some Adam. The other is the measure of the self's standing and authority. Without another such being, the issue of authority cannot arise—there is only the simple movement of desiring objects and acting on those desires with or without success. In that setting, the gap between what the self-conscious individual takes itself to be and what it is, is opened and closed so quickly that the issue of its being aware of itself as an institutor of erotic significances cannot properly arise. At that level, what is at stake is solely the validity of the erotic assessments, not the creature's *right* to issue assessments as such. Once another comes on the scene, however, no self-enclosed action will do: the division between what this being takes itself to be, its self-conception of itself as an institutor of significances, and the reality of truly being thus is exposed to the other's regard. The only desire that matters in that setting is the desire to have the other recognize the self's standing as a self-consciousness. But this means that between the self and itself, between the desire to be such a being and the reality of truly being such a being, stands the other.

This is the crux of Hegel's theory of recognition, his account of how it is that my relation to myself is mediated by the other, not psychologically, not because I care deeply about how the other sees me and how I would feel crushed if she repudiated my existence. All that may be true, but it is not Hegel's deep claim. It is because of the erotic structure of consciousness that there opens a gap, a division, a small but radical abyss between *taking* myself to be thus-and-so, which is a work of desire, and my being thus-and-so; as a consequence I am not a unified or simple being, a thinking substance, say, but can only be myself by practically achieving a unity between taking myself as an authoritative maker of significance claims and being an authoritative maker of such claims. The difficulty of this self-division is, again, that I cannot close it by myself: between my appearing and my reality stands the other because what is at stake is not the fact of who I am, but my standing *as* a subject. This is what makes us intrinsically vulnerable beings subject to humiliation and devastation. Making this conception of self-consciousness empirically plausible and socially vivid will require a developmental story demonstrating how the other *can* intrude between self-as-desired and self-in-itself (where the "in-itself" includes how and what the self desires to be), and how that structural dependency plays out in social practices. Nonetheless, neither of those stories can get started without the conceptual analysis of what a self-consciousness is.

III. Risk and the Necessity of Life for Self-Consciousness

We are still missing a fundamental step. It is now clear why the *desire* for recognition is necessary for a being to become self-aware as an institutor of erotic significances, but what *actions* could satisfy this desire? Pivot the logic of recognition back onto the question of life. I began this stretch of argument by wanting to claim that the desire for recognition is a transfigured version of the desire for life, the insistent drive for self-preservation. Brandom's Hegelian thesis, that self-consciousness is best understood as a particular development of the tripartite structure of erotic awareness that governs animal life, accomplishes that task in formal terms. Hegel famously underscored the radical nature of this development in arguing that "the individual who has not risked his life may admittedly be recognized as a person, but he has not achieved the truth of being recognized as a self-sufficient self-consciousness" (§187). The first clause of this statement is meant to claim that recognition of personhood occurs through routine social practices in which each recognizes any other's status or standing as possessing the authority to make claims and is in turn recognized herself. Adam and Eve do not have to risk their lives in order to recognize one another. The second clause is claiming that the meaning of "life" changes when institutors of erotic significances take their own takings of how things are as claims requiring acknowledgment from others. If one is committed to one's claim, then one must be ready to face challenges to it, to defend it, to reconcile it with other claims one has made or with the claims of other authorities whom one recognizes; this is how the desire for life becomes the life of reason, where reason is, in the requisite sense, oriented by desire. But what happens when not this or that claim is contested, but one's authority to make claims—one's standing as a self-sufficient self-consciousness—is challenged?

Hegel's assumption here is that unless one were willing to risk one's life for the sake of one's standing as an authorized institutor of significances, one could not finally *be* a self-conscious institutor of such significances. Only by being willing to sacrifice one's life for a value that is not life itself does one reveal one's standing or status as one who lives by values to which one is committed; only through revealing that does one *self-consciously* lift oneself out of the drive for self-preservation and bind oneself to the world of meanings and values that are authoritatively instituted by beings who recognize one another as having the authority to do so, thus coming to inhabit a norm-governed world. One's *status* as an institutor of values must become the primary value if one is to answer the challenge as to whether one has the authority to make claims and institute values. Having that authority practically means being able and willing to perform the difference between commitment to some value that the self takes itself to be and having that value as only a means to more life (and so being determined by the desire for life after all); having that authority for oneself means knowing what it is to decide in favor of that value, sacrifice other values for it, let that value alone orient one's choices. While for animals the drive for self-preservation is constitutive of their relation to their being, for humans, being moved by the desire for just life itself is the paradigm case of movement without commitment, of being determined, of one's self-consciousness not being truly self-sufficient. The risk of life is what carves out and makes explicit what self-sufficiency is for self-consciousness, and hence what freedom or independence is. Hegel's thought here is that the idea of authority emerges through a claim to normative self-sufficiency: my determining which desires are desirable negates the determination of the drive for self-preservation through the institution of mechanisms of self-determining valuation. Because only the other can validate the performance that enacts the difference between being living and being more than living, then risking one's life is the effort to make visible that it is nothing but one's *status* that is at stake, where the meaning of that status is its power to *oblige* others, to noncausally compel their actions, to have one's very standing and status be a reason for the other's action. One's standing—sometimes depicted as the demand or summons of the human face or human body—*counts* only if it alone is a sufficient constraint on others' actions toward you, your standing becoming a limit and reason with respect to their acting, say, compelling them to not touch you, or coerce you, or quash you underfoot, compelling them to engage you through offering reasons and promises and resentments and excuses. Without the recognition of standing, there are only causally efficacious ways of moving and changing states of affairs, and only through the recognition of the standing of oneself and the other as self-consciousnesses are there values in the world apart from life and death.

The point of Hegel's great conceptual device of staging a life-and-death struggle for recognition—in fact, in Hegel, a struggle for freedom or independence—is to demonstrate self-consciousness's power of negation, its power to depart from the demands of life for the sake of nonvital ends or values, and further, to self-consciously institute the possibility of living a life in accordance with values and ideals, including one's standing as one who confers values on things and commits oneself to those values. The risk of life is the mechanism for *marking* the transition from nature to culture, from self-certainty to self-consciousness, from being moved to act to having reasons to act, from purposive to normative life even *after* all those transitions have taken place. The risk of life performs the difference, revealing the truth of self-consciousness (in part). The risk of life shows the difference between the two by the sheer fact of the willingness to sacrifice life for something higher; and in the willingness to sacrifice life for a nonvital end is shown how the very idea of values as something for the sake of which actions are done is necessarily bound to the idea of commitment to those values. Valuing, commitment, and sacrifice thus form a constellation that explains how the idea of self-consciousness must be taken as a status or standing with respect to like-oriented others.

Nonetheless, neither freedom nor emphatic recognition of self-consciousness is achieved through one combatant slaying his opponent. Rather, the whole gambit of the risk of life is resolved by both combatants coming to recognize the utter futility of this killing-or-be-killed performance and by one of the combatants surrendering, letting himself become the unrelenting other's slave. The *relationship* between master and slave as the institution of sociality is the truth of the risk of life, what it must come to if it is going to be meaningful at all for those participating in the original battle. *Spiritual* life and death, as Hegel terms it, the possibility of degradation, dehumanization, radical humiliation, devastation and soul death in relation to realized recognitive life, displaces biological life and death as the sphere of the human. The puzzle here is that the two stages of Hegel's account—the risk of life in battle and the resolution of the battle through the institution of the relation of master and slave—are meant to tie together two apparently contrary statements:

> *And it is solely by staking one's life that freedom is proven to be the essence*, namely, that as a result the essence for self-consciousness is proven to be not being, not the immediate way self-consciousness emerges, not its being absorbed within the expanse of life—but rather, it is that there is nothing on hand in it itself which could not be a vanishing moment for it, that is, that self-consciousness is merely pure being-for-itself. (§187; italics JMB)

> In this experience self-consciousness learns that *life is as essential to it as is pure self-consciousness.* (§189; italics JMB)

Something in the nature of self-consciousness requires its separation *from* life in the manner that the risk of life realizes, while also requiring the recognition that life is *"as essential"* to it as the ideal of being a *"pure"* self-consciousness. The futility of the life-and-death struggle demonstrates that the idea of being a *pure* self-consciousness is illusory; the precise character of this illusion, the very illusion of traditional metaphysical dualism, is that the combatants interpret their being living beings as a mere external condition, a mere causal requirement for being a self-consciousness, thus interpreting self-consciousness as in-itself essentially not life. If that were the case, then self-consciousness could not amount to a *doubling* of the tripartite structure of erotic awareness, but rather would be its abstract negation. For Hegel, the requirement for self-consciousness is that it *"sublates* [the tripartite structure of erotic awareness] *in such a way* that it *preserves* and maintains what has been sublated and which thereby survives its having become sublated" (§188). In saying that life is essential to self-consciousness, Hegel is claiming that even if the risk of life is essential to the repertoire of self-consciousness, and hence even if life can be sacrificed, any such sacrifice would, finally, have to be *for the sake of another form of living;* if they are not to be finally self-defeating in the way that the life-and-death struggle is, nonvital values must be or functionally refer to modes of living, to forms of self-conscious *life*. The good of a form of self-consciousness is its being a good way to live.

Brandom's analysis of the risk of life misses Hegel's thoroughgoing entwining of life and self-consciousness, treating life in precisely the same manner as do the errant original combatants, failing to integrate life *into* self-consciousness in a manner that would make self-consciousness a formation of living. Brandom construes the risk of life not as a constitutive and recurring moment in the life of self-consciousness—a way of marking the value of a value, and defending value orientation in general—but as definitive for what is essential to self-consciousness and what not: "By being willing to risk one's life for something, one makes it the case that the life one risks is *not* an essential element of the life one is thereby constituting, while that for which one risks it is" (SDR, 28). Although he notes that Hegel's analysis comes in phases and stages, Brandom nowhere later qualifies or modifies this claim.[14] It is no accident, then, that his prime example of the risk of life is the Japanese samurai code of *Bushido*, where for a wide variety of reasons a warrior can be required to commit ritual suicide. While powerfully revealing how valuing can require and accomplish the overcoming of the desire for life, the meaning of valuing cannot just be that overcoming without, again, becoming self-defeating, becoming a hatred of life (which is a routine consequence of attempts to secure the dignity and autonomous standing of the human). This is precisely the view of the relation between self-consciousness and life that Hegel is seeking to overcome, and hence why a little later, in the section on the "unhappy consciousness," he emphatically demonstrates how self-defeating and futile and absurd is the effort to think of oneself as other than an embodied, living being. Hence, the risk of life also has the genealogical significance of marking how one might come to believe that self-consciousness was ontologically distinct from life: because bodily life can be sacrificed to a value (can be doubted as essential to self-consciousness), and sometimes needs to be sacrificed if the edifice of recognitively instituted value relations are to remain in force, the inference is drawn that life is not essential to who we are. This thought is as false here as it is in Descartes' second *Meditation*.

Using *Bushido*, Brandom demonstrates how the risk of life is necessary to demonstrate the negativity and freedom essential to self-consciousness: if life, which is a condition for self-consciousness, can be freely surrendered, then anything can. But life is essential to self-consciousness and not just, therefore, a "vanishing moment." If the vanishing moment truly vanishes, then there is no self-consciousness. Brandom does say that Hegel's fable of the life-and-death battle is "metonymic" for a more general structure whereby self-consciousness is formed through commitments that may require risk and sacrifice, and that it is through a history of commitments, risks, and sacrifices of various kinds that an individual's or a collective's spiritual identity is forged and fashioned. But saying this does not by itself draw life back into the very structure of self-consciousness in the manner that Hegel requires, and nothing that Brandom says elsewhere does so either. In accordance with his analysis of the risk of life, the doubling of the tripartite structure of erotic awareness becomes a work of structural homology—self-consciousness having the same structural shape as erotic awareness—rather than a canceling and preserving, a raising up in a manner that would truly make self-consciousness desire itself. And without an account of how life is sublated into the very structure of self-consciousness, we fail to have an account of how the desire for recognition can be the fulfillment of the drive for self-preservation.

IV. Being and Having a Body

We have already seen *why* the desire for recognition must come to replace the desire for life for self-conscious beings; and the method of doubling the tripartite structure of erotic consciousness as a clue to the structure of self-consciousness provides a prima facie reason for claiming that self-consciousness is desire itself (a claim I have just argued that Brandom himself forfeits). What is missing is the structural coordination between Hegel's two statements: the necessity of the risk of life to reveal the freedom of self-consciousness from the determinations of life, and the discovery that life is essential to self-consciousness. *How* is self-consciousness life *and* more than life? Hegel nowhere provides an explicit account of this coordination in the *Phenomenology*. In elaborating the harm of rape and torture in the previous chapter, I was relying on Helmuth Plessner's account of the socially mediated dual structure of human embodiment, our being and having bodies, as the key to understanding how bodily violations could be devastations of the person. Plessner's two masterworks, *Levels of the Organic and Man* (*Die Stufen des Organischen und der Mensch*; 1928) and *Laughing and Crying* (*Lachen und Weinen;*1941), accomplish the coordination of spiritual life and organic life that Hegel only ever stated, outlined (in the Encyclopedia *Philosophy of Mind*), and intrigued.[15] What I need to do here is provide enough of the core elements of Plessner's theory for the arguments in chapters 5 and 6, for, as things transpire, the dual structure of human embodiment is central to the notions of respect, self-respect, and human dignity. Plessner's theory, I will argue, demonstrates that the life and more-than-life structure of self-consciousness is realized in the relation between the two structural modalities of all animal bodily life, being a body and having a body, where the former becomes the actuality of life in self-conscious life, and the latter the realization of the more-than-life aspect of self-consciousness. In fine, what Hegel conceives of as the structure of self-consciousness is better understood as a way, the human way, of coordinating the two structural dimensions of all animal bodily lives. This satisfies Brandom's original thesis in a way that his own account does not. I will begin with an outline of Plessner's theory, only toward the end of the section making explicit its mode of completing Hegel's theory.

Plessner reconstructs the life and more-than-life structure of self-consciousness as referring to a human's becoming self-conscious about, and responsible for, the double structure of embodiment shared by humans and animals alike: the lived body (*Leib*) that is an ontogenetic development from and manifestation of the animate body (*Körper*). In line with Hegel's theory, the fundamental features structuring animal embodiment take on their particular human caste through the introduction of self-consciousness, where one's becoming self-conscious is equivalent to one's self-relation becoming mediated by another, or, more broadly, the "we-sphere," the shared world one participates in with others. Because the mediating authority of the shared world is what severs, denaturalizes one's bodily self-relation, the shared world (*Mitwelt*) acquires a "priority over the given fact of one's living body and the given fact of the outside world."[16] And further like Hegel, Plessner's theory, while unfolding from simple to complex (from lower to higher levels), nonetheless constructs the intelligibility of the development from the retrospective perspective of its endpoint: it is the "ex-centric positionality" of human embodiment—human self-conscious life—that illuminates the full meaning of the contrast and relation between being and having a body, between the animate body and the lived body. For Plessner, *the dual structure* of all animal life—the lived body and the animate body—*itself* becomes a component of self-consciousness; for humans, the coordination between the dual aspects of embodiment arises as a demand that must be self-consciously satisfied, rather than being, as with our animal fellows, satisfied automatically and naturally (i.e., instinctually).

For the purposes to hand, and in order to better forge the connection with Hegel, I am going to use a narrowed version of Plessner's general theory that takes its instruction from how the original account of embodiment was developed in *Laughing and Crying*. Although it is not Plessner's terminology, one way of considering the animate body is in terms of the involuntary body, the body that is self-feeling and self-active. This is the spatially extended body that breathes, blushes, sneezes, hiccups, snores, lactates, flinches, tires, awakes, falls asleep, excretes, has erections and wetness and orgasms, flinches, sweats, emits odors, suffers pains, gives birth. It is the living, organic body as living in and through its continued organic functioning, its maintaining of the internal coordination of parts and whole that is necessary for life. This is also the body that breaks out in laughter and bursts into tears, that laughs and cries uncontrollably (where what distinguishes laughing and crying from other involuntary occurrences is that their occurrences are *expressions* of the existential meaning of the dual structure of human embodiment, and thus come to be forms of self-consciousness about the nature of human self-consciousness). The lived or voluntary or intentional body, oppositely, is the body that accomplishes actions in the world, and hence the body that can disappear into the intentional objects those actions perform, the body that can immediately or directly play the rhythmic phrase of the sonata as opposed to merely carefully pressing down on each key with a different finger (which is also voluntary). In intentional actions, we can, to a greater or lesser extent, "forget" or "transcend" our body toward its object—cycling around the bend rather than anxiously leaning one's torso toward the right while halting the legs' peddling motion. The more accomplished we are in our activities, the more the body can disappear into them, the more it becomes absorbed in the action's meaning rather than its physical requirements. (This signals the appeal of flying as an ideal of action: bodily self-motion without gravitational resistance.) Animal action routines are protointentional in that animals too are absorbed in the object of the action—the cat stalking the crumpled bit of paper; indeed, it is tempting to hypothesize that the highest accomplishment of an intentional action—spontaneously and absorptively playing the sonata—is its coming to approximate, in its spontaneity and automaticity, a purposively instinctual animal action routine; this is why the idea of the lived body cannot be fully or adequately captured by the concept of the voluntary body. The voluntary body is the specific human modality of the lived body, the body through which the needs and demands of the organism in relation to the external world are satisfied.

One conception of the involuntary body is that which can interrupt the self-transcending movements of the lived body, returning the body to itself and its own needs and functioning. Because animal action routines can be interrupted by the demands and sufferings of the involuntary body too, the distinction, viewed narrowly, between the animate body and the lived body is one that applies as much to animals as to humans, which means that the animal-human distinction in Plessner does not track the emergence of dual structured embodiment out of some primordial univocally structured body (there is no such emergence, because animal life itself is already dual structured). Rather, the animal-human distinction refers to the different forms or modes through which the dual structure of being and having a body is realized: animals accomplish the coordination between being and having a body instinctually and automatically, while for humans the lived body becomes the voluntary body, the body whose actions are mediated through concepts and social rules; but once the lived body is transformed from purposive to intentional, the relation between the lived and animate body is no longer instinctually governed but must be achieved. Roughly, for humans, the *coordination* between being and having a body is accomplished as an ongoing task *in accordance with social rules*. For Plessner, our most basic and unavoidable bodily self-relation, which just is the relation between the animate body and the lived body, the involuntary body and the voluntary body, is socially mediated. Hence, even my relation to my own body is mediated through my relation to the other. It is this fact that so firmly installs the human as a mode of living in Plessner's theory, and marks his theory as the bodily analogue of recognitively structured self-consciousness.

Involuntary bodily processes exemplify the ontological fact that the human body is not something that even potentially can be fully within our control, fully within the ambit of will and reason, although some of it can to different degrees: we must breathe to live, but breathing can come under voluntary control. And, again, it is because they are so emphatically tied to the creation of new life that human sexual practices and their reproductive consequences have become a synecdoche for the organic stratum of human existence, since their indelible involuntariness remains outside not just the control of will and reason, but emphatically outside of what can be accomplished through human actions and doings at all. These aspects of bodily experience refer to ways in which I simply *am* a body that undergoes bodily life as opposed to my *having* a body that is an instrument for realizing my purposes in the world.

Despite the patent structural coordination between the two aspects of embodiment, one could imagine wanting to sever the voluntary body from the involuntary body so radically that rather than two aspects of embodiment, they would come to appear as belonging to different ontological registers: the involuntary body would come to stand for bodiliness itself, while the voluntary body, fully under control of the rational will and wholly immersed in the objects of its intentional acts, could disappear as body altogether. And this radical effort would naturally elaborate the routine experience whereby the involuntary body *interrupts* the actions of the lived body, where this interruption is experienced as one in which—as the body vividly manifests itself to consciousness through, minimally, a causal disturbance of intentional life, and at the extreme in the destruction of intentional meaning—we experience the animate body as alien to the life of consciousness and reason, as not "me" or "mine" but as the working of brute nature on and in me. Hence the body would come to appear as external to the life of meaning, experiences of the interruption of the voluntary by the involuntary thence coming to be coded as, say, the revenge of nature on culture. This, in effect, is the version of embodiment that derives from the long histories of patriarchy and monotheism where the dual structure of human embodiment comes to be figured as an ontological dualism. This is, in effect, the theory of mind/body dualism that has been the explicit logic of embodiment in idealist and rationalist conceptions of the human from Plato to Brandom.

It is what Plessner means to deny: my voluntary body is the instrumentalization of my bodily life for the sake of its living purposes. Further, my body is not only mine when I am in full control and possession of it, when I incontestably *have* it so that it disappears in its intentional objects, but I am my body in its states of disorder, determination, or simple physical givenness too; the heights of passion and the quivering delights of sexual engagement also involve moments of involuntary bodily occurrences and disorder. Laughing and crying are of particular import in spelling out the animate body because, unlike most other forms of bodily involuntariness, laughing and crying are *expressive* behaviors that are *directed at a situation*; laughing and crying are not direct and immediate causal responses to external stimuli, but mindful appraisals; as modes of taking and responding to states of affairs, laughing and crying are *about* something in the world. In this respect, they are like intentional forms of behavior. In their resolute aboutness, they are forms of behavior in which the whole person is at stake. Yet, the kinds of responses laughing and crying are make them the direct contrary to an intentional action performed by the agential body. Laughing and crying are forms of emphatic bodily involuntariness, of bodily reactions emancipating themselves: "man is shaken by them, buffeted, made breathless."[17] Rather than being ways of controlling the world and mastering a situation, laughing and crying involve retreats from engagement, the body collapsing in on itself, the person being internally shaken and heaved about in a state of (near) uncontrollable bodily disorder. Yet this involuntary disorderliness is taken as the fullest response to the situation possible.

Consider laughing and crying as providing the anthropological conditions and genetic intelligibility of comedy and tragedy, those synoptic visions of the world that mark human finitude by denying the possibility of complete human mastery over the world; the dispossessions of laughing and crying perform a bodily critique of all fantasies of human sovereignty. If laughing and crying are expressive behaviors, then the bodily loss of control they exemplify must itself be of expressive value. Hence, there must be about laughing and crying a precision and aptness as modes of response to contexts of a particular kind. For most problematic situations, there exist modes of instrumental response: fight, flight, endurance. These forms of responsiveness are also ways of resolving the relation between the being and having of a body: the agential body takes over, lifts the involuntary body into its grasp, and acts. "If, however," Plessner argues, "the situation cannot be brought to fulfillment, if it becomes unanswerable in itself, then speech and gesture, action and expressive movement, break down. Then there is nothing more to be done with the situation; we have no more to say to it, we don't know where we are with it."[18] Laughing and crying are responses to limit situations in which nothing further can be done, in which we are existentially helpless, albeit in a nonthreatening way. Nothing more fully responds to the irresolvable ambiguities of the human condition than laughter; nothing more fully responds to unremitting pain, to frustration, to unendurable loneliness, to loss, or to a reversal of fortune in conditions of hopelessness than tears. When all actions are useless or pointless or unavailable, when there is no further step the body can take to resolve and determine the situation, then what is required is the possibility of acknowledging and expressing the extent and character of what we cannot control or overcome: I can do nothing to bring back my beloved from the emptiness of death, so, finally, in wave after wave of violent sobbing, I acknowledge my inconsolable loss. To acknowledge the irreplaceable expressive powers of the involuntary body is to acknowledge that I truly am this body, and hence that the "I" of self-consciousness cannot be something altogether separable from it.[19]

For Plessner, this thesis belongs to a general account of the meaning of human embodiment in the context of organic nature in general, and the context of animal life in particular. All animals, insofar as their border is something that both underwrites their autonomy from their environment while opening them up to it, have a dual structure of both being and having their bodies. So the being and having of the body also refers to the body that perceives and suffers in relation to the body that acts and determines. The distinction between having and being a body is a derivation from the fact that living things have bodily borders separating them from their environment that must be sustained if they are to remain alive; this, again, is the thought that living beings are self-maintaining *forms*. Being alive and sustaining a bodily border are reciprocally determining features of organic life. Because sustaining its border is a necessary condition for a living thing—were the border to fully collapse or be irreparably ruptured, the living thing would cease to be—every living thing must establish and maintain *its position* with respect to its environment. Living things position themselves with respect to their environment.

Animals establish the position of their body with respect to the environment instinctually and thus automatically; in this respect, their relation to their environment is not a problem or question for them. As with the tripartite structure of erotic awareness, the meaning of the environment is taken from the perspective of the body in it; Plessner calls this "centric positionality," the body being and making itself the center of this world, centering the world around itself for the sake of its vital ends. Erotic significances and centric positionality are perspectivally convergent descriptions of the same phenomenon; the satisfaction of vital ends is how living things sustain their bounded relation to their environment. For all animal lives, every achievement of a relation to the immediate environment involves a coordination of the animate and lived body; while for the beasts this coordination occurs instinctually, for humans it is, ideally and for the most part, achieved intentionally. Humans have a position with respect to the environment *only* by *consciously or voluntarily taking* a position, by establishing themselves with respect to it. Consequently, human positionality has an "ex-centric" structure: "man has not a univocal, but an equivocal relation to his body . . . his existence imposes on him the ambiguity of being an 'embodied' [*Leibhaften*] creature and a creature 'in his body' [*im Körper*], an ambiguity that means an actual break in his way of existing."[20] The nature of the human is that the general dual structure of animal embodiment becomes vivid and manifest, and thereby becomes a problem, a question, and, above all, a demand that requires an active resolution (or the forfeiture of resolution in particular circumstances). As if recalling the meaning of Hegel's account of the risk of life, Plessner concludes this passage by stating "The brokenness of man's relation to his body is rather the basis of his existence, the course, but also the limit of his power." Our brokenness refers to the ontological fact that bodily self-relation is for humans an infinite *task*. Brokenness also refers to the existential fact that this task is often experienced as a fundamental surd or alienation in the very structure of human existence because it is a task that we do not always have the capacities to accomplish; we know as bodily beings that our lives are not fully our own, and we feel the weight of this as a rent or tear in our condition.

What Plessner refers to as our brokenness corresponds to what Hegel calls the negativity of self-consciousness. The negation at the core of self-consciousness is the negation of centric positionality, of the instinctual automatic resolution of the coordination between being and having a body. *Ex-centric positionality* is Plessner's term for self-consciousness; it is just the thought that the relation between the body I am and the body I have must be achieved—at every moment—and that achievement occurs through my consciousness of myself as both a center of an environment, with respect to my needs and desires, and decentered with respect to that environment, a way in which my body is also simply another object in a neutral environment. The body is a task because it lacks automatic self-congruence; there is for humans no "natural" answer to the question of how the being and having of the body are to be related or what its relation to the world here and now is to be; answering that question is what human life is, in miniature in everyday practice and culturally as the construction of the meaning of human embodiment. But this is also to say that the relation between our being and having a body is always a question and always a demand.

The rupture in the human bodily self-relation comes from the outside; even my bodily self-relation is mediated through a third: I can *take up* a position with respect to my environment—which is what it is to establish a relation between the body I am and the body I have—only in accordance with the possibilities of determination offered by the shared social world I inhabit. So along with the lived and animate body there is *the person*. Relations between humans are relations between persons, not between organisms; relations between persons are symbolically and normatively structured. If positionality relates to borders and boundaries, then establishing a position is establishing (i) the character of the boundary, (ii) the nature of the relation to the external object, (iii) the relation between the voluntary and involuntary body, and (iv) the relation to the demands of one's social others. All four of these moments are different aspects of the same operation; each determination of my relation to the environment is an effort of self-determination in which I attempt once more to bring my being and having of my body into congruence in accordance with socially constructed norms of appropriateness. Hence, each way of relating to the environment is simultaneously reestablishing the relation between the body I am and the body I have in relation to social rules and norms: delicately belching with hand over mouth after a rich repast; fiercely focusing energy, eye, and hand as I attempt, once again, to place the thread through the eye of the needle; or quivering as you run your nails down my back. Because the possibilities of establishing the relations between the body one is and the body one has are social and historical, here too the other stands between the self I desire to be and its actuality; that is, *the other mediates the relation between the body I am and the body I have by setting the terms for their mutual coordination.*

I am claiming, then, that the determining structure of human self-awareness turns on our capacity to set our voluntary body and involuntary body in relation to one another; that is, each human life is recognizably human only if it can *recognizably* present itself as having resolved the relation between the voluntary and involuntary body in intelligible ways.[21] An individual can only be recognized as a social agent if she can so present herself—that is, present herself to all relevant others as self-possessed, as having control over the *relation* between her voluntary and involuntary body in a manner that is socially sanctioned. Manifesting such control typically occurs simply by doing those voluntary actions that are appropriate in particular circumstances, and, more importantly here, by following local rules about where and when the involuntary body can manifest and express itself—laughing, crying, showing sexual excitement or anger or fear, releasing bowel and bladder, etc.—in only the appropriate places. The original and founding locus of human agency is its socially sanctioned establishment of the relation between the voluntary and involuntary body (between culture and nature, between the more than life of self-consciousness and life itself); failures in maintaining that relation typically result in feelings of shame, and, if radical enough, become socially disqualifying. It is because the stakes of maintaining an appropriate relation are constitutive of the human that, for example, in our culture toilet training—which is one of the earliest social markers for having mastered the relation between the animate and lived body—can become such a fraught moment in child rearing.

Plessner's *Levels of the Organic and Man* accomplishes what Hegel's *Phenomenology* and *Encyclopedia Philosophy of Mind* only promise: a demonstration that the thesis that *self-consciousness is desire itself* is realized in the thesis that *ex-centric positionality is positionality itself.* Plessner's notion of positionality makes thematic and explicit the bodily and hence material presuppositions that are passed over by the defiantly purposive and intentional character of the tripartite structure of erotic awareness. Here is

Robert Pippin provisioning the centrality of positionality without embodiment: "The idea is that all determinate consciousness is, let us say, positional, is something like *having a position* on what is its intentional object, or on what it is doing. It is to be understood as a taking, and it can only *be* positional, have a position, if this involves *taking a position* actively, or apperceptively. But this latter self-knowledge as an activity is not positional."[22] This is plausible but for the fact that the very idea of positionality is, apparently, assumed to arise with the idea of "taking a position" in logical space, where logical space appears somehow separated from the material space of doings in the world; but it is just this that cuts off the human from the animal, making the relation between the human and the animal imponderable. When it comes to human actions, the logical space of reasons is actualized as a complex material space in which individual bodily self-relations are realized through bodily comportment to other objects and bodies.

For Plessner, again, the issue here concerns the maintaining of a bodily boundary. For nonliving things, their boundary is identical with their contour or outline; for some things, like water or gases, even this is something of an exaggeration. For a living thing, however, its boundary is more than its outline or contour: "Its boundary is a part of itself, not merely a boundary between body and medium, but an actual boundary belonging to the body and setting it up against the medium . . . [A living body] is, through its relation to its boundary, *both* directed *out* beyond the body that it is *and* back *into* it again . . . For a living being, it is essential to have a way to confine itself (*sich begrenzen*) by *taking a position* (*Position nehmen*) which is more than simply having a position in space and time in physical terms."[23] All living things operate via the having of a position because all living things possess a self-referential structure whereby they sustain their boundary by the means through which they establish a relation to what lies outside them. Because all living things must have a position in relation to their environment, then *pace* Pippin, the issue is not positionality, but the means or mechanism through which a position is established. Plessner stages the human in relation to other forms of organic life, which all share the character of possessing a self-referential structure whereby inside and outside are continuously set into relation with one another. Human positionality is distinguished by being ex-centric: "The 'ex' in ex-centric positionality thus refers to an individual self's carrying out its life by relating back to itself [by having a position only by taking a position]. Since, however, it is a matter not just of the individual bodily self but also the creation of relationships with the environment, the 'ex' refers also to the things in the environment and the possible other selves contained in it."[24]

Since Plessnerian positionality turns bodily self-relations into a consequence of how a being positions (determines) its relation to the external world, to things and persons, it gives to the account of erotic awareness an appropriate and anyway unavoidable material anchor. *The risk of life can now be restated as the social mechanism through which human positionality is revealed as inalterably ex-centric, and the necessity of life for self-consciousness can be restated as the recognition that ex-centric positionality is nonetheless a formation of organic (centric) positionality that requires the achievement of a congruence between the body I am and the body I have.* Achieving self-congruence is the bodily form underpinning all other existential efforts whereby humans become who they are, whereby the unity of self-consciousness is achieved. We must fully acknowledge that the *necessary* congruence between the body I am and the body I have is a social accomplishment whose meaning and possibilities are determined as relations among persons. If the self-congruence between the body I am and the body I have is a *biological imperative* that is accomplished through obedience to socially sanctioned laws and forms, then the drive for self-preservation (the necessity of sustaining a boundary in relation to the external world) becomes the desire for recognition, the desire to have sanctioned those actions through which my bodily self-relation is achieved.

And this is equally to say that torture and rape are limit conditions of human interaction since in them the individual's relation to his other is one that explicitly bars self-congruence from occurring. Torture and rape are social practices that exploit the severance between the body I am and the body I have, the abiding prerogative of ex-centric positionality, against the person whose body it is by making self-congruence impossible. That is what is devastating; the continuance of the injury is the continuance of the experience that the conditions of self-congruence have been ruptured and can be ruptured by others again. I think of Brison's pirouettes as she walks down the road as the mark of her rapist situating himself again and again between the body she is and the body she has; with each pirouette, an acknowledgment of her bodily autonomy, her power to establish the relation between the body she is and the body she has, occurs through rights and permissions that others have the power to override and even destroy; each anxious pirouette thus marks the other's presence in a movement that is purely her own. In chapter 6, we shall see how this same set of concepts structures the elements of moral psychology: respect, self-respect, and dignity.

V. From Life to Recognition

One might reasonably complain at this juncture that for all its sophistication, it is difficult to see how the only permanent desire for a self-conscious being is the desire for recognition, and how the only unconditioned value of her standing or status as a self-consciousness is meant to reveal itself as ingredient in ordinary ethical practices, as the stuff of ethical life. I take it as obvious that ordinary life does not for the most part feel like a striving for recognition, and if recognition relations are the underpinning of everyday social practices, they are not obviously so. If they were patent, then the wide panoply of competing ethical orientations would not exist. I take these charges to be legitimate and to require answering. The answer to the question of why the striving for recognition is not typically manifest is easy: it is because human social relations are not routinely experienced as structures of (inter)dependence. Ordinary inhabitants of contemporary Western societies no more feel as if their standing with respect to one another is socially constituted and structurally dependent than did Hegel's original master and slave understand themselves as recognitively constituted beings. The master, although only a master through being recognized as such by his slave, feels himself to be independent, while the slave's effort is to work off or free himself from what he takes to be only a *contingent* relationship of dependence. The question here is not why these relations of dependence are not recognized; it is how they can nonetheless play the role they do in human affairs despite being socially repressed and overlooked.

My answer has two parts: the first is to pick up the large hint offered by the claim that the routine, effective mechanism of recognition is becoming recognized as a member of a particular social community (which coordinates with the already noted point that joint actions need not appear as joint actions to their participants). The second, to be prosecuted in the next chapter, is to demonstrate that everyday social practices have effectively invisible relations of trust as their ethical substance. In order to begin getting at the right way of phrasing the first thesis, let me instance an elegant passage from Jürgen Habermas that begins the attempt to provide a framework that would give force to the claim that moral necessity involves "a good that we cannot do without" (to borrow Aristotle's phrasing) in a manner that connects the natural and the social.

> I conceive of moral behavior as a constructive response to the dependencies rooted in the incompleteness of our organic makeup and in the persistent

frailty (most felt in phases of childhood, illness, and old age) of our bodily existence. Normative regulation of interpersonal relations may be seen as a porous shell protecting a vulnerable body, and the person incorporated in this body, from the contingencies they are exposed to. Moral rules are fragile constructions protecting *both* the physis from bodily injuries and the person from inner or symbolic injuries. Subjectivity, being what makes the human body a soul-possessing receptacle of spirit, is itself constituted through inter-subjective relations to others. The individual self will only emerge through the course of social externalization, and can only be *stabilized* within the network of undamaged relations of mutual recognition.

This dependency on the other explains why one can be hurt by the other. The person is most exposed to, and least protected from, injuries in the very relations which she is most dependent on for the development of her identity and for the maintenance of her integrity.[25]

Any reasonably naturalistic account of morality must begin with the fact that unlike other animals, humans are born prematurely; it is prematurity that explicates what is meant by the idea of "the incompleteness of our organic makeup." We are organically incomplete in two different ways: We are *permanently* organically incomplete in forever lacking the hardwiring—instincts and the like—that generates the requisite purposive behaviors that provide the means for survival and reproduction for our animal neighbors; for humans, (rational) social practices take the place of drives and instincts. While for animals learning allows for the completion of instinctual routines, for humans social learning, which leads to the acquisition of socially constituted and governed action routines, replaces the instinctual action routines of animal life. We are *temporarily* organically incomplete because the thoroughness of prematurity at birth (as a token of our permanent organic incompleteness) entails a temporally extended process in which the physical maturation necessary for individual survival occurs with and through socialization; *we become biologically viable* (fully functioning, "independent," and self-moving) only *by becoming socially viable*. Our organic makeup is completed, to the extent that it ever is, through socialization; we realize or actualize ourselves as natural beings socially.[26] Physical maturation, gaining control of our bodies in relation to the physical and social environment, occurs in tandem with and through socialization; hence through socialization we become the bodies we already necessarily are. Again, human beings not only are their bodies but, as self-conscious, ex-centrically positioned beings, they incrementally come to voluntarily have or possess their bodies; or to put it another way, humans can maintain their lived bodies through having voluntary bodies; hence acquiring the means for full bodily self-possession requires acquiring the means for (complete) rational self-determination. Subjectivity is rooted in our simultaneously being the bodies we have or possess, where our having a body is "the result of the capacity of assuming an objectivating attitude toward the prior fact of being a body."[27] I take this thought to be another way of phrasing the thesis that part of being erotically self-aware, with its scission between self-as-desired and self-in-itself, and part of what it means to have one's relation to oneself mediated from without is that, as we just saw, one's relation to one's own body also becomes something that is mediated, something that requires establishing, and hence something that must be achieved voluntarily, an achievement that, because it is mediated and developmental, comes in degrees both developmentally and practically. Some such thought is required for both the account of the eighteenth-century development of the social individuation of bodies offered in chapter 1, and for the accounts of torture and rape in the following chapters. I shall say more about this conception of embodiment below.

One urgent thesis that Habermas's suggestion makes plain is that a solely conceptual analysis of why we should regard self-consciousness as constituted through its relation to other self-consciousnesses is insufficient on its own. The very idea that the tripartite structure of erotic awareness is realized in human beings through relations of recognition requires an ontogenetic story in which the displacement, the canceling, and the preserving of that structure takes place; prematurity is the structural cancelation of the nature-instinct story, and socialization the mode in which it is preserved. Socialization understood as constituting a developmental process explains how and why the transformation from animal centric positionality to human ex-centric positionality occurs; it explains, again, how self-consciousness can be desire itself. Relations of recognition are the right way to establish the connection between life and sociality because striving for recognition is nothing but the social formation of the striving to live for social beings. As I will argue in the next chapter, undergoing a thoroughgoing process of socialization, becoming a fully self-moving or self-determining social agent, acquiring a sense of one's intrinsic self-worth, and coming to be recognized as "one of us" are all interrelated aspects of the broadly unified routine developmental sequence whereby the human infant develops into an adult member of society. Each aspect of this four-part developmental sequence is oriented differently:

Undergoing socialization processes involves learning a first language and acquiring all the basic social skills and understandings necessary to navigate a particular social world.

Becoming self-moving involves separating from the mother, coming to have control over one's own body, being able to perform those actions essential for social life for oneself, and hence possessing ordinary capacities for practical reasoning.

Acquiring a sense of self-worth involves having a sense that one matters to social others, hence a sense of how local others matter to one, and thus an orienting and determining sense of what is involved in understanding, according, and maintaining one's own life and the lives of those around one as possessing intrinsic value and significance.

Finally, we have the string that pulls together these diverse accomplishments: becoming recognized as one of us is coming to have all the implicit rights (and corresponding duties) that enable one to be an active member of society, that allow one's life to matter in the manner that the lives around one matter, that allow one to reasonably expect and receive treatment of the kind typical for a member of one's society, to learn how one's existence is counted by others as a salient and occasionally overriding reason to do or forgo particular actions.

Coming to be recognized is, one might say, the fulfillment or the completion promised by the three other developmental sequences. Although under narrow and urgent circumstances humans are moved to act by the immediate animal drive for self-preservation, under normal circumstances human living is accomplished through living a human life as a member of social group; hence, the drive for self-preservation becomes the desire to live the kind of life demanded and prized by one's social world. Hence, instead of an instinctually structured system of action routines, humans undergo some version of this four-part developmental sequence; but if being fully recognized as one of us is the string that pulls together all the other developmental sequences that enable one to live a social life, then the drive for self-preservation is finally realized as the desire for recognition.

Let me pursue this claim a little further. One attains humanity only by being treated as human, only by being *lifted* through socialization to the status of being (fully) human, being one of us. One attains the standing of being human by being, through socialization, recognized as human, and only by being so recognized can one be (fully) human. Insofar as each and every social practice has implicit within it rules governing who is entitled to participate in that practice (in what manner and to what degree), each social practice is at the same time, whatever its explicit content, also a practice of recognition (and misrecognition). Thus, by recognition I mean all those practices and forms of conduct with their associated cognitive and affective commitments that demonstrate, express, or help individuals to live out a particular form of social life and thereby form those individuals into full-standing humans. In order for the notion of "full-standing human" to tie back into a naturalist understanding whereby the human form of life is itself one more life-form, we can say that recognition refers to any interlocking set of practices that sustains the worth and value of human individuals by promoting the conditions through which they can be full and active participants in the society to which they belong, where the continuance of that society, its reproduction, is the manner through which species survival occurs.

One is a human by first being practically recognized as a human, where being so recognized is borne by judgments of a certain type, say, practice judgments. But the normativity of those judgments is an internal correlate of the standing of the object judged. Were it not for the fact that we secure our world through social practices, it would not be the case that the standing of humans as individuals depends on their being recognized. But the new normative register recorded by ethical practices, *the good we cannot do without, is being recognized by our social fellows as fully human*, where each must depend on the continuance of that recognition for her continued social existence.

Prima facie, this is what ethical practices are primarily if not solely about, and this provides the translation manual for individual survival and the continuance of human forms of life. Begin with the latter item: unlike other life-forms, humans reproduce their kind only as members of a particular social group; what is reproduced over time is not humankind as such but some particular social actualization of it. What kind of social group it is that produces and reproduces itself through shared practices will depend on place and time: tribes, clans, families, cities, principalities, nations, and states have each had their day. What matters is that it is the social grouping whose collective practices provide the means for the continued existence of itself and its members. Sometimes the boundaries of the group are firm and fixed, in other times and places, even demarcating where one social group ends and another begins can be all but impossible.

A human becomes capable of *surviving* as a practical agent in the world only through being recognized as being "one of us Gs," where G stands for an enduring social group with norms regulating who is and who is not a member, and what different forms of membership involve—male or female, master or serf, doctor or plumber, black or white, Hutu or Tutsi, Untouchable or Brahmin, one of us or alien visitor—in terms of (what counts as) full participation in the life of that social group. Simplifying this thought: one *survives* as an individual only through the possession of a specific social identity; one is *recognized* as human, one achieves standing as human, only through the medium of being recognized as a G of a certain kind. Recognition is the primary mechanism of human survival because through it one is provided with the conditions—typically role-bound rights and duties—of active membership in the ongoing life of a particular human community. The unrecognized wither; the partially recognized—those recognized and also misrecognized—suffer denigration, shame, humiliation, marginalization, diminished opportunities, lack of self-respect, and, at the extreme, may suffer some version of devastation; those who suffer significant patterns of misrecognition (through marginalization, exclusion, and degrading treatment) are denied access to routine means for attaining the kind of full self-respect that is the ideal upshot of unconditional social recognition—that is, that form of mutual recognition that would provide for parity of participation with all other members of the group. Because mutual recognition is a condition of existence, an intentional partial absence of recognition across a whole life or merely at one time causes an injury to the very being of the one misrecognized.

Ethical practices are primarily forms of recognition. Ethical practices are necessary because they provide the minimum necessary forms of recognition that enable an individual to be treated as a member in good standing of some relevant social group, in part or in full, and thereby *as* human, in part or in full. It is because individuals *require* recognition in order to have the social standing that enables participation in social practices of a kind generally available in a society, that recognitive norms are second-personal: they concern what I owe you, and only thereby what reason demands. This makes plain one of the crucial places where contemporary ethical naturalists go wrong: in thrall to the thought that the ethical has something to do with the good life for man, thereby meaning some notion of flourishing or full self-realization or perfection or becoming virtuous, they lose touch with the fact that moral practices, centrally and for the most part, contour human societies not at their heights, but from their depths, providing first and above all the bare necessary conditions for the possibility of a self-sustaining and self-reproducing human community, a community capable of providing generally for living and the continuance of individual lives in ways that are characteristically free from pain and capable of enjoyment in a manner coordinated by the needs for the continued functioning of the social group as a whole.[28] As Habermas's passage rightly promotes, ethical practices are best conceived of as the necessary medium underwriting the continuance of particular societies through promoting and securing the fragile existences of its members as members of that historically reproducing social group. Ethical practices primarily concern the necessary conditions for the possibility of the *already* normatively constituted lives—one's standing or status as a person ("one of us")—of dependent, vulnerable, and mortal beings in society; they are practices that thus function to sustain the status of society's members as they simultaneously maintain and promote those social arrangements necessary for social reproduction, all of which may be far removed from ideals of self-realization or flourishing or happiness or perfection or autonomy (although such ideal ends are often built into what being a good member of that society is; but even then, we should understand such an ideal as bending backward toward something like optimal conditions for the continued survival of the group with its characteristic form of life). Because being human is not given with the mere being alive, ethical practices sustain normative relations among the members of a community, their characteristic ways of recognizing one another as members of "this" normative order of things. But this normative world is primarily just how beings of a certain species live and reproduce their kind. Living a life as a member in good standing, in whole or in part, of some society is what most of us most of the time do, and it is that which ethical practices underwrite.

In part inspired by Elizabeth Anscombe's contentions that "morality" should be replaced by "justice," and "morally wrong" (a deontological thought) replaced by "wrongs someone" (a recognitive thought), Michael Thompson has suggested a grammatical formula to capture how relations of recognition give ethical substance to ordinary interpersonal relations. The normativity considerations of justice are, he argues, intrinsically relational or "bipolar," and so require a bipolar judgment form.[29] Thompson phrases the thought that the recognition of another as having the standing of a human occurs through the recognition of others as persons, where the primary judgment is *X is a person in relation to Y*, and hence "'recognizing someone as a person' is registering her as a person in relation to yourself."[30] Intersubjective recognition of one individual by another is the pivot through which a community generates the ethical norms regulating social action generally, because in making relevant judgments the other makes a "special sort of dent" on your agency, her moral standing normatively determining your action as determinately as a barrier will determine your action physically.[31] An order of justice—that is, the recognitive order of any social group G—is thus simply the indefinite totality of individuals capable of entering into such bipolar recognitive pairings in accordance with a roughly unified body of social rules and practices.

What follows from this is that what makes breaking a promise wrong, for example, has little to do with undermining conditions of enlightened self-interest or a procedure to which all could rationally agree or disappointing an other's well-founded expectations or breaking the trust that the promise had induced, however relevant all of these considerations are to the overall resilience that the practice of promising has for us. Rather, what most profoundly makes breaking a promise wrong is that it wrongs some one individual, the one to whom the promise was made; promise breaking withdraws the recognition given in making the promise in the first instance; it devalues an other by failing to sustain the recognition of her standing as a person, who she *is*. In breaking the promise, you harm the other by in effect denying that her expectations matter; but if they do not matter in your calculations, then she does not matter; hence, breaking a promise is failure to recognize her as a person. Promise breaking is an act of disrespect, and being an act of disrespect, it is morally injurious—it devalues the other. For the purposes to hand, the details do not matter. All that is required here is the acknowledgment that the moral authority of the practice of promising, including the kinds of ethical necessities it carries, is fully parasitic on what Thompson is calling a particular order of justice with its iterated pairwise sets of *X recognizing Y as a person*. That the practice of promising can normatively trump short- and long-term interests requires neither the magic of deontological rules from nowhere nor the authority of a rule all could share; what promising requires is the normative lift provided by structures of recognition of the appropriate kind. *X recognizing Y as a person* alone provides the kind of necessity, the kind of good we cannot do without (because it is necessary for social survival), that is missing from standard accounts of practical reasoning. And failures of recognition cause moral injury.

Let me gather together and rephrase my argument.[32] We can speak of the human in two different ways: in terms of a life-form and in terms of social practices, where "human" refers to one life-form among many others and to the members of a wide range of social practices. Both ways of talking are intertwined: the human life-form is defined by developing social practices. One can therefore say that to be human (in the first sense) means to be or become a member of an orderly set of social practices. Since being or becoming a member of an orderly set of social practices defines what it means to be a specimen of the human life-form, then to recognize (identify) the other as human means, finally, to recognize (in the sense of the German *achten*, to respect) the other as a participant in social practices. This gives us just the connection between life and recognition that Butler's Spinozist thought demanded: to persist in one's own being is only possible on the condition that we are engaged in receiving and offering recognition.

FIVE

Trust as Mutual Recognition

I. Introduction

Every day is an adventure in trusting thousands of others, seen and unseen, to act reliably.[1]

At the turning point in Nicholas Ray's *On Dangerous Ground* (1952), the hard-bitten detective, Jim Wilson, played by Robert Ryan, is speaking to a murder suspect's blind sister Mary Malden, played by Ida Lupino. Haltingly, she asks "How is it to be a cop?" He responds, "You get so you don't trust anybody." She replies, "You're lucky; you don't have to trust anyone. I have to trust everybody." The self-destroying and world-destroying consequences of radical distrust are exemplified in the movie's opening scenes as Jim's skeptical regard brutalizes Jim himself and everyone around him. The necessity of trust is what he must learn. That he learns it from a blind woman who must trust everyone—that is, who is vulnerable before the world and dependent on every other's goodwill—underlines the fact that the vulnerability she represents belongs to everyone. Her dependence makes vivid what is otherwise partially hidden: our existential helplessness. He recognizes this in her instantly, recognizes it as the source of his incessant self-repudiation, as what he has been unable and unwilling to acknowledge, which is why he does not pity her. He takes her blindness not as a disability but as an existential qualification we all possess in different ways and modes: we are essentially vulnerable and dependent beings who, as a consequence, will inhabit either a world of trust or a world of distrust, either a world of moment-by-moment unspoken and mostly invisible mutualities and reciprocities that enable everyday practices to unfold in accordance with their own norms and rhythms, or a world of ever-anxious self-protection where violence is the insurgent shadow of each human encounter. Interestingly, Ray has his characters describe this existential vulnerability in terms of "loneliness," as if the great work of civilization is not the escape from the existential loneliness that is the consequence of dependence and vulnerability, but the sharing of it. The bond holding us together, then, is not a mutual protection racket (the Hobbesian view of the world that Jim's city life expressed), but the acknowledgment and embrace of dependency and needfulness—with trust as the fullest and hence most resplendent expression of this acknowledgment and embrace, trust as the soul and substance of human togetherness.[2] This is the condition of the human that the drive for sovereignty, mastery, and independence—the fury of the rapist and the cold calculations of the torturer—seek to escape.

Ray's austere vision of human vulnerability, dependence and trust is the one to be pursued in this chapter; that his noir police procedural story *must* become a love story will also be the trajectory of my argument.[3] Of course, the condition and need for trust, its social primacy, has been near the center of my argument from the outset, from the moment of the overwhelming societal distrust of the sovereign law of torture that begat the humanitarian revolution that was most fully realized in the abolition of torture and the uprising of the rule of law, to the terrible discovery that human devastation just is, finally, loss of trust in the world.

In attempting to make good on the intuition that devastation is loss of trust in the world, I have tracked two lines of argument: first, that the moral injury of rape and torture involves a violation of the personhood of the victim, a denial of the standing or status of the victim as a person, *through* a violation of her bodily autonomy, a violation of the conditions under which she could have moral authority over the being and meaning of her body. The puzzle underlying this claim is that it was unclear how the sheer fact of depriving an individual of control over her body could be a violation of personhood that could be felt to be devastating. Second, in order for that claim to be coherent, we discovered the need for the idea that the standing or status of an individual is, as such, dependent on the recognition of others, that each is a second person as a condition for being a first person. In the previous chapter, we tied together the bodily autonomy thesis and the recognitive thesis by arguing that persons are authorities, the issuers of authoritative claims, judgments, acts; that is, persons are the kinds of beings whose deeds are defeasibly right, defeasibly true, defeasibly legislative, and that this is what is at stake in the idea of human individuals as fully immersed in a sea of practical norms pursuing lives in accordance with the norms of a particular society. But one can only be this kind of authority if one is recognized as such an authority through how others respond to one's acts. It follows from this that one's self-relation, one's standing or status for oneself, is dependent on those around one: one cannot issue authoritative claims if no one treats one's deeds and statements as possessing defeasible normative authority deserving a rational response. Entry into the second nature of recognitive social relations between and among persons occurs through its departure from first nature: human lives are the lives of living beings lived through and in accordance with social norms, where the primary locus for the acknowledgment and departure from first nature occurs in the relation between the involuntary body, the body I am, and the voluntary body, the body I have.

These constructions provide some of the conditions for the intelligibility of the devastation of rape and torture: because I am forever divided from myself, because who I am for myself is in part constituted through how I am recognized by relevant others, I am dependent on others for my standing as a person. Because the relation between the body I am and the body I have is a social task, the other who stands between how I take myself to be and how I am equally stands, exactly, at the juncture between my voluntary and involuntary body. The ex-centric positionality of the human body is the contouring of the relation between the lived and animate body in accordance with socially prescribed norms. In rape and torture, the other on whom I am dependent for my standing as a person appropriates for himself my having a body, my voluntary body, leaving me with only the body I am, a thing among things, thus depriving me of the minimum necessary conditions for personhood—which is devastating.

Or it would be devastating if at least one other vital condition were satisfied. Some part of devastation concerns the fact that in losing my standing or status as a person I am being devalued, not instrumentally devalued, not devalued as being an adequate means for the other to acquire some useful goods, but devalued *as a person*. The puzzle here is making sense of the *value* of being recognized as a person as somehow having a conception of worth or value that transcends the value of life itself. Even if it is a necessary condition for being recognized as a person that one be capable of sacrificing one's life for the value one takes oneself to exemplify, that alone only provides a negative or formal criterion for the value of personhood: it is a value that is greater than the value of life such that it is worth sacrificing one's one life for it. And something of that thought is meant to converge with the idea that human lives are lived in accordance with normative rules, principles, and reasons that are not reducible to rules for staying alive. But looked at from the outside, even if human lives are governed by normatively constructed social practices, why shouldn't those rules be seen as simply the requisite human means for satisfying biological imperatives? Why should one's standing as a person be the sort of thing worth dying for? Saying that the being of persons is their being recognized as persons does not so much answer this question as deepen it.

The one clue offered in the previous chapter arrived in my extended Adam and Eve scenario when Adam remained coolly indifferent to Eve's fury at his unwillingness to give her another bite of the apple. The point of that fable was not only to deny that recognition is the sort of essentially discursive affair Brandom supposes it to be, but equally to demonstrate that, underlying the claiming-making recognitive exchanges of the kind typified by the original apple-eating episode, there was a *pure* or *unconditional* demand for recognition, for Adam to respond to Eve's anger *because* it is the anger of another person—that purity or unconditionality is, after all, the point of the risk-of-life story. Even if the desire for recognition as a person—to be recognized as a full member of this community—is the way in which the drive for self-preservation is satisfied for humans, personhood is not a condition for anything apart from membership, apart from being capable of living a life in accordance with the normative practices of this community. Humans live in accordance with modes of living that outstrip the direct demands for survival that nonetheless must be satisfied individually and collectively. The mode or way of life is everything—it is constitutive of what one's being a person *is*—such that sustaining that way of life can be worth dying for, and being unable to live in accordance with its minimum conditions of having self-worth can make life no longer worth living; or, if one goes on living under such conditions, one can no longer feel oneself to be of worth, that something of the naked desire to live has taken over in ways that even for the individual can feel repugnant, undignified. All this follows just from the evident logic that there cannot be relations of recognition at all unless some recognitions are pure; and while this is a fair translation of Kant's thought that persons are ends-in-themselves into the language of recognition, one might still complain that something is missing. What is missing is the meaning of these structures of normative self and other relations *from the inside*. What is dissatisfying is that we have an account of the conceptual difference between instrumental and noninstrumental evaluation, and of how the latter is borne by practices of recognition, without having an account of the desires, motives, attitudes, and emotions appropriate to such a structuring of experience. What we do not have is a way of understanding all this from the first-person point of view such that the denial of recognition could both feel and be injurious, such that certain acts are experienced as devaluing, as denying the value one is, and some are even felt to be devastating, as undoing one's standing as a person.

If animal psychology is meant to explain the desires, motives, and emotions animals possess that move them to do those actions that are necessary to their individual and species survival, then, if the desire to live for humans is borne by the desire for recognition, *moral psychology* must be bound to elaborating the relation between the structures of recognition constitutive of human self-consciousness and the affective self-understanding of agents that gears them toward seeking and sustaining their sense of self-worth in relation to those others on whom they are necessarily dependent in the midst of a community governed as a whole by, finally, relations of pure recognition. My flat-footed conjecture is that humans consider and feel themselves to be of unconditional self-worth because their first caregivers treated them as being of unconditional worth, which is just to say that humans consider themselves to be of worth, to be ends-in-themselves, because in the first instance they were loved by their parents, loved well enough by those who first bore them into the world. And this will be sufficient for the purposes to hand if it can also be shown that love is a, indeed *the*, paradigmatic form of pure recognition, and that the work of first love is simultaneous with the work of primary socialization such that becoming a socialized individual and becoming a being who conceives of herself as having intrinsic worth are two sides of the same process.

But this was supposed to be an anticipation of an argument about trust, with love coming in at the end of the story. How are trust and love connected? Trust, I will argue, is the social actuality of first love, it is how individuals' self-understanding of their intrinsic self-worth in respect to others is realized in everyday practice; to trust another is to recognize them as a self-consciousness who recognizes you as a self-consciousness. Trust is the routine, ideally omnipresent yet mostly invisible ethical substance of everyday life. Trust is the ethical foundation of everyday living. Trust is trust in others before whom we are unconditionally vulnerable not to take advantage of our vulnerability. Given the exorbitance of this requirement—the forbearance of trust as the proper acknowledgment of our existential helplessness before one another—trust can only be effective if it remains unnoticed: trust must be the invisibility of trust. Trust, as we shall see, would not be *trust* if we were constantly calculating and speculating about it. Hence, the ethical foundation of everyday life is a set of attitudes, presuppositions, and practices that we typically fail to emphatically notice until they become absent. My explanation of the fact that although trust is the ethical substance of everyday living, it has been virtually ignored by philosophers is that they have been utterly taken in by trust's systematic invisibility; hence, modern moral philosophy typically begins its reflections with conditions in which trust has either become absent or, more standardly, is simultaneously *assumed* and *suppressed*. Modern moral philosophy is not simply remote from the actuality of ethical experience, it typically begins at the very juncture where actual moral life is invisible. Moral philosophy as now practiced is the morality of a world without its ethical substance. In stating the matter in this way, my philosophical strategy is analogous to Alasdair MacIntyre's "disquieting suggestion" at the commencement of *After Virtue* that our language of morality represents "fragments of a conceptual scheme, parts of which now lack those contexts from which their significance is derived."[4] The lost origin of morality, I want to argue, is not ancient Greece, but everyday relations of trust.

Defending such a claim would require a monograph on its own; what I can accomplish here is to motivate that thesis in a manner sufficient to support the role I am assigning to trust as what is destroyed in morally traumatic events. My argument will begin by attempting to give some phenomenological heft to my claim for the pervasiveness and necessity of trust; I will then try to secure this claim through a developmental account of trust, elaborating more fully the thesis that trust relations are indeed relations of mutual recognition as I proceed.

II. The Necessity, Pervasiveness, and Invisibility of Trust

The basic form of recognition supporting everyday life is that found in the mute mutual recognition that occurs in conditions of trust. Trusting and being trusted, and hence being in a condition of mutual trust, is the primary mode in which we recognize one another as persons (or, before the introduction of modern social forms, recognizing one another as [full] members of the community). It sounds odd to think of trusting mutual relations as a form of recognition, but it is this revision I want to add to our understanding of trust and recognition.[5] My simple guiding thought is: in its primary form, for X to trust Y is for X to consider Y as a person like herself, and to assume, ceteris paribus, that Y sees her as a person too, and that he will let her standing as a person affirmatively count in his (unreflective) treatment of her, as well as in his expectations regarding her treatment of him. But that is a formal claim; what about the content of trust as a particular attitude might make that claim plausible? And why should we even consider trust a relation of recognition?

One standard way of starting to answer the second question is to consider trust in relation to social contract. I understand social contract theory as a way of both affirming and denying the necessity of recognition for everyday life. It denies it because it considers the participants to a contract to be already formed, and at some level self-sufficient apart from the contract. It is necessary because without being accorded some standing by others whom the contractor accords a standing in return, life would be practically impossible; we need one another, and must depend on one another—above all, and especially, we need and depend on one another not to attack us. If it were not the case that trust represented a form of recognition, and hence a form of social bonding, the idea of contesting models of social bonding based on contract with a trust model would be a nonstarter. The debate between contract theory and trust is properly a contestation of where and what kind of recognition is necessary for a life together; do we recognize one another primarily through acts of will and reason, or do we recognize one another first in a more prereflective way, say, through habitual social practices premised on unnoticed attitudes and affects? Can bonds sustaining a life together emerge despite an original indifference in others' interest, or must we assume an original interest in one another, say, because we love and trust one another? Can there be a social world at all without there being bonds of love and affection somewhere near its foundations, and what can develop from such bonds? Does it make sense to think of a society as composed of, preponderantly, self-interested adults only, or is society intrinsically a place where relations between children and parents project society's original understanding of itself?

The argument that a social contract cannot be the first or primary way in which we set in place our relations with one another—recognize one another as coparticipants in a shared social world—is premised on the idea that we would only require a social contract in the full Hobbesian sense under conditions in which mutual trust had collapsed; indeed, the signature character of a Hobbesian war of all against all is not a continual state of battle, but a state of affairs in which no man can trust any other man. (Even in its most robust formulation, contract theory assumes a background of trust that has now become disintegrated; hence, even at its most fervent, contract theory concedes the primacy of trust, aches for its solidities, and seeks to find modes of social cooperation that can, desperately, replace it. Why else would one turn to considerations of contract?[6]) Systematic distrust is the primary element in states of civil breakdown. However, in such a situation, the idea of contract is hopeless because in it no man could trust any other man to keep his contract because the very conditions that make it necessary undermine the conditions for its success: "As background trust diminishes, costs of enforcement simply become too high for contracts to be effective."[7] Under conditions of pervasive distrust, an original social compact could never be formed in the first instance.

Nor could a central authority possessing a monopoly over the legitimate use of violence compensate for the lack of trust: without pervasive conditions of mutual trust, the level of fear necessary to produce an expectation of contractual reliability would be indistinguishable from a state of terror. At best, imposed social order might provide conditions under which a community could commence attempting to cultivate relations of trust (again)—acting *as if* we trust one another is a way of getting there—but that too is different from substituting contractual relations for trust relations. Contract, however socially important, is only ever fully effective against a background of trust. But, again, contracting with one another is a primitive form of recognizing one another as formally equal members of a social relation, and setting in place a practice of action coordination among individuals premised on that recognition. If trust is the premise for any social contract, then trust is the background set of recognitions of one another that makes contracting possible. Trust is indeed an attitude or ambience, but it is more than that; trusting one another is one of the ways we mutually recognize one another.

Take these brief comments as a reminder of a familiar philosophical conversation. I mention it here in order to focus on the thought that trust is the primary form through which we recognize one another as persons. As a first approximation, trust is a cognitive attitude that anticipates that the other will have and display goodwill toward me under conditions in which I am vulnerable. Annette Baier prefers a definition in which the issue of vulnerability is at the forefront: "Trust . . . is *accepted vulnerability* to another's possible but not expected ill will (or lack of goodwill) toward one."[8] As Baier goes on to comment, we can gather a sense of the forms of trust by looking at the varieties of vulnerability and the diverse grounds we have for not expecting others to take advantage of it; that is, we need to look at "the variety of sorts of goods or things one values or cares about, which can be left or put within the striking power of others, and the variety of ways we can let or leave others 'close' enough to what we value to be able to harm it."[9] The problem to which trust is an answer is that we are intrinsically vulnerable creatures whose ordinary lives in society necessarily expose us to the will of others with whom, typically, our connection is unchosen. Radical dependence on unchosen relations to others begins with infancy and childhood, and continues throughout life—no matter how absurdly and desperately this is denied and repudiated. This is patent to any inhabitant of a metropolis who walks the streets, takes public transport (bus or subway), works where they can, sends their children to public schools, shops in ordinary stores and markets. Compare this to the life led in a gated community: driving to a private place of work, a private country club, having provisions brought to one through the filter of security officers, and sending one's children to a private school. While some of this is just taking basic safety precautions in a dangerous world when one can, at another level the effort is to create the sense of oneself that through making all one's relations chosen—private arrangements—one is not radically dependent on others, or not dependent on them in the same way, choice lifting the weight of dependence by dressing it as a product of independence. Yet at each turn the gated community dweller is still dependent and still must trust neighbors, colleagues, security personnel, teachers, priests, repairmen, husbands and wives. The gated community existence translates the fantasy of the social contract into a practical form that remains shrouded in fantasy: we cannot remove the depth of our being intrinsically dependent creatures; choice can alter the terms of dependence, but finally the utter dependence on others, one's utter helplessness before them, cannot be overcome. Trust will be necessary. In different ways, torture and rape are also images of the repudiation of radical dependence, a repudiation of our existential helplessness before others. The existential burden of dependence is everywhere intertwined with the consciousness of vulnerability; one cannot fully protect oneself, overcome one's vulnerability, without repudiating conditions of dependence. Fantasies of independence or omnipotence begin in infancy and, given the vulnerability dependence tokens, can reappear throughout life. Sovereignty, for Améry, is the primary articulation of that fantasy.

Everyday life beneath its ever-shifting surface of routine and variation is full of terrible risks. Because we are not solitaries but depend upon numerous and indefinite others for the simplest acts of everyday living, we must let those others come in close enough—as close as jostling body-to-body on the subway, as close as tending to my small children's most intimate needs—so that we are exposed to whatever viciousness or cruelty or hatred or perversity or sheer indifference can stain a human soul. The outrage at the actions of pedophile priests and teachers marks the difference between trust and reliability: what is relied upon—because custom, habit, law, fear, or the pressures of self-interest have made the situation reliable and regular—can surprise and disappoint us when it fails (the train is late, the morning newspaper did not arrive, the vendor has given me the wrong change, the bread is stale, the letter never arrived, and so on); when a trust is broken, it is a betrayal, the breaking not of a causally reliable mechanism but of some deeper human bond. If that trust is broken, where do I turn? How do I live with school and church if I need to protect my own from the institutions whose task is to nurture and protect? How do I live here if my neighbors manifestly have ill will toward me? Each breaking of a trust is a tear in our way of being with others: friendships falter or end, marriages fracture, work relations dissolve, whole worlds are lost. When a trust is betrayed, something in the moral fabric binding us together is rent; if we are fortunate, the tear is minor, the lesson learned, and life continues as before with less ease, more reflective caution, more deliberative evaluation, but it continues. If we are unfortunate, it will seem as if no accessible life will ever again be granted—as in the lives of Améry and Brison.

Trust radiates out from the body as our original vulnerability to others; the need for trust begins with the inevitability of having others come physically close enough to cause physical harm and spreads out to each place where I have a care or fundamental interest whose harm would be, under the strictest interpretation, a harm to me. Since we are physically vulnerable before every other—Hobbes's correct (egalitarian) insight that in principle any man can kill any other—and because we cannot contract with every other the terms of mutual safety; because, further, we cannot fully anticipate how far-reaching our dependencies will be, then in order to provide space for everyday bodily habitation of the world, we need expansive and resilient networks of trust. One of the reasons why destructions of trust tend to be so disturbing is that, unlike contracts that are explicit, linear, and specific, trust relations tend to be implicit, casually spread out (like an atmosphere or mood), and nonspecific; that is, there is no specific thing we had trusted the other to do or forgo from doing. As Baier has it, trust "comes in webs, not in single strands, and disrupting one strand often rips apart whole webs."[10]

I am pressing the depth of vulnerability and risk in everyday life not because we do feel constantly threatened by all those who come dangerously close to us and on whom we depend, but because, usually, we do not, because, if we are among the fortunate, we rarely feel dangerously threatened, and there are only delimited portions of life where high vigilance is required. However, only by underlining the degree of potential danger to life, limb, and well-being lurking at every intersection of everyday life can we begin to bring into view the massive ethical edifice (which simultaneously is terrifyingly fragile) which has made those dangers invisible. (This, of course, was also Hobbes's strategy, but because he needed the active ill will of others for his argument to run, he needed more than potential threat: he needed to show the a priori validity of distrust. My aim is the exact opposite.) The space between the exorbitance of the danger and everyday obliviousness to the danger is the actuality of trust as the condition for everyday interpersonal engagement in the world. Trust, I am minded to say, is the original position of our relation to others; trust provides for our original insertion into social life. So thorough and so pervasive are trust relations, and so needful are we of them, that were we fully aware at each moment of the depth of the thoroughness of, pervasiveness of, and need for trust that, by the fact of full and persistent consciousness, trust would become distrust.

Let me refine that claim. Trust is a constitutive attitude or orientation to the world that acts as an interpretive filter through which we make sense of the brute appearing of others in close proximity. Because the attitude of trust takes others as persons who take you as a person, trust tilts each approach, each saying and doing of others into the most benign and trust-preserving interpretation available, just as, conversely, an attitude of distrust distorts each saying and doing into the most appropriate form of ill will consistent with the given circumstances. Trust and distrust are self-perpetuating modes of interpretation, suppressing or distorting countervailing evidence and highlighting attitude-preserving evidence. As primitive attitudes and orientations, they tend toward their own preservation rather than toward truth. However, there is a difference between them: trust tends to become visible only through breakdown, a movement from the invisibility of trust to its appearance as having been unjustified, thus leading to distrust; while distrust, once in place, is a form of vigilance, anxiety, an exacting awareness of threatened vulnerability; distrust is not fear, but the "wary suspicion"[11] of the other, a sense that there might be something in the vicinity to be fearful of. Distrust is doubt of the other's goodwill, and hence, whether it is local and episodic (just in this neighborhood or just with used-car salesmen or just with respect to other men looking at my wife) or pervasive, it calls for persistent vigilance and alertness. Distrust operates as a highly conscious interpretive filter to the same degree that trust tends to operate as an unconscious filter, as the presumption of the lack of a need to attend, be aware, scrutinize, question, evaluate. Trust is the orientational acceptance of the other as one who accepts you into her presence. Trust cannot be trust, accepting and open and blinkered in its interpretive outlook, without some degree of what retrospectively looks like gullibility or naïveté, without, in the light of particular failure, the possibility of retrospectively appearing to be too trusting, too lacking in the vigilance proportional to the harm possible.

This begins to hint at the fundamental difficulties in comprehending trust: how elusive it is (when operating ideally, trust is invisible) and how paradoxical its appearance from the perspective of deliberative reason. These two difficulties are coordinate. Part of understanding the rationality of trust is to demonstrate how a fundamental mode of orientation can only operate through its remaining dependent on insensitivity to present-tense deliberative scrutiny and evidential evaluation in a way that, again, will retrospectively consistently reveal it to have been rationally untoward—we *will* feel as if we have been insufficiently cautious and attentive to evidence, too trusting. Prospectively, things are much the same: in evaluating a situation it would only rarely appear that adopting the standpoint of trust could be fully justified since, whatever the contingent benefits, the costs of being wrong are always exorbitantly high, typically too high to be traded off against possible gain.[12] Of course, the gain would be having a life with others at all, but that is, precisely, the conundrum: if prospectively trusting appears to be too rationally risky, and retrospectively trust appears to have been naïve, how is trust possible? How can we live with others in a trusting way, and why would we? And yet, we must trust if we are to have a life at all.

III. Trust's Priority over Reason

Trust's prospective unavailability from the perspective of practical deliberation and its rational untowardness from the point of view of retrospective evaluation point to the kind of stance trust is and the kind of social achievement it performs. One way of stating this would be to say that the trusting person and the person without trust live in two different worlds. But that says too little if we think back to the trauma victim's loss of trust in the world; we had better say that trust is the condition through which we come to have a world in general, and to be without trust is to lose one's place in the world. Radical distrust is practical skepticism about others, a practical version of other minds' skepticism. In light of the deliberative paradox of trust—namely that we would only rarely, if ever, prospectively or retrospectively, be in possession of sufficient reason to adopt the stance of trust—its distinguishing features begin to come into view. Although a stance or an attitude, trust's basic mode of operation must be preconscious or unconscious, withdrawing from view in favor of the actions and interactions it allows to occur. If trust is a condition of everyday life, yet rebarbative from the perspective of practical reason, then trust must arise and insert our relations to others prior to our coming into possession of the standpoint of reason. Trust, one might say, is subject to rational correction and modification, but not to rational installation; reason is the caretaker of trust, not its creator (or ground). But if trust cannot be fully explained by reasons or assessed fully by reasons, then trust must be a primitive form of reaction, a prereflective attitude that enables certain types of phenomena to appear, say, others to be recognized as persons like myself in some ethically conspicuous way.

These issues knit together; let us nonetheless start by focusing on trust's tendency toward invisibility. Noting the indefiniteness and weblike character of trust, its form of interpretive self-preservation, its partial blindness to evidence, and its sheer pervasiveness in orienting our relations to others, Karen Jones comments that the harms others "might cause through failure of goodwill are not in view because the possibility that their will is other than good is not in view."[13] This thought underlies the very idea of what I will call *basic trust*. The blindness or obliviousness *proper* to trust covers over the very thing—our vulnerability before the potential ill will of the other—that gives conditions of trust their point and purpose. Trust in the goodwill of an other that we will not be harmed by him, when actual, is simply the thoughtless allowing him to come close, and so the forgetting of the potential for harm and the depth of vulnerability: we sit together at the restaurant table, order, eat, pay our bill; trust is simply doing those things, attending solely to them, the quality of the ambience, the food, our conversation, and not, for example, worrying if the other patrons will harm me or the cook poison me. (Do I need to walk around with a permanent food-taster? And who will taste her food?) What we have in view when we trust is simply the world; what we have in view when we distrust is the potential harm to us in the situation. Trust is self-forgetfulness, while distrust is a fraught consciousness of self that holds the world at a distance, where this contrast between world involvement and the inward turn toward the self tracks, precisely, the opening grammatical moment of the experience of pain. When we keep in mind what we would need to be aware of in order to be fully conscious of trust—namely *all* the terrible things that the trusted could do to us—trust cannot function at all; the insistent conscious affirmation of goodwill would become inseparable from its opposite; if you need to affirm the situation like that, then something is wrong with it. Trust's goodness in part turns on its keeping out of view that which calls it into existence. At this level, trust's invisibility is part of its ethical functionality, and again, part of what brings that thought into focus is consideration of the massive cost of distrust in time, resources, and sanity; it is the immense psychological costs of distrust that makes its proper attention to warding off potential pains irrational when not positively demanded by the context.

Functionally needing to be unconscious does not entail that trust rationally needs to be unconscious. On the contrary, Baier has proposed as a reasonable criterion for the rationality of particular trusting relations that they lose nothing of their appropriateness or value when, in particular circumstances, they become conscious. Take this to be an expressibility test for trust; as such, it is supported by the structure of its failure: "[if] the extent that what the truster relies on for the continuance of the trust relation is something which, once realized by the truster, is likely to lead to (increased) abuse of trust and eventually to destabilization and destruction of that relation, [then] the trust is morally corrupt."[14] The sort of thing at stake here is reliance on differentials in power and force, threat advantage, unequal need, etc. Trust does not assume actual equality between persons, but only that power differentials play no conditioning role in providing for the continuance of the relation that would contradict the presumption of trust itself.[15] Trust's great good, in fact, is that it locates the morally appropriate form of mutuality under or within conditions of pervasive inequalities in power or position; nowhere is trust more necessary than when all that we have to protect us from the other is her goodwill, her recognition of our standing as deserving a human response. Said differently, if trust concerns our vulnerability before the other, then trust pertains to conditions of dependence on the other, to, finally, our existential helplessness before the other. Trust relates to the moment of inequality—my dependence on you—in even the most equal of relationships. Hence trust—like the rule of law—is the perpetual work of equalizing the unequal.[16]

Consciousness of trust is not incompatible with it—the expressibility test literally joins full social consciousness with rationality. However, that expressibility should have that force with respect to trust points to the fact that the ordinary operating mechanism of basic trust is one of subconsciousness or invisibility, of leaving out of view what the consequences of ill will would be on any particular occasion. Consider an instance in which a friend has betrayed a trust; you are now extremely wary in your everyday dealings with her. However, an occasion arises—you need to organize an event together—where you suddenly find that you have been engaging with her for hours in the old trustworthy way. Once the realization dawns, you retreat, putting up your guard once more; however, you may discover twenty minutes later that you have again forgotten your distrust, and must re-alert yourself to it. It is hard work to stay distrustful all the time.[17] What makes the idea of momentary or short-term trust plausible is that it does not require anything affirmative from you; all that is needed is the forgetting of your rationally held distrust and the smooth functioning of the reciprocities and mutualities and coordinations of the practice being engaged in. But this is to say that distrust is not the simple alternative attitude toward trust; distrust is the privation of trust, an absence or rupture in the constitutive conditions of interaction.[18] Operationally, trust is not an endorsed attitude toward another because structurally trust relations obviate the need to take a stand upon the relation. Trust's role in our life depends upon its vanishing from view; generally we are not "aware of our trusting and seldom bring it sufficiently clearly before our minds to endorse or reject it."[19] It is, then, in the nature of trust as the ethical undergirding of everyday interactions that it recedes below or behind the actions and interactions it makes possible.

This thought also provides a wedge into the rationality paradox. From the perspective of reason, the only question could be "Can I take a trusting attitude toward this other?" But once the question is put in this way, the requirement of reason is that in order to trust, I must decide whether or not I can take an endorsed attitude toward her. The question of reason is a question of endorsing an attitude toward the other because once I place the other into question, I have already taken an ethical distance from her; I can only overcome that distance through coming to a judgment or decision in the affirmative. Nothing less will suffice. Trust functions by obviating the question, by relating us to potential interaction partners prior to and independently of the question of endorsement. Trust can do this only by operating as a baseline or primary attitude that does not require antecedent justification; on the contrary, as a primary orientation, trust is best conceived of as a primitive and original relation to the other, how others first appear to us, and hence part of the original physiognomy of social interaction. Trust is our simply having others appear to us as partners in some routine social interaction. From this original position, it is distrust that requires explanation and/or justification.

There is an obvious analogy here with Charles Sanders Peirce's views on epistemic belief and doubt, where the effort is to adjust belief to its practical function rather than to the requirements of rational validity autonomously conceived. In the same way in which trust allows us to accept others, so Peirce contended that the essential function of beliefs is to guide desires and shape actions. Trust and belief do not make us act at once, but they put us into a condition that enables us to act in the appropriate way when the occasion arises. For Peirce, real doubt motivates us to seek belief, and will not be satisfied until belief is restored since, again, the role of belief is to guide desires and shape actions. Doubt is resolved when we have a *settled* belief, whether or not the belief is emphatically true; belief is for the sake of action, not for achieving an epistemically felicitous state. Belief is not outside rationality, but it does come before it; to subject belief to doubt antecedent to concrete and weighty reasons for doubt would be to disable belief from playing its functional role. Hence, no belief needs to be justified ex ante; this is equivalent to saying that to adopt the standpoint of pure reason—in which every belief requires rational justification—is equivalent to adopting the standpoint of doubt without any grounds for doubt. Adjusting for the change of register, belief is to trust as doubt is to distrust. Hence, to ask for rational grounds for trusting an other is practically equivalent to adopting the standpoint of distrust, since it is premised on withdrawal from the other, placing her at a distance, and seeking reasons why it would be rationally appropriate to let her come close, dangerously close.

Karen Jones asks whether, because of its usefulness, a trusting attitude is the rational default position. Or should we say, given the extent of our vulnerabilities and the harms possible when we trust unwisely, that distrust should be the rational default position? Or is neutrality the rational default position?[20] She responds by saying that an appropriate default stance is too sensitive to circumstance and to the expected disutility of misplaced trust to make generalization possible. This strikes me as confused. The question of a rational default stance cannot be the question of what stance I *ought* to adopt in a given set of circumstances, since that would presuppose that the question of trust is a question of gearing the appropriate attitude for circumstances as they arise.[21] Everything I have said to here about trust's pervasiveness, its irreplaceability by contract, its structural role in ordinary life, which together terminate in trust's tendency to unconsciously orient everyday practice, all presses toward the conclusion that, developmentally and normatively, trust is the primary, defeasible condition of all social interaction, and in having that role it is prior to rational evaluation, and hence prior to what should or should not be the rational default position in any given circumstance. To say this is not to claim that all things being equal I *ought* to trust another unless I have sufficient grounds for not trusting her; even that formulation places trust in the ambit of (moral) reason and withdraws it from its role of prereflectively placing us in relation to others. Equally, to claim that trust is the primary and defeasible condition for social interaction is not to claim that trust has been factually the default position in the preponderance of historical conditions, or even that much of the time in which it was operative it would have passed the expressibility test. This last is to concede that relations can pass for trust relations, appear for all the world as if they were trust relations, but that they conceivably would have failed the expressibility test if performed, and hence were morally corrupt in some significant way (they in fact did depend on unacknowledged but operative power differentials). The possibility of just this occurrence is the worm in the apple of trust relations between perspicuously unequal partners; the mere thought of making the terms of the relation explicit, by itself, can turn trust into distrust. This is why trust, as a mechanism of moral equality, flourishes in and anticipates contexts where whatever features of social life that undermine trust can or will become subject to the demands of equality.

Put this last issue aside. Trust is the primary, defeasible condition of social interaction in the sense that trust is the spontaneous, prereflective attitude guiding responses to the appearance of routine interaction partners; trust relations are thence the ideal optimal form in which we recognize one another as persons under ordinary social circumstances. As the ground of ordinary interaction, trust does not require antecedent justification; trust is accepted as appropriate until such time as it is shown not to be appropriate. Distrust is the failure of trust, not simply a contrary attitude. Basic trust is the necessary presupposition of everyday intersubjective life; basic trust cannot be a reflective option, in the way that Jones supposes, without extracting humans from the constitutive conditions for social life in general. Since I have conceded that reason is the caretaker of trust, then the only plausible way of explaining how trust could come to play the role it does in our lives is to assume that institution of trust precedes reason.

Although such precedence could be merely logical or psychological, for reasons beyond those already canvassed, making it developmentally prior provides the thesis the explanatory leverage it requires. One might then assume that adult trust develops out of the innocent trust that infants are required to have in caregivers, and hence that trust is not an optional stance toward the world, but the attitudinal concomitant of coming to have a world at all. If this were the case, then basic, adult trust would be seen as developing out of innocent infant trust in order to occur at all. The presumption here is that we do not directly learn to trust, like we learn to crawl, because emphatically distrusting is developmentally impossible. If we necessarily *develop* attitudes that are trustful, then what is eventually *learned* in coming to have adult as opposed to innocent trust is distrust. Distrust, we might say, is the measure of the full impact of emergent independence out of radical dependence; distrust is the mirror of the reality of the radical independence from one another of radically dependent beings. Distrust is the corrective and refinement of trust. In learning distrust we are (forever) learning an adult, reflective form of trusting, to trust conditionally rather than unconditionally, and hence to moderate, qualify, segment, and localize our trust: there is a trust appropriate to lovers and friends that is different from the trust of co-workers that is different from the trust of diverse professionals and service persons (doctors, lawyers, salesmen, plumbers, postal workers, etc. are all trusted differently, and differently in different locales and circumstances) that is different from trust of strangers (and we trust strangers differently depending on the part of the city we are in or the situation in which we are joined) that is different from civic trust in the primary institutions in which we participate (which are diverse in themselves: trusting schools is different from trusting a bank, which is different from trusting local government).[22]

None of the developments that make trust selective remove trust from being basic; on the contrary, they demonstrate that, all other things being equal, trust is the default position that remains even after the costs of so doing become palpable in a manner to make revision (qualification, moderation, withdrawal) necessary. What occurs when revisions occur is that the scope of trust is modified and refined. Trust cannot be intelligibly banished without the self becoming damagingly disconnected from the world. Consider: how do we understand an individual who is radically distrustful under circumstances in which trust is warranted? Or worse, an individual who is distrustful under all circumstances whether that distrust is warranted or not? One could say that such radical distrust was simply irrational, but that cannot be quite right since, from the perspective of instrumental reason, in the long run it may appear to be safer and rationally simpler to be distrustful rather than trustful. Again, because present pain and damage trump and thus disqualify the claim of past satisfaction, which in turn affects deliberations about the future, then *rationally* distrust can appear the safer option—and it is *safer*, but that is because practical deliberation about whether to trust or not can only occur from the perspective of vulnerability and anticipated harm. Practical reflection makes danger too bright, which is why it becomes disabling if used as the general antecedent to all practical engagement and why a grand betrayal of trust can quickly spiral into systematic withdrawal and disconnection.

What we are thus inclined to say about the persistent mistruster is that the attitudinal set necessary to sustain basic distrust will be pathological: anxious, fearful, paranoid, cold, a disturbance of attitude that yet converges all too readily with objective calculation and rational justification. Recall that both trust and distrust are self-perpetuating in different ways, and hence both are systematically underdetermined by evidence and over-

step rational boundaries as would be set by fixing appropriateness in accordance with evidence. I am now saying that when trust is caught in its
overextension it is, precisely, a failure in scope or appropriateness that is
a structural consequence of trusting at all; hence we experience the retrospective sense of having been naïve or gullible. Trusting too much is, one
might say, the rational form of failure suitable to trust, and hence what
learning to trust judiciously inevitably and continuously involves. Conversely, when distrust oversteps its attitudinal parameters, it is not simply
irrational; its form of irrationality makes the stance pathological. Hertzberg states that the "distrustful person is someone who has been damaged
by other people . . . The destruction of our trust in others is a tragedy of
life."[23] The scope of overextended distrust is the measure of the damage
suffered. It is this asymmetry between the rational faults of trust and the
pathological faults of distrust that leads us to think of trust as the material a priori of social interaction. The asymmetry is morally necessary since
trusting too much is judging the other too kindly, being too inclined to
suppose the other's person-acknowledging goodwill, while distrust doubts
that the other can be responded to simply as a person among other persons. When one doubts the goodwill of the other, one tends to retreat from
a participant stance to a third-person stance; one thus shifts from trusting
to, at best, relying on the other, and thus considering the other as one who
is to be "dealt" with, manipulated, controlled, monitored, and protected
against as one might protect against an ill wind. (In between trust and distrust there is a large swathe of cases where neutrality is the optimal stance.
Under conditions of neutrality the presumption is that I can, more or less
confidently, rely on the others, and thus formally and outwardly treat them
in person-respecting ways. Neutrality involves taking an objective stance
that can be clothed in the paraphernalia of a participant stance. I am assuming that neutrality between trust and distrust, and routine reliability
are more or less coextensive.)

Analogously, while we would think of trusting relations coming to embrace more and more features of social life as an indicator of evolving and
improving social relations, a social world in which distrust was everywhere
necessary—in which no one could trust any other—would be a prime example of social pathology, a systematic deformation of the normative idea
of a functional social world. Notice that in such Hobbesian circumstances,
each individual might be fully rationally justified in being distrustful of all
others—one's children may be spying for the state, one's lover in league
with subversive elements. What thus makes the situation pathological is
not the distrustful cognitive set of each, it is that the circumstances them-

selves require each to maintain a state of doubting vigilance that makes the ordinary social goods in which we are essentially dependent on others—love, friendship, making music or laws or bridges or enduring institutions together—impossible or, if possible, only minimally so and at great cost.[24] But here too I would want to say that the distrustful person is damaged, in a sense by other people, but more broadly, damaged by history.

Trusting relations are the normatively basic mode through which individuals recognize one another as persons. This, again, is not the claim that we "ought" to trust others or that we "ought" to recognize others as persons so that we can trust them; both those ways of regarding trust construe it as one of a number of possible stances one might take toward a given situation, and that all other things being equal—that is, if the evidence warrants—it is the practically most advantageous stance to adopt. Trust precedes practical reason as its condition of possibility because the stance of trust is what first allows others to appear as persons to whom one responds in person-appropriate terms—that is, simply in ways that are appropriate to the activity in question: playing chess, doing an experiment, going over one's expenses, asking directions. Trust could not be trust with its attitudinal partiality if it were subject to reflective evaluation prior to its cultivation. Again, it belongs to the logic of trust that it is perspicuously perceived in its absence, and it is part of the natural history of trust "that we come to realize what it involves retrospectively and posthumously, once our vulnerability is brought home to us by actual wounds."[25]

What are the grounds for claiming, as I have been, that the object of trust is a *person* who perceives you as a person? Victoria McGeer offers a reasonable interpretation of the claim that trust involves the presumption of the other's goodwill toward one as saying that trust involves "recognizing the other's acknowledgment of oneself as a source of self-determined action, hence as a reflectively self-conscious person with reactive attitudes toward other people and the world."[26] In order to trust another, one must presume that the other would, in the course of their actions, *count* one as having the standing of a (relatively) self-determined being (as, roughly, one whose responses accord with the linguistic and practical rules governing appropriateness for that stretch of behavior).[27] And one must presume that others would tailor their actions accordingly; in so tailoring their actions, in taking you to be a limit to their actions, and further assuming that you will have appropriately similar attitudes toward them, then in trusting them you *are* recognizing them, respecting them, as a person, as, for all intents and purposes, an end-in-itself who takes the personhood of others, including you, into account. However, that is only a partial description of what trust requires; much of the moral heavy lifting in trust concerns how the truster understands the trusted to understand her, and thus how the trusted is expected to behave toward the truster—how her standing makes a dent in her deliberative agency. Trust concerns your understanding of your standing, worth, or value for the other in relation to your constitutive vulnerability as a person. Trust works from the perspective of the first person not only as one being a worthy agent but also, at the same time and with respect to that very standing as agent, as a potential victim, and hence institutes its ethical orientation by looking toward what treatment I (rationally) expect from others who view me in accordance with what I take to be my forever-vulnerable intrinsic worth, where expecting them to view me in the appropriate way includes their seeing me as someone who will regard them analogously. The intelligibility of trust as a form of recognition is how it connects constitutive vulnerability with the presumption of intrinsic worth.

IV. Trust in a Developmental Setting

In *The Struggle for Recognition*, which inaugurated the present resurgence of interest in recognitive theory, Axel Honneth places trust in a developmental setting in the context of his elaboration of a tripartite schema of ideal-types of recognition, each type possessing its own internal logic. Love, having rights, and being regarded as making a valuable contribution to the social life of the community—love, legal recognition, solidarity—are the three fundamental forms of recognition that in their plurality point to different ways or modes of recognition: emotional support, cognitive respect, and social esteem, respectively. Honneth further supposes that these different ways in which we are recognized as persons are practically fulfilled in different portions of the social world: intimate relations and family (love and friendship), the state (rights), and work and civil society (social esteem).

In this scheme, acquiring basic trust is a component of the logic of love as it unfolds in child development. Following object-relations theory, Honneth contends that infant development proceeds from a beginning stage in which mother and infant conceive of themselves as somehow merged in a state of undifferentiated oneness, at least in the physical sense that the infant's acts are fulfilled or completed by the "mother" and in the narrow psychological sense that neither conceives of her life as separate: all life's mattering occurs solely in their dyadic union. This is followed by a second stage of separation in which the infant, in trying to destroy the mother, who has begun to turn her attention elsewhere, reassures herself of both her and the mother's independent viability. Reassured in the light of her struggle for recognition with the mother, the child realizes that "he or she is dependent on the loving care of an independently existing person with claims of her own."[28] In order for the process of separation from the mother to succeed, the child must develop enough trust in the continuity of care that he or she is able to be alone without feeling abandoned or bereft or deserted or in danger of not having future needs met or not having feelings of attachment reciprocated. The child "trusts the loved person to maintain his or her affection, even when one's own attention is withdrawn."[29] Honneth elaborates this thought thus:

> But this certainty is, for its part, just the outwardly oriented side of mature confidence that one's own needs will lastingly be met by the other because one is of unique value to the other. To this extent, the "capacity to be alone" is the practical expression of a form of individual relation-to-self, similar to what Erikson conceived under the title of "trust." In becoming sure of the "mother's" love, young children come to trust themselves, which makes it possible for them to be alone without anxiety.[30]

Although trust here involves trust that the other will return, that one will continue to count for the other even when she is not present to you or you to her, the prize in so counting for the other is the capacity for being alone, becoming confident about being in the requisite sense a separate person because you accept the parent as truly separate from you. For Honneth, we can even date the emergence of the "I" from this moment when the child is capable of being alone, when a sufficient separate sense of self emerges that allows the "I" to consider itself in relation *to* its others. Separateness or independence or rough-and-ready individuality, of a kind so basic for the requisites of social life that even the most communal of societies must have and support it, is grounded in the trust that the bond of connection to the parental figures will remain firm through states of physical and psychological absence. And clearly, the thought that one feels oneself to *count* or *be of worth or value* even when one is not being physically cared for and attentively seen must be a pivotal moment in the development of a sense of self.

Let me concede that a crucial moment in development occurs when the child becomes capable of trusting its parental love sufficiently to tolerate being alone without feeling terrified, threatened, or injured by its temporary absence. Nonetheless, this sense of trust in the other and the self-trust corresponding to it do not quite match the idea of basic trust whose loss we saw was the principal consequence of traumatic torture and rape. In those circumstances, the traumatized subject is capable of being alone—but only of being alone; it is trusting others to come near that is the problem. Not only is trusting others not to harm one (or one's interests) closer to our ordinary understanding of what trust involves, the notion of self-trust does not fully correspond to Honneth's own further elaborations of his account. On a chart showing the structure of the three forms of recognition, Honneth specifies that the component of personality threatened by the absence of love is "physical integrity" and the corresponding form of disrespect "abuse and rape,"[31] which, given the account of trust we have been presuming, sounds perfectly plausible. Granted that assurance of one's being of intrinsic value or worth is a premise for the devastations of rape or torture, nothing about Honneth's object-relations–based analysis of the dialectic of love would lead one to suppose that physical integrity or trust that the other will not harm one was its core stake, as opposed to the capacity to be alone.[32]

Honneth's misprision in the analysis and placement of trust is part of a wider structural distortion in his tripartite scheme. A quick way of displaying the problem here is to consider how he gives to each of the three forms of recognition—love, rights, and esteem—a separate form of disrespect: abuse and rape with respect to love, denial of rights and exclusion with respect to legal recognition, denigration and insult with respect to the social esteem that comes with solidarity. This separating and isolating of forms of disrespect directly contradicts what we have already learned about the moral harm of rape—namely that it shatters basic trust in the world *by* denying the victim's right to bodily integrity and sexual autonomy; it essentially intends to denigrate and demean, and it necessarily expresses a denigration of the victim. Abusing physical integrity *is* a denial of right and *is* an act of demeaning. Rape patently deprives the victim of social integrity (the component of personality secured by rights) and dignity (the component of personality secured by social esteem).[33] Physical integrity is not an isolated and separable good apart from the right to bodily integrity and sexual autonomy (in whole or in part); physical integrity is socially possessed only on the condition that one is given the series of rights (however morally, ethically, legally, or religiously expressed) necessary for its protection and expression, and the possession of those rights is accompanied by one's others routinely expressing that valuation of the possessor that having those rights implies. In failing to connect the elements of his own account appropriately, Honneth misconstrues the phenomenon of recognition itself.

My departures from Honneth's way of prosecuting an account of recognition are, at least, threefold. First, becoming recognized as a person does not occur through the successful achievement—one after another in a cumulative process—of three separate forms of recognition, each with its own domain and logic. Rather, an individual's standing as a person is produced and sustained through diverse social practices that articulate different dimensions or strata of a single complex. The first and primary task of rights, in the broad, nonlegal sense of the term, is to elaborate and socially secure the goods originally achieved in the acquisition of basic trust in the world; one will only finally secure the standing before others that such trust in the world originally delivers through having the necessary rights.[34] Trust is presupposed in order to acquire rights, and *continued basic trust* in normal social interaction in private and public is a consequence of their secure and felicitous possession. Rights, no more than contracts, can replace trust, since trust in the possession of rights is essential to their actual operation. Generally, moral and legal norms are only actual and effective to the extent that we can have confidence that they are authoritative for our social others, and hence that we can trust that our social others are bound to them; this includes being bound to rebukes, grievances, angers, and punishments when those norms are transgressed (recall again Adam's indifference to Eve). This is not to reduce moral and legal rules to trust: they possess a specificity and concreteness that trust relations rarely do; they normatively articulate social space, they orient practices and provide justifications for actions, they justify practices of censure and punishment, they are a collective memory of the values constitutive of who "we" are. Rather, the thought is that the social actuality and ethical substance of a moral rule or right is, finally, the *normative expectation* that it will be effective, operative, and meaningful in social interactions, and that expectation just is trust in others.[35] Hence, part of the trust in others is trust that they will respond as morality dictates, but this is just to say, again, that the meaningfulness of those dictates is parasitic on our sense that others will abide by them. Trust, we might say, is the social presupposition, the basic structure of mutual recognition, on the basis of which moral and legal rules can arise and be socially effective.

Trust is a stratum of personhood, the basic one, produced only through having a "good enough" parental upbringing, but it is not tied to love as its internal correlate. Trust, when successful, detaches from its being acquired, and becomes a general normative orientation to interpersonal life.[36] Second, then, I understand morality, and hence the function of recognition, negatively as providing the *minimum necessary conditions for the possibility of agential life in a self-reproducing society*, as again, following Habermas, "a porous shell protecting a vulnerable body, and the person incorporated in this body." Honneth, conversely, contends that the experiences provided by the three forms of recognition make it possible for a person to "see himself or herself unconditionally, as both an autonomous and an individuated being, and to identify with his or her goals and desires."[37] Honneth supposes that one of the achievements of modernity has been the separation out of the three forms of recognition that were originally undifferentiated in archaic group moralities; so separated, they provide for a formal grammar of the good life in recognitive terms. This is attractive but unearned; apart from the effort of schematizing, Honneth provides no evidence that would turn the negative-protective function of morality—what individuals need in order to be (relatively) full-functioning members of a society capable of reproducing itself—into a model of the good.[38]

Third, while love is the first form of recognition the infant enjoys, neither it nor legal recognition is the primary form of recognition we experience. Trust itself is the primary form of recognition—and it is just this Honneth fails to see, and in not seeing, obscures. If this is right, then there should be a different way of mapping the relations between first love and the trust it generates, and trust as the normatively primary, defeasible condition of social interaction. More precisely, I want to consider the thought that a developmental perspective is intrinsic to the satisfying understanding of trust in adult social relations.

The situation of infants, lasting long into late childhood, is one of radical dependence on caregivers without whom they would not survive; indeed, "the human infant is not . . . an independently intelligible living unit . . . because the sense of his activity depends on the way in which it is interwoven with the activity of others. (The child . . . only gradually becomes independent of his mother's body.)"[39] It is the radicality of dependence that requires infants to affectively assume and anticipate that they will be cared for, their needs met, their pains soothed, their excited affections returned. In time, they come to feel the weight, steadiness, and actuality of parental concern: they feel what we call "loved." As Hertzberg rightly remarks, it would be incorrect to call infants' original behavior toward caregivers one of trust; and while it is true to say they "gradually evolve attitudes which may be called trustful,"[40] that leaps over the shape and stakes of development. Infants' dependence, their utter helplessness, requires them to anticipate that the parent will complete their needy incompleteness. What happens here is not that infants learn to trust their primary caregivers; rather, they first learn a fundamental antecedent to trust—namely, they develop a sense of their self-worth and value; in being able to count on their needs being met, the parental gaze returned, their feeling of excitement in the presence of the other reciprocated; in thus feeling loved they come to feel that they count and matter in the eyes of the other.[41] What is thus attained is the child's experiential sense of what the normal and suitable response to her presence is, and, in light of that treatment and response, her intrinsic worth. Expectations routinely fulfilled become a sense of being of worth or mattering, which is in turn affirmed and bolstered by the continuance of expectations being fulfilled, needs met, desires satisfied. Interactions between infant and primary caregivers set in place for the infant its standing as intrinsically valuable as simply the internal correlate of the treatment received from sufficiently attentive—loving—parents. So coming to have a sense of worth is the same as coming to expect to be treated in a particular manner. When the expectation is, so to speak, automatic, spontaneous, just a matter of acting and responding as normal, then, once the possibility of disappointment has been learned and absorbed, we can say that the child trusts her parents and intimate others.

What this developmental sequence encapsulates then is a movement from love, to self-worth, to an expectation of others responding to that sense of worth as manifest through their responses being responses to a person (a relatively self-determining, intrinsically vulnerable agent) who anticipates treating the other in kind. In brief, the developmental sequence, which I will say more about directly, must do more than provide for the ability to be alone; it must allow for trust to be, finally, the presupposition of one's *standing as a person* in relations with other persons.

The structure of this process of trust-in-the-making or "innocent" trust is unlike adult trust because significant distrust is not yet on the horizon.[42] Were the obstacles to innocent trust to be an insistent element in the psychological life of the infant, this would be because the parenting was severely incompetent, because it was severely disrupted or, worst of all, because there was abuse. In these cases, it becomes tempting to speak of an original or primary distrust of the world of a kind to radically call into question for the infant whether it counts, whether its needs will be met, whether it is safe; but this is not to pick out an alternative path to maturation, but rather to the endlessly documented thought that developmental circumstances of these (deformed) types produce pathological disturbances to the infant's psyche. That is another way of coming to understand innocent trust as normatively constitutive of social interaction; the platform of innocent trust is the background against which maturation and socialization take place.

Innocent trust is the accompaniment, the background music of good-enough parenting. As Baier states: "That infant trust normally does not need to be won but is there unless and until it is destroyed is important for an understanding of the possibility of trust. Trust is much easier to maintain than it is to get started and is never hard to destroy. Unless some form of it were innate, and unless that form could pave the way for new forms, it would appear a miracle that trust ever occurs."[43] Baier's thought is naturally to be construed as a causal claim, but it can be extended to state that the physiognomy of trust, its intelligibility, depends upon the sequence through which innocent trust, the need and acceptance of utter dependence, the expectation that others will respond appropriately, as need requires, becomes adult basic trust. That trust is an original relation to others—taken for granted, spontaneous, prereflective, felicitously receding behind the interactions it subtends—speaks to trust being the concomitant of the child's coming to have a world populated by others generally. Thus—and here is the upshot of the developmental claim—that trust *can* have the features it does, and thereby functionally play the role it does, is a consequence of basic adult trust inheriting from the dependent infant its primordial and felicitous acceptance of its dependence on others. Innocent trust and basic trust are sequential modes through which the attitudes necessary for coping with organic incompleteness are arrived at. There is and needs to be something childlike about trust—its always being too trusting—if trust is going to work at all. Trust carries into the adult world a remnant of the infant's unreflective, spontaneous acceptance of its primary others. Stating the matter this way is not to psychologize the kind of ethical substance trust is; rather, it is to acknowledge that the conceptual anatomy and functional characteristics of trust are only intelligible in a developmental setting.

V. On First Love: Trust as the Recognition of Intrinsic Worth

If humans are capable of suffering devastation, if they are capable of suffering from an irreducibly moral injury, which must, I have been arguing, be an injury to their standing or status as human (as a person, as being a full member of "this" social group), then the developmental sequence through which the human infant becomes a fully self-conscious being must be a process of normative constitution. Contemporary developmental psychologies widely share the Hegelian thought that the primary characteristics of human mindedness—adopting a first-person perspective, having the capacities to attribute intentions, desires, and beliefs to others disparate from one's own, feeling empathy with others' feelings, etc.—are *accomplishments* and *achievements*, at least, and in some cases are theorized as being inter-subjectively *produced* phenomena.[44] Although the details of each theory differ, in broad terms they chart a process that begins with the infant's ac-quiring some conception of its own body as it acquires increasing control over it (yielding the idea of a physical agent), then becoming increasingly engaged in affective-communicative interactions (yielding the emergence of a social agent), which in turn is refined as the infant becomes capable of treating the actions of others and itself as purposive and goal oriented (yielding some conception of a teleological agent), until, sometime dur-ing the second year of life, the infant becomes capable of ascribing men-tal states like desire and intention to others sufficient to understand those states as springs of action.[45] There is debate about how much to ascribe to infants at nine months as opposed to eighteen months, but the gist is agreed.

Amongst the leading accounts of which I am aware, there is an effort to hone their findings to capacities and abilities that are, finally, empirically discriminable. While this makes sense as a constraint on empirical inquiry, it necessarily leaves out of account what I am arguing is the primary work of socialization: the construction of a being who conceives of herself as possessing the kind of *intrinsic worth* necessary for continued participation in normatively governed practices in which there is a categorial divide be-tween intersubjective (second-personal, participant) modes of responsive-ness and objective (third-personal, instrumental) modes of manipulation. Capacities for intersubjective forms of interaction are, I have argued, finally dependent on beings who conceive of themselves as having a standing or status such that their sayings and doings are authoritative: defeasibly true, defeasibly right. If trust is the primary bearer of the intersubjective side of the categorial divide between intersubjective and objective modes of re-sponsiveness (those being the modes of responsiveness appropriate to per-sons and things, respectively), then we need a developmental account that can not only include the possession of one's coming to have a belief that one has intrinsic worth, but in which intrinsic worth belongs to the struc-turally normative conditions through which intersubjective, participant practices transpire. Again, persons not only have values, they *are* values. It is this joined normative and structural constitution of self-consciousness that developmental psychologies have thus far eschewed and that is neces-sary for an understanding of human devastation.[46] Hence the arguments in this section can offer only an ideal or formal account of what I take the requisite developmental sequence to look like, assuming that my major lines of argument are at least compatible with and ideally will converge with empirical inquiry.[47]

To recapitulate: From the perspective of trust, morality is developmentally leveraged from how the objects of others' actions conceive of their vulnerable worth, where vulnerability refers not just to an individual's features—her body, her agency—but to her worth itself, her standing as a value in herself. So, trust is the anticipation, the presumption, the naïve confidence that others will treat me as a person. The question, then, of how does all the complex moral machinery—treating one another as ends-in-themselves—ever get started begins to be answered developmentally: we come to have such grand ideas about our worth because loving-enough parents act that way toward their children. According to McGeer, parental love is turned into trust by parents behaving "*as if* the child trusts the parent—i.e. the parent acknowledges and acts towards the child as a person whose attitudes and actions towards the parent are not only self-determined, but also conditioned by the child's recognition of the parent's own personhood."[48] A central mechanism for the communication of these norm-governed behaviors—how the child is socialized into becoming one who understands herself to be a person among persons—is mimesis; mimetic interaction between parent and child teaches the child what it is to regard another as a person by so treating her and responding in personhood-preserving ways.

A child is socialized and acquires a sense of its worth through a variety of mechanisms and routes, including psychodynamic ones. I am here using mimesis as a synecdoche for the whole process because first, we now know that mimetic interactions begin at birth and remain an enduring mechanism of learning and socialization throughout childhood; second, as compared to other psychological mechanisms—identification, projection, internalizing, externalizing, fantasizing—mimesis is a relatively simple and empirically observable process; third, in mimetic interactions a "learning how to act" aspect is connected to a "connecting with the other" aspect of a kind necessary for explaining how, generally, an understanding of oneself as having a certain standing is connected with acting in normatively appropriate ways; and hence fourth, at first incipiently and eventually explicitly, mimetic interactions are themselves recognitive.[49] The mimetic portion of the construction of self-consciousness thus entails that processes of recognition are both the primary means and the upshot of child development.

While we assume that the primary caregivers are (some version of) mom and dad, with a strong mother-centric view now dominant, earlier societies employed forms of "alloparenting" in which diverse members of the group were equally active in providing essential nurturance and affective attention.[50] Which individuals and how many are involved in primary caregiving does not affect the structure of the experience the infant undergoes. What a satisfying account must do is connect trust with first love via mimetic interaction. The standpoint of trust is the incorporation by the child of its being seen through the eyes of love as worthy and valuable, where the presumption of being so valued becomes its being seen and counting for others as a self-determined vulnerable being who can and will respond to others as self-determined, vulnerable beings too. This complex attitude is imbibed as what being loved by parents comes to in the course of the child's becoming a relatively independent or self-determining being. (What being "independent" means will of course vary from culture to culture. My assumption, again, is that what is required for "full" recognition is being recognized as a "full" member of a community—that is, having all the rights and duties that go along with full membership sufficient for guaranteeing the opportunity to be a fully active participant in the primary practices of societal reproduction.) Trust is the attitude of mutual recognition that comes to be through socialization processes in which the child is loved as a person, and which is necessary to become a person.

The forms of attention to the child and their mimetic response by the child are a rhythmic being seen by the other and seeing the other in return, where each to-and-fro movement is the dance of coming to be seen as a person (e.g., eliciting an apt action from the child) and seeing the other as a person (responding to the action elicited suitably). Each parental act that seeks a mimetic response presumes that it is transcending the causal order of things; hence each such act is an invitation or summons to the infant to *act* in a corresponding way. In summoning the infant to act in some particular way as opposed to causally manipulating the infant in order to generate the desired response, each parental act exposes the infant to the space of reasons where actions bear *meaning* rather than causal significance, and thereby solicit a meaningful and not merely causal response. How else might we describe the focal eye contact and mutual smiling that occurs after the first two months of life? Or the mutual monitoring, affective mirroring, and turn taking that occurs in these months? Mimesis is thus, implicitly and progressively, already recognition, since it takes the child to be a self-moving center of action who becomes progressively more capable of responding to rational invitations to act in rationally appropriate ways. In early mimetic acts, the "rational" element is slim but emphatic: there is an invitation to act like "this"; in acting like "this" the infant is both responding appropriately and doing the action in question in the appropriate way. Two massive areas of normativity are thus built into each mimetic exchange: responding to free actions with free actions (and not with some bit of mechanical/reflexive behavior) and acquiring the sense that the actions are not just fitting for the context but can be done correctly or incorrectly.

Each to-and-fro exchange is thus an affirmation, a way of saying that the mimetic doing of "this" action has the sense "this is how this kind of action *should* be performed, what so acting is"; mimetic affirmation gives contextually constituted modes of acting normative authority. This needs qualifying and elaboration. Of course, the earliest mimetic acts, tongue protrusions and the like, must be hard-wired, but even these hard-wired responses are not simply that, since they involve purposive mechanisms that in time become effort and trying and attempting to get it right by the infant. While the mimetic tripwire is hard-wired, the infant all but mechanically responding to the invitation to mimic the adult action, the process instigated is not merely mechanical because its elements have ineliminable purposive and agential features, and rightness conditions; the neonate forerunner of intentional effort and success matters from the very beginning.[51] Mimetic interactions are thus components of an ontogenetic bootstrapping operation whereby the continual exposure of the infant to the space of reasons via mimetic invitations initiates processes that, incrementally and progressively, become full-blown intentional actions (and related to-and-fro action sequences) in the course of their doing.

Further, in order for the infant to try to match the parental model, she must already be involved in a complex cross-modal mapping, attempting to match what is perceived with her eyes to internal proprioceptive sensations (the "what it's like" to protrude one's tongue). Because successful mimetic interactions necessarily involve cross-modal mappings, registering equivalences "between the body transformations [infants] see and the body transformations they only feel themselves to make," we can hypothesize that "there is a primitive *supramodal body scheme* that allows the infant to unify acts-as-seen and acts-as-felt into a common framework."[52] While there is debate about when to ascribe to the infant such a supramodal body scheme (from the get-go or only when the infant has effective sense of its bodily boundaries), bodily self-awareness is a condition for the developmental processes that follow. As a consequence, Daniel N. Stern has argued that we should conceive of "primary consciousness" as a "yoking together, in the present moment, of the intentional object and the vital background input from the body. The body input specifies that it is *you* who is now having the experience of the intentional object."[53] Self-consciousness requires that experiences be grasped as "mine"; the mine-ness of experience, Stern argues, is rooted in the coordination between a sense of the intentional object—the rattling of the rattle—and bodily self-awareness—the infant's internal sense that it is its *effortful* kicking motion that is producing the rattling. Minimum coordination between the body I have and the body I am emerges early and forms an essential condition for what follows.

At roughly nine months, something of a social-cognitive (or recognitive-cognitive) revolution occurs as "infants start to follow the adult's gaze reliably (gaze following), actively attend to the adult's facial and vocal attitude expressions about unfamiliar objects or situations to modify their own behavior (social referencing), and act on objects in the way adults are acting on them (imitative learning)."[54] While, again, there is debate about how best to interpret this moment, it seems reasonable to hypothesize that at least by the middle of the second year of life in gaze following and social referencing the infant is becoming sufficiently capable of distinguishing its subjective life from the parent's to attribute to the infant the acknowl-edgment of points of view other than its own. And this would entail a si-multaneous decentering of the infant's own subjective perspective that is coordinated with its emphatically *sharing* intentional states with the adult (attending to an object because the other is attending to it). With social ref-erencing, the infant is explicitly taking the primary caregiver as *authoritative* in determining what an appropriate response to a new situation should be; that is, social referencing, which again is the moment in which something like a separate subjective orientation becomes established, occurs with an incipient installation of the other as authoritative about what kind of re-sponse is called for here. This is a moment that is proximate to that of Adam and Eve's apple exchange where three coordinated phenomena all come into being simultaneously: the acquisition of a subjective point of view different from that of the other; the capacity to respond to the other as other, taking the other as having a special standing that is needful for the infant; and the emergence of explicit rightness conditions ("Should I touch this? Should I cry now?").[55] But to say that these three moments arise together is equally to claim that becoming minimally self-conscious, conscious of oneself as a separate being, is to become exposed to the anxi-ety of separation, to come to experience the emphatic or constitutive need for another's returning a response as an affirmation of one's now-exposed separate existence.

These accomplishments create the conditions for even more explicit imitative learning. Imitative learning involves a slightly different normative coordination: there it seems right to say that mimetic acts through which infants learn *how* to perform certain actions simultaneously involve learning to do them *correctly*; the norm is given with the achievement of the performance itself. Since acting is learning how to act correctly, mimesis sets in place the two primary features of rational action: first, that actions are contextually sensitive, rational/meaningful responses to contextually sensitive, reasoned/meaningful summonses from an other, the infant getting, so to speak, that an intentional action is an address to her to act in a manner appropriate to the original invitation; second, that actions are normatively saturated, possessing intrinsic correctness conditions—acting is always acting rightly or wrongly.

Even assuming only the modest resources of mimetic interaction and affect mirroring, the nine-month revolution (or its elaboration at eighteen months) would appear to transform protorecognitive interactions into full-blown relations of recognition in which the infant's separation from the parent becomes explicit, so demanding that the connection between infant and parent be *achieved* in a way that introduces new forms and possibilities of failure; misrecognition is now possible in way it was not earlier. If, for example, efforts at social referencing are not responded to appropriately by the adult, if the adult does not recognize the intentional summons to respond, then the infant is left with "wild" affects, affects that, lacking a socially referenced subjective place, are deposited back on a being who lacks resources for coping with them; in this case, lacking such resources is equally injurious to the conception of self the infant was incipiently soliciting; if it cannot regulate its emotions, then it cannot construct a self whose separateness and connection to others is intelligible to it. Perceiving this form of threat is what it is to comprehend how a coherent self-conception depends on the achievement of successful forms of mirroring and referencing, and hence how the primitive structures of independence and dependence are installed simultaneously. But to concede this is equally to acknowledge the absoluteness or radicality of the dependence of the infant on others as a condition for its being.

What would make this scenario emphatically recognitive would be the reminder that mimetic interactions must equally belong within the order of desire. Even the simplest mimetic interactions between parent and child will, over time, embody all three aspects of what Judith Butler denominates "the desire of desire": desiring desire itself as more life, more vital affection; desiring what the other desires by making the other's desired doing the model for one's doing; and the converse of this, wanting the other to desire your desire by taking your desired action as the model to be imitated.[56] Coming to appreciate this feature of mimetic interaction is essential since, as we have already seen, to desire the other's desire, to desire that the other desires your desire, is the structural core of *pure* recognition; hence, the structure of desire governing mimetic episodes is what, finally, makes those episodes authority constituting, and thus truly recognitive. Further, the desire of desire in mimetic interaction is the precise mechanism through which the desire to live becomes the desire to be recognized. But this is to say that only by placing mimetic episodes in the order of desire is it possible to understand why the being of a self-conscious agent is dependent on recognition, and hence how self-worth, social existence, and recognition are interrelated. Let us consider the three aspects of the desire of desire in turn.

First, seeking out a mimetic interaction and, even more importantly, *succeeding and repeating, is desiring desire*, desiring to have one's desire enlivened, renewed, connected by being placed in relation to the other's desire; the connection with the other, the repetitious involvement in the mimetic cycle, doubles the desires and ratchets them up. There is an excitement in mimetic interactions, as the satisfaction attaching to successful acts seems to call for more: more desire and more acts and more satisfactions, as if the doubling from the outside somehow connected with the affect itself. The demanded repetitions—"Again!"—that are so central to mimetic interactions connect achievement and satisfaction with the urge of desire itself for satisfaction, the desire for desire which is the desire for more life, more vitality, more satisfaction—without end.[57] Part of the message here is thus that subjective interaction, the achievement of mutual recognition that occurs in successive mimetic interactions, is life, the liveliness of life. That *recognition is life* and *isolation a kind of death* is affectively true before it becomes socially true, and it is socially true because it was affectively true in the very constitution of self-consciousness.

Second, desiring to imitate the parent's action is desiring her desire, having her desire become the model for what the infant desires, viz., to do "this." In this mode, successful mimetic action is a normative achievement whose value is satisfying the desire implied by the original summons to mimetic interaction. In getting the action right, the infant satisfies mother's desire and thus becomes worthy. Practical success and self-worth are inseparable here. Third, conversely and even more importantly, parents will pick out stretches of infant behavior and imitate it, indicating that that action, say, hand-waving, is something worth doing. When this occurs, what the infant is taught is that the parent desires her desire, and so approves, values, and confirms her; her doing and her desire are worthy of being *models*—normatively authoritative—for what should happen. In being imitated, one is given the value of being a source of value, as being authoritative for how a stretch of acting normatively should be done. Becoming an agent is being *authorized* as an agent, or, what is the same, learning that acting is an exercise of normative (legislative) authority: the infant is authorized by having its doing mimetically repeated by the adult, and the adult is recognized in turn as an authority in being referenced by the infant. But being an authority is always qualified: an act is authoritative if and only if it is deserving of being taken up and repeated by the other; without the other's echoing response, nothing has been done or felt.

Putting together the learning how to act/acting rightly aspect of mimetic interaction with mimetic desire, it follows that each mimetic acknowledgment of a success is also affirmed as an individual achievement, so valuing the doer. In performing the action as it should be performed, the infant is affirmed as deserving because she is one who has the standing of one who has the capacity and expertise to perform "these" kinds of actions—all the smiling and congratulating and cooing and "Aren't you a clever girl?" business that accompanies the interactions, with this process itself heightened when the infant's action becomes the model and the parent the repeater. In complex mimetic interactions, the two sides are joined, and when joined successfully they naturally give rise to (and are driven by) the first moment: the desire for more desire, the desire for life-giving recognition itself. Mimetic affirmation normatively authorizes the standing of the infant as agent by authorizing her mimetic performances, her *standing*, value, and worth bound up with her increasing mastery over her body and her capacity to successfully engage in interactions with caregivers and with things in the world, and thereby her capacity to legislate appropriate action sequences. As the infant increasingly comes to see herself in these normative and value-saturated terms, she also comes to see her parents as co-respondents, beings who share the normative sense of how these forms of action are done, and hence how they are to be responded to accordingly. Thus, in the ongoing processes of mimetic responses—their increasing sophistication, their increasing real mutuality, their sharing of enlivening pleasure in interactive success—there is borne and shaped, in socially normative forms, the worth of the partners to the interaction: they become independent persons for one another. Hence, the mimetic dance is experienced by the child normatively as how it matters and expects to matter to others who matter to it; call this the mimetic dance of first love.

A core component of first love, the one carried by and realized in mimetic interactions in particular, is the anticipation of mattering to the other who matters in return; this structure of mattering to an other who matters to you becomes the child's assumption of mattering to others as she matters to her parents, and hence, finally, mattering as one person matters to another. But stating the position in these bald terms is to state them from the outside; hence it is to perceive the emergence of self-consciousness from the position of a third person. How might all this be expressed in first-personal terms? Let me try the following phrasing of the scenario we have been tracking. What is meant by an individual's being of intrinsic worth is that its doings *normatively demand* an echoing response from the other. Through the course of early mimetic interactions, the increasingly satisfied *expectation* that a doing will be responded to as worthy of being repeated—or that the mirroring of the adult action will be returned once more—must turn into a normative expectation, since that norming of the doings is what the mirroring is meant to establish. Mimetic responses, increasingly then, take on the sense of what is an appropriate or correct or right response to the original summons. (And small children, we know, are rule fascists: only the right way of doing X is tolerable.) My hypothesis has been that this transition from, let us call it, subjective psychological space to norm-governed intersubjective space provides the ground interpretation of the events succeeding the nine-month revolution.

Once this occurs, the infant has already incipiently formed a metarepresentation of itself to the extent that it is now aware of itself as separate from the adult; it seeks the adult's attention, and comes to see itself as being seen by the adult. In the language of desire and norm, the infant now begins to *take* its doings as authoritative, as worthy, to the extent that to find no echoing response from the other is *taken* as a rebuff or rebuke or denial of it. That is, once the awareness of separateness occurs, mimetic summonses become a way in which the infant is *staked*: a failure in response to a mimetic response here is like a denial of its being, a banning or expulsion rather than a mere unanticipated result or a disappointed expectation (to be *only* disappointed by others' responses assumes either indifference or resiliency). This is not a psychological fact, but a normative one: the rebuff is a denial of intrinsic worth. Thus the infant cannot act at this juncture without its *every* action becoming a staking of its standing. If loved well enough, there will be enough mimetic affirmations to make the originally fragile sense of self-worth simply the given presupposition of what it is to do ordinary activities. Isn't this scenario, from a different angle, just the Hegelian idea that self-consciousness involves a self-taking, a desire to be a self, that can be satisfied, finally, only by being taken up by another? And hence, isn't this scenario the Hegelian idea that the other stands between the self and itself as a condition for being a self-conscious being? While it is perfectly appropriate to call success here the providing of security, and failure insecurity, those terms alone will never provide a pathway into the structures of individual self-worth in relation to norm-governed experience. However, once we perceive the panoply of mimetic interactions running through the first three years of life as, finally, organized and driven by a desire for recognition, then the distinctive pathway into the normative is necessary: it emerges as the self emerges as a self-consciousness.

Of course, mattering to one's primary caregivers is not the same as mattering to others in the world; parental love remains specific and needful—we never seem to be able to be done with it—while becoming, eventually, the adult's need for love. Love has its own dynamic and trajectory. But as the original parent-child dyad becomes a triad, and then as the child begins interacting with siblings, playmates, or other adults, the presuppositions of mattering as connected to routine interactions are continually reformed so as to become the child's spontaneous presumptions about the proprieties governing everyday worldly encounters.[58] In this way, everything that has been learned about how actions mean, about appropriateness conditions, about responsiveness, above all about how one counts in interactions in relation to one's following the norms appropriate to them, becomes simply the taken-for-granted stuff of what acting in relation to others is. If this evolution through mimetic interaction of how the child matters to herself and others is accurate, then the child will trust in others just when she routinely sees them as simply further interaction partners, nonparental persons with whom she can interact as the activity dictates without further consideration; in so doing, she trusts them.

Trust is the self-understanding of the child as a person who is recognized as a person by others (which is why trust does not require any specific affective accompaniment); because her sense of self-worth and expectations are constitutive of who the child is, her trusting attitude necessarily involves how she (normatively) *expects* to be seen by (all) others. The expectation is, again, in the first instance, spontaneous and natural, just what a still-narcissistically tinged experience of others as potential interaction partners involves. But love being what love is, for a child who has undergone good-enough parenting, the expectation will be deep, as what is deserved, proper, *and necessary* (the good hangs on it). The necessity is normative and not merely psychological. I understand the depth of the expectation that one be treated in accordance with one's worth—the value deposit of love—to be the incipient source of the normative expectations connected with being a person. Because love-formed expectations are how the child thinks she should be treated, she carries those expectations outside the affective conditions of their inception. *Trust relations are love relations absent the affective bond that gives first love its specificity.*

Trust is the *conveyor and medium* through which the value world of love becomes the ethically normal world of interpersonal interaction. This entails not just that trust inherits and expands into a generative attitude the value assumptions and action expectations of the infant's education through love, but further that trust is the attitudinal sedimentation of those assumptions and expectations. Trust inherits and becomes the primary bearer of those prereflective value assumptions and action expectations; trust, then, is the social actuality of love's mimetic fashioning of an assured self-valuing social being. If this were not the case, there would not exist the tight connection between trust and personhood sufficient to explain how the traumatized loss of trust in the world is the direct consequence of the negation of an individual's standing as a person. In devastation, again, the victim is deprived of all the valuations and action expectations that are sedimented in her trust of the world; the transgression of basic norms of appropriateness simultaneously transgresses the normative conditions constitutive of an individual's sense of self-worth, and the loss of self-worth is emphatically indexed by loss of trust in the world. Devastation deposits the grown individual in the precise situation of having its entire being staked on some one or more authorities, and having its summons, which for an adult is, in the first instance, just its physical presence in the world with others, actively denied. Devastations are those occurrences in which singular episodes reveal how the self is constitutively dependent on others.

Trust, one might say, spontaneously takes the world to be one fit for a being who has been sufficiently loved in her formation as a person. *Because basic trust bears within itself the actuality of being well loved, the intrinsic value of an individual for herself is embedded in the daily routine of trust.* The work of first love is socially realized and confirmed in trusting relations. Although I am casting this in developmental and narrative terms, I mean this to be a conceptual point about the relation between love and trust: trust as the lesson of first love in how one comes to adopt the standpoint of taking oneself to matter, and expecting others whom one sees as persons to respond appropriately. Because the expectations are related to necessary conceptions of self-worth—the worth of one who has the standing appropriate to engage in normatively structured action sequences—they have normative authority; it is that authority that is underwritten, substantiated, and given social currency by the mostly implicit (trust-borne) and explicit ethical norms and principles. Because morality glimpses the normative sediment but not the trust, it transforms spontaneous expectations and inter-subjective patterns into monological external demands (say, the demands of practical reason). This is how morality becomes socially pervasive and unintelligible, empty, at the same time.

There could be no trust without the passage through love; trust thus bears not only the childlike remnant of its once having been innocent, it is a product of a particular process through which a human gathers her value through her treatment by her parents. Let me pace out this thought more directly. Being loved is being valued; being so valued becomes in-corporated into and associated with mimetically induced and normatively structured patterns of interaction. As the child becomes capable of a fairly full range of self-determined activities, those modes of interaction become those that occur between normatively constituted self-conscious beings— persons; in time the child takes those modes of interaction outside the family setting, expecting new others to fall in with patterns and normative expectations learned in the mimetic dance of first love. Learning to take those modes of interaction outside the family setting is learning to interact with relevant others in a manner roughly—normatively but not affectively or emotionally—analogous to the way one interacts with family members. In order to do so, the child must trust that those others will respond ap-propriately, and hence trust that although they are not adoring lovers the way parents are, she will nonetheless count for them; that she does count for them is revealed in their appropriate response patterns. Spontaneously expecting others to fall in with the patterns and expectations first learned in love is trusting them to do so—trusting them, we will come to say, to *respect* her intrinsic worth. Ordinary normatively regulated interactions— playing together, talking, sharing a chore or a routine—because they are forms of practice that operate on the basis of mutuality, bear a continuous ethical meaning to the child of her worth and mattering to her partners. This is why breaches of playground or classroom or sibling etiquette can feel brutally injurious to the child.

Trust is the ethical substance of ordinary interactions, and the more un-noticed it is, the more substantial its actuality. It is because trust is the ethi-cal premise of such interactions that breaches of normative rules governing a routine practice can be felt to be a betrayal, a slighting or putting down or dismissing. We are normatively invested in practices carried out in trust-ing conditions because lying beneath them is the presumption that follow-ing the rules of the practice *is* respecting me as one of its participants; and hence breaking the rules of the practice may signal that I no longer count as a person for you, which is what we discovered was the wrong of promise breaking in chapter 4. Trusting relations are the fundamental way in which individuals appear as persons in ordinary social circumstances. This is why basic trust—that one counts as a person for oneself with respect to others at all—is constitutive of the self, and its destruction a devastation to who one is as a person.

What trust pertains to, the reason why we require being recognized as a person by others is because we are dependent and vulnerable. As McGeer pointedly states, the adult "requires that his vulnerability to the trusted other be recognized as the vulnerability of one self-determined person to another. It is thus a vulnerability based on interests, needs, and desires which are importantly the truster's own and to which he trusts the other can and will be sensitive, guiding her actions accordingly."[59] Note that in expecting to be treated as a person, we expect others to be sensitive to our intrinsic vulnerability; hence *our standing and value as persons is in part constituted through our vulnerability*. Recognition of the needful kind is necessarily recognition of a finally unsurpassable vulnerability and helplessness before the other. Trust's invisibility is the fundamental mechanism we have for negotiating the difficulty and awkwardness of this fact. Nonetheless, our intrinsic value as persons necessarily includes vulnerability; I cannot recognize you as an end-in-itself if I do not recognize your vulnerability and perpetual exposure to harm. Trust is this. Love is this. It is sometimes said that the value of things is proportional to their scarcity; with humans, what ethical value we have is proportional to our vulnerability.

The reason why trust and not some other mode of recognition is primary is because I need to be counted as a person not for the sake of prestige or glory or moral fulfillment, but in order to survive, in order not to suffer injuries to my moral and natural being. It is the relation between our standing as persons, our vulnerability to others, and our bodily being that now needs further elaborating.

SIX

"My Body . . . My Physical and Metaphysical Dignity"

I. Why Dignity?

In "On the Necessity and Impossibility of Being a Jew," Jean Améry returns to the topic of human dignity that he had broken off in his discussion of torture. As he admits in his preface, he changed his mind about dignity in the course of writing the essays that compose *At the Mind's Limits*: "In the essay on torture . . . I brushed [dignity] off with a sweep of the hand, as it were, whereas later, in the essay on my Jewishness, I believed to recognize that dignity is the right to live granted by society" (AML, xiv).[1]

As we saw in chapter 2, the brush off occurs at his suffering "the first blow" as a consequence of his arrest by the Gestapo in July 1943. "I don't know," he proclaims, "if the person who is beaten by the police loses human dignity. Yet I am certain that with the very first blow that descends on him he loses something we will perhaps temporarily call 'trust in the world'" (AML, 27–28). The first blow crumbles Améry's trust in the world; with the experience of torture, that trust is lost for good, never to be regained (AML, 40; 46–48, 95, 99–100). Trust in the world, I have argued, is the ethical substance of everyday living; it is the primary locus of ethical experience, the place where our sense of intrinsic or unconditional self-worth that is the constitutive lesson of first love is existentially posed in our relation to relevant others, and hence what is experientially most at stake in the devastations that rape and torture impose. Even if the victim can regain some sense of his intrinsic self-worth, he can no longer have the confidence that this will matter to others, that his mere standing as a human is sufficient to support the existential proprieties of everyday living.

Trust in the world is the categorial attitude in which each individual's comprehension of their intrinsic self-worth is posed as internally conditioned by the regard of relevant others. Trust in the world is the switching station in which the self-worth learned from first love is transformed into the normative expectation that one's forever-vulnerable personhood will be treated with the respect that is its due. In comparison with loss of trust in the world, the question of human dignity can appear hopelessly abstract and vague.

One reason for dignity's abstract appearance is that, more explicitly than other fundamental moral concepts, dignity as it is now used, especially in human rights conventions and state constitutions, is a recent historical invention. The idea of connecting dignity with inviolability has Greek origins, but was installed in a recognizable way in the late Middle Ages by Italian city-states, republics, and principalities. "Republics," Darius Rejali reminds us, "carefully limited torture to noncitizens and slaves. Citizens had dignity and were thus inviolable, at least normally."[2] Along with prepubescents, the mad, and pregnant women, Roman-canon law generally exempted those having dignity from judicial torture. Possessing dignity in this setting was an acknowledgment of an individual's social standing; a dignified being was exempt from torture because either such persons are not the sort of beings who would lie about their deeds, or to torture a fellow citizen would implicitly rend the status system itself. The two thoughts were indiscriminately entwined. Dignity was a wholly civil status, but one which provided its bearer with a certain *legal inviolability*: the body of the citizen was placed beyond the reach of the state with respect to judicial torture. In most locations, the seventeenth century saw the dignity exclusion dropped. This gave literate elites a passionate individual interest concerning the use of judicial torture that they had not possessed earlier. Thus, when public tortures came to be viewed as destructive, and revolt against them widespread, a natural way of expressing what was legally required was to say that *everyone* now deserved the inviolability given by the possession of dignity. What subtly and imperceptibly changes with the generalization or universalization of dignity is that it shifts from a narrow civic-legal status into a moral status: each citizen is possessed of *moral inviolability*, with bodily autonomy and bodily integrity as immediate ingredients in the human being of each citizen; bodily violation thus becoming a denial of the victim's status *as human*. One might thus say that moral modernity involves the universalizing of the civil status position provided by the notion of dignity, where the force of the universalization requirement (that each is deserving of equal inviolability) is what makes the expansion a transformation from a positive-legal attribute into a moral-legal status, which is effectively what the efforts of the modern rule of law and human rights discourse amount to.[3]

Michael Rosen calls this the "expanding circle" narrative, in which, in response to the new sense of abhorrence at the sight of violation, the idea that each citizen-body should be inviolable, have dignity, comes to extend outward and downward "until it has come to apply to all human beings."[4] Application of dignity to all has, in fact, taken the better part of two and a half centuries to come into even notional effect. Constant among the earliest responses to the eighteenth-century declarations of the moral equality of all humans—including by Kant—were racist and sexist qualifications insisting that such equality should not be interpreted as entailing that all humans are equally morally mature and adult, and thus capable of taking on the full responsibilities, including political participation, that adulthood requires.[5] As a consequence, moral universalism was originally combined with an insistence on there nonetheless being *status* differentiations among men and women, whites and blacks, etc.—a method of qualification that is as old as universalism itself. This made the early uses of the notion of human dignity as signifying the universal moral equality of humans stubbornly equivocal: how could status equality be combined with status differentiation? If status differentiation was the mechanism for sidestepping or subverting the implications of moral universalism, then moral universalism could not or should not be interpreted in status terms; secularizing the natural law tradition—being born free and equal in rights—was thus taken to stand on its own as a moral condemnation of illegitimate social distinctions, with status distinctions remaining a mechanism of qualification and abridgement. Further, because dignity is irredeemably a status concept, even as it was expanded to signal the moral inviolability of all humans, it continued to stand in uneasy tension with more traditional moral concepts and notions: rules, commands, rights, duties, judgments, and virtues.[6]

It was not until directly after World War II, when the devastations of the Nazi genocide made connecting moral regard with status equality unavoidable—the *moral necessity* for treating each and every human being *as* a human being with equal moral standing—that the substantive moral universalism designated by the idea of the possession of human dignity was made explicit together with the minimum moral, legal, and political consequences entailed by that robust conception of universalism. Again, this history has been as complex as it has because neither moral universalism nor common moral ideas appeared to either require or be easily combinable with the vision of inviolability and equality of status that provides the idea of human dignity with its ultimate force.

In asserting that trust is the ethical substance of everyday life, I have been claiming that always and everywhere, sotto voce, status and morality have been, in fact, internally related, and that receiving the regard appropriate to one's station in light of social belonging has been the effective normative bond regulating social practices of all kinds. In the more technical vocabulary of the recognitive theory of self-consciousness: to be an authoritative maker of significance claims has typically occurred through being regarded as a full member of the relevant social group, where full membership is equivalent to having all the rights and/or duties—traditionally, narrowly attached to one's social role(s)—necessary for full and active participation in the practical life of that encompassing group. "Full" and "active" participation did not traditionally mean *equal* rights to participation. One is recognized as a member in good standing through participation in social practices whose participants' normative regard for one another is borne by their trust in one another, and their trust in one another demonstrated by the routine acceptance and social enforcement of the status, rights, and appropriate proximity of each consociate.

This emphasis on trust's centrality in connecting how self-conscious subjects' awareness of their intrinsic worth was related to the normative core structuring their relations to consociates should not lead us to forget how limited trust is as practical norm. As we have seen, trust's effectiveness depends on its invisibility, its capacity to operate through receding behind the social practices it makes possible. It is this that explains how trust can be both primary and extremely limited as an ethical notion: trust on its own cannot make explicit its assumptions and requirements without ceasing to be trust. For self-conscious beings who require an understanding of their standing and status in order to deal with status differences and inequalities, to deal with novel conditions and contingencies that require modification in existing practices, who must engage in practices of shaming, punishing, and excluding, and who have the further need to rationalize the authority of all those practices for the sake of socially transmitting and reproducing them, trust will be forever inadequate. The depth and power of trust is thus at one with its practical social insufficiency.

As a consequence, every society has invented a system of rules, norms, and practices through which it makes explicit its trust-borne system of mutual recognitions, misrecognitions, and nonrecognitions, and it has complemented its normative regulations with some narrative account as to why those regulations have the authority they do. Trust must be supplemented with explicit ethical rules, commandments, principles, ideals, and norms, and the whole normative complex must be rationalized and authorized. And even those elaborations are insufficient, since beyond them we further need to account for how the ethical norms governing trust-borne interpersonal relations concretely function in practice—that is, what ethical markers beyond trust and distrust orient the respect relations among consociates, as well as how they and the relevant ethical markers are related to the dominant social institutions of a society. It is through pondering this last issue that progress can be made in thinking through the ethical actuality of trust-infused social practices. Where should we look in order to elaborate the relation between trusting (and disrupted) interpersonal relations and social institutions that must, in some manner, be responsive to the same normative demands as those that structure the fine-grained interactions of everyday life?

Mediating between trust-borne expectations on the one hand, and the dominant institutions of a society on the other is a society's complex moral psychology: its language of insult, injury, shame, dishonor, disrespect, degradation, disgrace, embarrassment, indignity, mortification, and humiliation in relation to its language of honor and respect. The ethical actuality of a society's investment in its status-sustaining roles and ideals arrives through those expressions in which individuals register their experiences of misrecognition and moral injury. Although there are terms of recognition other than honor and respect, in general, the negative language of moral injury is more refined and nuanced than the affirmative language of moral praise and acknowledgment. I take the reason for this to be that we do not, in fact, have an account of what sufficient recognition looks like apart from the overstuffed closet of negative concepts that discriminate the forms, sources, and experiences of moral injury. For reasons we shall come to directly, this is a natural inference for a theory of recognition. Further, as argued earlier, the primary work of ethical notions is negative, protection from harm and injury, rather than being about (moral) self-realization or perfection. While devastation marks the extreme of the destruction of personhood, humiliation has come to replace dishonor as the paradigm form of a moral injury that involves a radical and painful diminishment of self-worth that stops short of devastation.[7] Devastation is the extreme of humiliation, and humiliation is the experience of the possibility of devastation. Humiliation is morally serious in itself—it is a form of moral injury and suffering—and for what it tokens: to feel oneself humiliated is to know that worse is possible.

In *The Decent Society*, Avishai Margalit attempts to construct a general social theory around the concept of humiliation. His opening thesis is useful for our purposes. He argues that a decent society is one in which the dominant institutions do not humiliate those whose lives fall under its auspices, while "a civilized society is one whose members do not humiliate one another."[8] A civilized society stands to a decent society as horizontally structured interpersonal relations stand to the vertical relation between individual lives and the dominant institutions of a society, or, what is the same, as the microethical life of a society stands to its macroinstitutional functioning. A decent (and civilized) society is not necessarily a fully just society, but unless and until the normative ideals of decency and civilization are satisfied, justice is meaningless. My argument has been that a civilized society is—and has been—one in which relations of trust are preponderant in interpersonal relations, where the burdens of distrust are fairly and equally distributed (i.e., disruptions to trust are not patterned by structures of group belonging), while a decent society is, for us moderns, one premised on substantive rule of law. As I will argue directly, the "Laws for the Protection of German Blood and German Honor," and the "Reich Citizenship Law"—which, following common practice, I will refer to jointly as the Nuremberg Laws[9]—were noteworthy for their attempt to use the law in order to cause maximum humiliation, humiliation patently portending devastation and death, at both the microinterpersonal level and the macroinstitutional level. The Nuremberg Laws comprehended, painfully and exquisitely, how the experience of indefatigable humiliation required not only legal abandonment but also a precisely aimed effort of savage social mortification.

Margalit considers three fundamental forms of humiliation, each of which has played a role in my argument as an element or cause of devastation: "treating humans as nonhuman, rejection [from the encompassing group], and acts intended to lead to lack of control or to highlight one's lack of control."[10] However differently, each of these forms of humiliation is tied to the undermining of an individual's conception of their intrinsic worth under conditions of radical dependency. One can only treat humans as if they were nonhuman—as thinglike, or beastlike, or as subhuman—in ways that are not just physically painful but decimating to the individual's sense of themselves on the condition that having a sense of intrinsic self-worth is constitutive of personhood in ways that normatively and existentially demand value-acknowledging forms of treatment; there can be no humiliation as the derogation of the human unless the *status* of being human is normatively and existentially constitutive of persons. Only when affirmative self-evaluation in relation to others is understood to belong to the very structure of subjectivity can these forms of moral injury take on the full character of their harmfulness. And, again, what makes these forms of harmfulness possible is that they are injurious because the standing of each is dependent on the regard of others; because we are dependent on others for our being human, forms of social exclusion and marginalization are experienced as humiliation: because the social operation supporting the principle of "separate but equal" is a work of exclusion, it is and is experienced as morally injuring. Constitutive dependency on others also makes the lack of self-control more than a physical fact: existential helplessness is a categorial stratum of personhood for beings who both have and are their bodies, where their having their body is dependent on the recognition of others. How systematically this is the case is another of the central themes of this chapter.

Margalit's way, and indeed the common way for expressing the thesis that humiliation assumes a background assumption of a value-saturated sense of self in relation to others, is to say that there is an assumption of "basic respect due to human beings, such that deviating from it results in humiliation." Margalit continues: "Humiliation is a concept based on contrast, and the opposite of humiliation is the concept of respect for humans. *If there is no concept of human dignity, then there is no concept of humiliation either.*"[11] Even in context, this claim about human dignity can seem as if shot from a pistol. It is not quite that since, some one hundred pages earlier, Margalit mentions that humiliating gestures violate the dignity of the victim, where "dignity is the representation of self-respect."[12] Exactly how this notion of representation is supposed to work is less than transparent. I take it that Margalit adopts the phrasing he does because he does not want to reify dignity into an independent value-bestowing property, an "inner, transcendental kernel"[13] whose possession would make an individual deserving of moral treatment. Nothing has done more harm to the discourse of human dignity than the assumption that there is some magical property, say the possession of the power of reason, whose simple possession by an individual suddenly gives her the standing of having intrinsic and inviolable worth. Call this the magical metaphysics of dignity. It is necessary to concede that at present this magical metaphysics is all too pervasive in dignity discourses. Given the fundamental role dignity plays in a wide range of legal and political documents, including the Universal Declaration of Human Rights and the German Constitution (*Grundgesetz* or Basic Law)—"Human dignity is inviolable. To respect and protect it is the duty of all state power."—there is an urgent need to shore up its conceptual and moral credentials without collapsing into magical thinking.

The turn to dignity after World War II was for the purpose of installing some fundamental conception of status and worth into the understanding of the specific moral wrongfulness and awfulness of the practices in the internment and death camps, and so to make ethically perspicuous in what ways those practices were radically humiliating and devastating prior to being genocidal. Genocide completes a process of dehumanization; the physical harm of dehumanization has the character it does because it did and was meant to cause absolute dignitary harm—or rather, to grasp dehumanization as structurally involving the harnessing of physical suffering to decimating humiliation is the thesis that here needs defending. As we saw vividly with torture and rape, the physical and moral forms of suffering and harm are in these kinds of cases interconnected; providing those considerations with a more robust conceptual texture is a further primary goal of this chapter.

In claiming that dignity is the representation of self-respect, Margalit means to be claiming that dignity is the way individuals represent their self-respect, where self-respect is an individual's respect for her own moral standing and worth. This entails that dignity arises as an object of respect: when respect is shown to the human standing of others, we are respecting their dignity. What this suggests—and this is the thought I want to track in this chapter—is that an appropriate understanding of human dignity requires a small constellation of interrelated moral psychological concepts: respect, self-respect, humiliation, and, I shall argue, love and lovability.[14] Call this the *dignity constellation*. What this constellation of concepts accomplishes is to structure and give form to the normative requirements of recognitively structured interdependent lives; the functioning of these concepts in practice provides for the actuality (or the failure) of trust relations. Again, such lives are not grounded and founded on anything other than the practices of recognition that make self-conscious lives possible in the first instance and that socially sustain (or crush) them.

Rather than attempting to directly conceptually reconstruct the dignity constellation, my procedure here will be to continue the exposition of Améry's personal phenomenology of the victim's existence as an accurate experiential guide to the nature of suffering in extreme situations. Améry discovers that dignity is an essential ethical figure that runs through the entirety of the Nazi project for the extermination of the Jewish people: from the Nuremberg Laws to the experiences in the camps to the political reality of Jewish life after the war. Even a cursory reading of Améry on dignity yields five stubborn theses: (i) human dignity is not a metaphysical and natural possession of human beings but a social accomplishment bound to structures of recognition; (ii) because human dignity is a social product, it can be destroyed; (iii) although human dignity would be nothing if not recognized by another, it cannot be the case that the meaning of dignity involves it being one-sidedly endowed, simply *given* by the other: individuals insist upon their dignity through resistance and revolt; (iv) human dignity has an ineliminable corporeal dimension; and (v) although recognition of human dignity occurs along a variety of dimensions, it achieves perspicuous representation in the discourse of human rights: rights are the primary articulation of the meaning of human dignity. I will say a little something about (v) in my concluding remarks, saving a full exposition for another occasion.

Améry's way of reckoning with the question of human dignity will allow us to give a perspicuous conceptual order to the materials on recognition, moral injury, trust, and love that have thus far guided our reflections by relating them to the other fundamental concepts belonging to the dignity constellation. Section II will introduce Améry's vision of the predicament of those deprived of their rights and dignity. In the following sections, I will attempt to provide conceptual clarification and justification for Améry's philosophical provocations.

II. From Nuremberg to Treblinka: The Fate of the Unlovable

Améry recalls sitting over a newspaper in a Vienna coffeehouse in 1935, studying the Nuremberg Laws that had recently been enacted in Germany. However much Améry self-identified as a good Austrian—he was born Hans Meyer, the only child of a Catholic mother and Jewish father—he recognized immediately that the Nuremberg Laws applied to him, and that, come what may, he would, from then on, be a Jew, and that being so had taken on a new dimension: society had passed a judgment upon him whose only tangible meaning was that "henceforth I was a quarry of Death" (AML, 85). Although millions of Jews have urged that they did not see what was to come in the Nuremberg Laws, Améry argues that it took no great political insight to see in them a death sentence.

> To be a Jew, that meant for me, from this moment on, to be a dead man on leave, someone to be murdered, who only by chance was not yet where he properly belonged; and so it has remained, in many variations, in various degrees of intensity, until today. The death threat, which I felt for the first time with complete clarity while reading the Nuremberg Laws, included what is commonly referred to as the methodic "degradation" of the Jews by the Nazis. Formulated differently: *the denial of human dignity sounded the death threat.* (AML, 86; italics JMB)

In pacing out what was involved in the denial of dignity, Améry entwines a political thesis with a thesis concerning the degradation of the Jewish character, demonstrating the conceptual and practical mutual dependency between two fundamental aspects of the Laws: depriving Jews of German citizenship—and hence all the rights and protections that go along with citizenship—and the more intimate prohibitions against not only marriage between Jews and Germans, but equally against extramarital intercourse between the two. Lovemaking between Germans and Jews was now prohibited. While miscegenation and genetic pollution were certainly an aspect of these prohibitions, those notions would have remained empty and idle unless the full ethical danger of skin-to-skin contact could be made palpable.

The prohibitions against intimacy between Germans and Jews is interpreted by Améry as a component of a process of systematic degradation whereby being Jewish was to be the bearer of an indeterminate contagion, an ethical danger in fleshly form, that could not be contained but required extinction: "By their very presence, our bodies—hairy, fat, and bow-legged—befouled public swimming pools, yes, even park benches . . . We were not worthy of love and thus also not of life" (AML, 86; a thought repeated almost verbatim in the next paragraph).[15] This seems a surprising thesis since it is usually assumed that respecting someone's dignity can be satisfied by moral and legal means alone, and that these can operate in relative autonomy from the intimate realm. But relative autonomy is not full detachability; for Améry, the existence of human dignity is not detachable from the *perception* of others as *in principle lovable*.

While my account of the constitution of intrinsic worth through first love sought to demonstrate how fundamental psychological concepts are intrinsic to the normative structure of self-consciousness, thus depsychologizing psychology, it could be argued against such a story that I have reduced moral concepts to psychological concepts. Améry here proffers the terms for a rebuttal of this criticism: love and respect for human dignity are psychologically intertwined because they overlap as status concepts that install and express the kind of value possessed by humans. Love and respect are *forms* of recognition: love is the attitude responsive to another's lovability as respect is the attitude that acknowledges another's human dignity.[16] The Nuremberg Laws, driven by the ratio that love is to lovability as respect is to dignity, begin with the background assumption that as a decent and civilized society, Jews exist in relations of interpersonal trust with their fellow German citizens supported by the rule of law applicable to all. Because relations of trust bear the moral weight of mutual respect between those whose own intimate relations are founded on relations of love and respect, relations of trust bear within themselves the layer of loving mutual regard that is the origin and continuation of the status of each as a person. The Nuremberg Laws could not succeed without severing the relations of trust between Germans and Jews. Because the moral weight of those relations could not be detached from their loving source and lining, destroying the relations of trust meant destroying that affective-axiological premise: Jews cannot be truly trusted because as they are in principle unlovable, they are outside the ambit of mutual respect for selves of equal intrinsic worth. But this is also to say that Jews can legitimately be deprived of all their civil and political rights because they are not deserving of moral regard. The deprivation of rights would remain morally unjustified unless the Jews were unlovable. Hence, the unlovability of the Jews is a necessary condition for their legal abandonment. This is the pulse of the story Améry tells; however morally abhorrent in their specifics, the underlying normative logic of the Nuremberg Laws is impeccable.

In broad terms, I understand love to be the realization and enjoyment of our being dependent on what is forever independent of us, while respect is the practical acknowledgment of others as self-valuing, intrinsically valuable others who are equally vulnerable and dependent beings. The logic of love is complex and much debated; however, the core elements necessary for Améry's thesis are not in significant dispute. To be lovable is to be worthy of love, to be the kind of being for whom a loving regard is fully appropriate. Oppositely, lovers *take* their beloveds as in some sense irreplaceable, and thereby come to regard the beloved as possessing intrinsic value. The lover benefits from loving the beloved because she is unique and irreplaceable, while the beloved benefits from being loved because her intrinsic and nonexchangeable worth is recognized. The satisfactions of love for lover and beloved have everything to do with human lives having a meaning and value that is not for the sake of anything beyond the love relationship itself. Love, David Velleman states, is "the awareness of a value inhering in its object; and I am also inclined to describe love as an arresting awareness of that value."[17]

Améry ties the understanding of dignity to love because modern love ushers us into the appropriate sphere of valuation of the person that a conception of dignity requires. Modern love takes the object of love to be of incomparable value, to be a self-existent end, an end worthy in itself and as itself. Love is not for the sake of anything, but rather in finding its object of incomparable worth, love is what makes any doings in relation to its object valuable. Jean-Paul Sartre states this emphatically: ". . . to want to be loved is to want to be placed beyond the whole system of values posited by the Other and to be the condition of all valorization and the objective foundation of all values."[18] If what love does is to locate and reveal the incomparable worth of its object, then that worth is presumed to have always been there; which is why, conversely, each of us desires to be loved (again). Only through being loved is our intrinsic worth intimately realized; being loved is the recognition of lovability without which it would remain a hope or wish without objective meaning or reality. To be human is thus to be lovable, and so we each await and search for the one who will discover our worth as we discover theirs.

Even as it is often obsessive and possessive, the experience of love is nonetheless the experience of having our narcissistic self-absorption undone as our affective attention is riveted to the irreplaceable other. It is through our attentive regard that the beloved's intrinsic and irreplaceable value comes into view. Love of course is partial, not neutral, but this partiality is at one with its form of attention to what is incomparable in the beloved. If love is what uncovers or brings into focus another's incomparable worth, then the correct moral inference to draw from the experience of loving and being loved is that each human is deserving of loving attention; conversely, then, the moral claim of each to equal treatment, to be treated with dignity, derives from or is, at least, equivalent to their lovability.[19] More emphatically, love alone is capable of realizing and acknowledging the intrinsic worth of any other in the first instance; it is not reason or the moral law or some abstract commandments descended from who knows where that strikes down our primitive narcissism; it is the experience of loving and being loved, of trusting and being trusted. It is for this reason that the logic of belonging and exclusion, of welcome and expulsion, track lovability. If an individual is found to be wholly unlovable—or ungrievable, where grief is the mark of love in loss—then they are in imminent danger of being expelled from the universe of moral consideration.[20] Améry is assuming that such is the picture of the human caste by our understanding of modern love. For us moderns having undergone the crucible of individuation, love is the first accomplishment of what membership accomplished in earlier social forms.[21]

If a person is intrinsically unlovable, then no one could find him irreplaceable; but if he is not irreplaceable in principle, if he is in principle unlovable, then at best his value would be relative to something else, exchangeable or substitutable, a means to some other valued end. Lovability has become an original marker for some notion of persons as having irreplaceable worth rather than relative value: lovability spells out the intrinsic value of the human in affective terms. But the structure of the distinction between the in principle lovable and the in principle unlovable is, famously, just how Kant distinguishes the kind of value that mere things have—namely a price—and the kind of value a person has—a dignity: "If [something] has a price, something else can be put in its place as an *equivalent*; if it is exacted above all price and so admits of no equivalent, then it has a dignity."[22] Kantian and related theories fabulize loving attention and the experience of lovability into conceptions of neutral cognition—treating each with reasons all could share—that mistake the primary moral logic at stake. I anticipated this result in chapter 4 with my defense of Michael Thompson's argument that moral or justice considerations involve bipolar judgments in which it is this very person before you that requires acknowledgment as a person, and that it is only such acknowledgments that can pressure our agency in one direction rather than another; only another's being *this person* can make them a person in a manner that can rationally check self-interested or thoughtless or blind desire in a responding agent in a manner that would make the check truly moral and not fantastical— that is, apart from divine commands or whisperings of the superego or fantasies about what reason requires. And, again, my way of pressing this conclusion is to urge that only on the basis of such a structuring of the moral does it make sense to say that an action is morally wrong because its wrongs *someone*. This is not to deny the existence of general rules or laws; it is rather to say that we should interpret them as providing a heuristic summary of the indefinitely reiterated pairwise sets of *X recognizing Y as a person*. To state the same thought differently: an order of justice is a formal elaboration of the commitments already housed in a society's trust-borne interpersonal relations.

Lovability is the ground of moral reason since it alone provides a value orientation that supplants the instrumental and is satisfying in itself. But this is to say more than that love relations ideally express and provide an intimate inroad into a society's moral discourse, as Kant thought the experience of beauty prepared us for morality. Rather, for us moderns, the practices of love, from first love through to romantic love, originate and structure the value orientations that underlie the language of dignity and respect. Love provides, in its rebuke to self-interest and narcissism, the conceptual terms, the forms of attention, and the structures of (anticipated) reciprocity that, when freed from love's urgencies and extravagances, prepare us for morality. Without the example of love, it is unclear how we moderns could fully embrace the demands of moral attention and moral respect without illusion. This is the conceptual background to Améry's assumption that the contrast between the lovable and the in principle un-lovable is a first wedge for comprehending what is meant by the denial of dignity. Roughly, the recognition of human dignity achieves publicly and impersonally what love achieves privately and individually; but the logic works from the direction of lovability: the public recognition of dignity is the institutional form appropriate to a civilized society in which interpersonal relations of trust realize the value assumptions that the lessons of love have already inculcated as the respect due to each one. And this is why expansions and widening of moral concern and appreciation typically occur when a singular member of an excluded class is suddenly perceived as lovable or grievable, so making her one of us.[23]

Améry thus acknowledges that the personal degradation of the Jews—"Our hideous faces, depraved and spoilt by protruding ears and hanging noses, were disgusting to our fellow men, fellow citizens of yesteryear" (AML, 86)—became the bridge into their being unlovable, as simply not the *kinds* of beings one might marry or have intercourse with, making the banning of marriage and intercourse not bald legal prohibitions but inevitable inferences from their moral expulsion from the family of man. The bridging operation through disgust is not arbitrary since disgust opposes love. As William Ian Miller states, "We can love and hate the same object at the same time, but we cannot love and be disgusted by the same object in any nondeviant . . . sense of love . . . Disgust is what revolts and repels; it is never benign."[24] Améry's relentless focus on the elements of disgust—hairy, fat, bow-legged bodies and hideous faces with "protruding ears and hanging noses"—turn aesthetic repugnance into moral disgust. Disgust resourced Jewish unlovability, and unlovability resourced moral expulsion. The moral and legal expulsion on the basis of their unlovability made Jewish lives essentially fungible. Or, somewhat differently stated, who cannot in principle be loved cannot in principle be a fellow citizen: the disgusting, what cannot be digested or absorbed, must be expelled not only interpersonally but institutionally, deprived of citizenship; but the deprivation of citizenship requires the denial of the ground of citizenship: dignity.[25] If the acknowledgment of dignity is equivalent to the acknowledgment of the intrinsic worth of the individual as a person, then the denial of dignity entails, first, the denial that any individual Jew is possessed of irreplaceable worth, and hence, second, that if they lack intrinsic worth, then they are dispensable, a fit subject for death. This elaborate logic, with its complex set of inferences, was compressed into Améry's reading of the newspaper announcing the Nuremberg Laws on that September day in 1935; a death sentence had been passed on him.

Améry argues that if the set of equations concerning the denial of dignity hold, then we can infer the inverse: "If I was correct that the deprivation of dignity was nothing other than the potential deprivation of life, then dignity would have to be the right to live" (AML, 89). If the acknowledgment of human dignity requires, minimally, an acknowledgment of the right to live, then the denial of dignity really is a death sentence: an austere and terrifying logic leads from the withdrawal of citizenship to the death camps, from "the proclamation of the Nuremberg Laws . . . all the way to Treblinka" (AML, 88).

III. Without Rights, without Dignity: From Humiliation to Devastation

The laws against marriage and sexual intercourse were the merely formal and legal expression of the attempt, through propounding their profound unlovability, to humiliate the Jews to the extent that they came to be seen as deserving expulsion from civilized society (in Margalit's austere sense). The depriving of the Jews of their civil and political rights was the formal side of what became an elaborate effort of institutional humiliation that terminated in the Jews' absolute expulsion from decent society. Humiliation can sound like a hopelessly abstract way of comprehending the dehumanizing practices leading up to the Nazi genocide. Yet, or so I want to argue, however physically brutal and brutalizing camp life, however extensive the suffering caused by the punishing regimes of forced labor under conditions of near starvation, these forms of suffering were not the distinguishing character of the kind of violence prior to extermination that the Nazis perpetuated on their victims. The governing effort of the Nazi project, beginning with the Nuremberg Laws, was systematic humiliation sufficient for the destruction of the dignity of the victims, and thereby sufficient for their devastation.

When Améry argues that torture was the essence of the Third Reich (AML, 24), he is making two interrelated claims: first, that the actual practices of torture, of the kind he suffered, should be understood to exemplify and fulfill the Nazi ambition with respect to the Jewish people—that each must be made to undergo an effort of devastation; but second, that evidence for this must lie outside the torture chambers themselves, since they were little changed from what would have occurred five hundred years earlier. Rather, the structural organization and intended effects of the concentration camps transformed the structural organization and intended effects of torture into an institutional practice for the treatment of the many rather than just a one. It was in order to underline this thesis that Améry placed the "Torture" chapter after the first essay, "At the Mind's Limits," which offers a phenomenological recounting of how the routines of life in the camps effectively decimated the victim's sense of self-worth and thereby individuality, achieving in actuality what the Nuremberg Laws had legislated in principle: the dying of death as a meaningful horizon of a human life—"The soldier died the hero's or victim's death, the prisoner that of an animal intended for slaughter" (AML, 16)—and the destruction of human dignity: "You do not observe dehumanized man committing his deeds and misdeeds without having all of your notions of inherent human dignity placed in doubt. We emerged from the camp stripped, robbed, emptied out, disoriented . . ." (AML, 20).

What was novel in the camps were the mechanisms whereby institutional practices of humiliation could be arranged so that the threatened devastation that is the promise of every act of humiliation could be realized. While Améry described the effects of these mechanisms, no one has better elaborated their logic than Hannah Arendt in *The Origins of Totalitarianism*.[26] Agreeing with Améry, Arendt states that what was most shocking in Nazi practice was that the "insane mass manufacture of corpses is preceded by the historically and politically intelligible preparation of *living corpses*" (OT, 447; emphasis JMB). I take "living corpses" to be one, extreme, version of the third-person perception of devastated human beings. Arendt contends that these were "politically intelligible" practices because their preparation followed a comprehensible logic: the destruction of the juridical person (OT, 447), followed by the murder of the moral person in man (OT, 451), followed by the destruction of unique identity, the spontaneity through which a person might still call an action "mine" (OT, 453). Arendt's analysis reveals that the meaning of this final destruction of individuality had systematic significance only as the conclusion of the destruction of the human that began with the ruin of the juridical and moral persons.

The three stages of Arendt's logic can be shown to involve the systematic and purposeful deployment of each of the three dominant forms of institutional humiliation: rejection or expulsion from the encompassing group, treating humans in thinglike, beastlike, or subhuman ways, and calculated attacks on individuals' capacities for self-control—all in a manner designed to humiliate, traumatize, and devastate, which is to agree that there are other reasons one might undertake such actions; whatever the reason for the action, however, it will likely strike its victim as humiliating, since even when the intention is not to humiliate, the action ignores the moral standing of the victim. If I am right in claiming that humiliation and devastation are elements of a continuum, then the political intelligibility of camp practices requires the dignity constellation as its background assumption: only beings having self-respect and a sense of their dignity *can* be devastated.[27] Once we comprehend camp practices in this light, then, conversely, we are better prepared to recognize the truth about torture as the essence and subtext of bureaucratically rationalized institutional practices. And this, in turn, allows us to comprehend the extent to which the eighteenth-century emergence of the rule of law as the determinate negation of sovereign torture is the *exact* analogue for the emergence of human rights—as a particular version of the idea of the rule of law—as the determinate negation of Nazi practices, a reading of The Universal Declaration of Human Rights I will sketch in my conclusion. What I need to accomplish here is the demonstration of how Nazi practice imbricates the dignity constellation, and hence how the elements of that constellation are to be construed.

Arendt provides a categorial analysis of the grim logic of Nazi practice that perfectly matches Améry's experience-based reflections. According to Arendt, the goal of totalitarian rule, which was tested and put into practice in the camps, was the striving to organize the infinite plurality and differentiation of human beings in a manner that would effectively decimate those forms of self-respect necessary for claims to individual worth; the outcome of such a project would be a situation in which all the victims were just one individual: total domination. What would bring this about is a state of affairs in which each and every person could be reduced "to a never-changing identity of reaction, so that each of these bundles of reactions can be *exchanged* at random for any other" (OT, 438), or, what is the same, the creation of a situation in which the individual would be "nothing other than a specimen of the species" (OT, 465).[28] In brief, the principle needed is the creation of the complete exchangeability and hence fungibility of all victims. The camps were the central institution of totalitarian organizational power because they put into practice that reduction of the many to the one, or, equivalently, they realized that state of affairs in which, in actuality, a living human would become no longer a lovable being, because she was no longer in any recognizable sense a unique and therefore irreplaceable individual for herself and for all others.

The modern rule of law does more than acknowledge human dignity, it *institutes* it through situating the citizen body as beyond the reach of the state, guaranteeing that even when individuals are directly under state control in the penal system they remain objects of respect. The juridical person is, from the perspective of the state, a person with dignity. And it is precisely this conception of the person that the Reich Citizenship Law restricted to those of German blood, implicitly casting Jews, Gypsies, gays and lesbians into a legal netherworld. The destruction of the juridical person began by depriving the Jews of all their political and civil rights. If laws prohibiting marriage and sexual intercourse had tacitly removed Jews from civil society, the Citizenship Law formally expelled them from the state: they no longer belonged to the encompassing group of which they were nonetheless functional parts. Although not named in the law, the Jews were nonetheless its target.

The Nuremberg Laws' creation of rightless persons took on an exorbitant form in the camps: first by making certain categories of persons outside the protection of law and hence, through denationalization, exposing them to the lawlessness of arbitrary rule; and second by placing the camps themselves, like the military prison in Guantanamo, outside the normal penal system, considering the inmates in them to be no longer covered by standard juridical procedures in which a definite crime would entail a predictable penalty, and, by extension, no longer extending to them all the standard rights—of treatment, defense, due process, and appeal—that criminals normally have. One might express this by saying that it was *no-nagents* who were placed in the camps, individuals who had been legally deprived of the capacity for normal or even criminal action: Jews, carriers of diseases, Gypsies, representatives of dying classes, etc. Apart then from some "natural" characteristics, the individuals placed in the camps were innocent in every sense. What thus made the operation of the camps a question of humiliating terror is just that: one was chosen, experimented on, punished, forced to labor, not for any reason pertaining to one's active life, not for anything one had done or failed to do, but just because of who, in some reductive sense, one was. The humiliation of racial profiling is the same: one is subject to treatment independent of one's doings; one's innocence is the condition for one's greater guilt. Once an individual's actions are no longer the condition for his treatment in the penal system, then he is effectively legally a nonperson; even his sufferings do not matter since he has no rights to protest them.

Arendt understands the murder of the moral person as demanding the destruction of human solidarity through incapacitating the operation of conscience. She argues that a condition of moral meaning is that we be able to give death meaning, which in part means that the difference between life and death functions as the necessary minimum value distinction through which the value of others can begin to come into focus: they matter if and only if their being alive matters. If my action is one in which the boundary conditions of life and death are unable to operate, then I am unable to judge what actions are obligated, permissible, or impermissible, in which case the minimum conditions for conscientious action are defeated. Nazi logic here comprised two elements. First, the border between life and death is erased by destroying the idea that death is a fate that belongs to a particular individual. Arendt notes that all previous forms of warfare and tyranny recognized the significance of death in this way: "The Western world has hitherto, even in its darkest periods, granted the slain enemy the right to be remembered as a self-evident fact that we are all men (and *only* men) . . . The concentration camps, by making death itself anonymous . . . robbed death of its meaning as the end of a fulfilled life" (OT, 452). I shall return below to the issue of why death belongs to the individual whose death it is, and hence why the right to be remembered belongs to human dignity.

Anonymity empties death of its ultimate significance: if no unique person dies, then nothing of intrinsic value disappears from the earth. Anonymous deaths are those for which no grief is called for, since it was not a being of intrinsic (self-)worth who died. Anonymity is one aspect of the destruction of death—of making death not the worst thing a human might suffer. Second, what went along with it was the engendering of situations that demonstrated to the victims that they could not judge in accordance with the boundary conditions for moral intelligibility that life and death provide—for example, situations in which one's choice was always between murder and murder: "Choose which of your children will die; if you fail to choose, then both die. If you commit suicide, both die. . . ." A situation is thence constructed in which each individual might be forced to become the weapon of death for what she loves most or, at least, for another innocent like herself, thereby making all actions and choices morally in vain. If your judgments and actions cannot count life as a good worth having and death as an evil to be shunned, then action loses a constitutive possibility of moral salience. Worse, what such situations construct is the destruction of the very idea of loving attention, of attending to another as a being of intrinsic worth. When a loving regard is impossible, its objects disappear: one can only be lovable if loving attention to one is possible. Without it, one's humanity is abandoned. It is not merely the bonds of attachment that are severed, their severing intends the profound emptying of the categories of loving subjects and loved objects, and hence of the forms of moral attention and moral counting they normatively adumbrate. The Nazis thus forced their victims to share their vision of each as being exchangeable, fungible, expendable. Under such conditions, one is forced to act for arbitrary reasons, which is to say, without sufficient moral reason. The fortunate were allowed utilitarian calculations: sacrificing a beloved for the lives of a group of strangers.

The last stage is the destruction of individuality; it was the cruelest of the camps' practices. If Arendt's analysis of the destruction of the juridical and moral person is correct, then one might hazard that the conditions for the recognition of individuality had already been destroyed, since the forms of regard and the forms of action constitutively necessary in order for one to be a self-respecting agent and to be treated with dignity had already been eliminated. In fact, there is a further step because even under these conditions it is conceivable that an individual could act with dignity, say, by going to her death with dignity. A further destruction is thus necessary in order to make the humiliation devastating.

The destruction of individuality begins with the removal of all distinguishing characteristics: clothing, hair, even one's proper name. In the early days of the camps, Arendt states, this destruction depended on torture and sadistic treatment, of continually reducing the individual to her suffering bodily self. But this phase gave way when the SS took over the administration of the camps, when sadists where replaced by functionaries, ordinary men: "The old spontaneous bestiality gave way to an absolutely cold and systematic destruction of human bodies, *calculated to destroy human dignity*; death was avoided or postponed indefinitely" (OT, 454; italics JMB). The camps, she says, were transformed from playgrounds for sadists into drill grounds. Punishment became mechanized routine; starvation and relentless laboring were compounded into a set of practices that left just the empty husk, "ghastly marionettes with human faces, which all behave like the dog in Pavlov's experiments, which all react with perfect reliability even when going to their own death, and which do nothing but react" (OT, 455). Although one hears in this description something of Arendt's disdain for those who failed to rebel against their own destruction, there is nonetheless a chilling emptiness in the perception of masses having become individually and collectively incapable of acting with dignity, of being emptied of their humanity. Here is Martha Gellhorn describing the survivors in Dachau shortly after its liberation:

> Behind the barbed wire and the electric fence, the skeletons sat in the sun and searched themselves for lice. They have no age and no faces; they all look alike and like nothing you will ever see if you are lucky . . . In the hall sat more of the skeletons, and from them came the smell of disease and death. They watched us but did not move; no expression shows on a face

that is only yellowish, stubby skin, stretched across bone. What had been a
man dragged himself into the doctor's office . . .[29]

Beings without faces are no longer fully human. These are beings who
have suffered utter devastation and then passed beyond it; they appear
numb to the total degradation they have undergone. Gellhorn's dry prose
captures the haunting unreality of these bodies who are no longer persons,
their insensibility a fragment of relief to us and a fragment of salvation
from suffering for them—except we know what they do not: what awaits in
the near future is an awakening to their devastation.

But even this state of affairs is not the end of the matter. The exorbitance
of Nazi practice was that it turned the legislative *denial* of dignity into the
practical *destruction* of dignity—ending with mass, *anonymous* death. The
manner of their slaughter and disposal fulfills the logic of the destruction
of dignity preceding it. In trying to picture this final state, which Arendt
tactfully elides from her account, I inevitably find myself screening once
more the terrible scene from Alain Resnais's documentary film, *Night and
Fog* (1955), in which we see a bulldozer pressing a pile of dirt and human
bodies forward until they tumble, helplessly, uselessly, into a large ditch in
the ground. What is unspeakable here is that our response to these scenes
is not one of pity or grief, but rather one of horror and disgust.[30] And that
is what is terrible: the Nazis turned their ideology of racial disgust into a
practice that transformed lovable beings into objects of disgust. They made
their morally atrocious vision of the Jews into an emphatic reality such
that even those utterly opposed to what they stood for are forced to share
their vision—Jews became faceless, and then became garbage. On seeing
either the same or very similar documentary footage as Resnais uses in his
film, the mother of the playwright and essayist Lionel Abel commented "I
don't think the Jews can ever get over the disgrace of this." Abel comments
in return that "She said nothing about the moral disgrace to the German
nation . . . only about . . . a more than moral disgrace, and one incurred by
the Jews." After quoting these passages from Abel's memoir, *The Intellectual
Follies*, Saul Bellow added his judgment:

> I too had seen newsreels of the camps. In one of them, American bulldozers
> pushed naked corpses toward a mass grave ditch. Limbs fell away and heads
> dropped from the disintegrating bodies. My reaction to this was similar to
> that of Mrs. Abel—a deeply troubling sense of disgrace or human demotion,
> as if by such afflictions the Jews had lost the respect of the rest of mankind,
> as if they might now be regarded as hopeless victims, *incapable of honorable*

self-defense, and arising from this, probably the common instinctive revulsion and loathing of the extremities of suffering—a sense of personal contamination and aversion. The world would see these dead with a pity that placed them at the margin of humanity.[31]

No witness has moral authority over the meaning of an event, and perhaps out of either overfamiliarity or moral repression—we must not permit ourselves to feel such revulsion for fellow beings, or admit to such feelings—the Bellow response is less common than it was. Nonetheless, it is hard to gainsay its accuracy. The turning of these human forms into so much garbage completed the process of robbing death of its meaning and thereby destroying the dignity of these humans. To deny this claim would be, I want to urge, to deny one of the fundamental moral significances of the Nazi genocide.

The grievable human is still human; when we act for the sake of another, say by attending a memorial for a dead beloved, we are still acting "for her sake" even though she is dead.[32] Grief responds to the dead human as still human, still deserving of being treated with dignity; the work of mourning, as Antigone's example continually reminds us, is the work of preserving the human dignity of the dead. The bulldozer's brute shifting of the lifeless bodies is not even a final indignity suffered by them, but something worse: the human form rendered into sheer meaningless stuff. Martha Gellhorn describes the bodies left in the crematorium in Dachau thus:

> There suddenly, but never to be believed, were the bodies of the dead. They were everywhere. There were piles of them inside the oven room, but the S.S. had not had time to burn them. They were piled outside the door and alongside the building. They were all naked, and behind the crematorium the ragged clothing of the dead was neatly stacked, shirts, jackets, trousers, shoes, awaiting sterilization and further use. The clothing was handled with order, but the bodies were dumped like garbage, rotting in the sun, yellow and nothing but bones, bones grown huge because there was no flesh to cover them, hideous, terrible, agonizing bone, and the unendurable smell of death.[33]

IV. Dignity and the Human Form

"What is dignity, really?" (AML, 88) Améry asks in contemplation of what first befell him in 1935. Some of the lineaments of his view are now clear. The dignity of persons refers to some notion of intrinsic worth or high standing, the value persons have as persons that makes them deserving of the kinds of respect that go along with moral regard. A fundamental expression of human dignity is given through the possession of rights. Respect for persons is not the same as respect for rights, because even those lacking a particular bundle of specific rights may think of themselves and be thought of by those around them as deserving of those rights, as having their dignity harmed but not destroyed by having their rights withdrawn; their dignity remains, demanding and calling for recognition. As I will detail in the next section, it is important to Améry that while he and his fellows could be deprived of their political and civil rights, that did not *immediately* spell the end of their possession of human dignity. While the possession of dignity is neither automatic nor a metaphysical necessity, but some sort of social accomplishment, that accomplishment is not wholly one sided: society bestowing dignity, and the individual receiving it; dignified and self-respecting behavior belongs to the logic of dignity as much as being treated with dignity and thereby having one's dignity affirmed. Human dignity has interlocking subjective and objective aspects that can be severed but not reduced to one another.

Human dignity can be destroyed. We respond to its objective destruction with reactions of shock, horror, and disgust, with a feeling of shame that one human might have done such a thing to another human, and too, as Bellow's response concedes, in those who must identify with the victims, with a feeling that we are disgraced and humiliated. Many things are disgusting that have nothing to do with destruction of dignity; and worse, as the Nazi project for making Jews disgusting to Germans demonstrates, disgust can all too easily be recruited for the sake of demeaning and humiliating those racially and sexually different from us. Disgust is a mobile human response that is all too easily co-opted for regressive purposes, and hence should not be regarded as possessing independent moral authority as to which acts are acceptable and which not.[34] My proposal here is not that my or Bellow's revulsion is autonomously authoritative. Rather, in reconstructing the path from humiliation to devastation, from devastation into numb mortification, and finally, through the final emptying of death of any human meaning, to the utter destruction of human dignity represented by the "garbage" of human corpses, an actual moral fate was played out for which finding in the final scene something in the area of revulsion and disgust is an intelligible response and failure to find anything in such scenes overwhelmingly morally repugnant could be taken as a chilling moral indifference. If disgust, shame, humiliation are ways of hiding oneself or saving oneself from further direct viewing, then sometimes the desire to close one's eyes or hide from sight is humane.

In claiming that human dignity can be destroyed, and that even as morally refined a witness as Martha Gellhorn felt compelled to describe the final disposition of those bodies as "garbage," I am returning to my critique of Jean Hampton's Kantian thesis that intrinsic human worth can appear to have been degraded but cannot really suffer degradation or destruction. That this, by now, should strike us as wildly implausible is obvious. What I want to pull from the final destruction of human dignity represented by the bulldozed corpses tumbling into a ditch is the extent to which *perception* of human dignity and its absence is tied to the perception of the human body. When we respond with horror and disgust to the bulldozed corpses, we are responding to the human form, which in standard settings is the site of what possesses incomparable worth—as in principle lovable—as here worthless, without human standing, as simply unable to sustain the nomination of dignity. The horror is the joining of those two things: the (normally and normatively) intrinsically valuable appearing body suddenly appearing as valueless stuff, garbage.

Disgust at the sight of the degraded human body is a wholly moral response: a visceral repugnance at the sight of *what ought not to be*. In order for the perception of the destruction of dignity in this setting to be sustained we need a heightened version of Wittgenstein's dictum: "The human body is the best picture [*Bild*] of the human soul."[35] The word "best" is too weak for what is philosophically required: the human body is the necessary appearance form of the human soul, of human freedom and subjectivity; that is, in some fundamental way, the dignity constellation is necessary for an appropriate appreciation of how the human body means—the human body is normatively saturated in ways that the dignity constellation gives articulation to, and, conversely, the dignity constellation cannot adequately operate except through its being bound to bodily behavior and the various bodily dispositions essential to a human life. As we shall come to see, essential to this story is some understanding of the dead body and the dignity befitting a human corpse.[36]

For a pathway into the intricacies of these claims, I want to begin with an argument of J. G. Fichte's. In *Foundations of Natural Right*, Fichte argues that what distinguishes the human body from the animal body is that the form of each type of animal body is fully determinate, having evolved in order to carry out a closed set of law-governed action routines. For the beasts, with only minor exceptions (vestigial organs and properties, etc.), bodily forms are wholly bound to the determinate functions they satisfy, and, conversely, each biological or animal function is satisfied through a determinate bodily form (or its determinate surrogate). The utter integration of form and function in animals is the exquisite beauty of evolution, each bodily complex becoming decipherable, finally, as an ideal solution (adaptation) to a challenge to species survival.

It is just this that is not true of the human body according to Fichte, because humans are not limited to following out predetermined, law-governed sets of action routines. Humans are free in the precise sense that they are capable of inventing an indefinite number of new modes of action, new ways for parts of the body to be arranged with respect to one another as elements of an integral whole. Fichte's argument commences from the idea that there is an indefinite number of possible conceptually mediated, nonbasic actions.[37] Consider the complex actions that go along with highly elaborated bodily activities like dancing (doing a pirouette in ballet, or a shuffle hop in tap dancing), playing a musical instrument (the movement of the fingers involved in playing a piano versus playing a saxophone, or the fingering necessary to play classical guitar), using a tool (turning a screwdriver), performing surgery, playing a sport, not to speak of more mundane activities like cooking (slicing and dicing), sewing, writing, speaking, and singing. Assume, first, that there is no definitive end to the possibility of such complex activities, that new ones are continually being invented in response to new types or species of practices (X-game sports, for example) or new technologies. Second, for each complex action the body performs, what is an independent, moving part of the body changes: for some actions, one or more fingers move while the arm and shoulder remain steady, in others, the whole arm moves while fingers and wrist are firm, while in still others, the wrist and fingers move as the arm moves (say, in shooting a jump shot). The relation of the body to its parts is a whole-part relation, but one that continually changes relative to the complex action being performed. Finally, to say that the notion of part must be relativized to the complex action performed entails that while the precise range of basic motions a part performs is not infinite (there are severe physical/structural constraints), it is indefinite—the lifting, bending motion of the arm while flicking the wrist, the fingers waving forward seems unimaginable apart from the activity of shooting a basketball. A body conforming to these three requirements is necessarily "articulated."[38] A human body (*Leib*), a voluntary body then, is "a closed articulated whole . . . within which we posit ourselves as a cause that acts immediately through our will."[39]

If new forms of actions are possible, then for the human body there cannot exist a one-to-one correlation between bodily form or part and specific action or vital function, a fact implicit in both the distinction between basic and nonbasic action and, even more, in the denial that there are such things as basic actions. In this respect, the human body must be in itself materially indeterminate with respect to the movements of its parts and the relation between the parts and the whole; each novel action is a further determination, a forming of an indeterminate potentiality that exceeds each previous actuality. Fichte summarizes this thought eloquently: "All animals are complete and finished; the human being is only intimated and projected."[40] This is Fichte's version of the thought that the unity of the human body is a practical achievement that is never complete.

Fichte's central claim is thus that the shape of the human body—upright posture, arms and hands freed from direct functional tasks, "the spiritual eye and mouth that reflects the heart's innermost stirrings"[41]—together with the indeterminate articulations in action is *the material form of rational freedom*, how self-consciousness materially appears. Rational freedom is not an inference from bodily behavior, but the intrinsic sense of bodily movements performed by the human form. This weighing of the human bodily form tends to be overlooked because while the tight fit between form and function is, for each animal kind, capable of being deciphered, that there is a tight fit between the human form, how the human body appears, and the *absence* of an immediate function associated with each part is necessarily oblique. It is certainly *logically possible* that something like our notion of bodily freedom and meaning might be housed in a differently structured body—cartoons and science fiction work this thought to death; in fact, however, we have no idea whether those envisioned states of affairs are actually (causally) possible.

The capacities of the human body to act in accordance with conceptual determinations entails a capacity for formability such that both conceptual content and an openness to re-formation are returned to the body as indelible features of its overall appearing. It is because crucial parts of the human body (hands, mouth, eyes, etc.) are freed from direct functional imperatives that the body as an ongoing shifting of relations of whole and part in relation to conceptually determined activities and meanings, the shape of the body as a whole, can be simultaneously completely material while not being functionally determinate like other natural bodies. Is this not just to say that, conversely, because in the specified sense it is not natural, not fully determinate because it is not fully determined by a closed set of causal laws, the human body must be conceived of as the appearing of the human soul? But this should not be surprising: how could human life be saturated by cultural meanings but the bodily-material bearer of the human actions that realize those meanings be materially indifferent to that fact in its forms of appearing? What Fichte wants from his argument is, however partial, the acknowledgment that we cannot coherently describe or analyze the appearance of the human body without acknowledging these macro-aspects of its appearance: the broad range of culturally specific, voluntary activities that human beings do and how they do them must be perceptually manifest, however indefinitely, in the kind of object carrying out those activities.[42]

Consider the alternatives. Could the human body be simply a neutral or functionally blank shape in which what and how it is affected, and what it does and how it does it, have no internal connection with its form of appearance? Objects can have surprising and hidden powers, but what makes that fact singular is that it is not the rule, and it requires explanation—how could something looking like "that" act like "this"? And standardly, we find good structural answers to such questions. By focusing on the external, performance, material, world-forming aspects of action (rather than on the purpose, intention, rule, meaning, willing aspects), Fichte closes the gap between inner and outer, making the character of bodily performance itself the necessary and best image, the appearance or look, of what is, from the opposing angle, purposive and meaningful.[43] Fichte, we might say, looks at the relation between action and embodiment from an "engineering" or "design" perspective, but the design is for a body whose range of actions is essentially open, and hence the bodily bearer of those actions must be, in the requisite sense, indeterminate (or plastic, if that seems a preferable expression). By considering action outwardly, he shows the "black box" idea of the human body to be unintelligible. But the classical name for the black box conception is, of course, just the idea of the body as a (law-governed, causal) machine as opposed to an immaterial mind. A body capable of doing all the types of action a human body can, and further capable of doing new types of action requiring new arrangements of part and whole, cannot be a machine—that is, it cannot be conceptually determinate in the way in which something must be determinate in order to be a law-governed (living) machine.[44] I take this conclusion to be precisely what would be expected in thinking of human self-consciousness as arising from and being a certain kind of interruption of erotic striving, where the inhabiting of a shared world comes to have a determining role in the kind of living body one is.

In making strong dualist accounts implausible, Fichte simultaneously deflates the skeptical force of weak dualist accounts. Because action is conceptually and not mechanically determined, and the conceptual is context dependent, Fichte must concede that not all particular human actions are transparent in their meaning. A certain type of skepticism thrives by taking particular failures of transparency as the ground for generalized doubt, requiring that meanings be located solely in the minds of agents, which in turn requires reverting to the black box conception of the body. Having removed the black box idea, Fichte can urge that context dependence and nontransparency should be construed from the opposite direction. Being indeterminate, opaque, enigmatic, or misleading are features of human performances; they are exactly the kinds of opacity, indeterminacy and breakage that are possible for the doings of beings whose performances bear *contextual sense*. Not knowing how a machine works or not knowing the function of a certain set of animal movements is not the same as not knowing the meaning of a human performance; in the latter case, knowing the details of context, narratively or culturally, is the usual requirement for interpretation (rather than explanation). It is the shape of the human body, its articulated part/whole form, that entails that its performances are conceptually determined, purposive, and context dependent. Some context-dependent doings are species universals, while some are not; which actions are species universals and which are not itself belongs to the fit between the human body and the form of life of beings having such a body. The appearance form of the human is thus the source or ground for the kinds of indeterminacies and differences that have been used to deny its universality. The appearance of the human body is the appearing of a self-determining, rational being; thus the human *body* cannot appear without the *human* appearing.

From this, it immediately follows that every act of misrecognition, every violent work of domination, exclusion, expulsion, denial, or rejection, every effort of collective humiliation, every mass enslavement, massacre, or genocide must, a fortiori, be premised on an anterior emphatic recognition. Nothing is more human than to deny the other her humanity, but it is always another human who is so denied, not a thing or beast. The desire to dominate, humiliate, and exclude are not efforts to prevent nonhumans from joining the human fold, but efforts to exclude *other* humans from *our* human fold. In this respect, it is tempting to claim that the most insistent bearer of human universalism is the human body performing the routine actions of everyday life. Just this was Wittgenstein's extravagant and austere new insight.

This is certainly also Fichte's view; he concludes this run of argument by urging that the "human shape is necessarily sacred to the human being."[45] It is our tacit acknowledgment of that sacredness, that dignity intrinsic to the human form, to state the same in more modest terms, that causes disgust when that dignity is destroyed, when the human form, despite its destiny in rational freedom, appears as stuff of a kind wholly outside the ambit of freedom and meaning. But as we shall see directly, being outside the ambit of freedom and meaning is also intrinsic to the human body, and it is this fact that orients the structuring of the human body by the dignity constellation.

V. The Body without Dignity

Referring to the multitude of stateless peoples created during the Nazi period, Arendt argues that the "loss of national rights was identical with the loss of human rights," the former entailing the latter: "The Rights of Man, supposedly inalienable, prove to be unenforceable—even in countries where constitutions were based upon them—whenever people appeared who were no longer citizens of any sovereign state."[46] Arendt's thought here is that unless human rights are transformed into positive rights that have the force of law behind them, they are idle, useless at the very moment when they would matter most. If rights are entitlements on the basis of which their possessor can make a claim, then there must be some responsible body that is in principle obligated to hear and respond to that claim. Rights of the citizen are the actuality of human rights; without the translation of the latter into the former, human rights remain manifesto rights, rights individuals *deserve* to have but currently lack. The obvious basis on which individuals might lodge a claim that they deserve to have their human rights respected by being made into positive law, that they have a right to have rights, is their possession of human dignity; to deny an individual her rights is to impugn her dignity, her intrinsic and equal worth with her fellow humans.[47]

However, even if the inference from dignity to rights is valid, the situation with human dignity is, according to Améry, not dissimilar to the situation Arendt diagnosed with respect to rights. Dignity, he says, can be bestowed only by society, and that insisting upon one's dignity no matter what anyone says or does "is an empty academic game, or madness" (AML, 89). Although the possession of human dignity is not exhausted by or reducible to the possession of rights, respect for individuals as persons goes beyond respecting their rights; nonetheless, what any society makes of the claim that each is possessed of human dignity is to a significant extent provided discursive shape and practical meaning by the rights it officially acknowledges its citizens to have and its readiness and ability to enforce those rights' claims when they are challenged or disrespected. As we have already seen, Améry took it as a matter of fact that the withdrawal of the rights of citizenship intended and brought about a denial of dignity. When fundamental rights are denied a group of citizens (or the relevant rights are denied visitors), this can only gnaw away at the dignity of those so denied: legal inequality becomes humiliation and thus a moral injury because systematic discrimination attacks the presumption of equal worth of the excluded group. Without an operative notion of moral injury, we would miss the true harm that the denial of rights involves.

The denial of rights, however, does not entail the direct destruction of dignity—although it is an injury to it—for two reasons; in elaborating these reasons, I will draw on Orlando Patterson's *Slavery and Social Death: A Comparative Study*. I think the analogy of slave existence with victims of the Nazi genocide will help sharpen the analysis while providing ample reasons for considering Améry's views as having a wide applicability. First, then, insofar as an excluded group is capable of sustaining relations of mutual recognition *among themselves* through which each individual life is regarded as lovable and grievable, dignity is sustained. This is central to the two-sided account of slavery that Patterson provides. On the one hand, his analysis of the process of enslaving closely parallels Arendt's account of the Nazi destruction of the person. Slaves are socially dead persons; the slave is violently withdrawn from his social milieu; he is "desocialized and depersonalized," and then installed into the community of the master "as a nonbeing."[48] Slavery is an intense and relentless work of degradation and dishonor. The institutional processes of enslaving had the piercing intention of depriving slaves of standing, honor, and worth. Enslaving meant to be dignity destroying, and the form of moral injury suffered by slaves was directly related to practices of relentless degradation. We can make little sense of the harm of slavery if we reduce it to simply the lack of freedom; freedom matters as a component of an individual's conception of their self-worth and dignity.

Yet, on the other side, however injured the slave's sense of dignity, the master's view was not fully internalized, the humiliation and indignity rarely devastating, and thus rarely complete. First, although formally isolated and forced into a liminal social existence, the slave cherished and cultivated whatever community remained available: "The fierce love of the slave mother for her child is attested in every slaveholding society; everywhere the slave's zest for life and fellowship confounded the slaveholder class."[49] The slave's (vertical) relation with the slaveholder was not his only social relation, and arguably, the slave system could not have reproduced itself unless it permitted ordinary mothering practices—the teaching of the lessons of first love; further, at least a significant minority of slaveholders in the American South permitted families to remain intact. Those (horizontal) practices—and the even odder one of requiring slaves to practice Christianity and so conceive of themselves as God's children—along with whatever other community the slaves managed among themselves, provided resources for the production of lovable and grievable lives, hence securing sources of dignity. Lovability is the primary source of self-respect and dignity, and it can survive, however riven, direct attacks on the social standing of the victim if he or she possesses some mutually recognitive community, some belonging, some fabric of interpersonal relations premised on trust. Dignity is the moral expression of lovability; it is the moral standing an individual inherits from a good-enough upbringing that can be realized in the trust relations of the community of slaves. The case of slavery, and later of a viciously segregated society, provides a robust example for thinking of respect for individual dignity in trusting interpersonal relations as a public version of the self-worth derived from the work of love; there are no other resources available to account for the moral facts.

Solidarity with those who share one's condition of humiliation thus makes dignity—however injured and loosened—possible even under the most extreme and deracinating conditions of oppression. It is just this that Améry intends when he asserts the necessity of his being a Jew—it is necessary for the recovery and sustaining of his dignity: "My solidarity with every Jew whose freedom, equal right, or perhaps even physical existence is threatened is *also*, but *not only*, a reaction to anti-Semitism, which . . . is not an opinion but the predisposition to commit the crime of genocide. *The solidarity is part of my person* and a weapon in the battle to regain my *dignity*" (AML, 98; italics JMB). If dignity is a social construction whereby a group bestows on its members the status of possessing intrinsic worth, then it can only survive, finally, in a community capable of upholding relations of mutual recognition at some fundamental level. This is the connection between the two sides of my argument in chapter 4: self-consciousness is essentially realized through acts of mutual recognition, and belonging to an appropriate community is the central mechanism through which the requisite norm-instituting and sustaining relations are realized; relations of recognition are essentially intersubjective relations between two concrete individuals, but because they involve acknowledgments of authoritative standing they typically operate through social practices that are either directly normatively infused through their distribution of roles and entitlements, or they possess a background of trust of the appropriate kind, or both.

Patterson's second reason for why the denial of dignity does not directly cause devastation and the destruction of dignity, although it often did—which will eventually bring me to the center of Améry's account—is that its very denial can produce a countermovement of resistance: "Confronted with the master's outrageous effort to deny him all dignity, the slave even more than the master came to know and to desire passionately this very attribute. For dignity, like love, is one of those human qualities that are most intensely felt and understood when they are absent—or unrequited."[50] Following Hegel, Patterson thinks of slavery as a trial by death: "Out of this trial the slave emerged, if he survived at all, as a person afire with the knowledge of and the need for dignity and honor. . . . The *existential dignity* of the slave belied the slaveholder's denial of its existence."[51] Dignity is qualified as existential rather than moral here for two reasons: first, the stakes of dignity pertain to a self-consciousness of one's intrinsic self-worth, and second, the threat to dignity is existential; it is a threat to one's *existence* as a person. Thus, to suffer the humiliation of slavery is to undergo a process of repeated negations of one's standing as a person. It is that process itself that makes the slave intensely aware of what is being denied to him, both as something suffered and as what the slaveholder possesses and he lacks. The institution of slavery had the moral contours it did through its status constructions of role and identity: the slave-holder's honor derived, in part, from the degradation he heaped upon his slaves; and the slave's degradation derived from what was done to him and how he was perceived by the slave-owner. The slave's sense of his or her dignity emerged at the precise locale where private lovability and communal dignity met with institutional degradation—a civilized society existing within an indecent one. It was because the slave system continued to produce, despite itself, some existentially charged sense of dignity that the mechanisms of social death were meant to vanquish that, eventually, the slave system routinely found itself required to make manumission an intrinsic part of its institutional operations. For the sake of socially reproducing and stabilizing the system of slavery, enslavement came to have disenslavement as institutionally necessary for its continuance. Patterson twists this argument one step further: we owe our modern conception of freedom to slavery and former slaves—only those who had been so brutally denied freedom would need to and did give freedom the unconditional conceptual and practical meaning it now has for us. Even if true only in part, it would be hard to deny that our understanding of the *value* of freedom in relation to the demands of respect for human dignity took moral salience through the cruel history of slavery and the struggle for its abolition.

The Nuremberg Laws were certainly a component of a system producing social death, but manumission was never part of its internal logic. The Laws were, as Améry rightly insists, a death sentence. Under those conditions, solidarity with his fellows was insufficient for the Jew; his moral survival required acknowledging the world's judgment and actively fighting back. If the first blow revealed to Améry his existential helplessness, "to hit back," the "moral power to resist" (AML, 90) became the vital source making possible the recuperating of his dignity. For Améry, hitting back becomes a bodily mode of self-affirmation; he baldly states, in words that are at first almost morally unintelligible, that *"my body, when it tensed to strike, was my physical and metaphysical dignity"* (AML, 91; italics JMB). Human dignity is so routinely assumed to be something external to the body that we are initially left without any easy way of reading Améry's claim. It is a deep part of Occidental thought that, premised on a presumptive clean dualism between mind and body, we should cleave an absolute separation between physical integrity and metaphysical dignity. Améry is pressing a case that these dualisms misconstrue dignity, the moral metaphysics of the body, and hence the meaning of violence.

At stake in Améry's argument is the reverse side of the thesis about the body without dignity. We have just seen that the dead body that appears as heaped garbage, as so much stuff, is disgusting, and that disgust is connected to the absence of dignity. The question then arises: in the absence of *what* does the body come to appear as incapable of sustaining dignity? The most natural answer to this question—namely that it is the human body without life and thus without agency that is intrinsically undignified—is at best partial, and largely false. While a dead body can *do* nothing to preserve its dignity, there are nonetheless dignified and hence dignity-preserving ways of treating the dead body. Ancient Greek literary sources emphasize the necessity of a proper burial and refer to the omission of burial rites as an insult to human dignity (*Iliad*, 23.71). Whatever memorial rites a society assumes—burial, cremation, dressing the corpse in Sunday best, cleaning it and stripping it naked—the practices all assume that failure to realize them involves an act of disrespect and desecration. It is massively tempting to cut short this argument at the outset by simply denying that the dead, lacking consciousness, can suffer anything; it is we who suffer their bodies being treated in dignity-destroying ways. And we suffer those things because, projecting ahead, we would not want our bodies so treated at our death. Why not? Why should I care what happens to my body once I am dead? The thesis that burial rites are either superstitious or quaint sentimentality is tempting but unsustainable. Eventually, I shall want to argue that our dignity-preserving treatment of the dead is but a particular manifestation of a general and indeed essential feature of human dignity. And once we understand how the care for the dead is a component of a wider moral effort, our moral attitudes toward, for example, the dying, the infirm, the diseased, the radically disabled, will become far more perspicuous.

What is accomplished by burial rites that makes them, somehow, dignity preserving? Although incomplete, for reasons I will come to, in his prelude to his analysis of Antigone's unswerving attempt to bury her brother Polynices, Hegel suggests three compelling metaphysical elements involved in burial rites. The primary stakes of burial rites concern the question: to what extent is death a wholly natural event? How does the otherwise natural event of an individual's death relate to his or her cultural belonging? All humans die, and however they die, their death is a natural fact, and hence the work of natural processes and forces operating within the human body. Stabbing causes bleeding, but it is the loss of blood that causes the body to finally fail, to stop living. If this natural aspect of death were ultimate, then death would have nothing to do with the life lived; rather, it would be nature assuming or reassuming its absolute authority in sheer indifference to the work of culture. But this distorts the meaning of a life as something lived between birth and death; death is not only a sundering or breaking of the continuum of living, an interruption of life—although in many cases it can seem exactly like this—but what brings a human life to *its* inevitable end: it is the living of a life that ends in death, and that fact is internal to the meaning of any life. Hence, the first task of burial rites is to transfigure a natural event into one internal to cultural life—that is, to add on to the natural occurrence, the happening of death to the body, its belonging to a culture, a distinctly human life. This occurs by supplementing the natural fact of death with the *deed* of human consciousness: "Hence, it is the duty of the family member to augment this aspect, so that even his [the dead one's] ultimate being . . . shall not belong solely to nature and remain something nonrational, but shall make it so that it too may be something that has been *done*."[52] In supplementing fact with deed, burial rites rescue death from the sheer contingency (or necessity) of the morass of natural happenings and endow it with meaning as the completion of this particular life. We are not responsible for the death itself, but through burial rites and mourning we are responsible for placing the life and the death together into a whole, unifying or bringing into considered relation the natural and the cultural; it is in that sense that the death becomes something done.

The other elements of Hegel's account follow naturally from his thought that burial rites involve the addition of a cultural action to the natural happening. Second, by making death, or the passage from life to death, into a work, something also accomplished, the community returns to or preserves for the dead one his or her individuality, their being someone with a proper name, lifting them out of the anonymity and chaos of nature. The great effort of separating the remains of victims of mass accidents exemplifies this desire for individuation, as do, in their own way, "unknown soldier" gravesites: placeholders for an absent name. In Western cultures, individuation is a primary way in which the demand for death to become deed is accomplished. Third, following directly from the claim of individuality, the action of burial sustains the dead one's place in the community: "By this action it makes him a member in a polity, which to a greater degree overwhelms and keeps in check the powers of the particular elements of matter and the lower living creatures which sought to be set free from him and destroy him."[53] In fine, burial rites function as acts of recognition through which the dead one remains one of us, her membership in the community extending beyond life, so that, conversely, we might become a community of the living and the dead. Through the *action* of burial rites, the dead remain individuals, not mere stuff; their being dead is acknowledged and normatively framed; once normatively framed, the dead typically arouse sorrow and grief, not disgust. Treating the dead with respect, whatever respectful treatment involves in a particular society, is the cultural mechanism through which a life is marked as a human one even in the moment of its loss of life. No souls or traits or metaphysical kernels could be operative here; this is an extreme moment in which dignity is bestowed on a human body in the very moment it returns fully to the natural world.

Burial rites negotiate the relation between nature and culture, providing the naturally occurring human body, even in its state of decease, with cultural meaning. That almost universally these are assumed to be urgent requirements on the living indicates that the stakes here—between the naturally occurring body as subject to natural forces and that same body as belonging to a distinctly cultural human life—are more general: something in the very idea of human dignity, of the standing of the human as human, hangs on successful negotiation between natural fact and cultural deed. But this fact needs to be ratcheted up one further level: while the urgency of the burial rites speaks to the necessity for both separating and connecting culture with nature, one source of confusion creating the necessity is that the dead still have a human look. Corpses are uncanny because with their altogether human figure—face, neck, torso, arms, legs, hair and nails—they seem very proximate to the living, very like us, just missing something. A recently dead corpse never appears quite dead enough, never quite fully on the dead side of the life/death binary; or, we might say, corpses inhabit a liminal state between life and death, revealing that distinction not to be an either/or but a continuum. From here it can be argued that a further purpose of burial rites is making that continuum into a binary, making sure that the realms of life and death, and culture and nature remain firmly distinguished from one another.[54] It is this all-too-human feature of the corpses and of the camp inmates that horrify onlookers: in the tumbling corpses we experience the emphatic continuum and the emphatic separation between the living and the dead, something so human being something so utterly dead (not human, garbage), while the survivors have the look of a corpse yet remain on the living side of the binary. So another interpretation of Lionel Abel's sense that the Jews would not be able to recover from the disgrace is that they would not be able to restore a firm separation between Jewish life and the realm of death, that they were lodged in a continuum in which death would forever cling to them.

VI. My Body: Voluntary *and* Involuntary

It is because the heaped and bulldozed bodies were deprived of all three of the dignity-preserving features of burial rites—with that heaping and bulldozing representing the terminal moment of a process of relentless degradation intending the devastation that every humiliation promises—that they became human forms fully abstracted from cultural belonging and thereby turned back into unconditionally natural stuff. But why should that be a cause of revulsion? Following Hegel, I argued that what salvages the dignity of the dead is the communal imposition of cultural agency with respect to their natural demise, with respect to what in fact exceeds the power of agency to directly control it. This is equivalent to saying that human dignity concerns not sheer autonomy or freedom but something more like the appropriate relationship *between* agency and what is forever beyond the power of agency to directly control it. In order for this thought to have the appropriate scope it requires, we need a fuller understanding of how dignity and embodiment are related, one that begins with the presumption that there are dimensions of human embodiment that are essential to personhood and yet forever involuntary. This is where my argument concerning embodiment in chapters 3 and 4 broke off.

Let me remind you of how I attempted to motivate the significance of the involuntary body. Following Susan Brison's lead, I argued that the historically most prominent characteristics of female bodily experience are those that are significantly involuntary: menstruation, pregnancy, child-birth, and lactation. Rather than thinking of these processes as an exception to the terms of human bodily life (an odd conceit anyway), they should be understood as exemplars of constitutive features of the body that are not directly under the control of our powers of voluntary agency; they happen of their own accord, and because they happen in this way they require specific forms of, I now want to say, *cultural* acknowledgment. Human bodies lack firm boundaries—they are wildly leaky and porous—and some fundamental bodily behavior is emphatically involuntary and/or disorderly: laughing and crying are, again, the privileged examples—*I* cry in grief; *I* laugh at your joke. Although we give in to the disorderliness of laughing or crying, or are overwhelmed by them, nonetheless they are intertwined with intentional objects: the death of a beloved, the meaning of a joke. My fullest response to the phenomena in question is a state of bodily disorderliness.

If defecation, orgasm, pregnancy, childbirth, laughing, and crying can be regarded as examples of *affirmative bodily involuntariness*, things we accomplish or want to engage in or let happen, and hence modes of involuntariness that we accept as part of our humanity, disease and disablement tend to be construed as modes of *deficient bodily involuntariness*. (And, again, I understand hatred of the body—religious or patriarchal—as premised on the absorption of affirmative bodily involuntariness into deficient bodily involuntariness, making the involuntary body generally abject, a stain or stigma to be repudiated or overcome.) Involuntary bodily processes should thus be taken to exemplify the ontological fact that the human body generally is not something wholly within the direct ambit of reason to control. These aspects of bodily experience, I have argued, are best understood through the adoption of a dual-axis conception of human embodiment: in one mode, I *am* a body that undergoes bodily life, while in another mode I *have* a body that is an instrument for realizing my purposes in the world.

On this conception of human embodiment there are two irreducible axes: the voluntary body, which is the body I have, and the involuntary body, which is the body I am, where each way of relating to the environment is simultaneously reestablishing and redetermining the relation between the body I am and the body I have. Part of what Plessner intends in calling human positionality ex-centric—decentered—is that we will not find either a final or stable metaphysical or practical bodily unity; our bodily self-relation is naturally underdetermined and therefore forever moment-by-moment in need of determination. This dual structure should be understood developmentally: we *come* to have a relation to our body, have it, and further come to have a relation to that relationality; this is another aspect of the constitutive character of human prematurity: I come to be by coming into a relation to the body I already am, and hence I am a self by having a relation to the relation between the body I am and the body I have. Human self-consciousness, my self-awareness, includes my awareness of my body as mine, and my further implicit awareness that that mineness must be continuously established and reestablished, where that work of establishing and reestablishing involves modes of *self-presentation through which I present my distance from bodily natural necessities or natural processes as a way of continuously relating to them.* Each moment of waking life imposes the requirement to arrange my body, to coordinate the body I have with the body I am. Habit and practice may hide, defer, or temporarily erase the decision, but each morning as we wake we take responsibility once again for standing, moving, establishing our body with respect to its world. Further, since determining my relation to my body is my self-consciously determining my relation to my environment, then the mineness of my body is also a normative claim: my body can be mine only if I can determine its relation to the world; and I can determine that relation only if I am permitted and free to do so. Since the norms in accordance with which the congruence between voluntary and involuntary is to be determined are socially legislated, then, acknowledging natural constraints, what counts as self-control and what stands outside what requires control is socially established; and, even more emphatically, what counts as a legitimate domain of bodily mineness is also normatively established. The social scope and norms determining the mineness of any individual's body simultaneously determine the scope and *meaning* of self-control. What is thus essential here, given that the relation between the voluntary and the involuntary body is an essential component of establishing a relation between the self I take myself to be and the living self I am—where this is necessarily mediated by my others in accord with social norms—is the claim that (whatever the scope of the norms determining bodily mineness and the requirements for self-control) every society must have such organized norms; it could not be a recognizable social world without them. That is the upshot of Plessner's thesis concerning ex-centric positionality.

The determining structure of human self-awareness thus turns on our capacity to set our voluntary body and involuntary body in relation to one another; that is, each human life is recognizably human only if it can recognizably present itself as having resolved the relation between the voluntary and the involuntary body in intelligible ways. On this account, being able to follow social rules or being able to originate intentional actions or being able to act autonomously are not modes of enacting a permanent separation between culture and nature, separating once again reason from necessity; rather, they represent taking responsibility for the ongoing character of that relation, a relation, I am claiming, that never stops happening.

An individual can only be recognized as a social agent if she can consistently so present herself—that is, present herself to all relevant others as self-possessed, as having control over the relation between her voluntary and involuntary body. Manifesting such control typically occurs simply by following local rules about where and when the involuntary body can manifest and express itself—laughing, crying, exposing one's sexual organs, showing sexual excitement or anger or fear, releasing bowel and bladder—in only the appropriate times and places. Although there is a vast moral apparatus relating to self-control, in the first instance the issues are not directly moral but concern an individual's self-consciousness of herself as a bodily being whose modes of embodiment are socially contoured rather than naturally determined. The original and founding locus of human agency is its socially sanctioned establishment of the relation between the voluntary and involuntary body. As I suggested before, it is this, of course, that can make toilet training a central moment in childrearing; one enters into the minimal terms of self-presentation necessary for acceptance into the social world by being able to control the time and place of those bodily excretions, and to lose control of that power can be socially disqualifying. That the founding of self-consciousness involves establishing *some* normatively determined relation between the involuntary and voluntary body also *explains* why we bury our dead. Self-conscious life originates and closes with practices and rituals where the relation between involuntary and voluntary, nature and culture are paramount.

The founding act of human life and the core of the notion of human dignity is the taking responsibility for oneself by showing one is capable of establishing and sustaining an appropriate relation between the voluntary and involuntary body, the body as a culturally organized bearer of meaning and the body whose natural being finally exceeds our powers of determination. Being able to follow social rules or act intentionally or behave autonomously are not ways of spelling out the unconditional separation of human meaningfulness from natural force, the space of reasons distinguishing itself from the space of law; rather, each human action involves taking responsibility for the ongoing character of the relation between culture and nature, a relation that never stops happening even in the most minimal action. Each human action has as its reverse side its given nature, from the gravitational pull of my body that is overcome in each step

I take, to remaining upright and standing, to the causal feel of each object as it is held, pushed, kicked. What holds in miniature for each individual action—having its intentional and material aspects—holds for human doings generally: human life is a mode of life, a form of biological living and thus subject, moment by moment, to *all* the exigencies of biological living. Culture, in its wide rather than narrow significance, is thus, primarily and necessarily, our way of organizing and acknowledging the character of the relation between culture and nature; or to put it more accurately, the nature/culture distinction should not be regarded as a self-standing cultural universal, but rather as something that is a universal because of the immanent requirement that all humans have to coordinate their insuperable dimensions of bodily involuntariness with their social agency.

Dignity—or honor, or social standing, or social membership—long before the discourses of freedom, autonomy, and self-determination became available, was bestowed on those able to regulate in socially recognizable ways the relation between the autonomous body and the body that is forever beyond final control. To belong to a culture, any culture, is to be able to heed its ways of negotiating the relation between culture and nature as it affects the body of the individual agent. We *are* as humans the ongoing effort to coordinate the voluntary and involuntary in socially acceptable—rule-governed, collectively self-determined—ways. (Morality, and the moralization of the human body and action, is simply the reduction of this ongoing effort to the relation between rational norms and bodily affects, the passions as remnants of nature.) Death, as the ultimate marker of the involuntary, of our forever belonging to nature, while materially absolute, is formally just one further occasion where *we* need to establish what each of us individually and all of us collectively continually establish at every moment: our relation to our involuntary natural being. Hence, Hegel's thought that what burial rites concern is putting in place a deed or action or work where there had been a natural happening is in miniature what we routinely do as social creatures; in this respect, burial rites are an exemplary form of social action. Burial rites are dignity preserving in the same way that the rules regulating sexuality, the passions, childbearing and childrearing, laughing and crying, eating, excreting, caring for newborns, the ill, and the infirm are. There are ways of *acting* with respect to the ill and infirm that are dignity preserving because in those cases, as with the dead, we must provide the increment of agency the individual cannot provide for himself; we establish the relation between cultural practice and natural force that the individual can no longer establish on his own, even if that means simply excluding, covering over, or hiding him from sight. Our being called upon to do so is simply a recognition that the body before us is human, one of us; its humanity, which is given through its physical form, requires that the coordination between voluntary and involuntary be established even if the individual is incapable of so doing himself. To not give to the body in question the increment of cultural form would make it anomalous: appearing human, but nonetheless not human—just stuff, and hence disgusting. Our intervention in borderline cases where agency is impaired is, nonetheless, a pervasive feature of human social life, and not an extraordinary occurrence.

The involuntary body, strictly on its own, is, for the most part, manifestly undignified; it nonetheless is brought within the ambit of culture, and its standing thereby protected, by being given a culturally appointed locale: *here* is where we make love, weep uncontrollably, rage with anger, laugh hysterically, defecate, give birth, menstruate, suffer fevers, do amputations, etc. Private spaces, as they may be termed—a bedroom or bathroom or theatre or hospital or graveside—are those places in which the involuntary body—which extends to the passions (rage, jealousy, desire, fear) in their excessive modes—can act or be without jeopardizing the standing of the agent as social agent or having such involuntariness spread to where it does not belong. Undignified behavior is not socially disqualifying in itself—in the appropriate setting it can be required, even joyous. Hence, culturally appropriate behavior is not the same as microscopically rule-governed behavior, requiring, as some moralities do, that all actions be accomplished intentionally—with full self-control and foresight. The coordinating, coding, and fixing of the appropriate relation between voluntary and involuntary is robustly more fine grained than a generalized requirement for self-controlled behavior: to not weep with grief or quiver with excitement or burst with anger can also be found disqualifying.

To say human dignity requires the establishing of a relation between the voluntary and the involuntary body in *socially* recognized ways is equivalent to claiming that human dignity inheres in the capacity of the individual to be self-presenting, as capable of establishing an appropriate relation between the voluntary and the involuntary. Self-presentation, which is the ordinary performance of being a self-conscious agent, thus operates in two directions simultaneously: it is my relation to my own capacities to establish appropriate relations between my voluntary and involuntary body in relation to my socially relevant (authorized) others. My self-relation is thus mediated by my relation to others: I am for myself a dignified being only if I am recognized by you as being one; and what you recognize is just that my choices and abilities to follow the rules and norms operative here spell out my capacity to be a social agent as such. As David Velleman states the thesis, you have a "fundamental interest in being recognized as a self-presenting creature, an interest that is more fundamental, in fact, than your interest in presenting any particular public image."[55] To be unable to be self-presenting is worse than courting social disapproval; it can be disqualifying.[56] Typically, if the failure is my own doing then it will be (temporarily) disqualifying; if the failure is caused by another or by conditions for which I am not responsible, then the extent of disqualification will depend on the mores of the culture: when and under what conditions it provides covering and so dignity for those deprived of it. Dignity, in its widest sense, is thus not a moral addition to the repertoire of social action; rather social action is constituted by some local version of what it means to act with dignity—that is, what is incumbent on every social member with respect to the relation between their voluntary and involuntary body with respect to every other member of the society.

Although in its contemporary usage the notion of human dignity is a patent construction out of the early modern usage referring to the social status of elite members, I am now claiming that the phenomena picked out by the ideas of acting in a dignified manner and treating others with dignity should be seen as referring to the originating and founding acts constitutive of self-conscious agency. In its core meaning, to be a self-conscious agent is to demonstrate that one can sustain the appropriate norm-governed relations between one's voluntary and involuntary body. Because the self-congruence between voluntary and involuntary occurs in accordance with social norms, one's relation to oneself is socially mediated. The primary manifestation of the desire for recognition, the very desire that culturally supplants and reorients the drive for self-preservation, is the desire to be recognized as a self-presenting being—self-presentation as the social actuality and paradigmatic performance of self-consciousness. Hence, the theory of recognition is a theory relating to the social contouring of the human body; an individual's socially mediated bodily self-relation is the fundamental mode of her installation into a normative world not of her own making.

What, we can now ask, is involved in *caring* about one's dignity? In caring about being a self-presenting person? Our standard way of expressing the absence of such caring is to say that such an individual is a being for whom the notion of *self-respect* no longer functions. Self-respect is the active form of the sense of oneself as being possessed of intrinsic worth under conditions of threat; self-respect is the active expression of one's lovability when that very claim to standing is challenged.[57]

VII. Bodily Revolt: Respect, Self-Respect, and Dignity

Améry recalls the moment in Auschwitz when the prisoner foreman Juszek—"a Polish professional criminal of horrifying vigor" (AML, 90)—hit
him on the face for a trifle. Cringing and taking it, muttering to himself
that despite these degradations he was still a person, that he still possessed
some remnant of dignity, would be here capitulation and defeat. To survive
morally, he would have to physically appeal his case against the society and
the world that had condemned him. I want to quote this passage in full.

> In open revolt I struck Juszek in the face in turn. My human dignity lay in
> this punch to his jaw—and that it was in the end I, the physically much
> weaker man, who succumbed and was woefully thrashed, meant nothing to
> me. Painfully beaten, I was satisfied with myself. But not, as one might think,
> for reasons of courage and honor, but only because I had grasped well that
> there are situations in life in which our body is our entire self and our entire
> fate. I was my body and nothing else: in hunger, in the blow that I suffered,
> in the blow that I dealt. My body, debilitated and crusted with filth, was my
> calamity. My body, when it tensed to strike was my physical and metaphysi-
> cal dignity. In situations like mine, physical violence is the sole means for
> restoring a disjointed personality. In the punch, I was myself—for myself and
> for my opponent. (AML, 90–91)

For Améry, hitting back represented a mechanism for asserting his fundamental worth in a manner consonant with the general notion of dignity. Améry's self-assertion is an act of demonstrating his self-respect, his
particular relation to self, in a manner that establishes that he expects to
enjoin or demand or claim respect from another. Améry assumes that it is
through acts of self-respect that respect from the other is claimed; and what
the other would respect, if the claim were recognized, would be the agent's
human dignity—that is, an acknowledgment that he was a self-respecting
being. Dignity is thus an evaluative hinge connecting self-respect with respect, where the recognition of the other's bodily integrity—her affirmation of the indelible *mineness* of her body—is the normal minimum necessary condition for respecting her dignity. If the human form, all by itself,
summons respect, hitting back *demands* it.[58]

Standard accounts in this area focus on respect—for the moral law or for
another person—as primary; I take self-respect as experientially central and
respect as derivative because the hinge of human valuing takes effect from
self-valuing, from the institution of self-consciousness as an awareness of

oneself as intrinsically valuable in a manner that involves, in the first instance, the trust-borne normative expectation that one will be treated and responded to accordingly. Assuming the analytic primacy of self-respect is, of course, continuous with the procedure I have adopted throughout of reconstructing moral ideas from the perspective of the potential victim of wrongful action rather than from the perspective of the moral prohibitions imposed on agents tempted to wrongful actions. Self-respect and dignity concern what is threatened when an individual is attacked in their standing as a person. My hypothesis is, then, that dignity is the public representation of lovability, where dignified behavior is the expression of a self-valuing agent when that value is *not* threatened; it is the moral standing an individual inherits from a good-enough upbringing. On this account, having an adequate sense of self-respect is to have a sense of oneself as lovable or possessed of dignity: self-respect is the active expression of that standing.

In a noteworthy passage, John Rawls identifies self-respect as the most important primary political good—that is, a good securable only through political means that is worth having whatever one's rational life plan may be. Rawls states "It is clear then why self-respect is a primary good. Without it nothing may seem worth doing, or if some things have value for us, we lack the will to strive for them. All desire and activity becomes empty and vain, and we sink into apathy and cynicism."[59] Rawls was almost certainly pondering the fate of the socially dispossessed in this remark. Although he provides almost nothing in support of this thesis, Rawls's intuitions seem to me important and apt. Finding sufficient reason for them is at least part of my ambition here.

It is sometimes said that self-respect is a proper valuing of the self, a confident conviction that one's self is of worth or value, and that having this conviction is a necessary condition for valuing one's activities and pursuits. If the "necessary condition" clause of this claim is to carry weight, then self-respect cannot be, for example, the having of a pro-attitude toward an object, the self, constituted independently of valuing it. Pro-attitudes usually arise as a consequence of achievements or comparisons; if self-respect is a condition for activities having value, then it must be prior to them. Self-respect thus must be distinct from the concrete feelings relating to self-worth like those of pride or self-esteem that we achieve through worthy performances. One can possess self-respect without there being any specific doings or achievements, or any feelings that are regular accompaniments to its possession or expression. Each of these ways of thinking about self-respect makes it too logically or conceptually external from the having or maintaining of a self, from the fact that persons *are* values.

Gabriele Taylor helpfully comments, "To respect the self is not to think either favorably or unfavorably of the self, but to do that which protects the self from injury or destruction, just as to respect others is not to think well or badly of them, but is at least to abstain from injuring or destroying them, whether physically or morally."[60] The value accorded to the self in self-respect is manifest in protective activity. As a threshold valuing constitutive of the self, self-respect *appears* negatively, in reaction to what might threaten it. Metaphorically, self-respect is akin to a boundary or skin enclosing the self which, if breached, would mortally wound one. However metaphorical in appearance, the idea of a boundary must be essential if we are to make sense of how being a self-consciousness is a development out of erotic consciousness where the goal is no longer the sustaining of one's physical boundary with respect to all others, but sustaining one's boundedness as a self-conscious agent. Having self-respect is like being healthy: while one sometimes does feel healthy, alert, and vigorous, being healthy typically refers to a normal state of the body; one becomes aware of that normal, functional, pain-free bodily state most vividly when it is under threat. Self-respect is analogous: its primary reference is to a normally had state of the self, its being as it ought to be, that typically only becomes an issue when there is a threat to it, which must now be understood as a threat to its standing as a being of intrinsic self-worth. Hence, the question about self-respect becomes: what do the activities undertaken to protect self-respect tell us about its usual status?

In a passage that is conceptually parallel to Améry's but that has a wider conceptual reach, Bruno Bettelheim ties the question of self-respect to what is called for in order to avoid becoming a *Muselmann*.

> To survive as a man, not a walking corpse, as a debased and degraded but still human being, one had first and foremost to remain informed and aware of what made up one's personal point of no return beyond which one would never, under any circumstances, give in to the oppressor, even if it meant risking and losing one's life. It meant being aware that if one survived at the price of overreaching this point one would be holding on to a life that had lost all meaning. It would mean surviving—not with lower self-respect, but without any.[61]

This passage focuses on three structural features of self-respect worth emphasizing. First, in speaking of "one's personal point of no return," Bettelheim is not referring to any particular practice (keeping clean), or moral norm (not stealing from fellow inmates), or virtue (loyalty to friends), or identity (remaining true to one's faith), or ideal (remaining a true communist), although any of these could become someone's point of no return. When self-respect is at stake, which is to say, when one's standing as a person is at stake and under threat, *any* value horizon can be chosen as one's point of no return. The idea of a point of no return is meant to signify that, under threatening conditions, some ideal or value horizon *must* be picked out as where one will stake oneself. But this is to say two things. First, it says that self-respect is not itself a separate moral content that can be aimed at directly the way one aims at particular values and ideals. Rather, self-respect concerns the relation of the self to whatever values and ideals it has chosen (or, under conditions of particular exigency, have been chosen for it).

Second, self-respect is the active articulation of the idea that selves are normatively constituted through picking out and binding the self to some one or more values and ideals. Under normal conditions, we can express our sense of self-worth simply by participating in ordinary activities in trust-borne ways and by following the norms governing self-presentation, the norms governing the appropriate ways of bodily disposing of ourselves, aligning our voluntary and involuntary body in all the ways socially sanctioned. When one is especially diligent in this regard, one is said to have a keen sense of one's dignity. But not all situations are normal in this way; when they are not, our humanity and dignity take expression through the support, confidence, and conviction that we give *to* ideals that are structurally important for the overall character of our lives. Self-respect, then, is not typically an independent motive for action; under usual circumstances, I undertake an action for the sake of the valued state of affairs it aims at. Self-respect, very differently, expresses an individual's *adherence to* some value commitment as essential to him or her, and because it is essential, because the self is staked to that value, it is identity and status constituting.[62] Self-respect must involve, in the final instance, adherence, the binding of the self to an ideal that becomes its border and limit; it is the valuing of some value as constitutive of one's being as a norm-conforming, value-conferring being, a being for whom values are *for* but who should not be taken as solely a value for another. All these are ways of expressing the idea that one possesses intrinsic value, that one is a value in oneself, or, finally, that one is a lovable being. Acts demonstrating self-respect require the valuing of the self as a value-oriented, value-constituted being; self-respect reveals the self valuing some norms, ideals, or features of itself as fundamental to itself as a valuer, one whose very self is bound up with determining itself in accordance with normative materials (or materials that are treated as possessing normative significance). To be a valuer is constitutive of what it is to be a human agent. To use Velleman's vocabulary: to be a value is acting as a self-presenting creature, where doing so under particular circumstances is more important than whatever image one might present.

The second structural aspect of Bettelheim's account is that the idea of a "personal point of no return" specifies self-respect as, finally, a threshold value, one possessing a negative and limiting character. Because self-respect has no content of its own, but rather gives content to a structure (the identification of the self with a value horizon), it is most clearly manifest and fully operative in those cases where the constitutive relation is in jeopardy. The limit is revealed in what threatens it and forces or brings about a protective response. While routine activities can show that one possesses self-respect as an underlying character trait (for example, taking care of one's appearance), its specific quality appears only in its threatened transgression and the ensuing response. And that, again, is because the being of a self-consciousness concerns the standing of an individual as possessed of an authority that demands a normative response from all others. At certain crucial moments, as my Adam and Eve fable anticipated, one demands pure recognition, recognition of oneself as a self-consciousness, as a person.

Having self-respect reveals itself in actively valuing the self in a specific ideal under conditions of threat, say, repeated humiliations for the color of one's skin, one's language, one's religion, one's manner of dress, one's sexual orientation, one's need to work for another in order to survive. If the value horizon constitutive of the self were breached or violated, whether that value horizon is chosen or imposed, then a fortiori that which gives point to all one's activities would be dissolved as well. More accurately, if the value horizon were breached, then one's standing as one who regulates her actions in accordance with some value horizon would be breached. It can sound mysterious to say of individuals that their possession of human dignity entails their moral inviolability. How can something so patently violable be thought inviolable? *Inviolable* has two senses, one normative and one descriptive: descriptively, to be inviolable is to be secure from violation, while the more modest normative sense refers to the prohibiting of violation. Kant's moral metaphysics collapses the two meanings into one; one should not violate what cannot be violated (the second clause undermining the urgency of the first clause). But we are morally violable, and what is violable but should not be violated is the standing of an individual, a standing expressed through self-respecting activity. Self-respecting activity displays or makes manifest the normative boundary of the self by making the boundary formed by adherence to an ideal a limit that must not be breached. Without the limit in place, no norm or ideal can bind or orient activity because binding and orienting are derivative from self-respect. Thus, what a breach in the value horizon entails is that values, norms, ideals, and the like are no longer sufficiently valued by the agent in order to regulate her behavior. But that is equivalent to saying that she no longer values her highest values, and hence no longer values herself. It is this thought that supports Rawls's conclusion that lack of self-respect deprives all activities of meaning, undermining the point of pursuing them. If self-respect is the binding of the self to a value horizon constitutive of its identity—*who* the self is as such as a self worth having—then once that valuing is breached or corrupted, all activities lose their *point*: no end appears as valuable to the self. If no end appears as valuable, then no end is worth pursuing.

Muselmänner are the most extreme instance of this; sometimes they are described as possessed of an infinite lethargy or tiredness, an exhaustion not of the body but of the soul; living happens to them. What Harry Frankfurt has termed "wantons"—those who do not care what desires drive them—are also best understood as failures of self-respect, as are the despairing socially dispossessed who were the object of Rawls's original description. Failures of self-respect are a matter of degree, from the gnawing depression that comes from a sense of the world's indifference to one's existence, to everyday efforts of currying favor, to the craven pursuit of recognition no matter the cost, to, finally, the extreme instance of being dead to the world because one lacks any conception of one's own value and mattering. The *Muselmann* is this. While the addict is one model of the failure of self-respect, the more common, I think, occurs with depressive despair, on the one hand, and when the desire for recognition overpowers the very structuring of self-valuing that recognition is meant to ensure on the other. What all these instances manifest is the inability to properly value the self *in* the values and ideals that structure its existence. Ends must not only be worth pursuing, but they must be actively held to be worth pursuing, and, when threatened, so holding them must itself *appear*. If self-respect is the necessary condition for anything being held to be worth pursuing by the self, then a value can show its worth or significance finally only by showing its contribution to the lives of individuals having self-respecting forms of life. That is what makes self-respect a constitutive mechanism through which humans value their lives.

Equally, this construal of the boundary character of self-respect explicates the third component of the analysis: why Bettelheim explicitly, and

Améry implicitly, associate it with the risk of life. A life is a distinctly human one only insofar as it insists upon more than survival, and hence only insofar as life is given value through some horizon of meaning. In chapter 4, the idea of the necessity of the risk of life for the sake of pure recognition arose in consideration of the transition from the tripartite structure of erotic life to its being doubled in the structure of self-conscious living. For a self-consciousness, life cannot be the highest good; its preservation at all costs can be the depredation of the human. Hegel's account of the risk of life for the sake of pure recognition is often accused of being a philosopher's fantasy about the origins of self-consciousness without real application to empirical life. If one supposes that Hegel was there meaning to redescribe Hobbes's account of the state of nature, or, worse, that the real application for a genetic account of self-consciousness belongs to developmental psychology, then the idea of the risk of life as somehow *necessary* might seem fantastical. Even if one thinks these criticisms are answerable, as I do, one still might find the connection between the risk of life and the structure of self-consciousness Hegel offers remote. Although the situations Améry and Bettelheim describe are extreme, their locating the risk of life as a necessary element in the structure of self-respect—the good hangs on it—makes it deeply proximate to all everyday living. Self-respect, on the reading I am offering, is meant to realize Hegel's structural analysis of self-consciousness because self-respect just is self-consciousness as manifested under conditions in which the standing of the self is threatened. Self-respect should be taken as the standard ethical manifestation of the structure of self-consciousness itself. This allows the notion of the risk of life to achieve a greater ethical perspicuousness than heretofore.

To speak of the risk of life in this manner is not simply to claim that human beings have values, and that having them leads sometimes to believing they are worthy of sacrificing one's life for; that construal, which is the explicit target of my argument here, makes values and valuing too external to the self. Again, it is the thought of the unbreakable intimacy between having a self *überhaupt* and the value horizon forming the identity of the self that is required. It is not the sheer goodness or highness of values or a lofty origin or rational force that permits them to trump mere survival; nor, analogously, could it be their possession of the formal property of being universalizable and/or acceptable to all. Rather, their force and necessity is parasitic on how proximate they are to what gives any self his or her ethical identity, some contextually necessary ideal as constitutive of who the self is for herself and the threatening other, and so her way of establishing some normatively recognizable relation between the body she is and the body she has for herself that allows her to appear to the other as possessed of a normative boundary—as having person-conferring status or standing. And in concrete circumstances, the limit can be virtually empty apart from its function within self-respect: not lowering one's eyes or bowing or moving, not speaking or remaining silent; there is a line that must not be crossed, no what matter the line itself looks like—a line in the sand will do. More generally, I would not have a recognizable human life if I could not take some values as identity constituting, some values as expressive of my intrinsic worth and lovability, if I could not find some way of establishing my relation to what I naturally am, some way of expressing that as a self-consciousness I am a living and more-than-living being, all in a manner sufficient for, to borrow Hume's exacting phrase, being able to "bear (my) own survey"[63] with respect to any other. To be able to bear my own survey is to find concordance between my proclaimed values, my ethical identity, and the acts I perform; it is to achieve a self-congruence between the self I take myself to be and how I am taken by others, between appearance and reality. Acting to protect one's self-respect is the morally paradigmatic instance of self-unification. Acting that appears as self-respecting explicitly enacts the separation and connection between nature and culture, life and self-consciousness as they become manifest for and in the body of the agent in relation to a threat from without.

In broad terms, if our identity and humanity require protecting in a manner analogous to the way in which our bodies require protecting from physical harm, then, in ways that I hope are now familiar, there must be forms of harm that are intrinsically ethical, forms of harm that affect the standing of the self for itself as a lovable being, and thus as a self-respecting being, as a being with dignity. Someone can be self-respecting only if she acts to protect herself from ethical harm, from humiliation, degradation, and, finally, devastation—that is, protects herself from having her self-respect and dignity destroyed. I must not only be able to bear my own survey—doing those actions that reveal the uncrossable boundary—but in so doing I am prohibiting the other from crossing that boundary, and so staking myself on it. If for the other there is no boundary, no limit to be respected, then I cannot indefinitely believe there is such a boundary without falling into radical self-deception. But this states the thesis too weakly: if self-respect possesses an ineliminable negative aspect such that it is actualized through protective action, and that protective action is in relation to the other, then *self-respect is just the subjective dimension of the social standing of an individual as a person possessed of dignity*. Self-respect is my sense of my intrinsic worth under a condition of threat; it is, thus, my subjective sense, and the outward expression of that sense, that I *deserve* respect, and when I receive the respect I *morally* deserve, it is my dignity—my standing as a human—that is being acknowledged. This is the second way in which Rawls's analysis is correct: self-respect is a primary political good. Unless each citizen were provided with the minimum necessary conditions for self-respect, they could not pursue a life *worth living* for themselves; since that is the necessary condition for a civil life, then for each citizen self-respect is a good no matter what other ends or goods are considered essential for their lives. One natural way of stating this thought is to say "Human dignity is inviolable. To respect and protect it is the duty of all state authority."

Self-respect thus cannot remain a mere inner conviction; the self-respecting individual must *visibly* present herself as human and worthy of respect. Consider again Velleman's thesis that you have a "fundamental interest in being recognized as a self-presenting creature, an interest that is more fundamental, in fact, than your interest in presenting any particular public image." Self-presenting is the visible and appearing form of the self-valuing of one who takes herself to be possessed of dignity, and the fact of self-valuing/self-presenting in particular circumstances trumps any particular value or image because human dignity is nondetachable from self-respect, and self-respect lies in sustaining oneself as one who lives through self-valuing in opposition to any contestation of that claim. Self-respect is the defensive mode of being a self-presenting being.

Améry's hitting back gives this thesis one further twist: the claim of bodily integrity can become the minimum condition for all further claiming of respect. As he is casually abused by Juszek, Améry no longer has a choice as to where to draw a self-respecting line; if a "trifle" will do to generate physical abuse, then anything will; if anything will do, then he is as existentially helpless as he was when hanging from the iron hook during his torture. His body as such has become, exactly, his entire self and entire fate. The hitting back is not an act of self-defense; Améry knew, and it came to pass, that the likely outcome of striking Juszek would be an even worse thrashing (and it could easily have provoked worse than a thrashing—his destruction). *Arousing* that worse thrashing, summoning it, is almost the point, a marker of success: it is no longer casual abuse raining down on him, but the attempt to flatten and degrade what had stood upright. Juszek's crushing—at least here—implicitly recognizes Améry's dignity (as what becomes manifest in his self-respecting action) as what is to be denied and destroyed. The stakes of hitting back are solely moral; it is about his survival as a moral being and hence as something other than a *Muselmann*—perfectly fulfilling the terms of Bettelheim's analysis.

Implicitly, Améry recognizes that the work of dignity and self-respect must locate itself in the relation between his involuntary body—"My body, debilitated and crusted with filth, was my calamity"—and his voluntary body—"My body, when it tensed to strike was my physical and metaphysical dignity." The body that is his calamity and the body that is his metaphysical dignity are his very body in its two irreducible modalities. The hitting back takes the physical fact of his body and attempts to give to it a metaphysical worth by claiming it, by asserting that a border has been violated, and redrawing it as, emphatically, the border he *takes* it to be. In hitting back, Améry is saying "No!" to the depredation of his self, and hence denying the denial of his dignity that Juszek's casual strike implied. In so doing he issues a claim that his body is morally and rightfully *his*.[64]

Améry takes the movement from the body that is his calamity to the body that is his metaphysical dignity as a movement from the fragmentary and disjointed to an appropriate kind of unity and integrity. It is, then, through an act of physical violence that he can restore his disjointed personality, the humanity of his personality. That violence can take on this meaning; that an act purely negative and destructive in itself can have the effect of affirmation depends in part on context—defying Juszek's negation of him—and in part on the body's having a moral anatomy of the kind I have been urging: the hitting back creates a new unity of the involuntary and voluntary body which is, here and now, Améry's self-presentation. Juszek's responsive thrashing to Améry's hitting back had, at least, the intention of denying Améry's claim that his body is *his*, and so his to present this way and not that. Bodily integrity is not a physical fact, but a moral unity in material form. To recognize the body of another as his own, to acknowledge another's bodily autonomy, is to recognize it as unconditionally vulnerable, and as thereby his calamity; and, simultaneously, in its capacity for self-movement in accordance with a recognizable set of norms and values, to see it as his metaphysical dignity. The body tensed to strike only matters because the body is also our calamity. If human encounters were without liability, without the possibility of hurt, injury, suffering, there would be no reason for morals, no lovability, no striving for self-respect, no desire for recognition. But that the body as calamity is also capable of presenting itself, of actively determining itself, entails another register of significance beyond the physical, beyond bodily pain and suffering: the human body necessarily possesses a positional sense of its mineness through which it becomes the originary vehicle and medium for moral meaningfulness; that very capacity for self-movement and self-presentation in relation to the body as calamity is thus what demands recognition.

This makes the parallel with the earlier account of bodily form complete: the human body in its figuration is an image of rational freedom; the figure of the human body is thus the passive appearing of a body that is constitutively Janus faced: it is always the appearing of a body that possesses irreducible voluntary and involuntary dimensions. The appearing of the human form under normal circumstances is the appearing of what possesses intrinsic worth—a thought that is simply assumed throughout the history of sculpture and painting from the Greeks to the present. The human body is the image of human dignity, and its treatment as mere stuff disgusting to the human eye. Self-respecting action is the assertion of that very idea of self, of making actual the relation between the voluntary and involuntary body implied by the human form. Such is Améry's body as he, in a momentous act of terror and resistance, strikes the face of the world that would deny him his dignity.

Moral Alienation

Human beings are the sorts of beings who can undergo devastation: they can be destroyed in their standing as a person; they can have their dignity and self-respect destroyed. When one loses one's dignity, one also loses one's trust in the world. Dignity is the representation of self-respect, where self-respect is the stance of one who takes herself to be of intrinsic worth and acts accordingly. Thus, to respect human dignity is to respect an individual's standing as being possessed of intrinsic worth. Respect for dignity and self-respect are the third-person and first-person perceptions of the same intrinsic worth that requires the insistent affirmation of the self and the continuous acknowledgement of (respect from) others to be sustained in existence. Self-respect requires the affirmation of bodily autonomy, while respect for dignity requires the recognition of bodily integrity. Because even the human corpse can be dispossessed of its dignity, then we must understand the human form as the originating bearer of human dignity, and hence as a summons to dignity-respecting regard and treatment.

To be human is to be recognized as human. While proposed and striven for though activities displaying self-respect and dignity, one's status and standing as a human would not survive without the continuous and persistent recognition of one's defining social others. Being human is a social accomplishment achieved through socially sanctioned behavior, in particular behavior demonstrating adequate command of the rules governing voluntary bodily activities in relation to the outpourings of the involuntary body. Under ordinary circumstances, trust in the world is the ethical substance of everyday life; trust is always trust that the other will respect one's standing as human and regulate her actions accordingly. Trust is most powerful and meaningful when it can recede utterly below the shared, cooperative, and public activities that compose the dense practical actuality of human lives. Failures and breaches in the trust regime cause moral injuries; moral injury—from the pains resulting from physical assaults, to humiliations, degradations, and devastations—is the actuality and revelation of the constitutive normative, value-laden materials from which each human life is fashioned. The experience of moral injury is the experience of one's value constitution, one's dignity as a social status in its dependence on the recognition and goodwill of others.

Because trust accomplishes its great ethical work through invisibility, through withdrawing beneath the activities it makes possible, all societies complement the trust system with a system of moral rules and principles that make explicit the primary sources of moral injury to which individuals are liable through explicitly prohibiting them, and the kind of respect each is owed in order to be a full and active participant in society through the assignment of rights and duties. However else communities have believed their moral rules, principles, commands, and practices were grounded and ordered, in fact, unless they did protect individuals from recurrent sources of moral injury and successfully underwrote the recognitions necessary for social participation, and thus resourced the trust system as the ethical substance of everyday life, they would quickly become dysfunctional. In making explicit the primary forms of moral injury and the moral regard due consociates in a manner ensuring full social participation, a morality system puts the whole force of social authority behind the mutual recognitions that are the normative cement holding the community together. In traditional societies it makes no significant difference that the presumed ground of authority (God, tradition) and the actual ground (normatively contoured practices of mutual recognition) are different so long as the morality system itself adequately tracks the sources of moral injury through its prohibitions, and successfully distributes the requisite rights and duties.

In modern secular societies, however, the morality system has entered into crisis because rule-based moralities and the grounding of morals in reason and rationality is functionally weaker than, and practically disconnected from, the experiential urgencies of ethical experience. This, again, was the driving concern of Anscombe's "Modern Moral Philosophy" and Nietzsche's concern in his diagnosis of civilizational nihilism—the path through which the highest values devalue themselves, leading to ethical ideals losing their authority and affective force.

One way of pressing Anscombe's and Nietzsche's view is to argue that the rule-based, deontological and utilitarian forms of modern moral philosophy are now forces of moral alienation; that is, they are forms of moral reflection and self-understanding that *separate* persons from their deepest moral commitments rather than being mechanisms for solidifying and undergirding moral beliefs. Utilitarianism, I want to argue, *undermines* our collective experience and understanding about the meaning of torture in relation to the rule of law, while a morality of principles undermines women's experiential knowledge of the moral harm of rape, while tacitly leaving the deformation of patriarchal assumptions about embodiment and reason untouched.

I. The Abolition of Torture and Utilitarian Fantasies

If it was not known earlier, we certainly learned from the Nazi atrocities that human beings can have their dignity destroyed, that they can be humiliated, devastated, and then turned into garbage. In learning this we simultaneously learned that being human in its robust evaluative sense is a status subject to destruction. Jean Améry's *At the Mind's Limits* tracks these consequences of the Nazi genocide with unblinking rigor. Elaborating the presuppositions of his reflections has determined the trajectory of this work. Once we discover that the intrinsic worth of the human is dependent on the entire range of social practices—beginning with the first love necessary for engendering an intrinsically worthy life, and terminating with care for the dead—through which bodily autonomy and physical integrity of the human are emphatically recognized, sustained, and expressed, we simultaneously recognize that the fundamental pulse of moral life turns on the recognition of moral injury as what should not be suffered by any being having the human form, that no being having the human form should suffer humiliation, degradation, devaluation, or devastation.

The collective horrified response to the Nazi atrocities was not as universal as it might have been; its full moral impact on our collective moral self-understanding was deferred for two decades and it is still incomplete.[1] Nonetheless, one small group did recognize the stakes and meaning of what had occurred, and in response penned and then with political brio managed to get international agreement for the Universal Declaration of Human Rights. The Declaration should be construed as a repetition of that moment in the eighteenth century when citizens responded to the sight of sovereign torture not with festive delight but with repugnance and moral alarm. It thus becomes plausible to interpret the Declaration as the determinate negation of the Nazi genocide in a manner sufficient to allow for the emergence of human rights that is thus analogous to the way in which the determinate negation of sovereign torture provisioned the uprising of the rule of law. Even more emphatically, it makes sense to consider the driving impulse of the Declaration to fashion human rights as the expression of a universalist commitment to the rule of law. In the Declaration, the rule of law is the institutional form through which the claim of human rights receives expression and recognition. Human rights are, in actuality, the effective content of substantive rule of law.[2]

After stating that "all human beings are born free and equal in dignity and rights" (Article 1), and that "everyone has the right to life, liberty and security of person" (Article 3), the Declaration goes on to spell out the minimum necessary conditions entailed by these two affirmative provisions—namely that "no one shall be held in slavery or servitude" (Article 4) and that "no one shall be subjected to torture or to cruel, inhuman or degrading treatment or punishment" (Article 5). The opening five articles provide the moral premises of the Declaration: without them one cannot begin, but with them a robust rights' architecture becomes possible. Assuming the opening articles form a moral prologue makes sense because there then follows a series of articles that quickly gather together and translate the upshot of our moral consensus into a series of *legal* human rights, rights to legal personhood. These are summarized pointedly in Article 6: "Everyone has the right to recognition everywhere as a person before the law."[3] I understand the plain meaning of Article 6 to be that all humans have a right to have (legal) rights.

The opening dozen articles of the Declaration operate as negations of the Nazi perversions of law and state power, as, we might say, negations of their negation. While fashioned one at a time, they arguably amount to more than a series of discrete items.[4] There is a deep if rough logic, a philosophical argument of sorts, running through the opening articles of the Declaration that recapitulates in a formal mode the experiential exigencies of the emergence of rights in the eighteenth century. Roughly, we spell out the dignity of the human through the moral intolerableness of slavery, torture, and cruel treatment or punishment; the joint banning of these forms the basis for and is the equivalent of the rule of law coming to replace the rule of one man over another: the slave body and the tortured body are emblems of a (devastating) power of one person over another that neither any individual nor any state should have. For no one on earth to have such legitimate access to the body of any human is for each to be entitled to be a legal person. The rule of law, so understood, is what we mean by recognizing the intrinsic worth—the dignity—of each; the rule of law is offered as the primary institutional bearer of our humanitarian moral consensus. The rule of law sometimes has this connotation for the citizens of democratic states, and even more often for those living under tyrannical or totalitarian regimes who come to see the rule of law as what they are deprived of: they know all too well the difference between the sovereign law of torture, law as pure positivity, and the rule of law. Sometimes too the rule of law does not seem to carry this moral weight: because positive laws can, formally, have whatever content the sovereign body decides, law can be a form of domination, destruction, and devastation. Over the past two centuries, that the law has too often been a form of domination, control, and repression is beyond reasonable doubt. As a consequence, the thought that the rule of law is the primary institutional bearer of our humanitarian moral consensus does not share the transparency or agreement possessed by its moral premises.

The eighteenth-century rights revolution and the fashioning of the Declaration were both motivated by the necessity of providing moral substance to the idea of the rule of law against the background of, on the one hand, five centuries in which the European legal system included unspeakably cruel torture practices as an integral and fully sanctioned element in its methods of interrogation and punishment, and, on the other hand, a regime that used the law to install and forward transparently barbarous purposes; the Nazi use and abuse of the law is a recurrent deliberative theme among the Declaration's drafters. From a particular angle of vision, it seems urgent to be able to argue that the legal systems of early modern Europe and Nazi Germany were not simply different from the kind of rule of law we have come to prize, but perversions of the very idea of law itself, even if, in the case of the late medieval and early modern legal system, that label only becomes applicable retrospectively. In both cases, the prohibition on the use of torture is a component of an effort to infuse the understanding of the rule of law with a demanding moral vision: the civil inviolability of the citizen-subject that is implied by the prohibition on torture provides a first marker for what is demanded by the recognition of human dignity, which in its turn becomes the moral fundament for the idea of the rule of law; hence, the governance of the rule of law in which all citizens are possessed of legal personality—and all persons everywhere entitled to recognition as legal persons—becomes the primary bearer of what is required for the recognition of human dignity. On this construction, the statement that "everyone has the right to recognition everywhere as a person before the law," which did not appear in the original drafts of the Declaration and the inclusion of which was strongly debated, becomes the pivot connecting the unassailable moral propositions opening the Declaration with the six succeeding articles that lay out the principal *legal* human rights: equality before the law, effective legal remedy, the presumption of innocence until proven guilty, a fair trial, etc. All these, I should remind you, were the substance of Beccaria's fashioning of criminal law and the content of his argument for the abolition of torture and the death penalty. The rule of law so understood is the cornerstone of a decent society. Those opposed to the inclusion of Article 6 thought it both redundant (its central claim implied by the list of legal rights) and semantically opaque. To those who insisted on the inclusion of Article 6, the Nazi production of civil death, through the deprivation of all civil rights to designated groups, is the paradigm of the denial of human dignity and the exclusion of individuals from the human community.

The new idea of human dignity was both presupposed by, and a product of, the constellation of ideas and experiences that enabled the banning of torture to be connected with the moral charging of the rule of law in the eighteenth century; in light of the atrocities of World War II, the Declaration attempted once more to forge a morally saturated, dignity-protecting conception of the rule of law—a trajectory and construction that my moral argument has meant to repeat. In order for that history and my repetition and moral reconstruction to make sense, something like the following must be the case: moral modernity, or, what is the same, the moral foundation of political modernity, is perspicuously realized and articulated in the series of acts whereby, throughout Europe, torture was banned. Torture became, and sotto voce remains, *a* if not *the* paradigm of moral injury, of what must never be done to an individual because it is intrinsically degrading and devaluing: it harms the human status—the dignity of the human—as such by intentionally harming the present exemplification of it.[5] Torture does more than morally injure, it devastates individuals in their standing as human. Even when torture is regarded—however mistakenly—as morally justified, it remains violation, degradation, and devastation. Because judicial and penal torture were state actions, the prohibition on torture spells out the limit of state action: if the state has rights over the bodies of its subjects, however restricted and conditional, then, finally, those citizens have no rights since there is no effective limit on state action. The body of the torture victim is the meeting place of state and citizen, and hence the place where the morally saturated body of the citizen meets the legal apparatus of the state: either the rule of law recognizes bodily autonomy as its own moral basis—broken laws standing for broken bodies—or the law becomes a vehicle of sovereign authority that knows no limit. Thus, it is the morally charged conception of the rule of law that holds together the ban on torture with the recognition of human dignity: remove the prohibition on torture, and neither the liberal state nor modern moral life is intelligible. This is what I meant in claiming that the rule of law must be understood as projecting the moral framework for an ethically distinct form of life.

To state that there should be an absolute ban on the use of torture by the state misstates the meaning of the abolition of torture. If my reconstruction of the inner logic of the early sections of the Declaration is even near correct, it follows that the right to life and liberty is given moral *meaning* by the banning of torture, slavery, and cruel and unusual punishments, which in turn provides the minimum contours of what it *means* to regard humans as possessing moral dignity that should not be violated, where so regarding them requires as its *necessary minimum institutional expression* the claim that "everyone has the right to recognition everywhere as a person before the law." The first five articles are not a series of very basic rights; rather, they form the moral premises through which the right to life means the right to be treated with dignity, which requires for its actuality the right to have rights. In the first six articles, a negative ethics driven by the extreme instances of torture, slavery, and barbarous penal practices gives a minimal form—the form of bodily autonomy and bodily integrity—to the idea of human dignity, and the idea of human dignity is then given institutional actuality in the idea of legal personhood and the right to have rights. Finally, given how the very idea of the right to legal personhood is generated, it follows that nothing will count as a valid legal system unless it operates in accordance with the substantive conception of the rule of law that is spelled out in the following articles. As I argued in chapter 1, following Beccaria and Jeremy Waldron, torture is conceptually and morally incommensurable with legality. There can be no state-sanctioned torture that does not undermine the legality of the state as such. The ban on torture is necessarily absolute, not from moral qualms or prudential wisdom, but because without it the very idea of the rule of law would dissolve. What I have meant to accomplish in these pages is to demonstrate that the conception of human dignity that emerges in this way is viable and necessary: torture destroys human dignity, and that is why it is morally wrong.[6]

Yet the practice of torture continues, and reasonable people think that the absolute ban on torture involves a naïve propounding of moral absolutes in a world that has long ago given them up. Ignore their mistake about the meaning of moral notions. The great puzzle is: why does torture remain? What makes torture a continuing temptation? How do we explain the centuries-long persistence of torture? What is it that makes us animals that torture? Why do we find ourselves unable to resist the temptation to torture? The persistence of torture, I want to argue, is best understood as a—perhaps indelible—illusion of the moral imagination. It is one of the deformations that the human imagination is irresistibly drawn to despite its proven disutility and barbarity. The continued practice of torture and the presumption of its moral permissibility depend on two interconnected fantasies that are deeply etched into our moral imagination. The first concerns the experience of suffering and the inflicting of great pain; the second derives from utilitarian modes of moral reflection. Utilitarian reflections, I want to argue, tell us nothing morally meaningful about torture—its legitimate uses, its limits, its control, its form of harm—because they operate in this setting *only* as a skeptical device, a moral evil demon, whose force is to dissolve the intelligibility of the framework within which moral and legal rules have authoritative meaning. Utility's only moral meaning is to create moral alienation.

In the pain scenario, we imagine ourselves in the position of both victim and torturer. I know that there are persons who have resisted torture and are, apparently, unafraid of the pain, but I am not so constituted: I assume that even if much counted on my resisting, I am so terrified of pain, especially the kind of pain caused by old-fashioned methods of torture—fingernail pulling, scalding water, burns, drilling into a live tooth (that scene from *Marathon Man* [1976] remains terrifying), a nail hammered into my sexual organs, not to speak of beatings of various kinds—that I am certain that I would submit; indeed I would surrender all even before I was touched. (Recall Améry's easy capitulation before his torturers.) Perhaps I might try deceit for as long as I could, but assuming my torturers would not be so easily satisfied—they would want to test the veracity of my claims with further inflictions of intolerable pain—I would submit. I cannot imagine holding out for long.

From the other side, I know that if a kidnapper had my children planted in a place in which they would die *soon* (say, from lack of oxygen) and I had no other resources available—no reason to think I could simply persuade the kidnapper to surrender the information because he had nothing to gain by giving me the information—then being without resource, I would turn to torture, to some crude infliction of intolerable pain as a way of getting him to talk. When the situation is urgent and we sense ourselves without resources, we are imaginatively driven to consider the use of violence and the infliction of pain as the action of last resort. I would do whatever it takes to save my children, and I would feel morally justified in so doing. In imagining ourselves on both sides of the equation, we are relying on our knowledge of the awfulness of pain, its intolerableness, our vulnerability before others, on others' vulnerability before us, and on our untapped capacity for cruelty (and, truth be told, vengeance); all this is imagined in a setting in which we believe ourselves to be without reasonable alternatives.

The second aspect of moral illusion is a product of utilitarian forms of argument, especially as represented by the ticking bomb situation. The power of this scenario *depends* on its eliminating *all* the contingencies operative in a real-life situation: we have the individual who knows where the bomb is, we know time is short and that numerous lives will be saved, there are no alternatives available, etc. In so eliminating all the counterfactual possibilities that would constrain or prohibit and throw the use of torture into doubt, the ticking bomb scenario de facto operates as a *retrospection*; that is, what it really imagines is a situation in which using torture in the described circumstances *will* have saved numerous lives, and therefore our decision *will* have been vindicated. By operating with an effectively retrospective picture, the ticking bomb example attempts to show that there are circumstances where torture *would have been morally vindicated*; and if we can imagine some such circumstances, then logically torture must on some occasion truly be morally permissible. Logically, if there are situations in which an action would have been morally vindicated, then there are rare, extreme, and isolated situations in which committing that action is morally permissible that have no implication for further institutional practice.[7] Conversely, to imagine circumstances in which we would have been morally vindicated in doing a morally atrocious act must entail that, in those circumstances, had we not acted, we would have been morally liable for the death of numerous innocent persons. The ticking bomb situation surreptitiously constructs a situation in which not torturing would have been morally wrong, propounding a dogmatic moral absolutism concerning the rights of the terrorist and a self-righteous moral insensitivity to the lives and rights of the victims.

I assume that these two moral fantasies work in harmony: the first engages our moral psychology, showing that torture has a place in the lives of human beings, roughly, because we are intrinsically vulnerable beings who are utterly dependent on others, and because the exploitation of vulnerability on the one side and power over others on the other side belong to the moral economy of intersubjective life. The reality and fear of pain and our willingness to cause pain to others in extreme circumstances are how the idea of torture gets its claws into our imagination. The ticking bomb takes that minimal moral psychological imaginary and gives it a robust institutional setting in which utilitarian, cost-benefit calculations have legitimate purchase (because numbers do sometimes count, sometimes do trump other moral considerations; sometimes the lesser evil is all there is). The point of convergence between the two fantasies is the lack of alternative in the first and the elimination of all contingencies (the retrospective vindication) in the second. I assume, finally, that these are not mere fantasies; they capture something about how we do act in extreme situations, situations, I am suggesting, that are inevitably already saturated with these imaginary features. Add to this saturation other real-life conditions— soldiers poorly trained and under great stress, hatred for an enemy, fear of having done less than is necessary to protect loved ones, militaries stocked with those who chose it in order to act out fantasies of power and vengeance, politicians not wanting to appear weak, racism, etc.—and we have the awful brew that has made torture a too-prevalent phenomenon in the political life of the modern world.

If I am right that the entirety of the utilitarian argument is fueled by a combination of desperate and extravagant fantasy, then the most urgent question is simply: what are we to make of this fact? How are we to construe this form of argumentation? I take it that the desperation and extravagance of torture arguments are not in themselves meant to provide, at least in the first instance, an affirmative argument in favor of the use of torture; or more precisely, they are not intended to provide justifications for the installation of institutional and legalized torture practices (although there are instances of such argumentation[8]). Rather, their whole and entire weight is, at least in the first instance, for the sake of locating a moment in which we are forced to abandon those constitutionally bound legal practices determined by ordinary moral commitments by providing a logically and psychologically compelling limit case in which all the normative constraints and moral saliencies governing ethical-legal reflection dissolve in the face of a reality incommensurable with their rational force, where the very idea of taking account of significant moral features of a situation no longer makes sense, where moral attention and moral judgment themselves are no longer appropriate. In effect, consequentialist trains of argument are not directly moral arguments, but rather efforts to demonstrate that the parameters and scope of standard legal-moral argument are not absolute but finite: of necessity, it must be *logically possible* for there to be conditions in which we could not expect guidance from existing moral and legal norms, where our standard capacities for moral attention and moral judgment are inadequate to determine what actions are truly necessary in order to save the maximum number of human lives possible in so-described dire circumstances.

The first thought that needs underlining here is that, shockingly, consequentialist/utilitarian forms of argument in this domain functionally operate in exactly the same way—as we earlier saw—that Nazi practices for dehumanizing their victims operated; namely, in order to destroy the moral person, the Nazis constructed circumstances in which the victims were forced to surrender their moral commitments and attachments by making them potentially responsible for some greater harm, hence forcing them to operate with only a hope of committing the lesser evil, to let no individual lives matter and only aggregates appear. That is, as both Améry and Arendt detail, the Nazis constructed a *counter*-moral world and a *counter*-rational world in which both ordinary prudential reason and emphatic moral judgment were systematically disabled, forcing its victims again and again to betray what morally and affectively mattered most to them. This is, in effect, how consequentialist argumentation works; its exorbitance is for the sake of locating a logically possible counterexample to ordinary moral deliberation. Its extravagances are *meant to produce moral alienation*, dislodging and undermining the conditions that make moral reflection effective and necessary.

Apart from reminding us of the finite character of moral-legal institutions, practices, and norms, what conceivably can be *learned* from such extravagance? What these forms of argument no longer even attempt to demonstrate is that our actual legal institutions, practices, and ideals should or could be otherwise, that there could be a rational way of justifying and *institutionalizing* torture and rape—rape as a form of torture is never even mentioned in these reflections—and hence that the use of arguments from collective self-defense could, for the case of an institutionalized legal practice, override the more stringent arguments required for the justification of torture that acknowledge that it is a practice that operates through shredding the fabric of the human status of the victim in order to produce a being who is no longer fully human. How exactly could we make doing that a part of an institutionally legalized practice? As Michael Ignatieff pointedly states: "For torture, when committed by a state, expresses the state's ultimate view that human beings are expendable. This view is antithetical to the spirit of any constitutional society whose raison d'être is the control of violence and coercion in the name of human dignity and freedom."[9] Apart from the general incommensurability, there are too all the practical moral incommensurabilities: How exactly are we to *morally* produce experts in the dismantling of the human status of others? What are *we* doing in producing such experts, and what are we doing *to* those persons who we expect to carry out such practices? How exactly are we to train them, prime them, and then make sure they are *never* tempted or allowed to use their terrible expertise until the wildly imagined circumstances in which they are to be permitted to use their expertise arrives? The overwhelming judgment here is that conceiving such institutional arrangements is impossible.[10] Whatever consequentialist argumentation accomplishes, it is *not* the justification for the legalization and institutionalization of torture practices.

But if not for the sake of legitimizing institutional torture arrangements, what are we to make of consequentialist argumentation? In order to bypass all the morally counterintuitive repercussions that would derive from the institutionalization of torture, recent argumentation has shifted from institutional design and policy to the solitary conscientious agent who agrees that we cannot build legal systems of torture, but who also insists that however morally circumscribed legal practices are, the domain of the moral must remain, at least in part, supralegal.[11] The purpose of the argument from conscience is to have it both ways: we can never have the certainty that the full set of justificatory considerations necessary to morally vindicate an act of torture have been satisfied, but in the relevant sorts of circumstances, we can imagine that an individual's conscience tells him that the cost of not torturing is so immense that he must, as a matter of conscience, torture. It is further presumed that once the torture is done and the circumstances eliciting it closed—agreeing that all the relevant knowledge here must remain retrospective—the conscientious torturer expects to be judged by his community for breaking the law prohibiting torture, and further will accept the community's judgment.

Ignore the fact that in democratic regimes, the governing principle is one of collective responsibility for state violence and that the purpose of instituting such collective responsibility was precisely to avoid giving sovereign power over to any one individual. Ignore too that the conscientious torture scenario effectively involves a reversion from the institutional sphere back to the intimate sphere, with its overabundance of vicious affect, which I have claimed is the natural home of torture fantasies. Nonetheless, what are we to make of the argument from conscience? What *tempts* us in this scenario is that it concedes all the criticisms of consequentialist arguments for torture but one: there must a *limit* to ordinary legal and moral practice. We know, surely, the argument runs, that there are occasions when good men and women must do terrible things, ghastly things, wholly immoral and wrong things for some greater good. Because doing these terrible things cannot be legislated and the circumstances of their commitment fully anticipated, they can only be done as a matter of individual conscience, and, I would hope (the conscientious defender urges) that I could be such a conscientious agent should the occasion demand it. In this setting, reliance on the conscience of a single individual expresses the separation between morals and law, and the excess of moral autonomy beyond lawfulness. The conscientious torturer is now some hybrid of an Abraham willing to sacrifice some Isaac and some Jesus willing to sacrifice himself; the torturer is now portrayed as a tragic hero. The pathos of this is part of the moral seduction.

What the figure of conscience does is permit all the uncertainties of empirical judgment to sit comfortably within the urgencies of conscientious moral certainty: with fear and trembling, conscience demands that this torture is what must be done. The ambition of the argument from conscience is to place all the difficulties of the institutional argument out of moral reach by placing them within the mind of the conscientious agent. Hence, the conscientious torturer joins moral skepticism with moral dogmatism and then offers himself up to retrospective judgment. I hear in the assimilation of the torture argument to the claim that sometimes tragic choices are inevitable—which is the best version of the argument from conscience—not the hard-won voice of a resigned moral realism, which is what we are meant to hear, but the working of what I claimed at the outset to be an insistent form of moral illusion.

Said differently, the only possible success that consequentialist arguments in this domain could have would be to be moral solvents, dissolving all the moral and legal principles, rules, judgments, and achievements that fail to meet the demands of their extravagant counterfactual claims and overheated imagination. But that success—the claim that at some point, surely, there is a necessity for torturing because there will be a time when the only issue will be a weighing of lives saved against lives lost, with all other constraints draining away—will always prove too much: once the moral barrier is crashed through, *anything goes* as long as the principle of utility itself is satisfied; hence torturing and killing innocents related to the terrorist seems possible, but if that is acceptable, then why not raping and violating women and children related to the terrorist, doing terrible things to small babies, committing small-scale genocides of innocent populations related to the terrorist, why not a bargain where one trades some of one's community for the sake of saving more of them, and on and on? The consequentialist solvent cannot resolve itself back into the territory of moral restriction—no torture of the innocent, no excessive use of force, certainty that all the constraints are satisfied—without abrogating its original skeptical foray. The ticking bomb's retrospective structure was always for the sake of putting aside constraints that no forward-looking deliberation could match, recognizing that this leads to the detour into conscience, which can only be meaningful if effective deliberative constraints can be set aside (they are what must be up to the judgment of the conscientious torturer); but once the setting aside is accomplished, no meaningful logic of constraint can operate. Anything goes; just do the numbers. In the desperate effort to find a good case of torture, we should hear not a tragic defense of the worth of human dignity and what is required for its protection, but the blistering force of moral skepticism dressed in the guise of cool worldliness.[12]

II. Moral Alienation and the Persistence of Rape

Because the imaginary of torture remains, and because torture coheres with the ideals of the security state, torture will continue to have its official and unofficial defenders for the foreseeable future. And if the demands for a security state come to dominate over the ideal of a democratic state governed by the rule of law, then torture could once more become a legitimated engine of state. If I am right, in this domain, consequentialist habits of thought function solely as mechanisms for alienating us from the hard-won legal truths of the Declaration. Nonetheless, in the case of torture, the most recent direction of legislation nationally and internationally has *tended* to slowly, reluctantly, veer back toward sustaining and strengthening abolition. With sufficient political vigilance, one might even hope that the practice itself might be forced to the extreme periphery of state practices.[13] In this case, at least, the arc of the moral universe appears to be bending toward justice. The same cannot be said about rape; and if this is so, then perhaps the judgment about the fate of torture is less secure and more morally illusory than it at first appears.

While the law against rape is absolute, it remains virtually idle: the vast majority of rapes are never reported; of those reported, few are prosecuted, and of those prosecuted, fewer still are convicted. At best estimate, counting in unreported rape, only between 3 and 5 percent of rapists ever spend a day in jail.[14] And we now know that things are, in this regard, even worse in the U.S. military. Despite claiming a policy of "zero tolerance," in 2012, there were 26,000 sexual assaults, with fewer than 1 percent resulting in a court-martial conviction. Over their entire career, one in three women soldiers are sexually assaulted.[15] In the wider population, somewhere between one in five and one in six women will suffer rape or attempted rape in the course of their lifetime (slightly down from a generation ago).[16]

Rape persists in staggering numbers despite its unequivocal legal and moral condemnation; despite its universal condemnation, the prohibition against rape appears to lack the force of the prohibition against torture even though it is widely known that rape is used as a method of torture. There is then a *massive moral disconnect* between the legal and moral status of rape, and the persistence of the practice of rape. Nor is there any reason to suppose that either race or class is a significantly exacerbating factor: college-aged white women suffer from rape at an even slightly higher rate than the wider population; it is not some *they* but *we* who rape.[17] Something in the moral understanding and perception of rape is wildly askew, as if somehow abstract moral knowledge and concrete moral perception were here so systematically disconnected that the former cannot and certainly does not successfully inform the latter. Although there are immense legal issues surrounding the reporting and prosecution of rape, my judgment here is that the phenomenon in desperate need of explanation is the persistence of rape, with my hypothesis being that the persistence of a rape culture depends essentially on what I am calling the moral disconnect between abstract moral knowing and concrete moral experience, especially among the perpetrators, with the further lemma that one element in the moral disconnect is a failure to appreciate how morally injurious rape is.

Failure to appreciate how morally injurious rape is, how it is at least standardly and perhaps always devastating, depends on a whole raft of pervasive social scripts and perceptions: that sexual exhibition is a direct invitation, that even rape is a form of sex and must, therefore, be ultimately enjoyable, that the only available alternatives for men are to be sexually aggressive or a eunuch, that the refusal by women to be sexually cooperative under normal circumstances is a ground for resentment and anger, that there is a morally significant gap between physical force and other forms of coercion sufficient to make the use of the latter, no matter how forceful, legitimate and therefore different from rape, that women desire to be overpowered, and so on.[18] In a carefully done ethnography and analysis of sexual assault in a party-oriented Midwestern university, the authors carefully integrate three levels of analysis: personal characteristics, the standard dynamics of a "rape culture" (as in the scripts noted above), and the authors' primary focus, the structure of particular settings, such as parties at male fraternities amongst a party-going, homogeneous upper middle-class cohort in which much alcohol is consumed.[19] The analysis reads as utterly plausible: the fraternity setting, the gendered hierarchy, the structure of men assuming the role of aggressor and women assigned the role of sexual gatekeeper, the place of alcohol, with, finally, the unexpected judgment by women in this cohort that when assaults and rapes occurred (and they did in the course of the academic year), it was the victim who was to blame, not her rapist—this judgment operating as a mechanism for protecting the party culture as a whole. What is so disturbing about this study is that neither students nor researchers even thought to mention how morally atrocious rape was; the devastation of rape was invisible. For all intents and purposes, rape was viewed as the end point along a sexual continuum, with sexual assault and rape showing up as something like unwanted sex, or perhaps extraordinarily bad sex.[20]

The institutional conditions and the powerful cultural clichés structuring the social interactions that occur in them matter, but they could not circulate in the easy way they do if rape were *emphatically* understood as, at one level, more morally injurious than killing. Again, if the justificatory burden for torture is higher than that for killing, and if rape is a form of torture, then rape is—at one level—more morally injurious than killing: killing need not shred the fabric of the human status of the victim, while torture and rape do, either as an explicit intent or as implicit element of the practice.[21] It is difficult to imagine that rape could persist if it were universally held to be as morally abhorrent and as morally atrocious as torture. Adopting the slogan "rape is torture" would not be a bad beginning.

How are we to understand the failure to regard rape as being as massively morally degrading and abhorrent as it, in fact, is? While inadequate to the enormity of the issue, four streams of thought essential to my overall argument do seem central here: (i) the contrast between moral rules and moral injury, (ii) why rape is not sex, (iii) the moral perception of women's bodies, and (iv) the abuse of the public/private distinction in the understanding of fundamental rights. This last issue will take me back to questions about rape and the law. I will be focused and brief, with the full discussion these issues deserve reserved as a topic for another occasion.

The very opening of my argument in this essay began: Moral rules and principles, whether taken as natural laws or laws of reason, are without force and meaning in a wholly secular universe; the very idea that moral rules or principles form the core of morality is a holdover from a theological age. Commands without a sufficiently powerful commander are idle, and obeying rules is not transparently the same as acting morally. Even if there is an absolute moral rule that "rape is wrong" or its action-guiding equivalent, "one ought never to rape," the skeptical question cannot be evaded: what *morally happens* if I break the rule? I assume the answer "I would feel guilty" (or not) cannot be to the point. Rule moralists will urge that implied by the rule is the thought that in breaking the rule one fails to show due respect for the other. This is better, but in this setting, the notion of respect idles too. The college students in the above study considered that sexual self-respect comes from knowing the local rules for partying and sexual conduct—how to dress, who to party with, how much to drink, which fraternities are safe, who to sleep with and when, etc.—which, when adhered to, will garner appropriate respect from males.[22] But this is just the flip side of the judgment that victims *always* were asking for it: they lacked either the requisite knowledge or the self-esteem needful for sexual respect, and therefore deserved none. In Kirby Dick's *The Invisible War*, we are shown the military as routinely blaming the victim, in two cases charging rape victims with adultery, although they were single, because their rapist was married. In a final judgment, one victim's case is dismissed because rape, she is told, is a normal hazard of military service.

Torture and rape are always radical acts of dispossession, a severing of the victim's voluntary body from her involuntary body. Lack of consent entails the violation of bodily autonomy, the violation of bodily autonomy is fulfilled by the violation of bodily integrity, and the violation of bodily integrity involves dispossession: lesser bodily integrity means lesser bodily privacy, which means lesser human significance. We cannot even begin to gather the sort of wrong rape is until and unless it is regarded as morally injuring—devastating—to the victim in her standing as a human. No matter the mechanisms for its achievement, rape accomplishes a violent act of dispossession that degrades and devalues, treating another human as subhuman, or seeking to make her so. Without the language and understanding involved in an embodied conception of human dignity as realized through bodily autonomy—where the practice of consent in sexual practices is our primary mechanism for securing and fostering the norm of bodily autonomy and respect for bodily integrity—nothing of the moral devastation of rape can be understood or become socially actual for victims and perpetrators.[23]

The morality of rules, I am arguing, morally alienates perpetrators and victims from the actuality of moral injury and devastation, and thereby effectively empties moral experience *generally* of its intelligibility and meaning. Moral alienation is the actuality of morality in our social world. The persistence of rape is both cause and effect of moral alienation: without the morality of rules we could not secure a moral culture that nonetheless tolerates and suppresses the devastation of rape. But the persistence of rape, which requires the morality of rules for its continuance, derives from the eons-long degradation of women as, in being bound to their bodily life, being bound to nature in a manner that the morality of reason repudiates as without moral significance on its own.

Without beginning with some deep sense of bodily autonomy and vulnerability as fundamental to an individual's understanding of her self-worth, we cannot even begin to explain why rape, although deeply involving a woman's (or man's) sense of their sexuality, of how their body is sexually contoured, and hence what touching and penetrating it involves, is *not* itself the act of one person having sex with another. As Ann Cahill pointedly expresses it, "rape is sexual but not sex, from the victim's perspective."[24] It is not sex from the victim's perspective because it happens without her agency, without her giving herself, without her welcoming and wanting, without her consent. When that occurs, it is not that the act is missing some tincture of mental assent, some mental nod of affirmation. Rather, the victim is dispossessed of having full and legitimate public control over the appropriate relation between her voluntary body and her involuntary body. And when this occurs, her body is no longer her own. To be dispossessed of the power to control the relation between one's voluntary and involuntary body is to be dispossessed of one's standing as a person. Because even good sex involves surrender to bodily involuntariness, it can seem as if the moment a rape victim surrenders to her violation she is doing what she would do if the sex were voluntary, and hence that this is just unwanted sex. When the rape is manifestly an act of physical overpowering and invasion, a battering of her sexual organs, this is *manifestly* not so. It is an assault. But the act does not suddenly become sex when for fear of being battered the victim stops physically resisting, or when from fear she does not physically resist at all; the issue of consent concerns a public practice and not a private mental event. There is not only the syndrome of blaming the victim, but my hunch is that the metaphysical confusion that is a moral confusion about the meaning of surrender here is one of the factors in promoting the sense in the victim that she must have been at fault for not fully or properly resisting. So the moral illusion persists that there was always more she should have done.

One apparently utterly socially routine feature of the college party scene points to a deep structure of male domination and its metaphysical misogyny—namely that women were encouraged and indeed wanted to look "hot" (but not slutty), to look erotic, where failure to do so was to court social disapproval, while men could dress how they pleased, and were not, all things being equal, meant to flaunt their sexuality. Has it not always been so? In chapter 3, following the thought of Beauvoir and Judith Butler, I argued that the sexual framing of the female body was a component of a fundamental structure of patriarchy in which the whole of bodily involuntariness is projected onto women, with men culturally preserving for themselves the entire set of entitlements and self-understanding that compose bodily voluntariness. So viciously invariant are these cultural archetypes that the male conception of embodiment (a body is *mine* if and only if I can manage to ideally control it, to bring all of it within the purview of the rational will) became the Western metaphysical idea of what bodies are like, and hence what the appropriate relation between the mind or rational will and the body should be. All this, we know, simply denies the existence of the involuntary body as a distinct stratum of human existence. What allowed this prima facie implausible conception of embodiment to become universally accepted (by men) was that the burden of bodily involuntariness was deposited on women, leading thereby to the exclusion of women from full and equal standing in the polity. But this cultural severing of the voluntary and involuntary body into gender-different locales can only be indefinitely sustained if the involuntary body is both deposited as constitutive of female embodiment and further that this conception of embodiment is tacitly repudiated, abjected.

The persistence of rape would thereby seem to imply that, for at least some significant portion of the male population, to perceive a "hot" woman is to perceive a woman as already abject, as one whose body condemns her to involuntariness, especially the involuntariness of sex and reproductive events, and hence as destined for sexual invasion. To so perceive women is to perceive them as not entitled to moral control or bodily autonomy. Women's sexuality is realized through sexual possession by some man, making every woman always already possessed by men, theirs. In *The Invisible War*, a Navy rape victim records how after raping her, her assailant ran his hands over all of her body and then stated "All this is now mine." Rape, I have argued, is a man's effort to pin a woman to her abject body and to appropriate to himself the whole of bodily voluntariness, to affirm, again and again, his possession of and entitlement to it, a logic, I have argued, that is equally what "breaking" the victim in torture amounts to, and hence accounts for the sexual subtext of all torture. Even before the deformed perception of female bodily abjection has come on the scene, the work of moral derogation has been accomplished: women, dispossessed in general from having full access to bodily autonomy—what the differential dress code means to accomplish—have been equally dispossessed of full human dignity since full human dignity is in fact accomplished through having morally appropriate control over the relation between one's voluntary and involuntary body.

If anything like this train of argument is true, it follows that from the patriarchal perspective, *women are incapable of suffering moral injury*: already bound to bodily involuntariness, they might deserve some moral regard, as all humans do, but nothing in the nature of their way of being human prevents them from being violated, dispossessed, and devastated as such. The all-too-familiar moral construction whereby it is the husband or family who are dishonored by a woman's violation, and whereby—until very recently following the dictates of the marital exemption clause—a woman cannot charge her husband with rape, points to a deeper moral syndrome in the perception of female subjectivity, a syndrome I am calling "metaphysical misogyny." If, in what is a paradigm of moral dispossession, women cannot be regarded as suffering moral injury through rape, *then there is no socially effective category of moral injury*; or to put it more accurately, sexist and racist culture generates a deracinating moral alienation whereby our collective failure to recognize the moral substance of our fellow citizens entails the severing of ethical experience from its conditions of possibility. In disavowing vulnerability and bodily involuntariness as conditions and components of moral experience—which is what sexism, patriarchy, and racism do—we thereby make unintelligible to ourselves our own moral experiences and fiercest commitments. The name this alienation goes under is moral principles. Culturally, convergent with but independent of the ordinances of religious ethics, there are, for a huge swathe of the population, only moral rules, principles, laws, and commandments, entailing that the stakes of morality are, finally, solely issues of virtuous obedience and defiant (or indifferent) disobedience. The idea that morality is a matter of moral rules and principles and the societal abridgement or denial of women's bodily autonomy—their bodily abjection—re-enforce one another, effectively silencing women's moral experience and placing the social presentation of moral injury out of the discursive reach of all. The moral metaphysics of male embodiment—the moral metaphysics of the autonomous will—is itself a product of patriarchy, of disavowal, that necessarily prevents the very idea of moral injury from coming fully into view. Hence, in the name of principled morality, the suffering of women becomes invisible. Women *know* they have been violated and dispossessed without having reliable and usable discursive access to the kind of moral metaphysics of embodiment that would substantiate their knowing. Arguably, most men know that rape is wrong, even terribly wrong, without knowing that it is destructive of a woman in her standing and status as a person, devastating. Patriarchal domination is not just the transgression of a moral boundary; in so transgressing, it suppresses the experiences of moral injury and devastation as such, loosening them from the moral fabric of which they are composed, and thus generating a fundamental deformation in our understanding of the meaning of being human.

Unless and until rape is seen as dignity destroying, as violative, degrading, and devastating, the very idea of moral injury cannot accede to its authoritative place as the fundament of moral experience, even as it operatively continues to function sotto voce in the language of humiliation, degradation, mortification, etc. Yet—as a final thesis that is relevant here—I claim that something like the thought of moral injury—including the thought that rape is a form of torture—*is* implicitly present in the judgment that torture is the worst thing a human being can suffer. Built into our understanding here is the belief that the state must be denied authority over any individual's body, for unless one has some moral sense that his or her body is his or her own, beyond the touch of the state, nothing can be morally his or her own. And this fundamental sense of bodily autonomy, I have argued, is what is at stake in the prohibitions on torture, slavery, and cruel and unusual punishments, where these prohibitions are the moral ground funding the notion of dignity necessary for the claim that each is entitled to the right of recognition of being a person before the law. This right, however, cannot be secure without buying into an appropriate moral metaphysics of embodiment, and the persistence of rape is a clear block to that moral metaphysics being fully embraced. To state the issue bluntly, we are both utterly committed to, and utterly divorced from, the conception of bodily autonomy and integrity necessary for a coherent conception of human dignity. And the reason for this is patent: the full *public* right to bodily autonomy and self-possession in each person's relation to the state has manifestly failed to cross over into each person's *private* right to bodily autonomy. I will not repeat the elaborate, detailed, and blistering feminist critical analyses of how the distinction between "public man" and "private woman" has formed and deformed the tradition of western political thought.[25] I would only add here that what finally drives the public man/ private woman distinction is precisely the gendered metaphysics of embodiment in which men appropriate to themselves the whole of the voluntary body as a mechanism for the suppression and subjugation of women, while disavowing the need for an explicit recognition of the sort of bodily self-possession necessary to capture the wrong of rape, its work of dispossession. The public man/private woman distinction is effectively the legal legitimation of rape; it is the legal form of every rape culture.

Without a massive transformation in moral culture in which the morality of rules is replaced by a robust conception of human dignity as the respect due to each of us as dependent, vulnerable beings subject to the depredations of humiliation and devastation, rape will persist. Nonetheless, transforming our legal culture might form a modest wedge into the transformation of moral culture. What would an explicit and public rec-ognition of bodily autonomy and self-possession sufficient to capture the moral harm of rape look like? Although far from sufficient, a beginning would be made if each person had an absolute *right to sexual autonomy*, where full autonomy is taken to include "mental capacity, awareness of the available options, adequate information, and freedom from outside inter-ference with the process of choice," together with what I have argued to be at the core of our notion of the person, "a physical boundary, the bodily integrity of the individual."[26] By making bodily autonomy central without explicit mention of sexual autonomy, the law has targeted the defense of public man while privatizing (and even abjecting) the bodies of women. The sexual body has always been the bearer of our idea of the involuntary body; without explicit acknowledgement of sexual autonomy, the actuality of bodily involuntariness is denied and repudiated. In privileging bodily autonomy without sexual autonomy, the law has distorted the moral expe-rience and legal rights of women, letting rape remain effectively under the radar of the law until that moment where physical violence itself suddenly makes a woman's body legally visible. In many jurisdictions, it remains the case that rape requires force, where force is only taken as actual when imprinted on a woman's body, thereby making her words, decisions, and choices prior to that moment empty of any legal meaning—and for too many men, empty of moral meaning. By explicitly or even implicitly re-quiring signs of visible force or explicit coercion, rape laws deny men's and women's bodily autonomy and self-possession.

I owe the thesis that sexual autonomy should be an explicit right and that abridgments of autonomy rather than the use of force should be the criterion for recognition of valid consent to Stephen Schulhofer, whose *Un-wanted Sex* argues for it with power, analytic subtlety, and legal rigor.[27] As he states his core thesis: "In a regime that prohibits not only physical force but *all* unjustified impairments of autonomy, an impermissible threat is, by definition, an improper interference with freedom of choice . . . A wrong-ful threat intended to induce sexual compliance is coercive in itself, just as a wrongful threat intended to obtain money is sufficient in itself to con-stitute the criminal offense of extortion."[28] How to distinguish legitimate inducements from threats and what forms of economic pressures, nonvio-lent threats, and professional authority are going to generate violations of autonomy are complex matters that Schulhofer analyzes with convincing care. But if we include within sexual autonomy the "freedom to seek inti-macy with persons of our own choosing and to seek sexual fulfillment as a valued goal of an intimate relationship," then at least the outline of what it means to possess sexual autonomy can begin to emerge.[29]

But my reason for introducing the idea that there should be an explicit right to sexual autonomy was not to settle, in two short paragraphs, all the problems besetting rape law. Getting the law right is vitally important, but if the morals governing sexual encounters between men and women are as weak and flawed as they now are, little will change. The essential good of having an explicit right to sexual autonomy is to provide full institutional recognition of the sexual component of the right to bodily autonomy and integrity, thereby making the full meaning of bodily autonomy itself visible. A first step to giving moral injury the kind of physiognomy it requires is to make explicit that the harm of rape is a violation of bodily autonomy and integrity, legally and morally. Squaring our moral and legal intuitions with one another in this way would begin to make powerful and visible the injurable and vulnerable bodies that in their moral inviolability are the actuality of human dignity. Saying "rape is torture" advances the discussion by offering a fierce moral reminder that equally binds the force of public right to the protections of private right; nothing less is morally or legally apt.

In chapter 5, I argued that an essential measure of the moral well-being of a society was the extent to which its citizens enjoyed trust in the world, since it, again, is the ethical substance of everyday life: trust is the ethical actuality of persons recognizing one another as persons. I further stated that trust is an unequally distributed social good. Nothing more emphatically distinguishes the everyday life of men from women in our society—and the everyday life of most whites from most African-Americans—than their experience of trust in the world. Fear of rape belongs to the everyday comportment of most women: knowing when and where they can walk alone, and when and where not; whom it is safe to be alone with and who not. All women must routinely take precautions that most men never even consider.[30] Women's lives in our society routinely have a lining of fear that most men's lives do not. Nothing will count as confronting the full extent of our moral deformity that does not address the social reproduction of fearful lives and the unequal and unjust distribution of trust. To provide full and explicit legal and institutional expression of the right to sexual autonomy, and so make explicit and visible the character and possession of the bodily autonomy and dignity of each vulnerable citizen body, is a necessary step to providing a civilization in which each citizen can be free from the threat of humiliation, and each capable of having equal enjoyment of trust in the world.[31]

1. G. E. M. Anscombe, "Modern Moral Philosophy," in *Human Life, Action and Ethics: Essays by G. E. M. Anscombe*, ed. Mary Geach and Luke Gormally (Exeter: Imprint Academic, 2005), 178.

2. This is hardly a radical thought with Anscombe; here, for example, is John Austin considering a thought of Blackstone's: "Sir William Blackstone, for example, says in his 'Commentaries,' that the laws of God are superior in obligation to all other laws; that no human laws should be suffered to contradict them; that human laws are of no validity if contrary to them; and that all valid laws derive their force from that Divine original"; *The Province of Jurisprudence Determined and the Uses of the Study of Jurisprudence* (Indianapolis: Hackett, 1998 [original: 1832]), 186. Austin twists and turns around Blackstone's statement, never confronting the plain sense of the final clause.

3. Anscombe, "Modern Moral Philosophy," 176.

4. In the introduction to his *Life and Action* (Cambridge, MA: Harvard University Press, 2008), Michael Thompson comments that his strategy is in part inspired by Elizabeth Anscombe's contentions that "morality" should be replaced by "justice" and "morally wrong" (a deontological thought) replaced by "wrongs someone" (a recognitive thought). This is more explicit than Anscombe herself.

5. Anscombe, "Modern Moral Philosophy," 169.

6. This is the argument of Alasdair Macintyre's *After Virtue: A Study in Moral Theory* (London: Duckworth, 1981).

7. For a critical diagnosis of overridingness see J. M. Bernstein, *Adorno: Disenchantment and Ethics* (New York: Cambridge University Press, 2001), chap. 3.

8. William Blackstone, *Commentaries on the Laws of England*, vol. 4 (Dublin: 1773), 321.

9. *The Diary of Samuel Pepys*, vol. 1 (London: J. M. Dent & Sons, 1953), 102–3. While it is comforting to think of these carnivals of cruelty as things from a distant past, the history of lynching in the American South tells a different in story. In his contribution to *Without Sanctuary: Lynching Photography in America* (Santa Fe: Twin Palms Publishers, 2005), "Hellhounds," Leon F. Litwack records a variety of functions served by the lynchings, although the dominating motivation was unquestionably to create an insistent atmosphere of fear and intimidation that would keep blacks in their place. But this effort had its reflexive side; a white resident of Oxford, Mis-

sissippi told a visitor that "lynching still had a reaffirming and cathartic quality that benefitted the entire community" (27). The photographs, the latest from the 1930s, routinely show crowds whose mood and posture run from the self-satisfied to the determined and defiant to the smiling and celebratory; never is there a hint of horror, disgust, or shame. These photographs were often circulated as postcards, giving the affirmative and communal function of the lynching a new dimension.

10. The belief that "cruelty is the worst thing they do" is Judith Shklar's definition of a liberal: *Ordinary Vices* (Cambridge, MA: Harvard University Press, 1985), 43–44. Shklar's thought becomes the ethical leitmotif of Richard Rorty's *Contingency, Irony, and Solidarity* (Cambridge: Cambridge University Press, 1989).

11. Blackstone, *Commentaries*, 321.

12. Nearly a century ago, Beccaria's being forgotten was already attached to the success of his doctrines: Coleman Phillipson, *Three Criminal Law Reformers: Beccaria, Bentham, Romilly* (London: J.M. Dent & Sons, 1923), 100.

13. In *Contingency, Irony, and Solidarity*, Rorty says of the ironist that she "thinks that what unites her with the rest of the species is not a common language but *just* susceptibility to pain and in particular to that special sort of pain which the brutes do not share with the humans—humiliation" (92). This judgment is one I share; what is peculiar is that Rorty does not think this claim is subject to philosophical elaboration—despite that fact that being subject to humiliation is what separates us from the brutes. In chapter 6, I will draw on some of the formulations in Avishai Margalit, *The Decent Society*, trans. Naomi Goldblum (Cambridge, MA: Harvard University Press, 1996). Margalit argues that a decent society is one whose institutions do not humiliate those living in it.

14. Annette C. Baier, "Trust and Antitrust," in her *Moral Prejudices: Essays on Ethics* (Cambridge, MA: Harvard University Press, 1995), 99.

15. For an account of the history of humiliation see William Ian Miller, *Humiliation* (Ithaca: Cornell University Press, 1993), chap. 5.

16. As will become evident, nothing is more socially saturated with meaning than human bodily involuntariness.

CHAPTER ONE

1. Edward Peters, *Torture*, Expanded Edition (Philadelphia: University of Pennsylvania Press, 1996), 100.

2. Cited in Peters, *Torture*, 5.

3. John H. Langbein, *Torture and the Law of Proof: Europe and England in the Ancien Régime* (Chicago: University of Chicago Press, 1976), 10. Langbein attempts to argue that the abolition was a wholly "juristic" event brought on by changes in the law of evidence. In order to achieve this result, Langbein must discount penal torture as a form of torture—which is implausible in the extreme. As Mirjan Damaška, "The Death of Legal Torture," *Yale Law Journal* 87/4 (1978), 869, states in his critical review, "The law of evidence did not change; modes of punishment did. If one wishes to use dramatic language and speak of legal revolutions, there was a revolution in substantive criminal law and not in the law of proof."

4. Michael Foucault, *Discipline and Punish: The Birth of the Prison*, trans. Alan Sheridan (New York: Vintage Books, 1979), 3, quoting from *Pièces originales et procédures du procès fait à Robert-François Damiens*, 1757.

5. Foucault, *Discipline and Punish*, 6, quoting from L. Faucher, *De la réforme des prisons*, 1838.

6. Foucault, *Discipline and Punish*, 10, 14.

7. Foucault, *Discipline and Punish*, 11; italics JMB.

8. Foucault, *Discipline and Punish*, 12.

9. Foucault, *Discipline and Punish*, 48.

10. Lynn Hunt, *Inventing Human Rights: A History* (New York: W. W. Norton, 2007), 94.

11. Hunt, *Inventing*, 98. On this point at least, Foucault's analysis is in agreement with Hunt; *Discipline and Punish*, 61–64, 72–75.

12. Quoted in Lisa Silverman, *Tortured Subjects: Pain, Truth, and the Body in Early Modern France* (Chicago: The University of Chicago Press, 2001), 149 (italics JMB). The final three chapters of Silverman's study provide a fine-grained analysis of the transformation of the meaning of pain through a range of discourses—political, legal, medical—over the three centuries leading up to the abolition of torture.

13. Silverman, *Tortured Subjects*, 149. The word "pain" comes from the Latin *poena*, meaning punishment for offense. Ridding pain of that spiritual coloring became a moral demand on science once a causal-naturalist understanding of the body became possible. Pain's disenchantment reached a crescendo in 1847 with the discovery that ether gas could be used as a surgical anesthesia.

14. Silverman, *Tortured Subjects*, 175.

15. David Hume, *A Treatise of Human Nature* (Oxford: Oxford University Press, 1968), 3.2.9, 385.

16. Of course, the other significant upshot of individuation is the emergence of romantic love. That love and morality are systematically intertwined experiences is the argument of chapter 5.

17. Lynn Hunt, *Inventing*, 97. For the history of the reception of Beccaria, see 75–77.

18. But not unknown: the good Samaritan (*Luke* 10:29–37), aiding the half-dead stranger on the road, was interpreted from the beginning, by at least some exegetes, as portraying the outline of a Christian ethic.

19. Hunt, *Inventing*, chap. 2, "'Bone of their Bone': Abolishing Torture"; and Foucault, *Discipline and Punish*, Part Two, chap. 2, "The Gentle Way in Punishment."

20. Foucault, *Discipline and Punish*, 79–80 (italics JMB).

21. The first French translator of *On Crimes*, André Morellet, anxious that the work would be mistaken for a political pamphlet, radically reorganized the text in order to give it the appearance of being a systematic juridical treatise. As I argue below, this misconstrues the argumentative procedures that Beccaria is adopting.

22. See H.L.A. Hart, "Bentham and Beccaria," in *Essays on Bentham: Studies in Jurisprudence and Political Theory* (Oxford: Clarendon Press, 1982), 41.

23. For an excellent account of Beccaria's argument to which I am indebted, see Richard Bellamy's editor's introduction to *On Crimes and Punishments and Other Writings*, by Beccaria, trans. Richard Davies (Cambridge: Cambridge University Press, 1995). All unspecified page references in this section are to this edition.

24. Bellamy, Introduction, xi.

25. Hart, "Bentham and Beccaria," argues that this assertion of nonexchangeable human dignity is the systematic difference between the two accounts (51), and, sotto voce, concludes his essay with an implicit affirmation of Beccaria's view of "the moral importance of the fact that humanity is divided into separate persons and of the need for a doctrine of 'natural' human rights as a constraint on the pursuit of aggregate utility at the cost of individuals" (52). In Beccaria's *invention* of utilitarianism, what became the great issue for standard utilitarian theory was already resolved.

26. For a useful discussion of Beccaria's famous footnote and Bentham's elaboration of it, see Hart, "Bentham and Beccaria," 42–44.

27. Hart, "Bentham and Beccaria," 40.

28. While clearly the thought of Hutcheson, Helvétius, and his close friend Pietro Verri influenced him, Beccaria is patently making constructive use out of the principle of utility.

29. Although credited with inventing the deterrence justification of punishment, it is evident that Beccaria thinks necessity undergirds deterrence: if deterrence did not deter, Beccaria would not support it.

30. Foucault, *Discipline and Punish*, 30.

31. Beccaria's theory fully anticipates the eight formal principles of legality—generality, publicity, prospectivity, clarity, noncontradiction, practicability, constancy, and congruence (between legislation and enforcement)—that form the "inner morality" of law according to Lon L. Fuller, *The Morality of Law*, Revised Edition (New Haven: Yale University Press, 1969).

32. In "Political Judges and the Rule of Law," *A Matter of Principle* (Cambridge, MA: Harvard University Press, 1985), 9–32, Ronald Dworkin contrasts the "rule-book" (thin) conception of the rule of law with a "rights" (substantive) conception.

33. For a powerful defense of this procedure see Rahel Jaeggi, "Rethinking Ideology," in *New Waves in Political Philosophy*, ed. Boudewijn de Bruin and Christopher F. Zurn (London: Palgrave Macmillan 2009), especially 73–79. It was Jaeggi who urged on me the necessity of underlining the practical contradictions besetting the regime of sovereign torture. For more on the Hegelian background of determinate negation, see Paul Redding, *Analytic Philosophy and the Return of Hegelian Thought* (Cambridge: Cambridge University Press, 2007), 81–114.

34. Foucault, *Discipline and Punish*, 91.

35. Foucault, *Discipline and Punish*, 91.

36. See Joel Feinberg, "The Expressive Function of Punishment," *Monist* 49/3 (July 1965), 397–423. The classic defense of the expressive conception of punishment is found in Emile Durkheim, *The Division of Labor in Society*, trans. W.D. Halls (New York: The Free Press, 1997), and his *Moral Education*, trans. Everett K. Wilson and Herman Schnuer (New York: The Free Press, 1961). For a recent evaluation and partial defense of Durkheim in the context of the sociology of punishment today, including two stimulating chapters on Foucault, see David Garland, *Punishment and Modern Society* (Oxford: Clarendon Press, 1990).

37. Foucault, *Discipline and Punish*, 94.

38. Bellamy, Introduction, xxiii (italics JMB).

39. Beccaria is not here promoting the theological certainty required by Roman-canon law. On the contrary, he urges in chapter 14, "Evidence and Forms of Judgment," that, ideally, evidence for a crime should be accumulated through pieces of evidence that are each independent of one another, but together press toward the same conclusion. Thus "moral certainty is, strictly speaking, nothing but a probability" of the kind that we find in ordinary life as sufficient for the purposes of guiding "the most important enterprises of our lives" (34).

40. Self-incrimination was, in fact, *the ideal* of the Roman-canon criminal law system. The idea that we are to be protected against self-incrimination assumes some version of modern individualism in which the law is for the sake of the self, and where selves are morally entitled to seek their own self-preservation.

41. This is an understatement: the practice of slavery not only weakened the "cruel and

unusual" criterion to the point of only banning "excessive" violent practices (which by becoming "usual" could become acceptable), but more radically, those practices of legal qualification, hedging, and weakening then became the paradigms through which the law would come to tolerate inhumane penal practices and, finally, resource and legitimate contemporary torture practices. For this grim history see Colin Dayan's two important studies: *The Story of Cruel and Unusual* (Cambridge, MA: The MIT Press, 2007), and the more detailed *The Law Is a White Dog: How Legal Rituals Make and Unmake Persons* (Princeton: Princeton University Press, 2011).

42. Trans. Barry Richard (Harmondsworth: Penguin, 1963), 15.

43. Quoted in Jane Mayer, *The Dark Side: The Inside Story of How the War on Terror Turned into a War on American Ideals* (New York: Doubleday, 2008), 219. Although Mora did write an important memo objecting to the practices in Guantánamo, these sentences are later.

44. Jeremy Waldron, "Torture and Positive Law," in his *Torture, Terror, and Trade-Offs: Philosophy for the White House* (New York: Oxford University Press, 2010); all page references in this and the next section are to this essay.

45. Ronald Dworkin, *Taking Rights Seriously* (London: Duckworth, 1978), 23. Chapters 2 and 3 on "The Model of Rules" are relevant here.

46. Seth Kreimer, "Too Close to the Rack and the Screw: Constitutional Constraints on Torture in the War on Terror," *University of Pennsylvania Journal of Constitutional Law* 6 (2003), 295. It is Kreimer's argument I am here tracing.

47. Kreimer, "Too Close," 296. At one level, this is too optimistic; as noted earlier, the pattern of lynching in the South from the end of the nineteenth century to the early decades of the twentieth was intended as a recurrent degradation of the black body.

48. In part or whole, my quotations from Supreme Court decisions are to passages cited by Waldron or Kreimer. However, the decisions themselves are readily available on the Internet.

49. Seth Kreimer, "Too Close," 289.

50. Substantive due process, which is briefly considered in Frankfurter's decision in *Rochin*, is much disputed since it presumes that the court can assign rights not explicitly stated in the Constitution, thus expanding the scope of the Court's powers. Waldron's take here is to say that "if there is anything to the substantive due process idea, the claim that torture for any purpose is unconstitutional comes close to capturing the minimum" (240). Kreimer takes a more affirmative line.

51. Alan Dershowitz, *Why Terrorism Works: Understanding the Threat, Responding to the Challenge* (New Haven: Yale University Press, 2002); and "Tortured Reasoning," in *Torture: A Collection*, ed. Sanford Levinson (New York: Oxford University Press, 2006), 257–80. Both Waldron and Kreimer contest Dershowitz in their essays.

52. Foucault, *Discipline and Punish*, 16.

53. See the Senate Subcommittee Hearing "Reassessing Solitary Confinement: The Human Rights, Fiscal, and Public Safety Consequences" from June 2012, p. 2; the whole document can be found at http://www.judiciary.senate.gov/imo/media/doc/CHRG-112shrg87630.pdf. The last accurate numbers we have are from 2005.

54. (Charlestown: CreateSpace, 2011), 98. For the classic history of the American penitentiary, see David J. Rothman, *The Discovery of the Asylum: Social Order and Disorder in the New Republic*, 2nd ed. (Berlin: de Gruyter, 2002); for the British system, see Michael Ignatieff, *A Just Measure of Pain: The Penitentiary in the Industrial Revolution, 1750–1850* (New York: Pantheon Books, 1978). With Foucault's work, these studies document the immense gulf between normative logic, moral ambition, and empirical reality.

55. Foucault distinguishes three moments in the evolution of the modern penal system: the sovereign spectacle of torture; the poetics of punishments in which there is a match between crime and punishment of the kind favored by Beccaria and Bentham; and the pure incarceration system with its disciplines, surveillance, etc., as imaged by Bentham's Panopticon. He distinguishes these three systems this way: "mark, sign, trace; ceremony, representation, exercise; the vanquished enemy, the juridical subject in the process of qualification, the individual subjected to immediate coercion; the tortured body, the soul with its manipulated representations, the body subjected to training" (131). The reformers' poetics of punishment model never took hold, almost immediately collapsing into incarceration for no more complex reason than that deprivation of liberty in accordance with the severity of the crime is simpler to operate.

56. For a searing philosophical treatment of this claim, the reader should consult Lisa Guenther, *Solitary Confinement: Social Death and Its Afterlives* (Minneapolis: University of Minnesota Press, 2013).

57. This result is hardly surprising for two reasons: first, it still belongs to our "idea" of punishment as something that should impose hardship, deprivation, and suffering on the individual punished. But, second, this is to agree that despite our humanist qualms about corporal punishment, the penal system still "supplies a subtle, situational form of violence against the person which enables retribution to be inflicted in a way which is sufficiently discreet and 'deniable' to be culturally acceptable to most of the population" (Garland, *Punishment and Modern Society*, 289).

58. Foucault, *Discipline and Punish*, 128–29; italics JMB.

59. Foucault, *Discipline and Punish*, 129.

CHAPTER TWO

1. I take the equivocality of the achievement to be a consequence of a remaining divide in our understanding of state and law: a security state will operate with an instrumental and repressive conception of law, while a democratic understanding of the meaning of the state would lend its conception of law an emancipatory character. Roughly, the security state will take the procedural rule of law to *not* entail the substantive conception of equality and dignity projected by Beccaria's rule of law doctrine.

2. It matters to this claim that we read Beccaria as *constructing* the dignity of the self through the mechanisms of the rule of law, where the fully dignified self possessing moral inviolability would be an achievement of the pervasive implementation of that practice of law. It is this that makes the rule of law in its substantive sense rise to the level of being a form of life.

3. Jean Améry, *At the Mind's Limits: Contemplations by a Survivor on Auschwitz and Its Realities*, trans. Sidney Rosenfeld and Stella P. Rosenfeld (Bloomington: Indiana University Press, 1980). Further references in the text to this work will be abbreviated AML; page references are to this edition. The German original, based on a series of radio talks, was published in 1968 under the title *Jenseits von Schuld und Sühne* (Stuttgart: Klett-Cotta, 1977), *Beyond Guilt and Atonement*.

4. Améry is self-conscious about displacing the usual topic of discourses like his—namely the *Muselmann*—by his own experience (AML, 9).

5. If one were to begin one step back, then the first step would be urgent activity to avoid further hurt and danger—the A-delta fibers automatically triggering muscular responses of withdrawal and avoidance. But even this automatic withdrawal/avoidance set of responses is combined with unresponsiveness to other external stimuli;

pain carries out its urgent survival purposes through stilling other drives and modes of worldly interaction. This is why, conversely, the effort of attending to the world, distracting oneself, can be a successful mechanism for stilling pain's sensational influx, and why those in the midst of urgent and/or demanding activities sometimes will not feel acute pains until after the activity is completed. Both the overwhelmingness of pain and its refraction are intelligible survival mechanisms. For the overlap between the grammar of human and animal pain behaviors see Jaak Panksepp, "On the Neuro-Evolutionary Nature of Social Pain, Support, and Empathy," in *Pain: New Essays on Its Nature and the Methodology of Its Study*, ed. Murat Aydede (Cambridge, Mass: MIT Press, 2005), 367–87.

6. Chronic pain is pain without explicit or readily discoverable connection to a recognizable bodily injury. Nonetheless, chronic pains—back pains, phantom limb pains, et al.—are typically spatially experienced (even when the locale no longer exists). What chronic pain does is disable the standard protective and reparative actions coordinated with pains of particular types.

7. It is interesting to note that while some pleasures are place specific, like tastes being in the mouth, many are not. In part this is because much pleasure involves either a release from pain, thus permitting the localization of attention to recede, or from the satisfaction of achieving desired ends through action. Pleasure, I want to say, is a more mental phenomenon than pain, and hence is less tied to specific bodily locales. I take that asymmetry between pleasure and pain to matter to our thinking about morality and practical reasoning generally.

8. See Piotr Hoffman, *Doubt, Time, and Violence* (Chicago: University of Chicago Press, 1986).

9. Like everyone working on pain and torture, I am indebted to Elaine Scarry, *The Body in Pain: The Making and Unmaking of the World* (New York: Oxford University Press, 1985). References in the text to this work will be abbreviated BP. What is both telling and attractive about Scarry's study, making it a perfect companion for Améry, is its phenomenological procedure, and its virtual abstention from explicit moral reflection. World making and the unmaking of the world are her terms of reference.

10. Following the outline of the history of individuality and pain in the previous chapter, we need to remind ourselves here that pain *became* a marker for existential separateness, and that its so becoming is connected with sympathy emerging as a compensating or coordinated primary ethical virtue in the eighteenth century. My assumption is that in less individualist cultures, the grammar of pain is still operative but that it is embedded in a cultural fabric in which being in pain takes on a diversity of significances, and that these significances control, inhibit, enhance, and elaborate pain's basic grammar.

11. On this last feature see my "Amery's Devastation and Resentment: An Ethnographic Transcendental Deduction," *Tijdschrift voor Filosofie* 76/1 (2014), 5–30.

12. Ludwig Wittgenstein, *Philosophical Investigations*, trans. G. E. M. Anscombe (New York: Macmillan Publishing, 1958), §244.

13. David H. Finkelstein, *Expression and the Inner* (Cambridge, MA: Harvard University Press, 2003), in the finest expressivist account of mental life to date, says "We might speak here of a distinctive logical space in which we locate mental items and their expression along with the circumstances against whose background they have the significances they do" as belonging to "the logical space of animal life" (126–27). A version of the idea of "the logical space of animal life" will become prominent in my considerations in chapter 4.

14. As Finkelstein argues, expressing and asserting are not mutually exclusive (*Expression*, 95–96).

15. As should now be evident, 'devastation' is the term I am using to talk about traumatic experience. Although my interest is in the nature of the human such that it is liable to devastation and trauma, the fact that this is so inevitably raises the question about why some are devastated (Améry) and some, apparently, not. If some are not, does that show that those who are devastated are so because of individual weakness, say? My approach is as follows: Traumatogenic experiences do not produce devastation in each individual that undergoes them. Torture, rape, the death camps are each, paradigmatic traumatogenic experiences. Analysis of them needs to show why they are *structurally*—and thus routinely—trauma inducing and devastating, not that they *always* produce a devastation. Because traumatogenic experiences do not cause traumas in each individual that undergoes them, it is important not to morally charge either capitulation or resistance; if the events are objectively devastating in routine cases, then capitulation is neither blameworthy nor weakness, nor is resistance a matter of moral virtue or psychological strength (a person can fail to be devastated by a traumatogenic experience because they were so lacking in self-worth, it felt like something deserved). Demonstrating phenomenologically that devastation, via dispossession, is the meaning of torture is the purpose of this chapter.

16. In fact, Améry more or less has completed his analysis of torture before he arrives at the event itself.

17. This catalogue of the attributes of pain carefully follows—half quoting (usually without quotation marks), half paraphrasing—Scarry's analysis of its felt experience (BP, 52–56), interlacing it with Améry's personal account.

18. "Pain Has an Element of Blank," is in *The Poems of Emily Dickinson* (Cambridge: Harvard University Press, 1998), 501–2. It is quoted in full in Melanie Thernstrom's engaging compendium, *The Pain Chronicles: Cures, Myths, Mysteries, Prayers, Diaries, Brain Scans, Healing, and the Science of Suffering* (New York: Picador, 2010), 17.

19. For a fine overview and handling of this issue, with the right kind of naturalist acknowledgments against idealism, see Jennifer Hornsby, "Agency and Alienation," in *Naturalism in Question*, ed. Mario De Caro and David Macarthur (Cambridge, MA: Harvard University Press, 2004), 173–87.

20. I am taking this analysis of human embodiment from Helmuth Plessner, *Laughing and Crying: A Study of the Limits of Human Behavior*, trans. James Spencer Churchill and Marjorie Grene (Evanston: Northwestern University Press, 1970), 12–47. I will offer a fuller account of Plessner's conception of being and having a body in chapter 4.

21. Injury, in its literal sense, is not the only source of bodily pain; naturally occurring significant changes to quotidian bodily dispositions—menstrual cramps, labor pains—and illness (naturally occurring injury?) are even more regular sources of pain. The first point concedes that not every pain is a malfunction or injurylike in its meaning; but that does not entail that the pain itself is not aversive, or that such an event—menstruation, say—would not be "better" undergone without pain.

22. Christine Korsgaard, *The Sources of Normativity* (New York, Cambridge University Press, 1996), 148. My structural division between empiricism and rationalism parallels, but is not the same as, the central arguments about pain in analytic philosophy of mind. There, objectivism becomes a representational understanding in which pain sensations are essentially for the purpose of depicting the region of tis-

sue damage, and subjectivism the view that pained feelings prompt the appropriate behavior. For exemplars of these views see Michael Tye, "Another Look at Representationalism about Pain," and Don Gustafson, "Categorizing Pain," both in *Pain*, ed. Aydede.

23. Korsgaard, *Sources*, 148. Negative, painful emotions affect the same portions of the brain as pains themselves. For a recent study articulating how not just painful emotions, but social needs—the need for certain kinds of social connection—are part of our brain circuitry, see Mathew D. Lieberman, *Social: Why Our Brains Are Wired to Connect* (New York: Crown Publishers, 2013). Lieberman's neurological account converges fully with the account of recognition offered below in chapters 4 and 5.

24. Korsgaard, *Sources*, 149.

25. Korsgaard, *Sources*, 150.

26. Korsgaard, *Sources*, 149. The following ideas about pain are drawn from Korsgaard, *Sources*, 149–53.

27. Of course, such beings would eventually have acquired a good deal of inductive information about the ways their bodies can be harmed, but that matters little in this case, since there still could be no incremental inflictions of pains since the increments would be experientially idle.

28. Korsgaard, *Sources*, 147.

29. Korsgaard, *Sources*, 148: "Stoics and Buddhists are right in thinking that we could put an end to pain if we could just stop fighting."

30. There is also a life-threatening inverse pathology—congenital analgesia—in which injury does not cause pain. Deep immersion in an activity when a severe injury occurs can be accompanied by episodic analgesia, with pain emerging only after the event is completed. What is most surprising about episodic analgesia is that it can be instantaneous, and hence not a consequence of distraction or an effort of bringing the pain under control. See Ronald Melzack and Patrick D. Wall, *The Challenge of Pain* (London: Penguin Books, 2008), 3–9. Although the authors' "gate-control" theory is no longer in the center of research in the field (as it was when the first edition was published in 1982, a fact elaborated in Melzack's introduction to the 2008 edition), this remains an invaluable introduction to the contemporary study of pain.

31. This argument is worked out in beautiful detail in Nikola Grahek's *Feeling Pain and Being in Pain*, 2nd ed. (Cambridge, Mass: The MIT Press, 2007). As Grahek nicely makes the point here, it is not enough that a pain sensation discriminate the region of the damage; it must somehow represent the *significance* of the danger and damage. Only the emotional-cognitive dimensions of pain accomplish this task.

32. For most higher animals, expressions of pain, including pain-induced vocalizations, are treated not as calls for help but as a warning, typically against whatever in the vicinity produced the injury, and, in a different but still functional register, as notification that the injured fellow should be left alone to heal. In this respect, pain expressions in human life function in a manner opposite to their standard function in the lives of most higher animals. The explanation for the difference almost certainly derives from the extent and duration of human prematurity, on the one hand, and the extent to which survival skills are social rather than natural acquisitions, on the other hand. I shall say something more about this below.

33. A society in which the pain-aid connection was not in effect would have to be one that had adopted a stringent form of stoicism; but this is to imagine the pain-aid relation suspended or repudiated, and hence to acknowledge its initial authority.

34. The notion of "social contract" here is intended in an anthropological and not political sense: roughly, the very idea of what is involved in social existence as such.

35. In *Adorno: Disenchantment and Ethics* (New York: Cambridge University Press, 2001), chap. 6, I argue that the relation between pain and aid should be regarded as a structure of material inference: aid *follows* from an appropriate conceptualization of a stretch of pain behavior; hence aiding is part of the *meaning* of seeing an episode as one of pain behavior.

36. Infants and very small children who are not so tended, or worse, receive the opposite kind of treatment, will not develop naturally. Because receiving aid when in distress is a functional requirement for survival and development, then developing the expectation of aid is at least a naturally necessary corollary of all successful developmental sequences.

37. John Berger, *A Fortunate Man: The Story of a Country Doctor* (New York: Vintage Books, 1997), beautifully explicates the role of doctors in mediating between the isolated ill and society at large.

38. Judith Butler calls the severance consequent on social dispossession a state in which a life has become ungrievable. She articulates this thesis most movingly and powerfully in her Frankfurt Prize acceptance speech, "Can One Lead a Good Life in a Bad Life?" *Radical Philosophy* 176 (Nov/Dec 2012). Becoming ungrievable is patently an analogue of the state of affairs in which the pain-aid grammatical nexus is severed. For example, Butler states "This is someone who understands that she or he will *not* be grieved for if his or her life were lost, and so one for whom the conditional claim 'I would not be grieved for' is actively lived in the present moment. If it turns out that I have no certainty that I will have food or shelter, or that no social network or institution would catch me if I fall, then I come to belong to the ungrievable."

39. Améry is adopting the concept of sovereignty from George Bataille. For some reflections on this borrowing, see Melanie Steiner Sherwood, "*Ver-rücktes* Universe of Torture: Améry and Bataille," *On Jean Améry: Philosophy of Catastrophe*, ed. Magdalena Zolkos (Lanham: Lexington Books, 2011), 135–50.

40. Mark Osiel, "The Mental State of Torturers: Argentina's Dirty War," in *Torture: A Collection*, ed. Sanford Levinson (New York: Oxford University Press, 2004), 129–41, gives an "ordinary man", "banality of evil" account of some of the torturers in the Argentinean Dirty War (1976–1983). Often the torturers needed and received support from the priesthood in order to carry out their murderous work. I am not denying that the empirical psychology of torturers is multifarious. The contention is that there is a deep and abiding existential satisfaction operative in modern police torture, and that this satisfaction is a consequence of its deep structure. In order for torture to succeed, the victim must be broken, and the victim becomes broken only to the extent that all authority for the meaning and being of the relation between victim and torturer resides with the torturer. Seeking and coming to possess this absolute authority is to become sovereign. Hence, even nervous, guilty-feeling, anxious torturers must seek to become sovereign. The moral meaning of such an episode will be analyzed in the next chapter.

41. This also explains the kind of totality Nazism meant to be for itself, since belonging must feel like wholeness not dependence.

42. As I shall discuss further below, the "other" also plays out for the would-be sovereign his habitation in a body that he cannot, finally, fully control or call his own. Dependency on our bodies and dependency on others are continuous phenomena.

43. Although a robust reading of the idea of the welfare state can be interpreted as a sec-

ular replacement for religion in this regard. That would certainly explain the inverse proportion between religious belief and living in a welfare state in the contemporary world.

44. In the chapter entitled "Shame" in *The Drowned and the Saved*, trans. Raymond Rosenthal (London: Abacus, 1988), Primo Levi modulates from this kind of shamefulness to what has come to be called "survivor's guilt." That shame has these different dimensions will need accounting for.

45. The need to distinguish and connect predictive and moralized trust was urged on me by one of the anonymous readers for the University of Chicago Press. For reasons that will become clear in chapter 5, moralized trust is in part constitutive of the normative structure of human self-consciousness.

46. This, as stated, is implausibly strong. In chapter 4, I will elaborate the minimum necessary conditions of social agency with respect to the body that capture the claim underlying Améry's statement.

47. The CIA's "KUBARK Counterintelligence Interrogation" Manual (1963), section VII.A.7, 41. http://www.gwu.edu/~nsarchiv/NSAEBB/NSAEBB27/01–02.htm. There are now at least four print versions of this available.

CHAPTER THREE

1. See Jean-Paul Sartre, *Being and Nothingness: An Essay on Phenomenological Ontology*, trans. Hazel Barnes (New York: Philosophical Library, 1956), 402–4. To what extent Améry's account of his torture leans on this stretch of Sartre's thought is a topic for a later occasion.

2. Ruth Seifert, "War and Rape: A Preliminary Analysis," in *Mass Rape: The War against Women in Bosnia-Herzegovina*, ed. Alexandra Stiglmayer, translations by Marion Faber (Lincoln: University of Nebraska Press, 1994), 55. For an overview of war rape, the best account remains Susan Brownmiller, *Against Our Will: Men, Women and Rape* (New York: Fawcett Books, 1975), chap. 3.

3. Susan J. Brison, *Aftermath: Violence and the Remaking of a Self* (Princeton: Princeton University Press, 2002); references to this work in the text will be abbreviated A and followed by pages from this edition. Brison herself draws on analogies with Améry's torture (A, 46–47, 50, 65). That said, her work has come to play a role in the rape literature similar to Améry's in the torture literature; however, references to both systematically suppress their patent use of a thick conception of intersubjectivity in rendering their experiences. My account attempts to make good that deficit.

4. Arguably, torture and rape should be regarded as extreme, limit forms of epistemic injustice. For a general analysis of this phenomenon, see Miranda Fricker, *Epistemic Injustice: Powers and the Ethics of Knowing* (Oxford: Oxford University Press, 2009). I am again grateful to the anonymous reader for the University of Chicago Press for urging this addition to my analysis.

5. Judith Lewis Herman, *Trauma and Recovery* (New York: Basic Books, 1992), 53.

6. Herman, *Trauma and Recovery*, 52–53.

7. L.N. Henderson, "What Makes Rape a Crime?" *Berkeley Woman's Law Journal* 3 (1988), 225.

8. I shall argue in chapter 4 that the structural logic operative here converges with the account of slavery given by Orlando Patterson, *Slavery and Social Death: A Comparative Study* (Cambridge, MA: Harvard University press, 1982).

9. Herman, *Trauma and Recovery*, 34.

10. This claim could be compelling only if it could be shown that trust in the world is

a necessary condition for undamaged world relations that were the normal result of successful childhood development—that is, showing that trust in the world is the normal terminus through which children become normally functioning adults. I shall argue for this construal of trust in the world in chapter 5.

11. Annette Baier, "Cartesian Persons," in her *Postures of the Mind: Essays on Mind and Morals* (Minneapolis: University of Minnesota Press, 1985), 84.

12. Alan Wertheimer, *Consent to Sexual Relations* (New York: Cambridge University Press, 2001), 104–5; E.J. Ozer, et al., "Predictors of posttraumatic stress disorder and symptoms in adults," *Psychological Bulletin* 129 (2003), 52–73. Significantly, 65% of male victims of rape suffer from PTSD. How much confidence should we have in these numbers? What would it mean to undergo torture or rape and not be traumatized? Mary P. Koss, "Evolutionary Models of Why Men Rape: Acknowledging the Complexities," in *Evolution, Gender, and Rape*, ed. Cheryl Brown Travis (Cambridge, Mass: The MIT Press, 2003), baldly claims that "Current literature establishes that *all unwanted penetration is traumatic*" (196; italics JMB).

13. Wertheimer, *Consent*, uses the propensity of rape to produce PTSD as an indicator of its moral harm.

14. Didier Fassin and Richard Rechtman, *The Empire of Trauma: An Inquiry into the Condition of Victimhood*, trans. Rachel Gomme (Princeton: Princeton University Press, 2009), 276. Fassin and Rechtman understand the significance of the social emergence of trauma as a paradigm shift from history as the story of the victors to history as a historiography of the vanquished (275). For all intents and purposes, modern moral philosophy has not undergone this paradigm shift, remaining firmly in the victors' territory.

15. Gregg M. Horowitz, "A Late Adventure of the Feelings: Loss, Trauma, and the Limits of Psychoanalysis," in *The Trauma Controversy* (Albany: SUNY Press, 2009), ed. Kristen Brown Golden and Bettina G. Bargo, 38.

16. The premise of my argument here—that rape is not reducible to torture because there can be rapes where there is no evidence of force or signs of bodily harm—became part of international law through the International Criminal Tribunal for the former Yugoslavia. For an acute analysis of the implications of the Tribunal's findings see Debra Bergoffen, "Exploiting the Dignity of the Vulnerable Body: Rape as a Weapon of War," *Philosophical Papers* 38/3 (Nov. 2009), 307–25.

17. For a monumental telling of the history of stealth torture's emergence, see Darius Rejali, *Torture and Democracy* (Princeton: Princeton University Press, 2007).

18. This is only partially true since the majority of jurisdictions in the United States still require, either as part of their notion of nonconsent or as a separate criterion, forcible compulsion. For a useful survey of the issues, see Ethel Tobach and Rachel Reed, "Understanding Rape," *Evolution, Gender, and Rape*, ed. Brown Travis, 105–38. I take this issue up in my conclusion.

19. Joan McGregor, *Is It Rape? On Acquaintance Rape and Taking Women's Consent Seriously* (Burlington: Ashgate, 2005), 241. For a further consideration of the reasonable woman standard—and a vigorous defense of the law as protector of women's bodies—see Drucilla Cornell, *The Imaginary Domain: Abortion, Pornography, and Sexual Harassment* (New York: Routledge, 1995).

20. McGregor, *Is It Rape?*, 52–53.

21. In chapter 4, I argue that because we are self-interpreting beings, then how a self-consciousness interprets itself comes to belong the very being of that individual.

22. Jane Larson, "'Women Understand So Little, They Call my Good Nature "Deceit"'":

A Feminist Rethinking of Seduction," *Columbia Law Review* 93/2 (1993), 425 (italics JMB).

23. There is a growing literature that argues that social pains—the pain of grief or the pain of separation—are routed through the same brain mechanisms as physical pain. For a useful overview of the field, see Jaak Panksepp, "On the Neuro-Evolutionary Nature of Social Pain, Support, and Empathy," in *Pain: New Essays on Its Nature and the Methodology of Its Study*, ed. Murat Aydede (Cambridge, Mass: The MIT Press, 2005), 367–87; and Mathew D Lieberman, *Social: Why Our Brains are Wired to Connect* (New York: Crown Publishers, 2013). Because it has not yet been recognized as a recurrent kind, moral suffering has not been investigated in the same way.

24. A turning point in my dealing with the idea of moral injury was Judith Butler's *Excitable Speech: A Politics of the Performative* (New York: Routledge, 1997), especially the introduction, "On Linguistic Vulnerability," and chapter 4, "Implicit Censorship and Discursive Agency."

25. One advantage of this definition is that it is formally neutral between traditional societies in which communal membership alone formed the horizon for the ascription of rights and duties, and modern societies where, in principle, each human individual possesses that entitlement.

26. Jean Hampton, "Defining Wrong and Defining Rape," in *A Most Detestable Crime: New Philosophical Essays on Rape*, ed. Keith Burgess-Jackson (New York: Oxford University Press, 1999), 127. Hereafter all references to this essay will be cited in the text as DW.

27. Diamonds and gold acquire their supreme value by virtue of their rarity, on the one hand, and their "permanence"—the fact that, unlike other minerals, they do not spoil or corrode—on the other hand. From this perspective, it can appear as if Kant's moral metaphysics is seeking a "gold standard" for humans, despite and in opposition to the fact that we are living beings who do not possess any of those permanence-conferring features. Daniel Bernstein helped me to understand how the axiology of diamonds and gold functions.

28. Tort harms are legal harms that are not criminally wrong, e.g., a boat legitimately tied to a dock during a storm without the owner's permission that causes harm to the dock (DW, 122). I shall henceforth ignore this qualification.

29. Westin, *The Logic of Consent*, 149.

30. Westin, *The Logic of Consent*, 150.

31. I shall take up the issue of harms to the dead in chapter 6.

32. Westin, *The Logic of Consent*, 151; italics JMB.

33. Westin conflates two issues. First, what he provides is not an account of the material harm of rape but a *criterion* for determining whether a particular act is a rape for criminal purposes. Roughly, then, he conflates the criterion with the harm. Second, what he might have been thinking about in terms of dignitary harm is what other writers consider a secondary distress that some primary harms drag in their wake, viz., my indignation that someone should have violated my first-order rights. Being humiliated, denigrated, objectified, violated are all *primary harms*, the direct way in which certain types of acts damage us, and this is different from the reflective pain over one's first-order pain.

34. To forestall an obvious worry: First, I presume that we have sophisticated ways of distinguishing moral patients from moral agents, and hence of ensuring the dignity of those who lose some of their standing as moral agents—permanently or

temporally—and become moral patients. Second, the categories of moral agency and moral patience are relative: because we are existentially dependent physically and morally, because we are constitutively dependent on others, then all lives are dependent lives. I will elaborate this claim in detail in chapter 6.

35. Grahek, *Feeling Pain and Being in Pain*, 74.

36. One short way for making this claim is to recall that physical events—a train crash—can cause severe trauma, and trauma involves a devastation of the person as person.

37. Judith Jarvis Thomson, *The Realm of Rights* (Cambridge, MA: Harvard University Press, 1990), 205. For a fine treatment of moral injury in terms of bodily border crossing that has significantly influenced my argument, see McGregor, *Is It Rape?*, 220–26. Another useful treatment of the moral harm of rape as essentially bodily can be found in Ann J. Cahill, *Rethinking Rape* (Ithaca: Cornell University Press, 2001), chap. 5.

38. Nothing has done more damage to the reality corresponding to this thought than the assertions of legal positivism. My intention is take up this issue in future writings.

39. Which is to acknowledge that we do not characteristically seek to avoid all pains: some pains belong to natural functioning, some are signs of struggle and advance ("no pain, no gain"), some are welcomed as signs of aliveness, etc., but these all, NB, involve a coding or recoding of an original averseness.

40. Thompson, *The Realm of Rights*, 212.

41. Andrea Dworkin, *Intercourse* (New York: Basic Books, 1987—this edition 2007), 26–27.

42. Dworkin, *Intercourse*, 27.

43. Dworkin, *Intercourse*, 25–26.

44. Dworkin, *Intercourse*, 26

45. I presume the material basis for the persistence of this form of categorization is, to borrow Linda Alcoff's phrasing, "the differential relationship to reproductive capacity between men and women." See her *Visible Identities: Race, Gender, and the Self* (New York: Oxford University Press, 2006), 154.

46. For a trenchant defense of the kind of analysis of sex and gender I am assuming, see Sally Haslanger, *Resisting Reality: Social Construction and Social Critique* (New York: Oxford University Press, 2012).

47. Michel Foucault, Philosophy, Politics, Culture: Interviews and Other Writings, 1977–1984 (New York: Routledge, 1988), 200.

48. Dworkin, *Intercourse*, 154–55.

49. Although she builds her account from different materials, Cahill, *Rethinking Rape*, comes to an analogous conclusion (194). David Archard, "The Wrong of Rape," *The Philosophical Quarterly* 57/228 (July 2007), 374–93, uses Hampton, and Shafer and Frye (see note 52) to argue that rape attacks the sexually contoured integrity of the victim.

50. For a strong defense of the claim that rape is deeply cultural, and not universal, see Peggy Reeves Sanday, "Rape-Free versus Rape-Prone: How Culture Makes a Difference," in *Evolution, Gender, and Rape*, ed. Brown Travis, 337–61.

51. My conclusion here converges with the analysis of Carolyn M. Shafer and Marilyn Frye, "Rape and Respect," in *Feminism and Philosophy*, eds. Mary Vetterling-Braggin, Frederick A. Elliston, and Jane English (Savage, MD: Rowman & Littlefield, 1977), 341.

52. See the excellent discussion of this in Cahill, *Rethinking Rape*, chap. 5.

53. Judith Herman, *Trauma and Recovery*, 93.

54. In her "Throwing Like a Girl: A Phenomenology of Feminine Body Comportment, Motility, and Spatiality," in *Throwing Like a Girl and Other Essays in Feminist Philosophy and Social Theory* (Bloomington: Indiana University Press, 1990), Iris Marion Young provides a fine-grained phenomenology of female embodiment in the last portion of the previous century that chillingly captures the prerape experience of women that their bodies are not quite fully their own.

55. Shafer and Frye, "Rape and Respect," 334, argue that in our society the *meaning* of rape is bound to sexual difference, such that the political and cultural connotations of sexual difference should belong to our understanding of rape in *all* its forms.

56. What counts as socially undignified will vary from society to society, and remains historically changeable. For the transformations relevant to the considerations of chapter 1 of this study, see Norbert Elias, *The Civilizing Process: Sociogenetic and Phylogenetic Investigations*, trans. Edmund Jephcott (Oxford: Basil Blackwell, 1994). For the application of Elias's theory to the transformation of penal practices, in part intended as a challenge to Foucault's interpretation, see Pieter Spierenburg, *The Spectacle of Suffering: Executions and the Evolution of Repression* (Cambridge: Cambridge University Press, 2008).

57. Judith Butler, "Variations on Sex and Gender: Beauvoir, Wittig and Foucault", in *Feminism as Critique: Essays on the Politics of Gender in Late-Capitalist Societies*, eds. Seyla Benhabib and Drucilla Cornell (Oxford: Polity Press, 1987), 133. Simone de Beauvoir's *The Second Sex*, trans. Constance Borde and Sheila Malovany-Chevallier (New York: Vintage Press, 2011), 73–74, offers a genealogy in which the fundamental spiritual division of labor between men who are willing to risk their lives for the sake of a value (say, the idea of the community to which they belong) and women who are bound to processes of giving life: "[Early man's] activity has another dimension that endows him with supreme dignity: it is often dangerous . . . The worst curse on woman is her exclusion from warrior expeditions; it is not in giving life but in risking his life that man raises himself above the animal; this is why throughout humanity, superiority has been granted not to the sex that gives birth but to the one that kills." I take the dark irony of Beauvoir's final phrasing here as a potent reminder of what the patriarchal exclusion of living embodiment entails.

58. William Ian Miller, *The Anatomy of Disgust* (Cambridge, MA: Harvard University Press, 1997), after noting male disgust and fear of the vagina, argues (103–4) that men's greater disgust is over semen. Miller goes so far as to say that misogyny is rooted in disgust over semen. This is a version of the same thesis I am running here—namely that patriarchal attitudes and practices, as hierarchical and misogynist, are rooted in the repudiation of bodily involuntariness, as a self-repudiation, self-hatred, projected onto women.

59. David Sussman, "What's Wrong with Torture?" *Philosophy and Public Affairs* 33/1 (Winter 2005), 2–33. Hereafter, reference in the text to this will be abbreviated WWT.

60. The fullest elaboration of this argument can be found in Yuval Ginbar, *Why Not Torture Terrorists? Moral, Practical, and Legal Aspects of the "Ticking Bomb" Justification for Torture* (Oxford: Oxford University Press, 2010).

61. Adam Phillips, "On Tickling," in his *On Kissing, Tickling, and Being Bored* (Boston: Faber and Faber, 1993), 1.

62. My thinking on the awfulness of killing has been deeply influenced by Lt. Col. Dave Grossman, *On Killing: The Psychological Cost of Learning to Kill in War and Society* (New York: Little, Brown and Company, 1996), and discussions with my former student Nolen Gertz.

CHAPTER FOUR

1. For example, in her *Shattered Assumptions: Towards a New Psychology of Trauma* (New York: The Free Press, 1992), Ronnie Janoff-Bulman argues that "basic trust" in the world depends on three "fundamental assumptions": the world is benevolent; the world is meaningful; the self is worthy. Following attachment theory, these three assumptions are a consequence of an infant's earliest interactions with its caregivers. Without them, the infant does not attain to the world at all. Traumatic events "shatter" those assumptions; hence, even as a purely psychological occurrence, trauma for Janoff-Bulman is a normative event. What makes her account merely "psychological" is that the fundamental assumptions are just that for her—core beliefs acquired early. This makes traumatic events doxastic episodes that get their force from the early implementation of those beliefs together with the assumption that psychological life is conservative in its operations, strongly resistant to change, with the further condition that early acquisition entails affective primacy—the earliest beliefs are the most resistant to alteration. What torture and rape demonstrate is that the shattering occurs not because one is given overwhelming and undeniable *evidence* that one's belief that one is worthy is false; part of the agony of these events is not that they undermine self-worth beliefs directly, but rather that they shatter the conditions for the meaningfulness of those beliefs: the worth of the subject is epistemically fragile because it is constitutively dependent on the regard of others. In a profound way, self-worth is conditioned more by constitutive relations of *power and dependency* than epistemic reliability; it is this that a purely psychological account cannot make maximal sense of. Said differently, in a purely psychological account, the normative materials essential to the understanding of trauma become a sheer matter of entrenchment, and are thus lifted out of the interpersonal relations of power and dependency in which they have their primary role.

2. G. W. F. Hegel, *Phenomenology of Spirit*, trans. Terry Pinkard; §178; italics JMB. This translation is available online at http://terrypinkard.weebly.com/phenomenology -of-spirit-page.html. The paragraph numbers follow those in Pinkard's translation.

3. Hegel, *Phenomenology*, §177.

4. Judith Butler, *Undoing Gender* (New York: Routledge, 2004), 31–32. For Butler's related elaborations of Hegel on recognition see, for example, *The Psychic Life of Power* (Stanford: Stanford University Press, 1997), and *Giving an Account of Oneself* (New York: Fordham University Press, 2005).

5. Originally published in *Philosophy and Social Criticism* 33 (2007); my references to it, abbreviated SDR, are to the page numbers in *Recognition and Social Ontology*, eds. Heikki Ikäheimo and Arto Laitinen (Boston: Brill Academic Publishing, 2011).

6. For the import of this claim, to which I shall return, see Robert B. Pippin, *Hegel on Self-Consciousness: Desire and Death in the "Phenomenology of Spirit"* (Princeton: Princeton University Press, 2011), 68ff. Because Brandom is committed to a naturalistically based account of perception, Pippin argues that he is insufficiently sensitive to this claim (and hence to the structure of Hegel's overall argument). Nothing in my appropriation of Brandom is meant to deny Pippin's argument concerning the scope of self-consciousness, its sublation of consciousness within its practical mode of proceeding.

7. As Brandom notes, SDR 32, in relation to some trained rat behavior, the rat does not do the same movements it was trained to do (taking three steps and pressing the bar to release the food), but finishes the action sequence as called for (taking six

steps, if that is what it takes this time around), and that requires us to consider the routine as purposive rather than baldly mechanical.

8. Hegel, *Phenomenology*, §167.

9. Hegel's critique of Kant involves the idea that in making his Copernican turn, Kant altered the direction of fit between mind and world, making the world answerable to the demands of human mindedness, while suppressing the desiring/erotic structure that gives such answerability its prima facie intelligibility.

10. For an unpacking of this through Paul Grice's theory of intentional meaning, see my "From Self-Consciousness to Community: Act and Recognition in the Master-Slave Dialectic," in *State and Civil Society*, ed. Z. Pelczynski (Cambridge University Press, Cambridge, 1984), 14–39.

11. My phrasing here and the argument that follows was urged on me by Adam Gies.

12. Michael Quante, "'The Pure Notion of Recognition': Reflections on the Grammar of the Relation of Recognition in Hegel's *Phenomenology of Spirit*," in *The Philosophy of Recognition: Historical and Contemporary Perspectives*, eds. Hans-Christoph Schmidt am Busch and Christopher F. Zurn (Lanham: Lexington Books, 2010), 99, persuasively argues the instantiation of the "we" structure is one that is not necessarily perceived from the viewpoint of the participants in an exchange; and that, on the contrary, it is precisely Hegel's achievement to perceive in such exchanges a structure—Hegel's notion of "Spirit"—not readily available to its participants. This is one of the fundamental ways in which relations of recognition go unrecognized.

13. Pippin, *Hegel on Self-Consciousness*, 28.

14. Although approaching the matter from a different angle, I am here agreeing with Pippin's claim that "Brandom too distinctly isolates the sociality of self-consciousness" (*Hegel on Self-Consciousness*, 70). I am grateful to Karen Ng for urging me to clarify my difference from Brandom on this matter.

15. This is a minority interpretation of Plessner that I intend to detail in the future. For a strong confirmatory reading, whose formulations I will be relying on here, see Gesa Lindemann, "The Lived Human Body From the Perspective of the Shared World (*Mitwelt*)," trans. Millay Hyatt, *Journal of Speculative Philosophy* 24/3 (2010), 275–91. For a useful summary of Plessner's theory, see Axel Honneth and Hans Joas, *Social Action and Human Nature*, trans. Raymond Meyer (New York: Cambridge University Press, 1988), 70–90.

16. Lindemann, "The Lived Human Body," 282–83.

17. Plessner, *Laughing and Crying: A Study in the Limits of Human Behavior*, trans. James Spencer Churchill and Marjorie Grene (Evanston: Northwestern University Press, 1970), 66.

18. Plessner, *Laughing and Crying*, 67.

19. This thought will have large repercussions in our conception of action and agency since it will require acknowledging that agency and voluntariness come in degrees rather than being an absolute. As Jennifer Hornsby pertinently states the thought: ". . . in none of these cases [of acting irritably, drunkenly, tiredly, etc.] should we succumb to thinking of states and events that are items inside her and that cause her body's movements. When someone's springs of action are ones she would prefer to be rid of, it is understandable that we should liken them to constraints . . . But a person who appreciates that her conduct is out of accord with what she values, or is swayed by factors whose influence she regrets, admits her own motivations even if she does not approve of them. The desires and emotional states that explain what

she does are after all states of *hers*—of the human being whose capacities to make movements are exercised." Jennifer Hornsby, "Agency and Alienation," in *Naturalism in Question*, eds. Mario De Caro and David Macarthur (Cambridge, MA: Harvard University Press, 2004), 182.

20. Plessner, *Laughing and Crying*, 32.

21. I am here paraphrasing a line of argument from J. David Velleman, "The Genesis of Shame," in his *Self to Self: Selected Essays* (New York: Cambridge University Press, 2006), 55. I shall say something more about Velleman's argument in chapter 6.

22. Pippin, *Hegel on Self-Consciousness*, 64–65.

23. Hans-Peter Krüger, "Excentric Positionality and the Limits of Human Conduct: On the Spectrum of Human Phenomena between Laughing and Crying," in *Human Nature and Self Design*, eds. Sebastian Schleidgen, Michael Jungert, Robert Bauer, & Verena Sandow (Paderborn: Mentis, 2011), 37 (italics JMB). For an analogous but more fine-grained and scientifically informed account of boundaries, see Evan Thompson, *Mind in Life: Biology, Phenomenology, and the Sciences of Mind* (Cambridge, MA: Harvard University Press, 2007), 44–50.

24. Lindemann, "The Lived Human Body," 281.

25. Jürgen Habermas, "The Debate on the Ethical Self-Understanding of the Species," in his *The Future of Human Nature*, trans. Hella Beister and Max Pensky (Cambridge: Polity Press, 2003), 33–34. As lovely and compelling as I find this passage, I find nothing in Habermas's own thought that matches its demands.

26. For a nice handling of this idea see Neil Levy, "Culture by Nature," *Philosophical Explorations* 14/3 (Sept. 2011), 237–48.

27. Habermas, "The Debate," 50. The idea of being a body and at the same time having a body—*Leibsein und Körperhaben*—Habermas borrows explicitly from Plessner.

28. My criticism here is directed at the writings of Philippa Foot and Rosalind Hursthouse. For a detailing of these criticisms see my "To Be Is to Live, To Be Is to Be Recognized," *Graduate Faculty Philosophy Journal* 30/2 (2009), 357–390.

29. Michael Thompson, "What Is it to Wrong Someone? A Puzzle about Justice," in *Reason and Value: Themes from the Moral Philosophy of Joseph Raz*, eds. R. Jay Wallace, Philip Pettit, Samuel Scheffler, and Michael Smith (New York: Oxford University Press, 2004).

30. Thompson, "What is It to Wrong Someone?" 353.

31. Thompson, "What is It to Wrong Someone?" 348. Thompson is here interested in showing how bipolar judgments, XJY, have inferential powers that are unique to them.

32. I am indebted to Christoph Menke for this way of limning my thesis.

CHAPTER FIVE

1. Martin Hollis, *Trust Within Reason* (Cambridge: Cambridge University Press, 1998), 10.

2. There is more to say here: In the opening scenes, Ray presents a nuanced critique of what we now call "violence work," here represented by Jim Wilson and his two partners. Ray presses the claim that this type of work inevitably tears at the humanity of those who do it, police officer and criminal coming to take on the same lineaments and behavioral anatomy. What saves Ryan's two partners is the women in their lives; Wilson lives shabbily, alone. Women are civilization, while men police its borders. It is a dangerous and difficult division of spiritual labor. Wilson is so brutalized that he cannot fully recognize the saving grace women represent, and hence he cannot see what the purpose of violence work is apart from collective self-defense; only

by seeing the meaning of female bodily vulnerability and grace in the blind Mary Malden is Wilson able to perceive her as a woman. His falling in love with her is his recognition not of sexual difference, but of a shared humanity.

3. I take it as obvious that Ray means to be identifying the noir world as a Hobbesian one in which trust has either collapsed (because that is what cities do to persons) or been repudiated (because that is what patriarchy is).

4. Alasdair MacIntyre, *After Virtue: A Study in Moral Theory* (London: Duckworth, 1981), 2.

5. I have been anticipated here by Victoria McGeer, "Developing Trust," *Philosophical Explorations* 5/1 (January 2002), 21–38. McGeer's valuable essay also encouraged me to adopt the developmental orientation I elaborate at the end of this chapter.

6. There are non-Hobbesian versions of social contract theory that conceive of it as a reflective inquiry into the terms and conditions under which we could rationally agree to the norms regulating our life together in this society. This is how I interpreted Beccaria's social contract theory.

7. McGeer, "Developing Trust," 24.

8. Annette C. Baier, "Trust and Antitrust," in her *Moral Prejudices: Essays on Ethics* (Cambridge, MA: Harvard University Press, 1995), 99 (italics JMB). The four essays on trust in *Moral Prejudices* together with the essays of McGeer, Jones, and Govier (references for Jones and Govier are given below) have accomplished the conceptual heavy lifting on trust. My account sketches what they detail and supplements their accounts for the purposes of a theory of recognition.

9. Baier, "Trust and Antitrust," 100.

10. Baier, "Trust and Antitrust," 149.

11. Karen Jones, "Trust as an Affective Attitude," *Ethics* 107 (October 1996), 7.

12. My background assumption is that *psychologically*, pain trumps pleasure: a low probability of significant harm will trump even a good probability of pleasure because, truly, the ongoing consequences of damage are considerable while the gains of pleasure are dubitable. "Safety first" is not a bad rational motto; the difficulty is that if adhered to strictly, we might never begin to find out what comes second.

13. Jones, "Trust as an Affective Attitude," 12.

14. Baier, "Trust and Antitrust," 123.

15. Which is not to claim that attempting to change the power differential between persons would not be destabilizing to the trust relation; typically it is.

16. This also points to the fundamental moral weakness of trust: because trust allows moral equality between social unequals, under its benign effort of mutual acceptance, it can perpetuate damaging inequalities. My hunch is that effective conditions of (relative) trust between the sexes, above all between husbands and wives, have been one of the central mechanisms in preserving and re-enforcing sexual inequality.

17. The example is from Jones, "Trust as an Affective Attitude," 13.

18. Knud E. Løgstrup, *The Ethical Demand*, trans. Theodor I. Jensen (Philadelphia: Fortress Press, 1971), 19, states the thought this way: "Trust is not our own making; it is given. Life is so constituted that it cannot be lived except as one person surrenders something of himself to the other person either by trusting him or asking him for his trust . . . Trust and distrust are not two parallel ways life. Trust is basic; distrust is the absence of trust. This is why we do not normally advance arguments and justifications for trust as we do for distrust . . . distrust is the 'deficient form' of trust."

19. Jones, "Trust as an Affective Attitude," 14.

20. Jones, "Trust as an Affective Attitude," 20.

21. In saying this, I am not disputing that what Jones calls climate, domain, and circumstances are relevant to our reflective adjustment of trust, only that such considerations necessarily arrive too late to be determinants of whether to trust or not.

22. So the tension in my example of finding myself trusting a former friend occurs because even if no longer trustworthy as a friend, he is trustworthy when planning the event. The forms, degrees, and qualities of trust are diverse across different regions of experience. For a thoughtful canvassing of the diversity of forms of trust that gives each the requisite specificity, see the two books by Trudy Govier: *Dilemmas of Trust* (Montreal and Kingston: McGill-Queen's University Press, 1998) and *Social Trust and Human Communities* (Montreal and Kingston: McGill-Queen's University Press, 1997). For a fine account of the conditions for institutional trust, see Onora O'Neill, *A Question of Trust* (Cambridge: Cambridge University Press, 2002).

23. Hertzberg, "On the Attitude of Trust," 320.

24. I am not claiming that trust and distrust are exclusive alternatives; there is a good swathe of neutral, simple reliability lying between them. For a nice handling of this, see Jones, "Trust as an Affective Attitude," 16.

25. Baier, "Trust and Antitrust," 100.

26. McGeer, "Developing Trust," 33.

27. Being self-determined is a loaded way of describing human action; mostly we look for something simpler—namely that human beings respond in norm-conforming, socially acceptable ways. It just so happens that being an agent, being rational, acting in accordance with social norms, and being self-determined are (mostly) extensionally equivalent and conceptually mutually re-enforcing: the space of reasons is the space of freedom.

28. Axel Honneth, *The Struggle for Recognition: The Moral Grammar of Social Conflicts,* trans. Joel Anderson (Cambridge: Polity Press, 1995), 101.

29. Honneth, *The Struggle,* 104.

30. Honneth, *The Struggle,* 104.

31. Honneth, *The Struggle,* 129.

32. As Honneth might now concede, the psychological theory he is here operating with fails to match the requirements of a truly intersubjective account of self-consciousness of the kind demanded by Hegel's theory of recognition.

33. These uses of "social integrity" and "dignity" are Honneth's.

34. By "rights" here I intend ethical entitlements not legal instruments. I take it that all societies must provide their inhabitants with rights or rightlike protections, say, through duties all have toward one. So understood, rights can be expressed as religious obligations or customary practices, or role-specific rights and obligations; indeed, since role-bound rights and duties are the primary mechanism of recognition in traditional societies, I take role-bound rights and duties to be the original locale and ground of right, and later forms as attempts to generalize, formalize, and finally naturalize and universalize the narrow role-bound conception. Rights are forms of recognition.

35. For a nice handling of this claim, see Margaret Urban Walker, *Moral Repair: Reconstructing Moral Relations after Wrongdoing* (New York: Cambridge University Press, 2006), chap. 1, 3.

36. Adam Gies has suggested to me that he suspects a simple genetic fallacy on Honneth's part because trust emerges in the context of family and love relations that is its proper locale.

37. Honneth, *The Struggle*, 169.
38. In his recognitive account of the development of self-consciousness, Philippe Rochat, *Others in Mind: Social Origins of Self-Consciousness* (New York: Cambridge University Press, 2009), underlines throughout that our desire for recognition is driven primarily out of fear "of losing proximity with them, not gaining approval from them" (220) because although recognition is certainly a good, it is a good because without it we would cease to socially exist. I defend a negative reading of morals in "Suffering Injustice: Misrecogition as Moral Injury in Critical Theory," in *International Journal of Philosophical Studies* 2/3 (Sept. 2005), 303–24.
39. Lars Hertzberg, "On the Attitude of Trust," *Inquiry* 31 (1989), 316.
40. Hertzberg, "On the Attitude of Trust," 316.
41. Some development narratives—for example, attachment theory—state this moment in terms of a feeling of security; that seems true but insufficient with respect to the requisite developmental sequel.
42. McGeer, "Developing Trust," 32–33. This oversimplifies; infants unquestionably appear to instance feelings of anxiety about the affective reliability of their parents; these feelings are overcome—by coming to feel secure and loved—not judged false. So we perhaps should say something like: infants pass through (recurrent) moments of feeling what would be for an adult distrust on their way to coming to have a sense of self-worth. These moments, however, are resolved, not by the infant's adopting another standpoint, but by good-enough parenting, by providing the continuing assurance that permits psychological development to continue. The point here is that what I will call innocent trust and original distrust are more like alternating affective rhythms than possible stances. We do well to recall here that given its neediness, dependence, and lack of alternatives, the infant has little choice but to develop appropriately trusting attitudes toward caregivers. This explains the sometimes shocking resilience some children have to the poor care they were given, without ignoring all the appalling outcomes we now know about.
43. Baier, "Trust and Antitrust," 107.
44. The developmental account that comes closest to the assumptions of the theory of recognition offered in the previous chapter is Peter Fonagy, György Gergely, Eliot Jurist, Mary Target, *Affect Regulation, Mentalization, and the Development of the Self* (New York: Other Press, 2002). Their theory argues that the capacities of human mindedness, for "mentalization," are products of intersubjective interactions. Although the theory needs to ascribe to the infant some a priori mechanisms for picking out the relevant stretches of adult behavior to be mirrored, beyond that the account presupposes little; hence, the theory provides a bootstrapping analysis whereby the capacities for self-consciousness are "transmitted" and "produced" through developmental sequences that depend on mimetic interactions.
45. Fonagy, et al., *Affect Regulation*, 248.
46. These theories do have some psychological equivalents of normative constitution: secure versus insecure attachments, or, as we saw with Honneth, basic trust. Rochat, *Others in Mind*, has conceded the difference and the significance of self-worth: "In the social construction of our identity, we are immersed in a negotiation on the *value* of who we are, not just who we are as an individuated person. *Self-worth is a crucial and meaningful aspect of self-consciousness that eludes any sociobiological interpretations. Self-worth is at the core of the psychology that surrounds the issue of identity*" (214; italics JMB). Coming at the conclusion of a sophisticated attempt to explicate the social construction of self-consciousness, this is a telling admission.

47. Although I will say nothing further about it, the path constructed here is intended to correspond to that originally envisioned in J. G. Fichte, *Foundations of Natural Right According to the Principles of the Wissenschaftslehre*, trans. Michael Bauer (Cambridge: Cambridge University Press, 2000). Elsewhere, I have offered a reconstruction of Fichte's argument: "Recognition and Embodiment (Fichte's Materialism)", in Hans-Christoph Schmidt am Busch and Christopher F. Zurn (eds.), *The Philosophy of Recognition: Historical and Contemporary Perspectives* (Lanham: Rowan and Littlefield, 2010), 47–87.

48. McGeer, "Developing Trust," 34. In this stretch of argument I am closely following McGeer's compelling account.

49. A fourth reason is that in the tradition of Frankfurt School critical theory, T. W. Adorno consistently argued that mimetic rationality was a socially repressed but fundamental ingredient in cognition, providing access to irreducibly particular sensory states of affairs. My account here is intended as a partial vindication of Adorno's hypothesis.

50. Sarah Blaffer Hrdy, *Mothers and Others: The Evolutionary Origins of Mutual Understanding* (Cambridge, MA: Harvard University Press, 2009).

51. This sounds more skeptical than it should. Adam Gies has worked out an elegant four-part schema elaborating the sensory-somatic-motor equivalences composing what Andrew Meltzoff and M. K. Moore call "active intermodal mapping" ("Imitation of facial and manual gestures by human neonates," *Science, 198* [1977], 75–78):

(1.) *Organ-identification*—The infant first identifies the relevant organ.

(2.) *Organ-testing*—Identification is confirmed through "testing." The infant moves the relevant organ, without necessarily yet imitating the observed action, to confirm that there is a match with the observed organ.

(3.) *Gesture confirmation*—Organ testing culminates in further testing for gesture identification. The infant identifies the relevant gesture by testing "small" versions of it, working out the mechanics of the observed act.

(4.) *Gesture execution*—The infant combines the information in (1.)–(3.) to form a *motor representation* for executing the action.

These strike me as sufficient to label even an infant's earliest efforts as at least proto-actions. As Gies compellingly argues, what makes this possible is the "parental scaffolding," which relieves the infant of the original heavy cognitive lifting necessary for full-blown autonomous action. Gies's unpublished paper on the logic of infant mimesis is entitled "Imitation in Early Human Social Cognition—How Preverbal Infants are Initiated into 'Practices of Mind.'"

52. Andrew Meltzoff and Alison Gopnik, "The Role of Imitation in Understanding Persons and Developing a Theory of Mind," in *Understanding Other Minds: Perspectives from Autism*, eds. Simon Baron-Cohen, Helen Tager-Flusburg, and Donald J. Cohen (New York: Oxford University Press, 1993), 332–33. This essay presents an immensely useful summary of research on infant mimesis. For a modification of Meltzoff's and Gopnik's assumptions about the mechanisms operating here, see Fonagy, et al., *Affect Regulation*, 186–91.

53. Daniel N. Stern, *The Interpersonal World of the Infant: A View from Psychoanalysis and Developmental Psychology* (New York: Basic Books 1985; 2000), xviii (italics JMB).

54. Fonagy, et al., *Affect Regulation*, 225.

55. My account here is following the analysis of Stern, *The Interpersonal World of the Infant*, chap. 6.

56. The idea of desiring the other's desire is Hegel's. I am here following the schema offered by Judith Butler, "Longing for Recognition," in *Undoing Gender* (New York: Routledge, 2004), 137–38, 146, and 149.

57. I am here agreeing with Stern, *The Interpersonal World of the Infant*, that, first, there are vitality affects that need to be distinguished from categorical affects (anger, joy, sadness, etc.), and that the former have dimensions of activation and arousal (53–61); we can thus see how there is a *rush* of anger, a *wave* of sadness, or a *surging* of joy. Stern takes vitality affects to stand to categorical affects as adverbs stand to verbs. In Antonio Damasio, *The Feeling of What Happens: Body and Emotion in the Making of Consciousness* (New York: Harcourt Brace and Company, 1999), Stern's vitality affects are analyzed as "background emotions."

58. If Hrdy, *Mothers and Others*, is right that alloparents were the original human norm, and the narrow world of mother, father, and infant a late development, then in the first instance there is no larger story to tell about how this transformation from parental world to the wider world occurs since the wider world was there from the outset.

59. McGeer, "Developing Trust," 34.

CHAPTER SIX

1. Jean Améry, *At the Mind's Limits: Contemplations by a Survivor on Auschwitz and Its Realities*, trans. Sidney Rosenfeld and Stella P. Rosenfeld (Bloomington: Indiana University Press, 1980). Further references in the text to this work will be abbreviated AML; page references are to this edition.

2. Darius Rejali, *Torture and Democracy*, (Princeton: Princeton University Press, 2009), 50.

3. For an elegant defense of this narrative, see Jeremy Waldron, *Dignity, Rank, and Rights* (New York: Oxford University Press, 2012). For an underlining of the religious wellsprings of dignity and rights see Hans Joas, *The Sacredness of the Person: A New Genealogy of Human Rights* (Washington, DC: Georgetown University Press, 2013).

4. Michael Rosen, *Dignity: Its History and Meaning* (Cambridge, MA: Harvard University press, 2012), 8.

5. As Lynn Hunt, *Inventing Human Rights* (New York: W.W. Norton & Co., 2008), chap. 5, powerfully demonstrates, modern racist and sexist discourses arose in direct response to (and in Kant's case, as part of) the various declarations of moral universalism, taking on a precision, scientific veneer (e.g., biologism), and moral viciousness absent from earlier defenses of moral inequality on the basis of race or sex.

6. In contrast to Hampton's secularized theology, Elizabeth Anderson argues for a genealogical, "generalizing honor" reading of Kant on ends-in-themselves: "Emotion in Kant's Later Moral Philosophy: Honor and the Phenomenology of Moral Value," in *Kant's Virtue Ethics*, ed. M. Betzler (New York: Walter de Gruyter, 2008), 123–45.

7. On the history of honor, see Kwame Anthony Appiah, *The Honor Code: How Moral Revolutions Happen* (New York: W.W. Norton & Co., 2010).

8. Avishai Margalit, *The Decent Society*, trans. Naomi Goldblum (Cambridge, MA: Harvard University Press, 1996), 1.

9. Both Laws were dated September 15, 1935. The first bans marriage and sexual intercourse between Germans and Jews, while the second restricts Reich and state citizenship to those of German blood.

10. Margalit, *The Decent Society*, 146, and generally chap. 8.

11. Margalit, *The Decent Society*, 149 (italics JMB).

12. Margalit, *The Decent Society*, 52.

13. Rosen, *Dignity*, 9. For Kant the kernel is the moral law, or to put it more clearly, the rational will itself, while for Catholics it is the soul. Rosen does a patient job in unearthing and dismissing these claims.

14. Shame also belongs to this constellation of concepts, but my account of it will have to await another occasion. That said, Sartre's and David Velleman's accounts do a fair job of staking out the relevant territory, since both permit sense to be made of the brutal fact that in extreme cases it is the victims and not the perpetrators who feel shame.

15. Margalit, *The Decent Society*, 32, argues that contagion belongs to the logic of humiliation: "[Humiliation] is an emotion we may feel as a result of mere identification with others even if we are not the direct victims of the humiliating behavior. If we identify with the victim in that we share the characteristic for which he is being humiliated, then we also have a justified reason for feeling ourselves humiliated."

16. In my effort to demonstrate the systematic interconnection of love and respect as forms of recognition, I have been anticipated by Heikki Ikäheimo, "Making the Best of What we Are: Recognition as an Ontological and Ethical Concept," in *The Philosophy of Recognition: Historical and Contemporary Perspectives*, eds. Hans-Christoph Schmidt am Busch and Christopher F. Zurn (Lanham: Lexington Books, 2010), 343–67.

17. J. David Velleman, "Love as a Moral Emotion," in his *Self to Self: Selected Essays* (New York: Cambridge University Press, 2006), 94. Velleman does a fine job here of overturning both the Freudian drive conception of love and what has become the standard conative philosophical analysis of love, i.e., analyses that understand love as having the motive or aim of being with the other and wanting what is best for them. Of recent philosophical works on love, the most astute in dealing with conceptual issues raised by it is Troy Jollimore's *Love's Vision* (Princeton: Princeton University Press, 2011). For a critique of Velleman's overly Kantian and moralized view, see 133–34, and 154–55.

18. Jean-Paul Sartre, *Being and Nothingness: As Essay on Phenomenological Ontology*, trans. Hazel E. Barnes (New York: Philosophical Library 1956), 369.

19. See Jollimore, *Love's Vision*, 158–59.

20. In *Frames of War: When Is Life Grievable?* (New York: Verso, 2009), Judith Butler plausibly argues that the unanticipated discovery that another's life is grievable is a condition for the recognition of the intrinsic value of that life. Although structurally the grievable must be parasitic on the lovable, Butler thinks that in the order of experience grievability sometimes comes first. An obvious conceptual advantage to this way of framing the issues is that while love discovers, often belatedly, that the beloved's worth was inseparable from her finitude and mortality, her being *forever* independent, with grief the logic works backward: we discover our attachment, call it love, as a consequence of finding that "this" loss is unbearable, and further that grief can, thereby, more easily and more explicitly than love move beyond the intimate sphere (which is Butler's larger moral point).

21. For better and worse, we harness together strong individualism and strong universalism in order to preserve what was formally accomplished through explicit community membership. Nonetheless, it is only via that double movement that dignity emerges as a conception of intrinsic worth that raises the claim of the individual over and against the good of the whole, even if, as I am underlining, the individual receives that status from the whole of which he is a part.

22. Immanuel Kant, *Groundwork of the Metaphysic of Morals*, trans. H. J. Paton (New York: Harper & Row, 1964), 434.

23. Conversely, rules and laws protecting the dignity of each are meant to relieve us of the burden of having to perceive the lovability of each, since we cannot do this because there are too many others who are all too different to see fully. It is morally sufficient that we respect their dignity. But the transition from love to respect has, on my account, already been engineered through trust.

24. William Ian Miller, *The Anatomy of Disgust* (Cambridge, MA: Harvard University Press, 1998), 33.

25. Disgust tends to belong to ethical systems that employ some conception of natural order as necessary for moral order. Améry is construing the Nazis as from the get-go leveraging physical disgust into ethical disgust into grounds for the deprivation of rights.

26. Hannah Arendt, *Origins of Totalitarianism* (New York: Harcourt Brace Jovanovich, 1952). References in the text to this work are abbreviated OT.

27. Given the widespread actuality of childhood trauma, it is more accurate to say: only those *capable* of self-respect and a sense of dignity as essential ingredients in the constitution of their subjectivity can be devastated.

28. T. W. Adorno, *Negative Dialectics*, trans. E. B. Ashton (London: Routledge & Kegan Paul, 1973), 362, suggests exactly the same idea when he states "that in the concentration camps it was no longer an individual who died, but a specimen—this is a fact bound to affect the dying of those who escaped the administrative measure."

29. Martha Gellhorn, "Dachau" from May 1945, collected in her *The Face of War* (New York: Atlantic Monthly Press, 1988), 179–80.

30. William Ian Miller, *The Anatomy of Disgust*, argues that horror is a subset of disgust, "that disgust for which no distancing or evasive strategies exist that are not in themselves utterly contaminating" (26).

31. Saul Bellow, "A Jewish Writer in America," *New York Review of Books* LVIII/17 (November 10, 2011), 28, italics JMB. This is from the second of a two-part article excerpted from a talk Bellow gave in 1988. The italicized phrase is elaborated in the final section of this chapter.

32. My "for her sake" here follows Velleman, "Love as a Moral Emotion," 90, where he is arguing that in typical "for the sake of which" arguments—one does X for the sake of Y—the final object is usually understood to be the aim or goal of the action, what is brought about through the action. But this belies the different logic where the end is not what is brought about but rather the *ground* of the action.

33. Gellhorn, "Dachau," 184.

34. For a persuasive defense of this view see Daniel R. Kelly, *Yuck!: The Nature and Moral Significance of Disgust* (Cambridge, MA: Bradford Books, 2011) and Martha Nussbaum, *Hiding from Humanity: Disgust, Shame, and the Law* (Princeton: Princeton University Press, 2004).

35. Ludwig Wittgenstein, *Philosophical Investigations*, trans. G. E. M. Anscombe (New York, Macmillan, 1958), 178.

36. Rosen, *Dignity*, chap. 3, also comes to the view that essential for the comprehension of dignity is the treatment owed the dead.

37. For a fine defense of the notion of basic action that ties the notion of action to bodily movements in the way I am assuming here, see Lucy O'Brien, "On Knowing One's Actions," in *Agency and Self-Awareness: Issues in Philosophy and Psychology*, eds. Johannes Roessler and Naomi Eilan (Oxford: Oxford University Press, 2003), 358–82.

38. J.G. Fichte, *Foundations of Natural Right According to the Principles of the Wissenschafts-lehre*, trans. Michael Bauer (Cambridge: Cambridge University Press, 2000), 58.

39. Fichte, *Foundations*, 58.

40. Fichte, *Foundations*, 74.

41. Fichte, *Foundations*, 78.

42. For a more sophisticated version of the same argument that possesses a remarkable number of overlaps with Fichte, see Erwin W. Straus, "The Upright Posture," in his *Phenomenological Psychology* (New York: Basic Books, 1966), 137–65.

43. Standard solutions to the problem of other minds, in which human mindedness appears *in* actions rather than behind them, must in fact turn on this same thesis. For an early acknowledgment of this, see D. C. Long, "The Bodies of Persons," *Journal of Philosophy*, 71/10 (May 1974), 291–301.

44. Fichte's essential point would remain valid even after due concession is made for a more nuanced, less mechanical conception of animal life.

45. Fichte, *Foundations*, 79.

46. Arendt, *The Origins of Totalitarianism*, 292, 293.

47. The finest defense of Arendt's doctrine of the right to have rights based on dignity of which I am aware is Christoph Menke, "The 'Aporias of Human Rights' and the 'One Human Right': Regarding the Coherence of Hannah Arendt's Argument," *Social Research*, 74/3 (Fall 2007), 739–62.

48. Orlando Patterson, *Slavery and Social Death: A Comparative Study* (Cambridge, MA: Harvard University Press, 1982), 38.

49. Patterson, *Slavery and Social Death*, 337–38.

50. Patterson, *Slavery and Social Death*, 100.

51. Patterson, *Slavery and Social Death*, 100, 338 (italics JMB).

52. G. W. F. Hegel, *Phenomenology of Spirit*, trans. A. V. Miller (Oxford: Clarendon Press, 1977), § 452.

53. Hegel, *Phenomenology*, §452. For a fuller account, see my "'The celestial Antigone, the most resplendent figure ever to have appeared on earth': Hegel's Feminism" in *Feminist Readings of Antigone*, ed. Fanny Söderback (Albany: SUNY Press, 2010), 111–30.

54. I was pressed into this line of argument after reading Rudi Visker, "Art and Junk. Heidegger on Transition," *Phänomenologische Forschungen*, Jahrgang 2007, 39–59. I owe both the "not dead enough" thought and the argument concerning the further function of burial rites to him.

55. David Velleman, "The Genesis of Shame" in his *Self to Self*, 55. Velleman's essay means to be corralling the relation between the voluntary and involuntary body into a recognizably Kantian structure. However, since what matters above all, even for him, is that I present myself to you as a self-presenter in ways you can *recognize*, then the demand or summons to be self-presenting—to borrow Fichte's phrasing of the relation—is what is *socially* required in order to be a social agent, and so one of us, not what is morally required in order to conform to the moral law.

56. I am paraphrasing for my purposes a passage Velleman quotes from Thomas Nagel, "Concealment and Exposure," *Philosophy and Public Affairs* 27/ 1 (Winter 1998), 4.

57. Formally, my definition of self-respect aligns with Joseph Raz, *Value, Respect, and Attachment* (New York: Cambridge University Press, 2001), 157–59. The patent gap in Raz's theory is that he lacks any account of the origin of persons taking themselves to be values that are not just values for others; he lacks a conception of lovability. Margalit, *The Decent Society*, 35–39, usefully instances Uncle Tom as a case where

self-respect is manifested passively; Uncle Tom *knows* that he is loved by God, and hence assumes that nothing in this life can threaten his intrinsic worth.

58. Raz, *Value*, 161–64, provides a useful abstract of respect as involving the acknowledgment of a value that entails both reasons not to destroy it and to preserve it.

59. *A Theory of Justice* (Cambridge, MA, Harvard University Press, 1971), 440.

60. *Pride, Shame, and Guilt: Emotions of Self-Assessment* (Oxford: Oxford University Press, 1985), 81.

61. *The Informed Heart: Autonomy in a Mass Age* (Glencoe, IL: Free Press, 1961), 157. Primo Levi, *If This Is a Man* and *The Truce*, trans. Stuart Woolf (London: Abacus Books, 1987), 96, famously describes *Muselmänner* as "an anonymous mass, continually renewed and always identical, of non-men who march and labor in silence, the divine spark dead within them, already too empty to really suffer. One hesitates to call them living: one hesitates to call their death death, in the face of which they have no fear, as they are too tired to understand."

62. Taylor, *Pride, Shame, and Guilt*, 78, but without the status claim.

63. *A Treatise of Human Nature* (Oxford, Oxford University Press, 1968), 620.

64. For an analogous argument, almost certainly in Améry's mind at the time of writing, see Franz Fanon, *The Wretched of the Earth*, trans., Richard Philcox (London: Weidenfeld, 1968).

CONCLUDING REMARKS

1. For a detailing of this, see Jeffrey C. Alexander, "On the Social Construction of Moral Universals: The 'Holocaust' from War Crime to Trauma Drama," in his *The Meanings of Social Life: A Cultural Sociology* (New York: Oxford University Press, 2003), 27–84. See also Samuel Moyn, *The Last Utopia: Human Rights in History* (Cambridge, MA: Harvard University Press, 2010).

2. For analogous interpretation of the relation between human rights and the rule of law, see Tom Bingham, *The Rule of Law* (London: Penguin Books, 2011). Bingham was the Lord Chief Justice of England and Wales.

3. The immediately succeeding six articles spell out in more detail what legal human rights amount to: equality before the law (Article 7), the right to effective legal remedies for any abridgement of rights (Article 8), freedom from arbitrary arrest or detention (Article 9), the requirement for fair hearings before an independent judiciary with respect to all criminal charges (Article 10), the presumption of innocence (Article 11), and rights to fundamental areas of privacy (Article 12).

4. For the debates and argumentation leading to these articles, underlining their item-by-item, anti-Nazi origin see Johannes Morsink, *The Universal Declaration of Human Rights: Origins, Drafting, and Intent* (Philadelphia: University of Pennsylvania Press, 1999), chap. 2.

5. The *Declaration* plausibly places torture together with cruel and unusual punishments, and slavery. Together with rape and domestic abuse, these form a more-or-less unified syndrome of moral injuries—or so I have claimed. Because torture was historically primary in the eighteenth century and relates to core areas of criminal law, it has remained something of a moral marker for the syndrome as a whole, and thus intimately connected with our understanding of the modern state. My focus on torture was thus in part an archeology of the moral meaning of the modern state, not for the sake of excluding slavery, rape, and cruel punishments, but, on the contrary, as a mechanism for schematizing their moral presence.

6. My present intention is to take up the defense of the substantive rule of law in a companion volume to this one.

7. This is unrealistic in itself, since torturing takes practice, training, institutional provisions for research, etc. For a pointed account of the institutional prerequisites, see Jean Maria Arrigo, "A Utilitarian Argument Against Torture Interrogation of Terrorists," *Science and Engineering Ethics* 10/3 (2004), 543–72. Once one acknowledges all the real-life requirements for successful torture in a rare circumstance, one has thereby set in place structures, practices, policies, and political investments that entail that the situation is not a one-off, but part of a recurrent state practice. As Henry Shue argues in an essay that has the same argumentative shape as the one I am pursuing here, "The ticking-bomb hypothetical is too good to be true—it is torture conducted by wise, self-restrained angels . . . One can imagine rare torture, but one cannot institutionalized rare torture." Henry Shue, "Torture in Dreamland: Disposing of the Ticking Bomb," *Case Western Reserve Journal of International Law* 37/2–3 (2006), 231–39. He considers the issues I take up under the imagination under the notions of "idealization" and "abstraction".

8. For a good example, with all the elements of the fantasy fully at work, but without Dershowitz's cynicism, see Mirko Bagaric and Julie Clark, *Torture: When the Unthinkable Is Morally Permissible* (Albany: State University of New York Press, 2007).

9. Michael Ignatieff, *The Lesser Evil: Political Ethics in an Age of Terror* (Princeton: Princeton University Press, 2004), 143.

10. See, for example, the essays collected in Bev Clucas, Gerry Johnstone, Tony Ward (eds.), *Torture: Moral Absolutes and Ambiguities* (Baden-Baden: Nomos Verlagsgesellschaft, 2009).

11. For the best version of this, see Oren Gross, "The Prohibition on Torture and the Limits of the Law," in *Torture: A Collection*, ed. Sanford Levinson (New York: Oxford University Press, 2004) 229–53. Shue, "Torture in Dreamland," has Gross's argument as its target. For an earlier version of this form of argument see M. S. Moore, "Torture and the Balance of Evils," *Israel Law Review* 23 (1989), 280–344.

12. Apart from the numerous works already mentioned, the interested reader should consult Bob Brecher, *Torture and the Ticking Bomb* (Oxford: Blackwell Publishing, 2007); J. Jeremy Wisnewski, *Understanding Torture* (Edinburgh: Edinburgh University Press, 2010), which contains an immensely useful bibliography; Levinson (ed.), *Torture*; Michael Davis, "The Moral Justifiability of Torture and Other Cruel, Inhuman, or Degrading Treatment," *International Journal of Applied Philosophy* 19/2 (2005),161–78; Steven Lukes, "Liberal Democratic Torture," *British Journal of Political Science* 36/1 (2006), 1–16; and Christopher Tindale, "Tragic Choices: Reaffirming Absolutes in the Torture Debate," *International Journal of Applied Philosophy* 19/2 (2005), 209–22.

13. Although obviously of immense relevance, the Senate Select Committee on Intelligence's "Study of the Central Intelligence Agency's Detention and Interrogation Program" arrived too late—on December 9, 2014—for its findings to be incorporated into my conclusion. However, three strands of the findings stand out with respect to my argument here: first, that the use of torture did not provide either necessary or "timely" information for combating terrorism; second, that psychological studies concerning the inducement of "helplessness" were used in the design of interrogation procedures; and third, that a heretofore unknown practice of "rectal hydration" was used by interrogators. The practice of "rectal hydration" has no known medical purpose in these circumstances; its use was clearly to generate an analogue of rape,

so underlining my thesis that there is a deep structural overlap between rape and torture.

14. Susan Caringella, *Addressing Rape Reform in Law and Practice* (New York: Columbia University Press, 2008), 35–37.

15. Jennifer Steinhauer, "Sexual Assaults in the Military Raise Alarm in Washington," *New York Times*, May 7, 2013. See also the report from the Department of Labor, Trauma-Informed Care for Women Veterans Experiencing Homelessness: A Guide for Service Providers (http://www.dol.gov/wb/trauma/traumaguide.htm); and Soraya Chemaly, "Why #passMJIA? 50 Facts About Sexual Assault in the US Military," *Huffington Post*, November 15, 2013 (http://www.huffingtonpost.com/soraya -chemaly/military-sexual-assault-facts_b_4281704.html). The issue of rape in the military has received renewed attention in significant part due to the deeply disturbing documentary film by director Kirby Dick, *The Invisible War* (2012).

16. "Who are the Victims?," Rape, Abuse and Incest National Network (RAINN), www .rainn.org/get-information/statistics/sexual-assault-victims. See also the 2007 report from the National Crime Victims Research and Treatment Center, "Drug-facilitated, Incapacitated, and Forcible Rape: A National Study," at www.ncjrs.gov/pdffiles1/nij/ grants/219181.pdf. See also "Are We Really Living in a Rape Culture?," in *Transforming A Rape Culture*, Revised Edition, ed. Emilie Buchwald, Pamela R. Fletcher, Martha Roth (Minneapolis: Milkweed Editions, 2005), 5–9.

17. Following the National Institute of Justice report *The Sexual Victimization of College Women* (1997) by Bonnie T. Fisher, Francis T. Cullen, and Michael G. Turner.

18. See, for openers, Stephen J. Schulhofer, *Unwanted Sex: The Culture of Intimidation and the Failure of Law* (Cambridge, MA: Harvard University Press, 1998), chap. 3; Robin Warshaw, *I Never Called It Rape* (New York: Harper & Row, 1988).

19. Elizabeth A. Armstrong, Laura Hamilton, Brian Sweeney, "Sexual Assault on Campus: A Multilevel, Integrative Approach," *Social Problems* 53/4 (2006), 483–99. The authors report that campus rape and sexual assault numbers have not shifted for the past five decades.

20. One patent fault in the study, given its own orientation, is that the focus is on a female dormitory cohort without a consideration of a parallel male cohort, and hence without even an attempt at gathering the dominant and controlling moral attitudes.

21. By "morally more injurious" I mean *only* having a higher justificatory bar than killing (would anything ever morally justify rape?) and that the form of injuring involved necessitates the denial of dignity while killing does not. To be killed is, along a different scale, clearly worse (or should we say that it is often/sometimes so?). There is no such thing as a univocal scale for ranking moral injuries.

22. Armstrong, et al., "Sexual Assault on Campus," 493–94.

23. In "The Riddle of Rape-by-Deception and the Myth of Sexual Autonomy," *Yale Law Journal* 122/6 (April 2013), 1372–1443, Jed Rubenfeld argues that not sexual autonomy but a fundamental right to self-possession should be at the center of rape law. In seeing the harm of rape as a violation of bodily self-possession akin to the violations of self-possession that occur in enslavement and torture (1426–27), Rubenfeld's argument converges with central emphases of the one pursued in these pages. Nonetheless, Rubenfeld's effort to remove sexual autonomy and consent from their central place in rape law is mistaken: even if we agree that the ultimate *moral harm* of rape is self-dispossession, it does not follow that rape law should be bound to tracking that harm. Rather, the appropriate question becomes: what legal norms are best suited to protecting an individual's right to self-possession? Noth-

ing Rubenfeld argues shows that a robust conception of consent tied to an ideal of sexual autonomy is not best suited for this task.

24. Ann J. Cahill, *Rethinking Rape* (Ithaca: Cornell University Press, 2001), 140. Cahill goes on to provide sharp criticisms of both Catherine's MacKinnon's view that women never have any meaningful choice about intercourse in a patriarchal setting and Susan Brownmiller's view that precisely because a woman was denied her sexual agency, nothing *sexual* occurred; it was an act of force only, a bodily assault, battery. Cahill's distinction between an event's being sexualized—that is, having sexual *significance*—and its not being an act of one person having sex with another is important and well drawn.

25. I take the classic works here to be Susan Moller Okin, *Women in Western Political Thought* (Princeton: Princeton University Press, 1979); Carole Pateman, *The Sexual Contract* (Oxford: Political Press, 1988); and Jean Bethke Elshtain, *Public Man, Private Women: Women in Social and Political Thought* (Princeton: Princeton University Press, 1993).

26. Schulhofer, *Unwanted Sex*, 111.

27. For a pioneering earlier effort in the same direction, see Susan Estrich, *Real Rape: How the Legal System Victimizes Women Who Say No* (Cambridge, MA: Harvard University Press, 1987). For powerful defenses of autonomy in sexual relations, see Drucilla Cornell, *Beyond Accommodation: Ethical Feminism, Deconstruction, and the Law* (New York: Routledge, 1991) and her *The Imaginary Domain: Abortion, Pornography and Sexual Harassment* (New York: Routledge, 1995).

28. Schulhofer, *Unwanted Sex*, 131. As he notes earlier, rape laws requiring force fall well below the standards for property theft, where the law "punishes taking by force (robbery), by coercive threats (extortion), by stealth (larceny), by breach of trust (embezzlement), and by deception (fraud and false pretenses). All these methods violate my right because they impair—with no adequate justification—my control over my property" (p 101).

29. Schulhofer, *Unwanted Sex*, 121.

30. For documentation and analysis, see Schulhofer, *Unwanted Sex*, chap. 3; and Cahill, *Rethinking Rape*, chap. 5. Neither is operating with my thick ethical conception of trust; it is the experience of fear they home in on.

31. For an exemplary effort to bind equality (and so dignity) with vulnerability, see Martha Albertson Fineman, "The Vulnerable Subject: Anchoring Equality in the Human Condition," *Yale Journal of Law and Feminism* 20/1 (2008).